The Cult of the Virgin Mary in Early Modern Germany

What happened to the fervent Marian piety of the late Middle Ages during Germany's Reformation and Counter-Reformation? It has been widely assumed that Mary disappeared from Protestant devotional life and subsequently became a figurehead for the Catholic Church's campaign of religious reconquest. This book presents a more finely nuanced account of the Virgin's significance. In many Lutheran territories Marian liturgy and images – from magnificent altarpieces to simple paintings and prints – survived, though their meaning was transformed. In Catholic areas baroque art and piety flourished, but the militant Virgin associated with the Counter-Reformation did not always dominate religious devotion. Traditional manifestations of Marian veneration persisted, despite the post-Tridentine church's attempts to dictate a uniform style of religious life. This book demonstrates that local context played a key role in shaping Marian piety, and explores the significance of this diversity of Marian practice for women's and men's experiences of religious change.

BRIDGET HEAL is Lecturer in Early Modern History and Director of the Institute for Reformation Studies at the University of St Andrews.

Past and Present Publications

General Editors: Lyndal Roper, *University of Oxford*, and
Chris Wickham, *University of Oxford*

Past and Present Publications comprise books similar in character to the articles in the journal *Past and Present*. Whether the volumes in the series are collections of essays – some previously published, others new studies – or monographs, they encompass a wide variety of scholarly and original works primarily concerned with social, economic and cultural changes, and their causes and consequences. They will appeal to both specialists and non-specialists and will endeavour to communicate the results of historical and allied research in the most readable and lively form.

For a list of the titles in Past and Present Publications, see end of book.

The Cult of the Virgin Mary in Early Modern Germany

Protestant and Catholic Piety, 1500–1648

BRIDGET HEAL

CAMBRIDGE
UNIVERSITY PRESS

CAMBRIDGE UNIVERSITY PRESS
Cambridge, New York, Melbourne, Madrid, Cape Town, Singapore, São Paulo

Cambridge University Press
The Edinburgh Building, Cambridge CB2 8RU, UK

Published in the United States of America by Cambridge University Press, New York

www.cambridge.org
Information on this title: www.cambridge.org/9780521871037

First published 2007

Printed in the United Kingdom at the University Press, Cambridge

A catalogue record for this publication is available from the British Library

ISBN 978-0-521-87103-7 hardback

For my parents (all of them)

Contents

Illustrations

Acknowledgments

This book grew out of my PhD thesis, undertaken at the University of London. The project was first conceived under the guidance of Bob Scribner (1941–1998), and Lyndal Roper's brilliant supervision enabled me to bring it to fruition. Susan Foister and Susie Nash also provided essential encouragement and advice during my time as a graduate student. When it came to turning the PhD into a book, the comments of my examiners, Ulinka Rublack and Joseph Koerner, were invaluable, as was the institutional support of Newnham College, Cambridge. Since then I have been in St Andrews and Bruce Gordon and Andrew Pettegree have provided help and inspiration. I am grateful in particular for Bruce's stimulating comments on drafts of this book. Thank you also to Bettina Bildhauer and Christine Linton, who helped out with various language problems.

The research for this book was undertaken with the financial support of a number of institutions: the Associated Humanities Research Board, the Deutscher Akademischer Austauschdienst, Newnham College, Cambridge, the British Academy, the Carnegie Trust for the Universities of Scotland and the University of St Andrews. During my time in Germany many people provided help and guidance. In Nuremberg I wish to thank the staff of the Stadtarchiv, Staatsarchiv and Landeskirchliches Archiv. In Augsburg my thanks are due above all to the *Stammtisch* crowd. Helmut Zäh, Hans-Jörg Kunast, Benedict Mauer and Georg Feurer all generously provided me with information without which the local archives would have remained impenetrable. Moreover their hospitality made me feel at home. Rolph Kießling also offered valuable encouragement and advice. In Cologne Joachim Deeters and his staff made working in the Historisches Archiv a great pleasure. I am indebted to Klaus Militzer for his generosity in directing my inquiries. Thank you also to the staff of the Erzbistums Archiv, in particular Josef van Eltern, and to Gerd Schwerhoff who provided useful pointers for tackling Cologne's criminal records.

For enabling the book to appear in its final form I wish to thank Lyndal Roper, Michael Watson and the editorial board of Past and Present Publications.

I also wish to thank all those who helped with the task of assembling and paying for illustrations and permissions: Helmut Zäh, Frank Müller, Nina Rewizorska and Lorna Harris. On a more personal level, my thanks are due firstly to my parents, Felicity Heal, Geoff Heal and Clive Holmes, for all their support. Stefan Brunner's incomparable hospitality and Duane Corpis's friendship made my extended stay in Germany a joy, and while I was there the Hahn family generously gave me a home. Above all, I wish to thank my husband, Guy Rowlands, for his emotional and practical support throughout the writing of this book and for his intellectual advice, which has broadened my historical horizons.

Abbreviations

ARCHIVES, LIBRARIES AND MUSEUMS

ABA	Archiv des Bistums Augsburg
BPK	Bildarchiv Preußischer Kulturbesitz
GNM	Germanisches Nationalmuseum (Nuremberg)
HAEK	Historisches Archiv des Erzbistums Köln
HAStK	Historisches Archiv der Stadt Köln
RBA	Rheinisches Bildarchiv
StaatsAN	Staatsarchiv Nürnberg
StadtAA	Stadtarchiv Augsburg
StadtAN	Stadtarchiv Nürnberg
SStBA	Staats- und Stadtbibliothek Augsburg
UStBK	Universitäts- und Stadtbibliothek Köln
WRM	Wallraf-Richartz-Museum (Cologne)

EDITED PRIMARY SOURCES

CWE	*Collected Works of Erasmus* (Toronto, 1974–)
LB	*Desiderii Erasmi Roterodami opera omnia*, ed. Jean Leclerc (Leiden, 1703–6, repr. 1761–2), 10 vols.
WA	*D. Martin Luthers Werke. Kritische Gesamtausgabe* (Weimar, 1883–1983), 61 vols.
WA Br.	*D. Martin Luthers Werke. Kritische Gesamtausgabe: Briefwechsel* (Weimar, 1930–85), 18 vols.
WA Tr.	*D. Martin Luthers Werke. Kritische Gesamtausgabe: Tischreden* (Weimar, 1912–21), 6 vols.

JOURNALS

CR	*Colonia Romanica: Jahrbuch des Fördervereins Romanische Kirchen Köln e.V.*
JbKGV	*Jahrbuch des kölnischen Geschichtsvereins*
JbVAB	*Jahrbuch des Vereins für Augsburger Bistumsgeschichte*
MVGSN	*Mitteilungen des Vereins für Geschichte der Stadt Nürnberg*

Introduction

On the eve of the Reformation the Virgin Mary was, without doubt, the most frequently depicted, described and invoked saint in Germany. The proliferation of Marian images and devotional practices that occurred during the late Middle Ages testified to the deep attachment that people felt for the Mother of God. By 1500 most German churches had at least one altar dedicated to Mary and some, such as the parish church of St Laurenz in Cologne, had two or three.[1] Many of these Marian altars were adorned with splendid carved or painted retables showing scenes from the life of the Virgin, and some also bore richly decorated sculptures of the Virgin and Child. Mary also featured on façade sculpture, on stained-glass windows and on epitaphs. Small-scale paintings, mass-produced prints and cheap rosaries enabled the faithful to continue their Marian devotions outside the sacred confines of the church. Seven feast days commemorating the key events of Mary's life were observed with great solemnity: work stopped and people attended mass and heard sermons extolling Mary's virtues. Candles blessed on the feast day of the Purification and herbs blessed on the Assumption were valued by the populace not only for their spiritual significance but also for their alleged apotropaic power. Numerous other devotional practices also solicited Mary's aid and intercession. Through endowing Marian antiphons, through travelling to Marian pilgrimage shrines, through joining Marian confraternities and through reciting the rosary, both the clergy and the laity appealed to the mercy and authority of the Mother of God.

In 1500 a visitor to any German town or city would therefore have encountered numerous manifestations of Marian piety. While the importance of particular devotional practices varied from place to place, the invocation of Mary through images and rituals was a universal phenomenon. By the mid

[1] Bridget Heal, 'A woman like any other? Images of the Virgin Mary and Marian devotion in Nuremberg, Augsburg and Cologne, c.1500–1600', unpublished PhD thesis, University of London, 2001, pp. 91–2.

seventeenth century, the end of the period covered by this book, after the turmoil of the Reformation, Counter-Reformation and Thirty Years War, the situation was very different. Given the evangelical reformers' condemnation of Mary's cult, we might expect to find that all Protestant churches had been cleansed of images and liturgy honouring the Virgin. The reality, however, was much more complex. A visitor to a Protestant church in the biconfessional city of Augsburg in southern Germany would indeed have seen few, if any, Marian images. In the church of St Anna, for example, which was a Lutheran stronghold, the only Marian images on display between the period of the Reformation and the late seventeenth century were a roof boss of the Virgin and Child and an organ wing painted with the Assumption. Both survived only because they were located in a chapel belonging to the city's most powerful Catholic family, the Fuggers. In Protestant Augsburg, moreover, the only remnant of the rich Marian liturgy of the pre-Reformation period was the feast day of the Annunciation, which was interpreted as a festival of Christ. Moving 130 kilometres north to the Franconian city of Nuremberg, however, the same visitor would have encountered numerous Marian survivals, despite this city's consistent allegiance to the Reformation cause. Nuremberg's churches were still filled with images, many of them Marian, a fact that certainly surprised some early modern observers.[2] Images of the Virgin also continued to adorn the city's streets and homes, Nuremberg's population still celebrated three Marian feast days and blasphemy against the Virgin remained a punishable offence.

Throughout Catholic Germany Mary was, of course, still venerated and invoked, as she had been in the pre-Reformation period. But just as a seventeenth-century traveller would have noticed differences between the Marian imagery and liturgy of Protestant Nuremberg and that of Protestant Augsburg, so he would also have seen that Catholic devotion to the Virgin was far from homogeneous. For a paradigm of Counter-Reformation Marian piety he had only to look to Augsburg's Catholic cult. In Catholic Augsburg, as in nearby Bavaria, Marian feast days were observed with great solemnity, public processions invoked Mary using the Litany of Loreto, pilgrimage to recently restored and newly constructed Marian shrines flourished, and many people joined the Jesuits' Marian sodalities. By 1629 most of the city's Catholic churches had at least one new Marian altarpiece that used the dramatic and visually engaging compositions characteristic of the baroque to depict Mary's exalted status and power. A visitor to Catholic Cologne, by contrast, would have encountered numerous traditional manifestations of Marian piety. Cologne's churches were still filled with late medieval images, and pre-Reformation devotional practices such as the clothing of statues and the holding of elaborate processions with numerous images persisted despite the objections of reforming clergy. During

[2] See chapter 2, p. 108.

the seventeenth century distinctively Counter-Reformation expressions of Marian piety could certainly be found in Cologne, but there, unlike in Augsburg, Jesuit sodalities and baroque altarpieces never entirely displaced more traditional forms of Marian veneration.

This diversity of Marian devotional practice demonstrates that we need to eschew generalizations when considering the ways in which the Reformation and Counter-Reformation transformed the traditional cult of the Virgin. There has been a widespread assumption that the Virgin Mary disappeared from Protestant devotional life, and became, during the later sixteenth and seventeenth centuries, a weapon in the Counter-Reformation's campaign of reconquest. This assumption originates in part in the polemical writings of the Protestant reformers. As Jaroslav Pelikan writes, 'the most obvious characteristic of the picture of Mary in the Protestant Reformation was its critique and rejection of what it took to be the excesses of medieval devotion and teaching'.[3] For the evangelicals Christ was the only mediator between man and God. Luther described the invocation of Mary as 'abominable idolatry', and more radical reformers expressed their disapproval by destroying Marian images and shrines.[4] Given this polemic, it is perhaps not surprising that Hans Düfel, in his 1968 study of Luther's teaching on Mary, asked 'do not Marian veneration and Protestantism mutually exclude one another?'[5]

Our picture of Marian veneration in Catholic Germany, on the other hand, has been coloured by studies of the Counter-Reformation cults promulgated by the ruling dynasties of Bavaria and Austria, the Wittelsbachs and Habsburgs. Under Duke Maximilian I of Bavaria, devotion to Mary became a state programme. Maximilian promoted Marian pilgrimages, introduced new Marian feast days and required that all his subjects must own a rosary. During the Thirty Years War he invoked Mary as the champion of the Catholic cause. His army fought under banners depicting the Virgin, and the great Catholic victory at the Battle of the White Mountain (1620) was attributed to her intercession.[6] For the Habsburgs too, Mary served as a symbol of Catholic renewal and reconquest. Anna Coreth's 1982 study demonstrated that under Emperors Ferdinand II and Ferdinand III devotion to the Virgin became a key element of the 'dynastic political myth' that

[3] Jaroslav Pelikan, *Mary Through the Centuries: her place in the history of culture* (New Haven and London, 1996), p. 153.

[4] *WA*, vol. 52, p. 689 (*Hauspostille*, 1544). On the destruction of Marian shrines see Diarmaid MacCulloch, 'Mary and sixteenth-century Protestants', in *The Church and Mary*, ed. R. N. Swanson, Studies in Church History 39 (Woodbridge and Rochester, 2004), p. 198.

[5] Hans Düfel, *Luthers Stellung zur Marienverehrung* (Göttingen, 1968), p. 26 n. 33.

[6] On Maximilian's Marian veneration see Peter Bernhard Steiner, 'Der gottselige Fürst und die Konfessionalisierung Altbayerns', in *Um Glauben und Reich: Kurfürst Maximilian I.*, ed. Hubert Glaser (Munich, 1980) and Andreas Kraus, *Maximilian I. Bayerns großer Kurfürst* (Graz etc., 1990).

ascribed faith and Christian merit to Austria's ruling house.[7] The Wittelsbachs' and Habsburgs' militant use of Mary, especially during the era of the Thirty Years War, has encouraged historians to see a significant break between the Marian piety of the late Middle Ages and that of the early modern period. Johannes Burckhardt writes, for example, of the 'selective' reconstruction of Mary's cult in the aftermath of the Reformation that exalted the Virgin as Queen of Heaven, as patron of Catholic dynasties and as military helper.[8]

On the Protestant side, this bipolar model has been modified somewhat by works of historical theology that demonstrate Mary's continued significance for the leading evangelical reformers.[9] As Pelikan points out, we should not emphasize the negative aspects of Reformation Mariology 'at the expense of the positive place the Protestant reformers assigned to her in their theology'.[10] Luther's writings provide the clearest evidence of Mary's abiding importance. In his *Commentary on the Magnificat*, for example, which was published in 1521, he asserted that Mary could reasonably be called 'Queen of Heaven', and even sought her intercession.[11] Such statements enabled Protestant scholars writing during the middle of the twentieth century to claim Luther for the ecumenical cause. In her 1952 history of Protestant Marianism Reintraud Schimmelpfennig argued, for example, that Luther's Marian piety was as strong and as warm as that of the medieval venerators of the Virgin.[12] In 1962 Walter Tappolet produced an anthology of statements about Mary drawn from the writings of Luther, Calvin, Zwingli and Bullinger. The title of this anthology, *Das Marienlob der Reformatoren* [The Marian Praise of the Reformers], suggests that Tappolet, like Schimmelpfennig, was motivated by an ecumenical desire to develop some Marian devotion within twentieth-century Protestantism. Indeed, he explicitly stated that his collection was necessary because of 'the present situation of the churches'.[13]

While Tappolet's source collection is still of value, Schimmelpfennig's assertion that Luther venerated Mary to the same extent as his late medieval predecessors does not stand up to scrutiny. Already in 1968 Hans Düfel provided a more balanced account of Luther's attitude towards Mary, pointing out that

7 Anna Coreth, *Pietas Austriaca: österreichische Frömmigkeit im Barock*, 2nd edn, Schriftenreihe des Instituts für Österreichkunde (Munich, 1982); R. J. W. Evans, *The Making of the Habsburg Monarchy, 1500–1700* (Oxford, 1979), p. 73.

8 Johannes Burckhardt, *Das Reformationsjahrhundert: deutsche Geschichte zwischen Medienrevolution und Institutionenbildung, 1517–1617* (Stuttgart, 2002), p. 109.

9 For a useful survey of the writing on this topic see Beth Kreitzer, *Reforming Mary: changing images of the Virgin Mary in Lutheran sermons of the sixteenth century*, Oxford Studies in Historical Theology (Oxford and New York, 2004), pp. 6–11.

10 Pelikan, *Mary*, p. 157.

11 *WA*, vol. 7, pp. 573, 601.

12 Reintraud Schimmelpfennig, *Die Geschichte der Marienverehrung im deutschen Protestantismus* (Paderborn, 1952), p. 12.

13 Walter Tappolet, ed., *Das Marienlob der Reformatoren* (Tübingen, 1962), p. 5.

the Wittenberg reformer condemned the excesses of Mary's cult and invoked her primarily as an example of grace and faith.[14] Writing in 1994, Heiko Oberman reiterated that Luther's warm praise of Mary was based not on a Catholic notion of her own merit but rather on an evangelical view of her privileged status as a recipient of God's grace.[15] It is generally acknowledged that the other mainstream reformers were less vocal in their praise of Mary: more than half of Tappolet's anthology, for example, is dedicated to the writings of Luther alone. But Oberman and others have pointed out that Zwingli and Calvin also continued to accord her respect. For Zwingli, as for Luther, Mary was a model of grace and faith, as well as a witness who taught Christians how to follow God.[16] Calvin's visceral hatred of idolatry caused him to be much harsher in his condemnation of all remnants of medieval Marian devotion, but even he invoked Mary as a model of faith, and argued that because God had granted her honour we should do the same.[17]

Most recently Diarmaid MacCulloch has highlighted the ambiguous nature of the reformers' position with regard to Mary. On the one hand, they sought to demolish Mary's cult and to eradicate idolatrous devotions such as pilgrimage to the Fair Virgin at Regensburg. On the other, the threat of radical Protestantism led them to defend certain Marian teachings despite their non-scriptural origins.[18] Both MacCulloch's article and Beth Kreitzer's book, *Reforming Mary: changing images of the Virgin Mary in Lutheran sermons of the sixteenth century* (2004), also assess the historical evolution of Protestant attitudes towards the Virgin. MacCulloch suggests that after the early stages of the Reformation there was a 'general Protestant silence' about Mary. In England at least this silence was not broken until the seventeenth century. Kreitzer also observes a turning point around the middle of the sixteenth century: although Luther and his colleagues spoke warmly of the Virgin, later preachers were 'much more willing to criticize Mary and to suggest that she erred, or even sinned, in some of her behaviour'.[19] Both authors suggest that this shift in attitude was in part at least a response to the Tridentine church's aggressive promotion of the cult of the Virgin.

[14] Düfel, *Luthers Stellung*. Düfel concluded that because Luther had gradually developed into a 'Mariological minimalist' (p. 250), Marian veneration had no place in the twentieth-century Lutheran Church. For another discussion of the evolution of Protestant attitudes towards Mary see Stephan Beissel, *Geschichte der Verehrung Marias im 16. und 17. Jahrhundert* (Freiburg im Breisgau, 1910), pp. 100–11.

[15] Heiko A. Oberman, 'The Virgin Mary in evangelical perspective', in *The Impact of the Reformation*, ed. Heiko A. Oberman (Edinburgh, 1994), p. 241.

[16] Emidio Campi, *Zwingli und Maria: eine reformationsgeschichtliche Studie* (Zurich, 1997).

[17] Oberman, 'The Virgin Mary in evangelical perspective', p. 244; Peter Meinhold, 'Die Marienverehrung im Verständnis der Reformatoren des 16. Jahrhunderts', *Saeculum* 32 (1981), 56 and MacCulloch, 'Mary and sixteenth-century Protestants', pp. 203–4.

[18] MacCulloch, 'Mary and sixteenth-century Protestants', p. 213.

[19] Kreitzer, *Reforming Mary*, p. 24.

While studies based on the writings of the reformers enable us to reconstruct changes in the way that Mary was described by literate male clerics, we should be careful not to separate theology from piety, from religious devotion expressed in the form of ritual duties and observances. Piety was articulated through texts – sermons, hymns and prayers – but also through the religious practices of individuals and groups, from liturgy and pilgrimage to the donation and veneration of images.[20] As Scott Dixon observes, in early modern Europe most people experienced religion not in terms of 'abstract doctrine', but rather 'in the practical realities of ritual and custom'.[21] In 1939 Robert Lansemann published an extensive study of feast days during the era of the Reformation, in which he documented the survival of Marian liturgy using ecclesiastical ordinances.[22] The extent of this survival – most Lutheran churches retained three Marian feast days and some retained as many as five – suggests that even if, as MacCulloch and Kreitzer suggest, the reformers themselves de-emphasized Mary during the second half of the sixteenth century, some Protestant congregations still honoured her on a regular basis. Similarly Robert Kolb concludes, on the basis of his study of sermons, liturgy and devotional literature, that Lutherans abandoned the veneration of saints but not their commemoration. Lutheran church calendars, for example the ones produced by Caspar Goldtwurm in 1564 and by Andreas Hohndorff in 1587, continued to list saints' days, though they presented the saints as worthy examples of Christian piety rather than as powerful intercessors.[23] Kolb, MacCulloch and others also remark the survival of Marian imagery in some Lutheran areas, which is a central theme of this book.

On the Catholic side, the assumption that the militant Virgin invoked by the Wittelsbachs and Habsburgs typifies early modern Marianism needs to be re-examined in the light of recent studies that point to devotional diversity within the post-Tridentine church. German Catholicism has, as Marc Forster points out, often been regarded as homogeneous, in contrast with the obvious variety within the Protestant tradition.[24] Richard van Dülmen writes, for example, that 'unlike the Protestant Church, the Catholic Church was universally orientated, i.e. not shaped by regions or by territorial churches'. The life of Catholics in

[20] For a useful discussion of the concept of piety see Hansgeorg Molitor, 'Frömmigkeit im Spätmittelalter und früher Neuzeit als historisch-methodisches Problem', in *Festgabe für Ernst Walter Zeeden zum 60. Geburtstag am 14. Mai 1976*, ed. Horst Rabe, Hansgeorg Molitor and H.-C. Rublack, Reformationsgeschichtliche Studien und Texte, supplementary volume 2 (Münster, 1976).

[21] C. Scott Dixon, ed., *The German Reformation: the essential readings* (Oxford, 1999), p. 27.

[22] Robert Lansemann, *Die Heiligentage besonders die Marien-, Apostel-, und Engeltage in der Reformationszeit* (Göttingen, 1939). Unfortunately the only copy of Lansemann's unpublished second volume, containing the footnotes, was destroyed during the Second World War.

[23] Robert Kolb, *For All the Saints: changing perceptions of martyrdom and sainthood in the Lutheran Reformation* (Macon, GA, 1987) and Robert Kolb, 'Festivals of the saints in late Reformation Lutheran preaching', *The Historian: a Journal of History* 52 (1990).

[24] Marc Forster, 'With and without confessionalization: varieties of early modern German Catholicism', *Journal of Early Modern History* 1 (1997), 340.

northern Germany, he suggests, was not substantially different from the life of Catholics in the Tirol.[25] This tendency to regard Catholicism as monolithic has been fostered by the confessionalization paradigm. In 1993 Wolfgang Reinhard claimed that confessionalization – the parallel processes by which distinct Lutheran, Calvinist and Catholic ideologies and institutions were brought into existence – produced a new type of Catholic Church. The Catholicism created during confessionalization was, according to Reinhard, 'something totally different to the one church of the Middle Ages'. Through propaganda and censorship, through education and social discipline and through the use of rituals such as Marian pilgrimage, Catholic authorities created a new sense of Catholic confessional identity.[26]

Walter Ziegler and others have pointed out, however, that although in some Catholic areas, most notably Bavaria, church and state did, as Reinhard suggests, work together to enforce religious uniformity and to promote specific types of piety from the mid sixteenth century onwards, elsewhere 'confessionalization' occurred at a much slower pace. In the archbishopric of Cologne, for example, there were few significant reform initiatives and as a result Catholicism in the Rhineland retained its 'pre-confessional' character for many years.[27] Ziegler's proposal of two types of Catholic reform – early starting and Roman, as in Bavaria, or late starting and less Roman, as in Cologne – is too schematic, but his recognition that there was diversity within Catholicism as well as within Protestantism is important. Marc Forster's work confirms this, and does much more to elucidate the nature of early modern Catholic piety. In opposition to proponents of the confessionalization thesis, who tend to see religious identity as imposed from above by secular and ecclesiastical authorities, Forster argues that after 1650 local populations played a crucial role in shaping baroque piety. Even before 1650, however, Catholic devotion was far from uniform. The Tridentine reforms and the activities of the Jesuits helped to create a distinct Catholic culture amongst some of Germany's elite, but were not received equally well everywhere. We need to recognize, Forster suggests, that 'institutional reforms, new spiritual movements, and new forms of religious expression were filtered through local institutions and religious traditions as they spread'.[28] The result

[25] Richard van Dülmen, *Kultur und Alltag in der Frühen Neuzeit*, vol. 3: *Religion, Magie, Aufklärung 16.–18. Jahrhundert* (Munich, 1994), p. 59.

[26] Wolfgang Reinhard, 'Was ist katholische Konfessionalisierung?', in *Die katholische Konfessionalisierung: wissenschaftliches Symposium der Gesellschaft zur Herausgabe des Corpus Catholicorum und des Vereins für Reformationsgeschichte 1993*, ed. Wolfgang Reinhard and Heinz Schilling (Gütersloh, 1995), especially p. 437.

[27] Walter Ziegler, 'Typen der Konfessionalisierung in katholischen Territorien Deutschlands', in *Die katholische Konfessionalisierung*, ed. Reinhard and Schilling, p. 406.

[28] Forster, 'With and without confessionalization', 318. See also Marc Forster, *Catholic Revival in the Age of the Baroque: religious identity in southwest Germany, 1550–1750* (Cambridge, 2001).

was a multiplicity of religious styles, manifested not only in organizational variation but also, as this book will show, in differences in religious practice.

We should therefore not expect to find either that Mary disappeared entirely from Protestant devotional life or that the Jesuits succeeded in imposing their own form of the cult of the Virgin throughout Catholic Germany. In order to provide a fully nuanced account of the nature and functions of Marian devotion we need to abandon this crude, bipolar model, and look beyond generalized theology and polemic to the realities of daily life and worship within specific historical contexts. While doctrinal debates are, of course, key to understanding Mary's significance, we need to acknowledge that for the majority of the population of early modern Germany transformations in devotional practice were probably of more immediate import. In an age of widespread illiteracy, images, feast days and rituals such as pilgrimage had traditionally been the most obvious manifestations of Marian piety. The fate of these images and rituals – whether they were appropriated or destroyed by Protestants and preserved or replaced by Catholics – therefore provides the historian with an excellent means of assessing how people actually experienced and understood changes in Marian teaching.

The value of studying ritual has been widely recognized by early modern historians. An extensive literature on Marian pilgrimage, for example, testifies to the perceived importance of this particular rite, while Susan Karant-Nunn has explored the reordering of 'cultic observances' that occurred at the Reformation.[29] Such studies are vital to our understanding of popular culture, for, as Ed Muir has observed, 'unsophisticated Protestants and untutored Catholics identified themselves more by the rituals they observed than by the dogmas they asserted'.[30] On the visual side, historians of iconoclasm have highlighted the extent to which transformations in the environment of worship determined people's experiences of religious change. In her study of English iconoclasm Margaret Aston observed that 'the fabric of worship, its setting, circumstance and manner . . . was more striking, more unavoidably perceptible to most worshippers than specific or subtle alterations in the content of belief'.[31] It was,

[29] On Marian pilgrimage see, for example, Ludwig Hütl, *Marianische Wallfahrten im süddeutsch-österreichischen Raum*, Kölner Veröffentlichungen zur Religionsgeschichte 6 (Cologne and Vienna, 1985); Werner Freitag, *Volks- und Elitenfrömmigkeit in der frühen Neuzeit: Marienwallfahrten im Fürstbistum Münster* (Paderborn, 1991); Bayerisches Nationalmuseum and Adalbert Stifter Verein, *Wallfahrt kennt keine Grenzen: Ausstellung im Bayerischen Nationalmuseum, München, 28. Juni bis 7. Oktober 1984* (Munich, 1984). Susan Karant-Nunn, *The Reformation of Ritual: an interpretation of early modern Germany* (London and New York, 1997), p. 4.

[30] Edward Muir, *Ritual in Early Modern Europe*, New Approaches to European History (Cambridge, 1997), p. 181.

[31] Margaret Aston, *England's Iconoclasts,* vol. 1: *Laws against Images* (Oxford, 1988), p. 12. On iconoclasm see also Lee Palmer Wandel, *Voracious Idols and Violent Hands: iconoclasm in Reformation Zurich, Strasbourg, and Basle* (Cambridge, 1995); Cecile Dupeux, Peter Jezler and Jean Wirth, eds., *Bildersturm: Wahnsinn oder Gottes Wille?* (Munich, 2000); and P. Blickle *et al.*, eds., *Macht und Ohnmacht der Bilder*, Beihefte der Historischen Zeitschrift 33 (Munich, 2002).

however, Bob Scribner who did more than any other scholar to incorporate the evidence of the images themselves into the story of religious reform. Scribner developed the concept of the 'sacramental gaze', an act of seeing that could produce sanctification and healing, in order to explain the role of the visual in late medieval devotion.[32] Despite the Reformation critique of the veneration of images, their importance persisted into the sixteenth century, as his 1981 monograph, *For the Sake of Simple Folk: popular propaganda for the German Reformation* demonstrated. Protestantism had traditionally, of course, been seen as the religion of the word, but the first generation of Lutheran reformers recognized the didactic value of images and, Scribner argued, assigned them an important role in communicating religious reform.[33]

It is one thing to decode, as Scribner masterfully did in *For the Sake of Simple Folk*, images' iconography and explain their visual allusions. It is another, as Scribner himself acknowledged, to assess the impact that they had on their viewers.[34] The conviction that Lutheranism, in its attitude towards images and liturgy, made too many concessions to traditional religion was, of course, voiced first of all by sixteenth-century Reformed Protestants. Reformation historians have tended, with some justification, to follow these Reformed Protestants in regarding the retention of visible elements of the saints' cults – altars, altarpieces, statues and paintings – as 'Catholic survivals', and as evidence of the Lutherans' failure to transform traditional beliefs and practices.[35] But as Robert Kolb has pointed out, it is in fact very difficult to determine what impact these survivals had on evangelical congregations.[36] In Nuremberg's rural hinterland, as we shall see, a few statues of the Virgin did indeed continue to attract idolatrous offerings from pilgrims.[37] But we need to acknowledge that unless images are peppered with inscriptions, in the manner of Lucas Cranach's *Law and Gospel*, their meaning is always ambiguous. Placed in a new devotional context, and given a new interpretative gloss, a painting or statue of the Virgin and Child could be transformed from an object of idolatrous prayer into a proper commemoration of grace and faith.

Images' ambiguity – the difficulty of interpreting them and of assessing their impact – explains in part, perhaps, why relatively few historical studies make

[32] Robert W. Scribner, 'Perceptions of the sacred in Germany at the end of the Middle Ages', in *Religion and Culture in Germany (1400–1800)*, ed. Lyndal Roper (Leiden, 2001).

[33] For a recent discussion of this topic see Andrew Pettegree, *Reformation and the Culture of Persuasion* (Cambridge, 2005), pp. 102–27.

[34] Robert W. Scribner, *For the Sake of Simple Folk: popular propaganda for the German Reformation*, 2nd edn (Oxford, 1994), pp. 9–10, 248–9.

[35] On Catholic survivals see, for example, Ernst W. Zeeden, *Katholische Überlieferungen in den lutherischen Kirchenordnungen des 16. Jahrhunderts* (Münster, 1959) and Robert W. Scribner, 'The impact of the Reformation on daily life', in *Mensch und Objekt im Mittelalter und in der frühen Neuzeit*, ed. Österreichische Akademie der Wissenschaft (Vienna, 1990).

[36] Kolb, *For All the Saints*, p. 147.

[37] See also C. Scott Dixon, *The Reformation and Rural Society: the parishes of Brandenburg–Ansbach–Kulmbach, 1528–1603*, Cambridge Studies in Early Modern History (Cambridge, 1996), p. 172.

extensive use of visual sources. Moreover, once the historian moves beyond Scribner's 'cheap, crude and effective' woodcuts, he or she enters into the traditional domain of the art historian.[38] Here, the analysis of 'high art' – of painting and sculpture – requires an appreciation of style as well as of subject matter. As Michael Baxandall compellingly argued, to understand such images we need to acquire a 'period eye'. We need an awareness of the interpretative framework through which they were originally viewed, and this must include an understanding of the possible connotations of artistic style. Baxandall points, for example, to the Italianate (*Welsch*) and Germanic (*Deutsch*) styles that co-existed in sixteenth-century German sculpture, and to the negative associations that the former had for Germany's nationalist humanist historians.[39] In this study, the significance of style emerges in the context of Catholic images of the Virgin produced during the later sixteenth and seventeenth centuries. In Augsburg, and to a lesser extent in Cologne, gothic and renaissance gave way to mannerist and early baroque. What is the historian to make of this shift? Can it legitimately be seen as a reflection of contemporary religious, social and political change? Mannerism was primarily a visual reaction to perfect forms of the renaissance rather than, as Theodore Rabb suggested, a symptom of a profound unease within European society.[40] Yet we should be aware that a patron's choice of artist, and an artist's choice of style, may have historical as well as aesthetic meaning. In early modern Augsburg, for example, confessional politics played an important part in establishing the new styles within the city, as we shall see in chapter 4.

Although it is always going to be difficult to pinpoint the meaning of images, in terms of both their subject matter and their style, historians of religion cannot afford to ignore visual evidence. Real devotion was always physically engaging – a sensual experience – whether it was conducted in a whitewashed preaching hall or in a baroque cathedral. The visual environment shaped everyone's experiences of religious worship and of religious change. Images may have been commissioned by the wealthy elite, but they were, to a much greater extent than texts, accessible to all. In an age of limited literacy few people could read, but everyone could see. Moreover, the importance of images was widely recognized by sixteenth-century commentators themselves. As Luther argued, in a sermon preached in 1533, 'without images we can neither think nor understand anything'.[41] Albrecht Dürer, who echoed Luther's defence of religious

38 Scribner, *For the Sake of Simple Folk*, p. 5.

39 Michael Baxandall, *The Limewood Sculptors of Renaissance Germany* (New Haven, CT, and London, 1980), pp. 135–42. On the concept of the period eye see also Michael Baxandall, *Painting and Experience in Fifteenth-Century Italy*, 2nd edn (Oxford, 1988). For another discussion of the meaning of artistic style see Joseph Leo Koerner, *The Reformation of the Image* (London, 2004), p. 226.

40 Theodore K. Rabb, *The Struggle for Stability in Early Modern Europe* (New York, 1975).

41 *WA*, vol. 37, p. 63.

imagery, wrote that 'a thing seen is more believable and long-lasting to us than something we hear'.[42] Even, or perhaps above all, the iconoclasts acknowledged images' importance. Their violent attacks were testimony to their belief in the power of images.[43] Building on the Christian humanist critique of man's propensity to focus on external rites rather than on inner spirituality, reformers such as Zwingli argued that if images survived men would inevitably be drawn to worship them. For, Zwingli wrote in his *Brief Reply Given to Valentin Compar* (1524/25), 'man falls by his nature on the thing that is placed before his senses'.[44]

In emphasizing the importance of practical piety – of sermons, rituals and images – I do not intend to deny the significance of doctrine. During the first half of the sixteenth century the differences between Marian devotion in Nuremberg and Marian devotion in Augsburg were due partly, of course, to the fact that Augsburg was strongly influenced by Swiss and south German Reformed theology, while Nuremberg remained staunchly Lutheran. The doctrinal shifts in Marian teaching, from pre-Reformation to Lutheran and Reformed, are fundamental to our understanding of Marian devotion, and will be explored in detail in chapter 1. Theological differences do not, however, provide sufficient explanation for the diversity of German Marianism in the post-Reformation era. By the later sixteenth century, for example, Augsburg's Protestant church, like Nuremberg's, was Lutheran, but the two cities nonetheless had very different ecologies of Marian devotional practice. In order to understand this diversity, we need to contextualize theology and piety. We need to relate religion to other aspects of early modern life: social, political and cultural. While this book draws on evidence from many different German territories, it focuses in the main on three case studies – the cities of Nuremberg, Augsburg and Cologne – because of this need to reconstruct in detail the historical setting of Marian devotion.

Nuremberg, Augsburg and Cologne were three of Germany's greatest 'Frei- und Reichsstädte', cities that had no immediate territorial overlords. Imperial cities such as Nuremberg and Augsburg derived their political and economic privileges directly from the emperor, and owed allegiance only to him. Free cities such as Cologne, Strasbourg, Worms and Speyer had won their independence from episcopal overlords. They were grouped with the imperial cities, even though their independence was not always fully recognized by their former

[42] Quoted in Jane Campbell Hutchison, *Albrecht Dürer: a biography* (Princeton, NJ, 1990), p. 68.

[43] David Freedberg, *The Power of Images: studies in the history and theory of response* (Chicago and London, 1989), especially chapter 14.

[44] Quoted in Lee Palmer Wandel, 'The reform of the images: new visualizations of the Christian community at Zürich', *Archiv für Reformationsgeschichte* 80 (1989), 116.

rulers.[45] In comparison with the great territorial states such as Bavaria, these cities were small. But they were nonetheless key centres of trade, of commerce and of cultural and religious activity. Nuremberg, Augsburg and Cologne were all of comparable size and significance, but each had a different confessional history. Two, Nuremberg and Augsburg, played leading roles in the early Reformation.[46] Augsburg subsequently became biconfessional – there Protestants and Catholics lived side by side – while Cologne was the most important free city to remain loyal to Rome. There was, of course, no such thing as a typical city. Each of the Empire's approximately sixty to seventy free and imperial cities was unique, particularly in the nature of its relationship with surrounding princely territories and in its internal social and political structure.[47] This study will not, therefore, seek to describe post-Reformation Marian piety in terms of paradigms applicable throughout urban Germany or throughout the Empire as a whole. Rather, it will use these three case studies to explore in detail the ways in which the reform – both Protestant and Catholic – of Marian teaching and practice was shaped by local political, social and cultural circumstances.

With a population of perhaps as many as 40,000 during the early sixteenth century, Nuremberg was one of the largest cities in Germany.[48] Situated at the crossroads of a number of important trade routes, and with a flourishing metalworking industry, it was a vibrant commercial centre. It has been described as the 'quintessential' *Reichsstadt*: it owed its economic and political development to its imperial privileges; it was a favoured residence of the Emperor Charles IV of Luxembourg, who named it in his Golden Bull (1356) as the city in which each new emperor was to hold his first Diet; and from 1424 the imperial regalia were kept there.[49] Under Charles V the Empire's governing council and chamber court were situated in Nuremberg, and the Imperial Diet assembled there on a number of occasions up to 1543. Nuremberg was unusual in that it had no guilds: after an uprising in 1348/9 guilds and associations were banned, and henceforth Nuremberg's artisans were divided into groups placed under the

[45] Eberhard Isenmann, 'Die Reichsstadt in der Frühen Neuzeit', in *Köln als Kommunikationszentrum: Studien zur frühneuzeitlichen Stadtgeschichte*, ed. Georg Mölich and Gerd Schwerhoff (Cologne, 1999), especially p. 49. On the term 'freie Reichsstädte', which emerged in the late sixteenth century and is frequently used today, see ibid., p. 56.

[46] For a useful summary of recent research on the urban Reformation see C. Scott Dixon, *The Reformation in Germany*, Historical Association Studies (Oxford, 2002), pp. 98–114.

[47] Isenmann, 'Die Reichsstadt in der Frühen Neuzeit', pp. 39–42.

[48] Gerhard Pfeiffer, *Nürnberg – Geschichte einer europäischen Stadt* (Munich, 1971), pp. 194–5. Gerald Strauss, *Nuremberg in the Sixteenth Century: city politics and life between Middle Ages and modern times* (Bloomington and London, 1976), pp. 35–8 gives a significantly lower estimate: 25,000 plus 20,000 living in close proximity and tied to the city's life.

[49] Gerd Schwerhoff, 'Blasphemie vor den Schranken der städtischen Justiz: Basle, Köln und Nürnberg im Vergleich (14.–17. Jahrhundert)', *Ius Commune: Zeitschrift für europäische Rechtsgeschichte* 25 (1998), 42–3 and Günther Bräutigam, 'Nürnberg als Kaiserstadt', in *Kaiser Karl IV: Staatsmann und Mäzen*, ed. Ferdinand Seibt (Munich, 1978).

supervision of the city council.[50] This council was dominated by patricians, a fact that, as we shall see, played a decisive role in determining the nature of Nuremberg's Reformation.[51] Unlike Augsburg and Cologne, Nuremberg ruled over a very extensive rural territory, added to during the fifteenth and early sixteenth centuries by treaty, purchase and conquest.[52] The most significant threat to this territory, and to the city's independence, came from the rulers of the margravate of Brandenburg-Ansbach-Kulmbach. Nuremberg was situated in the middle of this margravate, and divided Ansbach from Kulmbach, frustrating any attempt to unify the two territories.[53] Already in the 1440s Nuremberg had come into conflict with Margrave Albrecht Achilles of Ansbach, and again in 1552 Albrecht Alcibiades of Brandenburg-Kulmbach attacked the city. On both occasions the territorial princes' advances were successfully repulsed, but at considerable financial cost to the *Reichsstadt*.[54]

Religious devotion flourished in late medieval Nuremberg, expressed though preaching, through liturgy and processions, through endowments and donations and through rituals such as pilgrimage.[55] The city's ties with the bishop of Bamberg were loose, and even before the Reformation the council played a key role in the management of Nuremberg's church, appointing lay superintendents to local religious institutions and presenting candidates for staffing the parish churches of St Lorenz and St Sebald. Evangelical ideas first took root amongst a small circle of prominent men, representatives of south German humanism such as Anton Tucher, Hieronymus Ebner, Caspar Nützel and Lazarus Spengler. These men gradually converted the majority of Nuremberg's magistrates to their cause and between 1520 and 1522 the council appointed Lutheran provosts and preachers, most notably Andreas Osiander, to key positions in the city's parish churches. Thanks to their efforts, local sympathy for reforming ideas increased. Nuremberg became the first *Reichsstadt* to adopt the Lutheran faith: the religious colloquy of March 1525 marked the official beginning of the city's Reformation and the church order produced in 1533 codified the liturgical and administrative procedures of the newly established Lutheran Church.[56]

50 Pfeiffer, *Nürnberg*, pp. 73–5.

51 Of the 42 councillors who sat on the Small Council, 34 were patricians and only 8 commoners. Strauss, *Nuremberg*, p. 58.

52 Nuremberg's territory comprised approximately 1,200 km^2. Gerhard Hirschmann, *Die Kirchenvisitation im Landgebiet der Reichstadt Nürnberg 1560 und 1561. Quellenedition*, Einzelarbeiten aus der Kirchengeschichte Bayerns 68 (Neustadt an der Aisch, 1994), p. 6.

53 Dixon, *The Reformation and Rural Society*, pp. 4–5.

54 Pfeiffer, *Nürnberg*, pp. 115–18 and 68–70.

55 K. Schlemmer, *Gottesdienst und Frömmigkeit in der Reichsstadt Nürnberg am Vorabend der Reformation* (Würzburg, 1980). On the annual display of the *Reichskleinodien* see Metropolitan Museum of Art and Germanisches Nationalmuseum, eds., *Gothic and Renaissance Art in Nuremberg, 1300–1550* (New York and Munich, 1986), pp. 14–15.

56 Emil Sehling, ed., *Die evangelischen Kirchenordnungen des XVI. Jahrhunderts*, 16 vols. (Leipzig and Tübingen, 1902–77), vol. 11 (Bayern I, Franken), pp. 126–283.

In Nuremberg Luther's own desire to combine religious reform with social and political conservatism found perfect expression. Moderate in its confessional stance, the council never allowed radical Protestant or sectarian teaching to gain a foothold within the city. Even more moderate in political terms, the city had, by the end of the 1520s, abandoned its role in the forefront of the campaign for Empire-wide reform. As Hans Baron pointed out, Nuremberg was firmer than either Saxony or Luther himself in refraining from any kind of active alliance policy that might have resulted in it having to take up arms against its political overlord, the Catholic emperor.[57] Nuremberg refused to join the League of Schmalkalden, the defensive coalition established by Germany's Protestant princes in the wake of the 1530 Diet of Augsburg.[58] After Charles V's victory over the league, Nuremberg was the first imperial city to declare itself ready to recognize the Interim issued by the 'violent' or 'iron-clad' Diet at Augsburg on 15 May 1548. Andreas Osiander found the council's partial restoration of Catholic ritual so distasteful that he left the city, settling permanently in Prussia.[59] The Interim remained in force until 1553 when the council, responding to popular pressure, restored the 1533 church order.[60] The Peace of Augsburg (1555), with its recognition of Lutheranism, brought no change in Nuremberg's religious situation, and the city successfully resisted all later sixteenth-century attempts at recatholicization. In 1609 it joined the Protestant Union, but tried, as far as possible, to maintain good relations with the emperor. Through a combination of diplomacy and luck Nuremberg managed to escape the worst traumas of the Thirty Years War. It was preserved, for example, from the belligerent *Religionspolitik* of Maximilian of Bavaria in the nearby Upper Palatinate and from other Catholic aggression in the wake of the 1629 Edict of Restitution by the arrival of Gustavus Adolphus. Although Nuremberg had to subscribe to the Peace of Prague in 1635 and abandon its allegiance to the Swedes, it fared well in comparison with other south German cities such as Augsburg.[61]

The Swabian city of Augsburg was somewhat smaller than Nuremberg, with around 30,000 inhabitants.[62] Like Nuremberg, it was an important economic

[57] Hans Baron, 'Religion and politics in the German imperial cities during the Reformation', *English Historical Review* 52 (1937), 405–6.

[58] Pfeiffer, *Nürnberg*, pp. 166–7. During the Schmalkaldic War (1546/7) Nuremberg was pressurized into providing financial aid for the league's members, but it simultaneously supplied both loans and weapons to the imperial forces.

[59] Ibid., p. 167; Gottfried Seebass, *Das reformatorische Werk des Andreas Osiander* (Nuremberg, 1967), p. 101.

[60] On the debate over the elevation of the host in Nuremberg see B. Klaus, *Veit Dietrich. Leben und Werk*, Einzelarbeiten aus der Kirchengeschichte Bayerns 32 (Nuremberg, 1958), pp. 222–7.

[61] Pfeiffer, *Nürnberg*, pp. 266–77.

[62] Barbara Rajkay, 'Die Bevölkerungsentwicklung von 1500 bis 1648', in *Geschichte der Stadt Augsburg: 2000 Jahre von der Römerzeit bis zur Gegenwart*, ed. G. Gottlieb *et al.* (Stuttgart, 1984), p. 252. For a useful comparison between Nuremberg and Augsburg see Gottfried Seebass,

centre. Its wealth was based primarily on its textile industry and on long-distance trade. Families such as the Fuggers, the Welsers and the Paumgartners profited hugely from this trade, and were amongst the richest commercial families in Europe. As creditors to emperors and popes, they gave the city a high political profile: five times between 1518 and 1555 the Imperial Diet met in Augsburg. The city's social structure was characterized by a particularly stark division between rich and poor. At one end were the wealthy merchants and entrepreneurs; while at the other were poor artisans, in particular numerous weavers. In Augsburg, unlike in Nuremberg, guilds participated extensively in civic government. Each of Augsburg's seventeen guilds sent twelve representatives to the Great Council, giving the masters of trades a clear majority over the patricians. Even in the Small Council the guilds were more strongly represented than the ancient families, though the guild members who reached this inner council were usually drawn from amongst an elite group of wealthy merchants.[63] Unlike Nuremberg, Augsburg had no rural territory. Of its immediate neighbours one in particular – the duchy of Bavaria in the east – posed a serious threat to its independence. During the late Middle Ages Augsburg's jurisdictional authority had also been challenged by its bishop, whose lands and administrative responsibilities extended far beyond the city itself. By the end of the fifteenth century Augsburg's bishop had withdrawn to his Dillingen residence, but the *Domstadt* with its cathedral chapter, composed of members of the nobility from outside Augsburg, remained an enclave of foreign authority. The other major ecclesiastical influence within the city was the great Benedictine monastery of SS Ulrich and Afra, which was an imperial foundation, exempt from the authority of the bishop. It housed the relics of Augsburg's chief patrons, the tenth-century bishop St Ulrich and the Roman martyr St Afra.[64]

Lutheran influences were at work in Augsburg from at least 1518, when the Wittenberg reformer defended himself before the papal legate Cardinal Cajetan in the Fugger palace.[65] There were evangelical disturbances in 1524–5, including a riot in August 1524, precipitated by the council's decision to expel the Franciscan friar Johann Schilling for his inflammatory pro-Reformation

'Augsburg und Nürnberg – ein reformationsgeschichtlicher Vergleich', in *Wolfgang Musculus (1497–1563) und die oberdeutsche Reformation*, ed. Rudolf Dellsperger, Rudolf Freudenberger and Wolfgang Weber (Berlin, 1997).

[63] Paul Warmbrunn, *Zwei Konfessionen in einer Stadt: das Zusammenleben von Katholiken und Protestanten in den paritätischen Reichsstädten Augsburg, Biberach, Ravensburg und Dinkelsbühl von 1548 bis 1648* (Wiesbaden, 1983), pp. 30–3. Lyndal Roper, *The Holy Household: women and morals in Reformation Augsburg*, 2nd edn (Oxford, 1991), pp. 7–11.

[64] R. Kiessling, *Bürgerliche Gesellschaft und Kirche in Augsburg im Spätmittelalter: ein Beitrag zur Strukturanalyse der oberdeutschen Reichsstadt* (Augsburg, 1971), pp. 27–34.

[65] For a useful summary of Augsburg's Reformation history see R. Kiessling, 'Augsburg in der Reformationszeit', in '*. . . wider Laster und Sünde'. Augsburgs Weg in der Reformation. Katalog zur Ausstellung in St Anna, Augsburg 26. April bis 10. August 1997*, ed. Josef Kirmeier, Wolfgang Jahn and Evamaria Brockhoff (Cologne, 1997).

preaching. Prominent in this riot, and in the other disturbances, were guildsmen, day-labourers and poor weavers. In the face of such 'popular' pressure the council tried for some time, under the leadership of the civic secretary Conrad Peutinger, to steer a middle course, pacifying the increasingly evangelically inclined populace by allowing Lutheran and Zwinglian preaching yet making every other effort to avoid alienating the Catholic emperor. While Augsburg's leading patricians – families such as the Fuggers and Welsers – remained staunchly Catholic, the council, with its elected guild representatives, finally decided in favour of reform. In 1534 a cautious Reformation was introduced, but the exact nature of Augsburg's confessional affiliation remained unclear. Under the leadership of preachers such as Michael Keller, Bonifacius Wolfart and Wolfgang Musculus, many local evangelicals had moved away from Lutheranism, aligning themselves rather with the practices of the Upper German cities, largely dependent on the theology of Huldrych Zwingli. In 1534 Martin Bucer was called from Strasbourg to help with the implementation of the Reformation. He persuaded Augsburg's council to consent, in May 1536, to the Wittenberg Accord, a unification formula drawn up between the Upper German and Saxon theologians in an attempt to resolve disputes over the nature of Christ's presence in the Eucharist. In 1536 Augsburg also joined the Schmalkaldic League. In Lutheran circles, however, the city's confessional allegiance was still regarded with some suspicion. Indeed when Augsburg made its final moves towards reform in 1537 such suspicion proved well founded. In its abolition of imagery, in the simplicity of its church ceremonies and in its new institutions – the Discipline Lords and the Marriage Court – Protestant Augsburg was more akin to its Reformed Upper German neighbours than to Lutheran Nuremberg.[66]

Augsburg's remaining Catholic corporations fled – the cathedral chapter, for example, moved to Dillingen – and for ten years the city was a leading centre of Reformed Protestantism. But in 1547 Charles V defeated the Schmalkaldic League. Augsburg was occupied by imperial troops, and in 1547–8 the Diet assembled there. The city's religious settlement and constitution were forcibly altered. Augsburg's bishop, Cardinal Otto Truchseß von Waldburg, and his cathedral chapter returned to the city. In accordance with the *Restitutionsvertrag* of August 1548 agreed between Otto and the city council, Augsburg's Catholic cult was renewed, and all churches confiscated in 1534 and 1537 were returned to Catholic use. In order to guarantee the implementation of the Interim issued by the Diet, and to punish those considered responsible for the

[66] Herbert Immenkötter, 'Kirche zwischen Reformation und Parität', in *Geschichte der Stadt Augsburg*, ed. Gottlieb *et al.*, pp. 391–400; Philip Broadhead, 'Politics and expediency in the Augsburg Reformation,' in *Reformation Principle and Practice: essays in honour of Arthur Geoffrey Dickens*, ed. P. N. Brooks (London, 1980). On the Discipline Lords and the Marriage Court see Roper, *The Holy Household*.

city's rebellion against imperial authority, Augsburg's guilds were abolished. Henceforth the Small Council was dominated by patricians, and adherents of the old faith enjoyed disproportionate political representation. The 1548 settlement ensured that the city's elite Catholic minority could shape civic politics, but also provided the basis for the lasting co-existence of Catholicism and Protestantism. A form of legal parity between the two confessions was confirmed by the Religious Peace of Augsburg in 1555, which limited the *ius reformandi* of the *Reichsstädte*, stating that in cities in which both Catholicism and the Augsburg Confession had previously been practised, members of both confessions must be allowed to continue to worship. The terms of this peace finally, therefore, compelled Augsburg's evangelicals to abandon Zwingli and adhere to the Lutheran Reformation.[67]

In the period immediately following the Religious Peace of Augsburg it seems that the council steered a careful middle course because of its desire to foster economic prosperity and social cohesion. It remained loyal to the emperor but confessionally neutral in its external politics, and within its own territory it tried to limit religious discord by mediating between individual citizens in cases of conflict.[68] At first, this was fairly easy to do as Augsburg's Catholics were numerically very weak: in the 1560s they comprised only about 10 per cent of the population.[69] It became increasingly difficult to contain confessional strife, however, as the Counter-Reformation really began to take hold. From 1559 to 1567 Germany's leading Jesuit, Peter Canisius, preached in Augsburg Cathedral, winning back thousands for the old church and instilling a new sense of self-confidence amongst Augsburg's confessional minority. The Jesuits' position was consolidated, with the help of the Fuggers, by the establishment of a college, *Gymnasium* and boarding school in 1579–82. The renewal of Catholic ceremonies, combined with a better understanding of differences in belief, inevitably brought about a sharper division between the two confessions. This division was spectacularly manifest in the *Kalenderstreit* of 1583/4, when many of Augsburg's evangelical citizens refused to recognize the Gregorian calendar, claiming that the pope had no authority to impose such a reform.[70] By the beginning of the Thirty Years War, Catholics comprised about 27 per cent of Augsburg's population, and with the promulgation of Emperor Ferdinand II's 1629 Edict of Restitution they were able to take full

67 Immenkötter, 'Kirche', pp. 401–4; Warmbrunn, *Zwei Konfessionen in einer Stadt*, pp. 98–114; Friedrich Roth, *Augsburgs Reformationsgeschichte*, 4 vols. (Munich, 1901–11), vol. 4 (1547–55).

68 Roper, *The Holy Household*, p. 26; Carl A. Hoffmann, 'Konfessionell motivierte und gewandelte Konflikte in der zweiten Hälfte des 16. Jahrhunderts – Versuch eines mentalitätsgeschichtlichen Ansatzes am Beispiel der bikonfessionellen Reichsstadt Augsburg', in *Konfessionalisierung und Region*, ed. Peer Friess and Rolf Kiessling (Constance, 1999).

69 Warmbrunn, *Zwei Konfessionen in einer Stadt*, pp. 135–6.

70 Immenkötter, 'Kirche', pp. 405–7.

control of the city.[71] Protestant preachers and councillors were dismissed and churches were returned to Catholic use. Augsburg's exclusively Catholic regime lasted until April 1632, when Gustavus Adolphus entered the city in triumph. Under Swedish rule, Augsburg's council was reconstituted as a Protestant body, Protestant services were resumed, and many Catholics fled. During the winter of 1634–5 Augsburg was subjected to a prolonged siege, as the Bavarian–imperial army attempted to recapture it. Thousands died of hunger and disease: by the time the Swedes surrendered in March 1635 the city's population was only about 16,000. The city was besieged again in 1646 by French and Swedish soldiers, but proper parity between the confessions was not re-established until 1648.[72]

With around 40,000 inhabitants, Cologne was Germany's largest city. Situated on the Rhine, it was a great centre of trade and commerce, and its strong trading links to the north and north-west – to Antwerp in particular – shaped its relationship with the Habsburg rulers of the nearby Netherlands.[73] Within the city, as in Augsburg, guilds played an important role. According to Cologne's 1396 constitution, there were 49 seats on the city council, most of which were filled by councillors elected by the 22 *Gaffeln*, political corporations composed of merchants' associations or guilds. The council could rule successfully only with the support of these *Gaffeln*, though in Cologne, as elsewhere, a small oligarchy effectively dominated the decision-making process.[74] Like Augsburg, Cologne had no rural territory: the council's administrative authority stopped at the city walls. As a bulwark of imperial authority on the north-west frontier of the Holy Roman Empire, the city represented an attractive prize for Germany's enemies. In 1473–7, for example, it was attacked by Charles the Bold of Burgundy.[75] The most serious threat to Cologne's security came, however, from its archbishop-elector. In 1288 the citizens of Cologne defeated their archbishop in battle and forced him to leave the city, but it was not until 1475 that Emperor Frederick II finally granted Cologne its *Reichsunmittelbarkeit* in gratitude for

[71] Warmbrunn, *Zwei Konfessionen in einer Stadt*, p. 136.

[72] Ibid., chapter 4, especially pp. 132–7 and pp. 62–75. For a full discussion of Augsburg during the period of the Thirty Years War see Bernd Roeck, *Eine Stadt in Krieg und Frieden: Studien zur Geschichte der Reichsstadt Augsburg zwischen Kalenderstreit und Parität*, 2 vols. (Göttingen, 1989) and his much abridged version, *Als wollt die Welt schier brechen: eine Stadt im Zeitalter des Dreißigjährigen Krieges* (Munich, 1991).

[73] Cologne was an important trading point for textiles, fur and leather and metalwork. Hermann Maria Wollschläger, *Hansestadt Köln: die Geschichte einer europäischen Handelsmetropole* (Cologne, 1988). Robert W. Scribner, 'Why was there no Reformation in Cologne?', *Bulletin of the Institute of Historical Research* 48 (1975), 218–19.

[74] Manfred Groten, 'Die nächste Generation: Scribners Thesen aus heutiger Sicht', in *Köln als Kommunikationszentrum*, ed. Mölich and Schwerhoff (Cologne, 1999), p. 111 and Scribner, 'Why was there no Reformation in Cologne?', 236–9.

[75] Peter Fuchs, ed., *Chronik zur Geschichte der Stadt Köln,* vol. 2: *Von 1400 bis zur Gegenwart*, 2nd edn (Cologne, 1993), pp. 18–20.

its role in the Neuss War against Charles the Bold, making it directly subject to the Empire and freeing it from the archbishop's territorial lordship.[76] Even then, plenty of potential for conflict over money and jurisdiction remained, and at two points during the sixteenth century the free city was nearly subsumed into a secularized hereditary electorate when Archbishop-Electors Hermann von Wied (reigned 1515–47) and Gebhard Truchseß von Waldburg (reigned 1577–83) tried to convert their territories to Lutheranism. Cologne was saved only by the intervention of the emperor, pope and, in the case of Gebhard Truchseß, of Bavarian and Spanish armies.

The city was known, for good reason, as 'Holy Cologne'. It had numerous ecclesiastical institutions, including its magnificent (if uncompleted) gothic cathedral, 19 parish churches and 29 cloisters. Between 4.3 and 10 per cent of its inhabitants were churchmen of one sort or another.[77] It had pilgrimage shrines that were of Europe-wide significance, in particular the relics of the Three Kings, kept in the cathedral, of St Ursula and her companions, supposedly martyred by the Huns for their Christianity, and of the soldier St Gereon and his Theban Legion. And throughout the early modern period Cologne remained, as its civic seal proclaimed, 'Romae ecclesiae fidelis filia'.[78] This faithfulness was by no means a foregone conclusion. From the 1520s onwards there were evangelical disturbances in the city – in 1529 two local evangelicals were executed – and from 1565 onwards native unrest was strengthened by an influx of refugees from the Netherlands. But the council stood firm, and never allowed Protestantism to win a proper corporate or institutional foothold. There was no Reformation in Cologne partly, as Scribner suggested, because of the council's strategic concerns – the need to protect the city's trade routes and to avoid alienating its powerful neighbours – and partly because of the nature of the city's religious life. With its high density of religious institutions, its conservative university and cathedral chapter and its papal nuncio, the city did not provide a fertile breeding ground for evangelical ideas.[79]

In the aftermath of the Cologne War (1583–9) Cologne's Catholicism was reaffirmed when it was allied to Bavaria by the election of a series of Wittelsbach

[76] Isenmann, 'Die Reichsstadt in der Frühen Neuzeit', p. 49.

[77] On 'Holy Cologne' see Klaus Militzer, 'Collen eyn kroyn boven allen steden schoyn: zum Selbstverständnis einer Stadt', *CR* 1 (1986); Rebekka von Mallinckrodt, *Struktur und kollektiver Eigensinn: Kölner Laienbruderschaften im Zeitalter der Konfessionalisierung*, Veröffentlichungen des Max-Planck-Instituts für Geschichte 209 (Göttingen, 2005), pp. 86–7.

[78] Wilfried Enderle, 'Die katholischen Reichsstädte im Zeitalter der Reformation und der Konfessionsbildung', *Zeitschrift der Savigny-Stiftung für Rechtsgeschichte. Kanonistische Abteilung* 75 (1989), 231.

[79] Scribner, 'Why was there no Reformation in Cologne?'. On the city's Catholicism see Gérald Chaix, 'De la cité chrétienne à la métropole catholique: vie religieuse et conscience civique à Cologne au XVIe siècle', thèse pour le Doctorat d'Etat, L'Université des Sciences Humaines de Strasbourg (1994).

archbishops. Under these scions of Germany's leading Catholic dynasty, new forms of religious devotion entered the city. In 1618, for example, Archbishop Ferdinand von Bayern, in conjunction with his brother Duke Maximilian I, founded Cologne's first significant baroque church, dedicated to Mary's Assumption and run by the Jesuits. But Cologne's religious life, unlike Augsburg's, was never dominated by characteristically Counter-Reformation forms of piety. During the seventeenth century the city, again unlike Augsburg, escaped the worst traumas of the Thirty Years War, distancing itself from its Wittelsbach archbishop and maintaining its neutrality with considerable care.[80]

The comparative study of the fate of Marian images and devotion in and beyond these three cities, undertaken in the main body of this book, will enable us to assess the role that Mary played in the development of diverse confessional identities and in the construction of boundaries between competing religious communities. Ever since Ernst Walter Zeeden's pioneering work on the survival of Catholic elements in Protestant religious life, confessional formation (*Konfessionsbildung*) has been a key concept for the historian of early modern religion.[81] While Heinz Schilling's confessionalization paradigm focused on social discipline and state formation, Reinhard's more church-centred version drew attention to the significance of *propria* or peculiarities – both structural and devotional – that distinguished one confession from another.[82] In this context, Marian piety was described as a rite of differentiation (an 'Unterscheidungsritus') that set Catholics apart from their Protestant neighbours. Reinhard and Schilling's edited volume on Catholic confessionalization cites, not surprisingly, the example of Duke Maximilian I of Bavaria's promotion of the Virgin's cult.[83] In Augsburg, as in Bavaria, Mary did indeed function as a marker of Catholic identity, most obviously for the city's Jesuit-influenced elite, but also for the populace, even before what historians such as Etienne François and Marc

80 Johannes Arndt, 'Köln als kommunikatives Zentrum im Zeitalter des Dreissigjährigen Krieges', in *Köln als Kommunikationszentrum*, ed. Mölich and Schwerhoff (Cologne, 1999).

81 Zeeden, *Katholische Überlieferungen*; Ernst W. Zeeden, *Die Entstehung der Konfessionen: Grundlagen und Formen der Konfessionsbildung im Zeitalter der Glaubenskämpfe* (Munich and Vienna, 1964).

82 For a useful English summary see Thomas A. Brady, 'Confessionalization: the career of a concept', in *Confessionalization in Europe, 1555–1700: essays in honor and memory of Bodo Nischan*, ed. John M. Headley, Hans J. Hillerbrand and Anthony J. Papalas (Aldershot, 2004), pp. 7–10.

83 On Marian devotion as an *Unterscheidungsritus* see Reinhard, 'Was ist katholische Konfessionalisierung?', p. 430. On Maximilian see Rainer A. Müller, 'De Christiani Principis Officio – Religion und katholische Konfession in ausgewählten Fürstenspiegeln der Frühen Neuzeit', in *Die katholische Konfessionalisierung*, ed. Reinhard and Schilling (Gütersloh, 1995), pp. 343, 346. In the same volume see also Marc Venard, 'Volksfrömmigkeit und Konfessionalisierung', p. 262 on France. Already in 1964 Zeeden suggested that Marian veneration was one of 'die positiv unterscheidenden Merkmale' of Catholicism. Zeeden, *Die Entstehung der Konfessionen*, p. 124.

Forster have described as the era of popular confessional identity (following the Thirty Years War).[84] But if the cult of the Virgin served, as Reinhard suggests, to distinguish Catholics from Protestants, how then did Germany's Lutherans manage to assimilate her images and feast days? And why did the Jesuits' militant Marian piety dominate Bavaria but not Catholic Cologne? We cannot understand the process of confessional formation without understanding the realities of religious devotion. And in order to understand the realities of religious devotion, we must recognize that Marian devotion was not merely a paradigmatic 'rite of differentiation'. Rather, the significance of the Virgin's cult derived from the conjunction of specific religious, political, cultural and social circumstances.

Recognizing this will deepen our understanding of the diversity and fluidity of both Protestant and Catholic piety, and will highlight the intricate interactions between art, religion and society. It will also force us to re-evaluate some of our assumptions concerning the impact of religious change on women, the subject of the final chapter of this book. The implications of the promotion and celebration of Mary, a highly idealized woman, have been much debated.[85] Feminist scholars studying the Catholic cult have tended to emphasize its negative overtones. The virtuous virgin mother presented, they suggest, an ideal to which no real woman could aspire.[86] Historians of the Reformation, by contrast, have suggested that the Virgin provided a positive role model, and allowed women the possibility of spiritual identification. When they abolished the cult of the Virgin, Protestant reformers created an exclusively masculine religious landscape, which was alienating to women.[87] This suggestion has been challenged by Christine Peters, who, in her study of English religion, points out that although 'female saints are tokens that female sanctity is attainable', the relationship between religious symbols and social reality is a complex

[84] Etienne François, *Die unsichtbare Grenze: Protestanten und Katholiken in Augsburg 1648–1806* (Sigmaringen, 1991) and Forster, *Catholic Revival.*

[85] Three collections of essays explore the issues surrounding Marian devotion and gender from various perspectives: E. Gössman and D. R. Bauer, eds., *Maria – für alle Frauen oder über alle Frauen?* (Freiburg im Breisgau, 1989); Hedwig Röckelein, ed., *Maria, Abbild oder Vorbild: zur Sozialgeschichte mittelalterlicher Marienverehrung* (Tübingen, 1990); Claudia Opitz *et al.*, eds., *Maria in der Welt: Marienverehrung im Kontext der Sozialgeschichte 10. – 18. Jahrhundert* (Zurich, 1993), part II.

[86] See, for example, Marina Warner, *Alone of All Her Sex: the myth and cult of the Virgin Mary* (London, 1976), p. 338 and M. R. Miles, *Image as Insight: visual understanding in western Christianity and secular culture* (Boston, 1985), p. 87. See also Anne Conrad, 'Nähe und Distanz – katholische Frauen im Spannungsfeld der frühneuzeitlichen Mariologie', in *Maria in der Welt*, ed. Opitz *et al.* for a more historically grounded discussion.

[87] See, for example, Merry E. Wiesner, 'Luther and women: the death of two Marys', in *Disciplines of Faith: studies in religion, politics and patriarchy*, ed. J. Obelkevich and Lyndal Roper (London, 1987), p. 303 and Roper, *The Holy Household*, p. 263.

one.[88] Mary may have been a woman, but as the Mother of God her appeal transcended all gender boundaries. Moreover, if, as this book suggests, experiences of Marian devotion were contingent, dependent on time and place, we must avoid oversimplified statements about women's relationship with Mary. Catholic women might have experienced Mary in a variety of ways: traditionally, for example, they could have participated in Marian confraternities, but under the influence of the Jesuits they were often excluded from communal and public manifestations of Marian piety. Some Protestant women might, as Reformation scholarship has thus far suggested, have lost contact with Mary, but others, particularly those living in moderate Lutheran areas, would still have seen images of her every day. To them, she was presented not as a powerful intercessor, but as a model of right belief and conduct, a housemother whose experiences were in many ways similar to their own. Local variations in religious practice were therefore key in determining what Mary meant to the inhabitants of early modern Germany.

88 Christine Peters, *Patterns of Piety: women, gender and religion in late medieval and Reformation England* (Cambridge, 2003), especially p. 96. For a useful discussion of symbols see Caroline Walker Bynum, Stevan Harrell and Paula Richman, eds., *Gender and Religion: on the complexity of symbols* (Boston, 1986).

1. *Transformations in Marian teaching*

Marian devotion flourished throughout late medieval Germany. Liturgy, sermons and images celebrated Mary's role in the story of salvation. Feast days commemorated the key events of her life: her conception and birth; her presentation in the temple at Jerusalem; Gabriel's announcement of Christ's birth; her visit to Elizabeth; her purification following Christ's birth; and her bodily assumption into heaven. Paintings and sculptures of these events filled pre-Reformation churches: surviving artefacts and inventories indicate that in 1510 a visitor to one of Nuremberg's churches might have seen as many as twenty individual images of the Virgin.[1] Leaving the church he or she would have encountered many more lining the city's streets: even in the mid nineteenth century there were still around forty late medieval *Hausmadonnen* – sculpted house signs depicting Mary – on display in Nuremberg.[2] And small-scale paintings and sculptures, mass-produced prints and cheap rosaries enabled laymen and women to pursue their devotions to the Virgin even within their own homes. These devotions focused above all on Mary's relationship with Christ – her care for her son during his infancy and her compassion for his later suffering – and on the power that this relationship gave her to intercede on behalf of sinners. While the importance of particular Marian observances varied from place to place, in the religious culture of fifteenth-century Germany the quest for Mary's merciful intercession was a universal theme.

Yet even within the Catholic Church Mary's cult attracted criticism. The humanist Desiderius Erasmus, who had written elegant Latin verse in praise of Mary at the beginning of his career, came to despise the excesses of the late medieval cult. In his *Colloquies* he ridiculed the superstitious supplications that his contemporaries directed at Mary, and poked fun at gullible Marian pilgrims and at the unscrupulous churchmen who exploited them.[3] Worship of the Virgin,

[1] Heal, 'A woman like any other?', pp. 33–46, 52–9.
[2] G. W. K. Lochner, *Die noch vorhandenen Abzeichen Nürnberger Häuser* (Nuremberg, 1855).
[3] MacCulloch, 'Mary and sixteenth-century Protestants', pp. 193–5.

and of her images and relics, distracted attention, Erasmus believed, from the true worship of Christ, and although he did not wish to cast Mary out of the church he certainly sought to reduce her significance within it. The attempts of such Catholic reformers to limit Mary's role ultimately foundered because of the turmoil caused by the Protestant Reformation, but some of the criticisms made by Erasmus lived on in later condemnations of Mariolatry. Both Heinrich Bullinger and Jean Calvin, for example, drew on Erasmus' denunciation of the worship of saints and relics.[4] The Protestant reformers, however, went much further than their Catholic predecessors. On the basis of their interpretation of Scripture they presented a radical challenge to the fundamental precepts of medieval devotion, in particular to the notion that Mary or any other saint could act as intercessor between man and God. Yet there remained a certain ambiguity in Protestant thinking on Mary: unlike other saints, Mary could never be entirely eliminated from evangelical piety since her veneration was so closely tied to that of Christ.

THE LATE MEDIEVAL CULT

By the late Middle Ages the story of Mary's life was firmly embedded in Christian culture. Liturgy, sermons and images commemorated key moments, from her conception and birth to her death and bodily assumption into heaven. Only a few of these moments – those associated with Christ – were recounted in the Bible. The early chapters of Luke's gospel describe the Annunciation and the Visitation and give the text of the hymn of praise that Mary spoke to God, the Magnificat. They also tell of Christ's birth, of his presentation in the temple and of the prophecy that Simeon made to Mary, that her heart would be pierced by a sword. John's Gospel describes the wedding at Cana, at which Mary asked her son to perform a miracle (2:1–11), and records that Mary was present at her son's crucifixion (19:25–7). According to the Acts of the Apostles (1:13ff.), she was also present when the Holy Spirit descended on the Apostles at Pentecost. Beyond this, the Scriptures have little to say about the Mother of Christ. Most of the other Marian lore that was taught on the eve of the Reformation derived from apocryphal sources, in particular from the second-century *Protoevangelium of James*. This text supplied the names of Mary's parents, Joachim and Anne, and told how Mary was born to them when they were already old. It recorded that Mary was presented in the temple at Jerusalem when she was only three, and remained there until her marriage to Joseph when she was twelve.[5] The story of Mary's bodily assumption into heaven after her death, which was witnessed

4 Ibid., p. 194.

5 Hilda Graef, *Mary: a history of doctrine and devotion*, 2nd edn, 2 vols. combined (London, 1985), vol. 1, pp. 36–7.

by the Apostles, gained popularity from the late fifth century onwards.[6] All of these accounts were disseminated through sermons and through compilations of saints' lives such as the influential thirteenth-century *Golden Legend* of Jacobus de Voragine.[7]

The most important events of the Virgin's life were commemorated by feast days. Late medieval German liturgical calendars prescribed the celebration of seven Marian festivals.[8] Four were long-established, having been introduced into the western church in the seventh century: the Nativity of Mary (8 September); the Annunciation of Christ (25 March); Mary's Purification (2 February); and her Assumption (15 August). Three were more recent additions, and testify to the flourishing of Marian piety that occurred during the fourteenth and fifteenth centuries. The feast of Mary's Presentation in the temple (21 November) gained popularity during the fourteenth century, and the feast of the Visitation (2 July) was established for the whole church by Pope Urban VI in 1389. The feast of the Visitation, like that of the rosary instituted by Pius V in 1573, was associated with Christendom's struggles against the Ottoman Turks.[9] The final feast, that of Mary's Conception (8 December), was celebrated in parts of Europe from the twelfth century onwards, but its observance did not become commonplace until the late fourteenth and fifteenth centuries.[10] The doctrine of the Immaculate Conception, with which this feast was closely associated, gained acceptance in the western church only slowly, and was not finally defined as an article of faith until 1854. The idea that at her conception Mary had been preserved from original sin through the special grace of God found its most eloquent medieval proponent in the Franciscan Duns Scotus (d.1308). But for Bernard of Clairvaux (1090–1153) and other opponents, the notion that Mary was conceived without sin, and therefore had no need of redemption, demeaned the saving work of Christ. The doctrine of the Immaculate Conception was approved by the Council of Basle in 1439,

[6] Ibid., p. 134.

[7] Jacobus de Voragine, *The Golden Legend: readings on the saints*, trans. William Granger Ryan, 2 vols. (Princeton, 1993), vol. 1, p. xiii.

[8] On the evolution of Augsburg's *Sanctorale* see F. A. Hoeynck, *Geschichte der kirchlichen Liturgie des Bisthums Augsburg* (Augsburg, 1889), pp. 241–83; on Cologne's liturgy see G. Zilliken, 'Der Kölner Festkalendar: seine Entwicklung und seine Verwendung zu Urkundendatierung', *Bonner Jahrbuch: Jahrbücher des Vereins für Altertumsfreunden im Rheinlande* 119 (1910), especially 134; Peter Weiler, *Die kirchliche Reform im Erzbistum Köln*, Reformationsgeschichtliche Studien und Texte 56/57 (Münster, 1931), pp. 122–33; F. J. Peters, *Beiträge zur Geschichte der Kölnischen Messliturgie: Untersuchungen über die gedruckten Missalien des Erzbistums Köln*, Colonia Sacra 2 (Cologne, 1951); W. Herborn, 'Fast-, Fest- und Feiertage im Köln des 16. Jahrhunderts', *Rheinisches Jahrbuch für Volkskunde* 25 (1985); Wilhelm Janssen, *Das Erzbistum Köln im späten Mittelalter*, vol. 2, part II (Cologne, 2003), pp. 480–1.

[9] Düfel, *Luthers Stellung*, p. 180; Remigius Bäumer and Leo Scheffczyk, eds., *Marienlexikon*, 6 vols. (St Ottilien, 1988–94), vol. 2, pp. 465–6; Graef, *Mary*, vol. 1, pp. 142–3.

[10] Donna Spivey Ellington, *From Sacred Body to Angelic Soul: understanding Mary in late medieval and early modern Europe* (Washington, 2001), pp. 53–4.

but its decree was not canonically binding because of the council's conflict with Rome. Nevertheless, by the end of the fifteenth century both the doctrine and the feast of Mary's Conception were generally accepted in the western church.[11]

Festivals were, as Bob Scribner pointed out, 'one of the most common kinds of religious experience to which everyone, high and low, learned and unlearned, clerical and lay had access'.[12] Most or, in some places, all of the seven festivals of the Virgin were designated as solemn feast days, and were celebrated under pain of sin for non-observance. Each festival began at vespers on the evening preceding the feast day. On the day itself the clergy recited the daily office of matins, lauds and six further liturgical hours, with texts and music proper to the event being commemorated. They also celebrated mass and preached sermons in the vernacular. These sermons highlighted key Marian themes. Notes taken during the final decades of the fifteenth century by the nuns of Nuremberg's St Katharina cloister record, for example, that they heard expositions of Mary's heavenly beauty and status as God's chosen one on the feast of the Assumption.[13] The finer points of the Latin office and mass may have been lost on the majority of the lay population, but the celebration of a solemn feast was nonetheless a spectacular event. Winged altarpieces, kept closed for most of the year, were opened to reveal their carved and richly painted interiors. The sexton lit numerous candles, and placed cloths and treasures – reliquaries and silver statuettes of saints – on the church's altars.[14] The clergy were clothed in richly embroidered chasubles and pluvials. Processions, often with images and relics, went around the church and its grounds.[15] In the collegiate church of St Maria im Kapitol in Cologne, for example, members of the church's most important confraternity, the *Marienbruderschaft vom silbernen Bild und zur großen Glocke* [Marian brotherhood of the silver image and the great bell], went to the church at eight in the morning on the festival of the Purification to receive candles and 'to go around with Our Lady's image', the silver statue of the Virgin to which their confraternity was dedicated.[16]

[11] Pelikan, *Mary*, pp. 189–200; Graef, *Mary*, vol. 1, pp. 298–302, 314–15; Ellington, *From Sacred Body*, pp. 54–60.

[12] Robert W. Scribner, 'Ritual and popular religion in Catholic Germany at the time of the Reformation', *Journal of Ecclesiastical History* 35, no. 1 (1984), 48.

[13] P. Renner, 'Spätmittelalterliche Klosterpredigten aus Nürnberg', *Archiv für Kulturgeschichte* 41 (1959), 209–10.

[14] See, for example, Albert Gümbel, ed., *Das Mesnerpflichtbuch von St Lorenz in Nürnberg vom Jahre 1493*, Einzelarbeiten aus der Kirchengeschichte Bayerns 8 (Munich, 1928) and J. Metzner, 'Stephan Schulers Saalbuch der Frauenkirche in Nürnberg', in *Zweiunddreissigster Bericht über das Wirken und den Stand des historischen Vereins zu Bamberg im Jahre 1869* (Bamberg, 1869).

[15] On processions in Augsburg see Hoeynck, *Geschichte der kirchlichen Liturgie*, pp. 177–89.

[16] Klaus Militzer, ed., *Quellen zur Geschichte der Kölner Laienbruderschaften vom 12. Jahrhundert bis 1562/63*, 4 vols., Publikationen der Gesellschaft für Rheinische Geschichtskunde 71 (Düsseldorf, 1997–2000), vol. 2, p. 917.

Before the Reformation there existed, alongside this formal liturgical cycle, numerous 'popular' forms of ritual. Key liturgical events might be dramatized. In Halle and Schwerin, for example, on the feast of the Assumption an image of the Virgin Mary was raised into the roof of the church. On the festivals of the Purification and Assumption there were important benediction ceremonies. At the Purification (Candlemas) candles were blessed to symbolize Mary's purity and Christ's role as light of world. These candles were subsequently used in the home for devotional purposes, but were also accorded a magical status. They were lit to ward off bad weather and evil spirits. At the Assumption bundles of herbs were blessed, in order to recall the flowers found by the Apostles at Mary's tomb and the fragrance said to have accompanied her ascent into heaven. These also were used for apotropaic magic, to protect buildings, livestock and crops and to avert all kinds of danger.[17] The fact that the Assumption was referred to in Nuremberg's reformed festival ordinance (1525) as the feast that 'we until now have called herb dedication' indicates the strength of this particular tradition.[18] During the mid fifteenth century, and again during the first half of the sixteenth century, there were, however, a number of attempts to purify popular ritual practices.[19] Evidence from Cologne suggests, for example, that by the second half of the sixteenth century herbs were no longer blessed at Assumption in the city's churches.[20]

The key events of Mary's life were communicated and commemorated not only through liturgy, sermons and popular ritual but also through images. Examples of many of the Marian iconographies that would have been familiar to a late medieval audience can be seen on the elaborate retable that adorned the high altar of Nuremberg's Frauenkirche until 1815. This retable had been donated to the church shortly before Nuremberg's Reformation by the merchant Jakob Welser and his wife Ehrentraut von Thumenberg. Although only parts survive today, the whole design, with its carved wooden frame and two sets of painted moveable wings, is recorded in Ulrich Krauss's 1696 engraving (figure 1). On ordinary weekdays, with the altar closed, visitors to the church would have seen the painted scene of the Lamentation that extends across the back of its outer set of wings as well as the representations of the Annunciation, the Visitation and the birth of Christ in its *Auszug* or carved superstructure.[21] On Sundays the first set of wings would have been opened to reveal an image of Mary's

[17] Scribner, 'Ritual and popular religion', 58, 62–3.

[18] StadtAN, Rep. A6, Sammlung der (gedruckten) Mandate, Urkunden und Verordnungen der Reichsstadt und Stadtverwaltung Nürnberg, 1219 bis Gegenwart, 1525 Mai 24.

[19] Scribner, 'Ritual and popular religion', 72–3.

[20] Herborn, 'Fast-, Fest- und Feiertage', 55. According to the *Missale Coloniense* printed in 1625 (UStBK, Bäumker 1080), herbs were not blessed in the cathedral or in the city's collegiate churches at that date (p. 635).

[21] Nürnberg (Kurt Löcher) Germanisches Nationalmuseum, ed., *Die Gemälde des 16. Jahrhunderts* (Stuttgart, 1997), p. 67.

Figure 1. Johann Ulrich Krauss (after Johann Andreas Graff), interior of the Frauenkirche, 1696 (GNM, Graphische Sammlung, Nuremberg)

death covering the two central wing panels with four smaller scenes from her life surrounding it (figures 2 and 3). The first of these smaller scenes represents Mary's conception by showing her parents, Joachim and Anne, embracing at the Golden Gate in Jerusalem. The second shows Mary's birth: Anne lies in a canopied bed beneath a blanket of gold brocade, and is attended by women who bring her food and drink and bathe the newborn baby. The third and fourth scenes show Mary entering the temple at age three and Christ's presentation before the high priest Simeon.

On feast days the altar would have been opened fully, as in Krauss's print. The inner sides of the inner set of wings showed the adoration of the magi, Pentecost, Christ's resurrection and Mary taken into heaven and crowned by the Holy Trinity.[22] At the centre of the altar was a carved image of the Virgin and Child standing on the moon and surrounded by rays of sun. This iconography, along with an abbreviated version showing Mary with only a sickle moon, was very common in Germany from the mid fifteenth century onwards. It conflates

22 Peter Strieder, *Tafelmalerei in Nürnberg 1350–1550* (Königstein im Taunus, 1993), ills. 601 and 2.

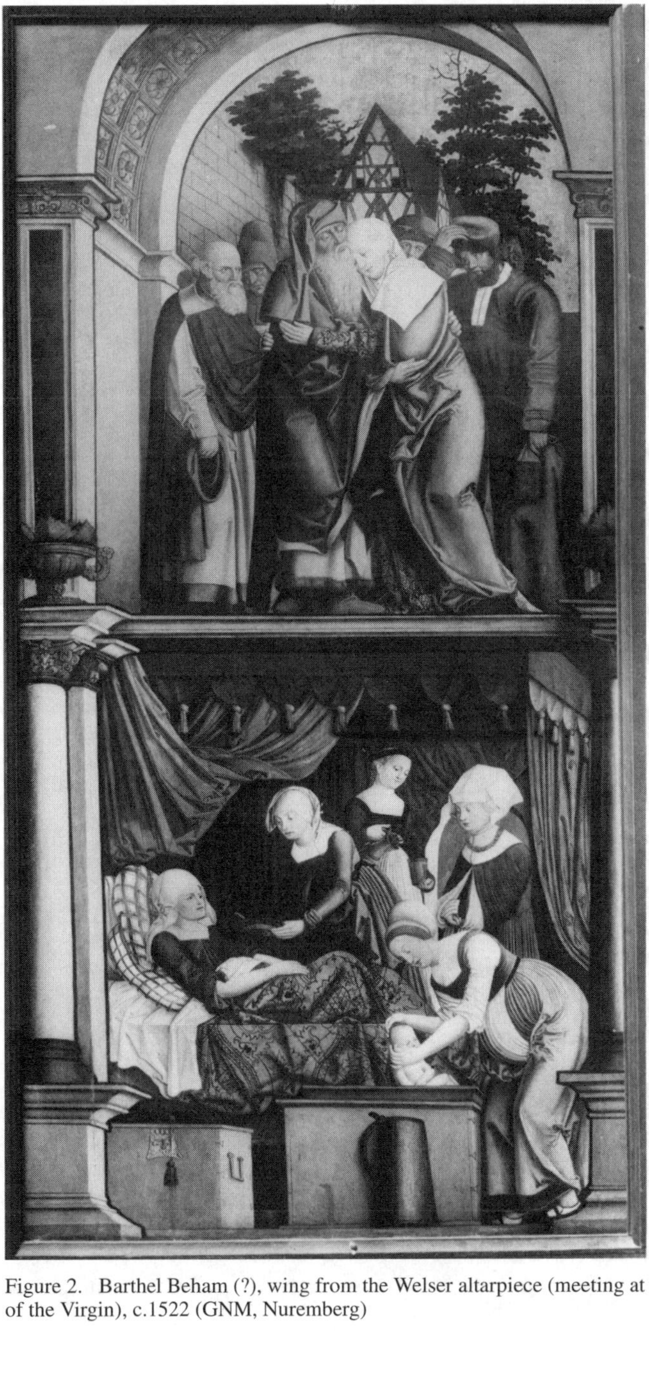

Figure 2. Barthel Beham (?), wing from the Welser altarpiece (meeting at the Golden Gate, birth of the Virgin), c.1522 (GNM, Nuremberg)

Figure 3. Barthel Beham (?), wing from the Welser altarpiece (presentation of the Virgin, presentation of Christ), c.1522 (GNM, Nuremberg)

the Virgin with the woman described in Revelation 12:1: 'and there appeared a great wonder in heaven: a woman clothed with the sun, and the moon under her feet, and upon her head a crown of twelve stars'. The woman gave birth to a son, who was taken up to God, and then witnessed the defeat of Satan. The identification of this mysterious woman with Mary was a part of biblical exegesis from the fifth century onwards.[23] The Woman of the Apocalypse, like Mary herself, was taken as a symbol of the church, and it is therefore likely that images such as the one at the centre of the Frauenkirche altarpiece refer to Mary's embodiment of the church. From the fourteenth century onwards such images were also, however, used to illustrate the doctrine of the Immaculate Conception.[24] If Mary was, as her identification with the Woman of the Apocalypse suggests, predestined before the creation of the world to be the mother of Christ, then she was untouched by original sin.

Images of St Anne with the Virgin and Child (the *Anna Selbdritt*), such as the one displayed on the column to the right of the choir in Krauss's engraving (figure 1), had also sometimes been used to refer to Mary's Immaculate Conception.[25] By the late fifteenth century, however, Anne was no longer a mere guarantor of her daughter's sinlessness. She and Mary's other close relatives were frequently celebrated in both liturgy and art. According to medieval tradition, recorded in texts such as Voragine's *Golden Legend*, Anne had remarried twice after Joachim's death. By her second husband she gave birth to Mary Cleophas, who married Alpheus and became the mother of the Apostles James, Simon and Jude. By her third she had Mary Salome, wife of Zebedee and mother of the other Apostle James and John the Evangelist. On the eve of the Reformation the feast day of St Anne was observed in both Augsburg and Cologne, and an Augsburg missal from 1510 contains votive masses that could be read in honour of Joseph, Joachim and the Virgin's sisters.[26] Paintings of the Holy Kindred were also popular throughout Germany, and, as we shall see in chapter 6, perhaps reflected an increased interest amongst their patrons in marriage, motherhood and the family. This devotion was, as Luther himself recognized, a relatively recent development: he lamented in a sermon on the Gospel of John printed in 1537 that 'we made saints of Anne and Joachim not more than thirty years ago'.[27] In theological terms, Anne's family successfully reconciled

[23] Graef, *Mary*, vol. 1, pp. 27–31.

[24] Gertrud Schiller, *Ikonographie der christlichen Kunst*, 8 vols. (Gütersloh, 1966–90), vol. 4, part II, pp. 157–9. See, for example, the *Missale secundum ritum Augustensis ecclesie Augsburg* (Augsburg, 1555), ABA, Fr 34, where a mass in honour of Mary's conception with wording similar to that prescribed for the feast of the Immaculate Conception today is preceded by a woodcut of Mary as the Woman of the Apocalypse.

[25] Schiller, *Ikonographie*, vol. 4, part II, pp. 157–9.

[26] *Missale Augustense* (Basle: Jacobus Pforzensis, 1510), ABA, Fr 30. On the veneration of Anne in Augsburg see Hoeynck, *Geschichte der kirchlichen Liturgie*, p. 254 and in Nuremberg Schlemmer, *Gottesdienst und Frömmigkeit*, p. 340.

[27] *WA*, vol. 47, p. 73.

New Testament references to the brothers of Christ with belief in Mary's perpetual virginity, but devotion to the Holy Kindred testifies above all to the preoccupation with Christ's humanity that was a *leitmotiv* of late medieval piety.

The relationship between Christ and his human mother was also, of course, central to this piety. Mary was no normal mother, as some images emphasized: a fifteenth-century altarpiece from the Cologne church of St Maria ad Gradus, for example, shows the Virgin and Child surrounded by Old Testament scenes symbolizing Mary's purity.[28] Much more common by the late fifteenth century, however, were images that depicted her as a tender human mother caring for her infant son. Albrecht Dürer, for example, produced a number of touchingly maternal prints and paintings of Mary with the Christ Child, sometimes with Joseph or Anne alongside. Dürer's images are never devoid of religious symbolism, but they do give prominence to the human relationship between mother and son. In a painting from 1512 all extraneous detail has been removed (figure 4). Against a dark background we see a young, halo-less Virgin, intently focused on the baby in her arms.

As well as emphasizing Mary's love for the Christ Child, late medieval devotion also focused on her suffering at her son's death. Images of the crucifixion, deposition and lamentation depicted Mary's agony, and the iconography of the *pietà* or *Vesperbild*, which was common in western Europe from the thirteenth century onwards, showed Mary alone with her dead son across her lap. Mary's suffering was also invoked in liturgy and in the cult of her seven sorrows, which flourished in Germany during the fourteenth and fifteenth centuries. In 1423 a synod in Cologne introduced the feast of Our Lady of Sorrows into the diocese, while a 1510 missal from Augsburg gives a votive mass that could be read in honour of the compassion of the Virgin.[29] Images of the *Mater dolorosa* – Mary with her breast pierced by the sword foretold in Simeon's prophecy – were common. An example can be seen on the column to the right of the choir in Krauss's engraving of Nuremberg's Frauenkirche (figure 1). Here, as in an altarpiece commissioned from Dürer by Frederick the Wise of Saxony, the central figure of the sorrowing mother is surrounded by smaller scenes depicting the causes of her sorrow, from the flight into Egypt to the events of Christ's Passion.[30]

Poignant textual accounts and visual depictions of Mary's care for her infant son and of her compassion at his crucifixion served not only to engage viewers' empathy but also to evoke the Virgin's role in the drama of salvation. Because of her motherhood and because of her co-suffering with Christ Mary had won the right to intercede on behalf of sinners. God had made her, as the great Strasbourg

[28] *CR*, 11 (1996), 67–8.

[29] Janssen, *Das Erzbistum Köln*, p. 481; *Missale Augustense* (Basle: Jacibus Pforzensis, 1510), ABA, Fr 30.

[30] Fedja Anzelewsky, *Dürer: his art and life*, trans. Heide Grieve (Fribourg, 1980), p. 79.

Figure 4. Albrecht Dürer, Virgin and Child, 1512 (Kunsthistorisches Museum, Vienna)

preacher Johann Geiler von Keysersberg said in a sermon on the feast day of her Assumption, the one who 'advocated the whole of human salvation before him'. Moreover, she was 'not an ordinary advocate, but a strong and powerful one, so that she has never lost any cause'.[31] The notion of Mary as *mediatrix* was a central theme of late medieval piety. Her son could refuse her nothing, and her intercessory powers were confirmed by her Assumption and coronation as Queen of Heaven. Seated at Christ's right hand she tempered his justice with mercy.[32] The salvific significance of Mary's relationship with Christ is made explicit in images of their double intercession, in which the Virgin and her son plead before God the Father on behalf of mankind. Mary shows Christ

[31] Quoted in Kreitzer, *Reforming Mary*, pp. 127 and 207 n. 119.
[32] Ellington, *From Sacred Body*, p. 107.

Figure 5. Master of the Holy Kindred, intercessory image, c.1464–75 (WRM, Cologne)

the breast with which she nursed him and Christ shows God the wounds he received at the Crucifixion. In a version attributed to the Cologne Master of the Holy Kindred we see a ladder of salvation (figure 5): the prayers of the kneeling donor are received first by the saints surrounding him on earth then by Mary before they reach Christ and God. From her position kneeling before God's throne, Mary gestures downwards towards the donor, emphasizing her role as mediator between heaven and earth. In images of the *Schutzmantelmadonna*, or Virgin of Mercy, Mary shelters supplicants beneath her outspread cloak. The wings of a plague altarpiece by the Ulm artist Martin Schaffner combine these two iconographies (figure 6). Mary holds her breast and looks towards Christ while protecting the pope, Emperor Maximilian I and their followers beneath her blue mantle. Her intercession averts the arrows of plague, the millstone (a reference to Revelation 18:21) and the swords sent by God to punish sinful mankind.

Figure 6. Martin Schaffner, two wings from a plague altarpiece, c.1513–15 (GNM, Nuremberg)

As images of the *Schutzmantelmadonna* suggest, securing Mary's intercession was of central importance to late medieval Christians.[33] Devotional practices intended to invoke Mary's aid proliferated. Through pilgrimage, through the veneration of images, through processions, litanies, antiphons, confraternities and the recitation of the rosary people sought Mary's miraculous intervention in their daily lives and her effective intercession when it came to the Four Last Things: death, judgment, heaven and hell. Throughout Germany, but above all in Bavaria, pilgrimage to Marian shrines flourished on the eve of the Reformation. Because Mary's body had been assumed into heaven there were few relics for the faithful to venerate, and pilgrimages focused instead on images of the Virgin and Child or of the *pietà*. The fourteenth-century statue of the Virgin and Child at Altötting in Upper Bavaria was one of the most important. Altötting's first reported miracle occurred in 1489 and from 1490 pilgrimage to the shrine flourished. The site attracted pilgrims of all social classes, from peasants to the Emperor Frederick III. In his miracle book published in 1497 Jackob Issickemer boasted that 'people from many lands and foreigners of every estate . . . came to report and rejoice that they were helped by the Virgin Mary after invoking her and promising and vowing to visit her shrine with their offerings'.[34] The benefits procured through devotion to the Virgin of Altötting ranged from relief from illness and injury to release from prison. Southern Germany's other important Marian shrines included Tuntenhausen near the episcopal seat of Freising and Regensburg in the Upper Palatinate. In Regensburg the chapel of the Fair Virgin was built on the site of a destroyed synagogue: the link between Marian devotion and anti-Semitism was, as we shall see, an important one on the eve of the Reformation. Cologne had its own miraculous Marian statue, the Milan Madonna supposedly brought back from Italy together with the relics of the Three Kings in 1164, and during the fourteenth and fifteenth centuries pilgrimages to Marienbaum, Marienhelde, Marienstatt and Nothberg in the Rhineland also emerged.[35]

While Marian *Gnadenbilder* – grace-giving or miraculous images – attracted pilgrims from all around, other statues of the Virgin were also venerated at a local level in the hope of securing Mary's favour. *Gnadenbilder* were, of course, richly adorned with votive gifts: the Madonna of Altötting, for example, wore velvet robes and received an ornate gold chain as a gift from Emperor Maximilian I shortly before his death in 1519.[36] Church inventories indicate, however, that

[33] See, for example, the discussion of Dietrich Kolde's *Christenspiegel* in Janssen, *Das Erzbistum Köln*, p. 485.

[34] Quoted in Steven Sargent, 'Miracle books and pilgrimage shrines in late medieval Bavaria', *Historical Reflections* 13 (1986), 461.

[35] See chapter 5 and Amt für rheinische Landeskunde, ed., *Wallfahrt im Rheinland* (Cologne, 1981).

[36] Sargent, 'Miracle books', 460.

statues in urban churches received similar, if more modest, offerings. Nuremberg's Frauenkirche had two statues of the Virgin and Child, which between them had twenty-six sets of robes, as well as veils, crowns, rosaries and other ornaments.[37] The Cologne parish church of St Laurenz had three Madonnas, one of which was described in inventories as the 'parish Mary', suggesting that it was especially venerated. An inventory from 1528/30 records that this 'parish Mary' was dressed in a red velvet robe embroidered with pearls and had another robe that was made of black velvet with a golden border. The other Marian images had similar accoutrements. On feast days and when the statues were carried in procession they were also adorned with gilded crowns (some decorated with pearls), necklaces and rosaries.[38] These robes and ornaments had surely been donated by local devotees. In 1491, for example, members of the Marian brotherhood at the Cologne church of St Brigida contributed jointly to the cost of making a robe for an image of Our Lady. Heinrich Loufstayt and his wife donated a gold-painted silk cloth that the same image was to wear on its head when it was carried in procession by members of the brotherhood. And in 1531 the Madonna acquired a robe decorated with pearls, donated by a widow, Drutgin.[39] Stephan Isaac, a Cologne priest and critic of the excesses of the traditional cult of the Virgin, was surely right when he claimed in 1586 that the inhabitants of the city believed that one 'did the dear saints in heaven a favour when one decorated or clothed their images'.[40] The robes and treasures were a type of votive offering, presented to a specific image as a mark of affection or veneration, but given value ultimately by the favour thereby extended to Mary in heaven and by the expectation that in return for this favour she would intercede on the donor's behalf.

Mary's favour was also sought through supplicatory processions, litanies and antiphons. On the eve of the Reformation processions constituted an important part of religious life.[41] In addition to the relatively small ones that took place within specific churches on solemn feast days, there were also larger and more spectacular processions that wound their way through the cities' streets. Some were part of a regular liturgical cycle, for example the processions with the relics of saints Sebald and Deocarus that took place in Nuremberg each year, or Cologne's great sacrament procession, the *Gottestracht*, which was held on the second Friday after Easter. Others, the *Bittprozessionen*, were organized in times of crisis or political need at the behest of city councils, to avert war, plague or bad weather or to encourage God to look favourably on a particular event or endeavour. In 1522, for example, Nuremberg's council ordered its

[37] Heal, 'A woman like any other?', p. 58; StaatsAN, Rep. 44e, Losungsamt, Akten, S.I.L.130, Nr. 7a and S.I.L.131, Nr. 10.

[38] See below, pp. 223–4.

[39] Militzer, ed., *Quellen*, vol. 1, pp. 289–96.

[40] Stephan Isaac, *Wahre und einfältige Historia Stephani Isaaci* (1586), fol. 14r.

[41] Schlemmer, *Gottesdienst und Frömmigkeit*, p. 261.

entire clergy to participate, with their relics and vestments, in a procession from the Sebalduskirche to the Lorenzkirche to secure God's favour for Charles V's journey from Spain to the Empire.[42] Images of the Virgin often played a prominent role in such processions. In Cologne, for example, the silver Madonna from the church of St Maria im Kapitol was carried in procession by members of the confraternity dedicated to it 'when Our Lord is carried around the city and Our Lady's image with it [i.e. during the *Gottestracht*] or when Our Lady's image is carried around with the saints and with the patrons of Cologne [i.e. during *Bittprozessionen*]'.[43] *Bittprozessionen* also frequently invoked Mary and the other saints through litanies, series of petitions recited by the priest with repeated refrains interjected by the choir or congregation. The most popular was the Litany of All Saints, some versions of which called on Mary repeatedly.[44]

Mary was also invoked through antiphons, Latin texts that, by the late Middle Ages, had become an accepted part of lay devotion. The most popular was the *Salve Regina*, which called on Mary as 'mother of mercy', as 'our life, sweetness and hope' and as 'our advocate'. The *Salve* was often sung during liturgical processions, and, like the *Bittprozessionen*, was used in times of crisis. In 1483 and again in 1520 Nuremberg's council instructed its clergy to sing the *Salve* each day after vespers because of plague epidemics.[45] By the eve of the Reformation numerous perpetual endowments had been made for the *Salve* to be sung in Germany's urban churches.[46] In Nuremberg, for example, Peter Harstörffer the Elder donated a *Salve* to the parish church of St Sebald in 1479 and Peter Imhoff and Ulrich Kiffhaber gave another to St Lorenz in 1505. The donors specified that the *Salve*, with accompanying sequences and hymns, should be sung by chaplains and boys every Saturday, the day on which the weekly Commemoration of the Virgin was observed. The St Sebald *Salve* was also to be sung on the eve of every Marian festival. *Salve* endowments, like perpetual masses, were given for the benefit of their donors' souls. Harstörffer made his endowment 'to praise and honour God the almighty, Mary the virgin ... and all the heavenly host, also to help and comfort my, my forefathers' and all devout souls'.[47] Donors also sought to encourage people to attend the singing of the *Salve* by acquiring indulgences. Presence at the St Sebald *Salve*, for example, brought with it an indulgence of fifty days on a normal Saturday and of one hundred on particular festivals. While the *Salve* was by far the most popular Marian antiphon, endowments were also made for the singing of others, for example the *Alma redemptoris mater*, which asks Mary, 'the open door of

42 Ibid., p. 278. 43 Militzer, ed., *Quellen*, vol. 2, p. 910.
44 Graef, *Mary*, vol. 1, p. 232; Hoeynck, *Geschichte der kirchlichen Liturgie*, p. 187.
45 Schlemmer, *Gottesdienst und Frömmigkeit*, pp. 275–6.
46 See, for example, ibid., pp. 195–6; Paul von Stetten, *Geschichte der Heil. Ro^{e}m. Reichs Freyen Stadt Augsburg* (Frankfurt and Augsburg, 1743), p. 244.
47 Schlemmer, *Gottesdienst und Frömmigkeit*, pp. 296–9.

heaven and star of the sea', to help her fallen people and to have mercy on sinners.[48]

Confraternities provided another outlet for expressing devotion to the Mother of God. These religious associations played a prominent part in the religious life of Germany's late medieval cities, especially in Cologne, where there were over 120 of them during the first half of the sixteenth century.[49] Mary was frequently chosen as patron: nearly one-third of Cologne's confraternities were dedicated to her.[50] The chief religious objective of the pre-Reformation confraternity was the commemoration of the dead: members participated in burial services and attended annual masses in honour of departed brothers and sisters. Each confraternity also venerated its patron with masses, processions and gifts. Devotion to Mary was expressed in various ways. Some confraternities venerated particular cult images, carrying them in procession and maintaining lighted candles before them. Some undertook to provide for the singing of Marian hymns and antiphons. The *Marienbruderschaft Salve Regina* at Cologne's Groß-St Martin promised to ensure that the *Salve* was sung every day after vespers in St Peter's choir in order 'to praise and honour almighty God, Mary his merciful mother and all the heavenly host'.[51] Statutes of the *Marienbruderschaft Salve Regina* at St Maria im Kapitol decreed that at the confraternity's annual feast a priest must sing the antiphon *Regina Caeli*, the offertory hymn *Recordare Virgo* and the antiphon *Salve Regina* 'in worship of the mother of the almighty God, so that she prays her dear child for brothers, sisters, the living and dead of this worthy brotherhood'.[52] In addition to these religious objectives confraternities fulfilled certain social needs: members were often drawn from a particular group or trade and integration was encouraged by compulsory attendance at an annual meal hosted by the elected masters. Some confraternities also cared for the poor: the 1535 statutes of the *Marienbruderschaft zu den sieben Freuden (Salve Regina)* [Marian brotherhood of the Seven Joys] at the Cologne parish church of Klein-St Martin decreed that on each of the seven Marian festivals alms should be distributed in the churchyard.[53]

The rosary confraternity founded in 1475 by Jakob Sprenger, prior of Cologne's Dominican convent, *Provinzial* of western and southern Germany and co-author of the infamous *Malleus Maleficarum*, promoted a particular form of Marian piety. This confraternity was exceptional in both organizational and spiritual terms.[54] Following the example of his fellow Dominican Alanus

[48] Ibid., pp. 299–300. In 1491 Hans Imhoff left money for daily singing of *Alma* before start of Divine Office at St Lorenz.
[49] Militzer, ed., *Quellen*, vol. 3, pp. xi–xvii.
[50] Mallinckrodt, *Struktur und kollektiver Eigensinn*, p. 119; Militzer, ed., *Quellen*, vol. 3, p. xxi.
[51] Militzer, ed., *Quellen*, vol. 2, pp. 1053–4.
[52] Ibid., vol. 2, p. 961. [53] Ibid., vol. 3, p. 260.
[54] Mallinckrodt, *Struktur und kollektiver Eigensinn*, pp. 67–72.

de Rupe, who had established the first rosary confraternity in Douai (Flanders), Sprenger chose to abandon the traditional principles of geographical and professional or social limitation. In order to join the confraternity all that an individual had to do was have his or her name entered in a book, of which there were two in Sprenger's province, one in Cologne and one in Augsburg. There was no entry fee, so even the poorest could participate, and there was no fixed organizational structure to which members were obliged to commit themselves (although the Dominicans held four vigils each year to assist the souls of the dead brothers). Sprenger's rubric urged members simply to pray three rosaries per week. Members of this confraternity, both ecclesiastical and lay, are shown kneeling beneath Mary's cloak in a triptych painted in around 1500 for the Dominican cloister church of Heilig Kreuz (figure 7).[55] Thanks largely to the efforts of the Dominicans, the recitation of the rosary – 150 Ave Marias, interspersed with 15 Pater Nosters, sometimes accompanied by meditation on the joys and sorrows of the Virgin or on the mysteries of the life of Christ – became a popular devotional practice.[56] An individual devotee could win indulgences through reciting the rosary, as Erhard Schön's 1515 woodcut demonstrates (figure 8). Here we see the crucified Christ, with God the Father and the Holy Spirit above, in the centre of a garland of roses. Christ is surrounded by prophets, patriarchs, apostles, evangelists, saints, martyrs and angels, and below are two groups of clerical and lay worshippers, led by the pope and emperor. At the bottom of the print angels rescue souls from the flames of purgatory, and the inscription records the number of years and days by which the devotee could shorten his or her time in purgatory through praying the rosary. By joining the rosary confraternity the devotee multiplied the effect of his or her prayer. The cumulative prayer of thousands – Sprenger claimed that in 1476 8,000 people in Cologne and 3,000 in Augsburg had joined, though no membership lists survive to confirm this – could not go unheard. As a defence of the brotherhood written by Michael Francisci de Insulis in around 1480 put it: 'it is impossible that the prayers of many shall not be heard'.[57]

On the eve of the Reformation most inhabitants of the Holy Roman Empire would have participated in forms of devotional practice intended to secure

[55] *CR*, 10 (1995), 262.

[56] On the history of the rosary see Erzbischöfliches Diözesanmuseum Köln, *500 Jahre Rosenkranz: Köln 1475–1975* (Cologne, 1975). For much of the sixteenth century the Ave consisted of only Gabriel's greeting to Mary. The non-biblical part, which asks Mary to pray for sinners at the hour of their death, was in use as early as the fifteenth century, but was officially added to the Roman breviary only in 1568. Janssen, *Das Erzbistum Köln*, p. 483 and Erzbischöfliches Diözesanmuseum Köln, *500 Jahre Rosenkranz*, p. 54. On rosary devotion in Nuremberg see Schlemmer, *Gottesdienst und Frömmigkeit*, p. 340.

[57] Militzer, ed., *Quellen*, vol. 1, pp. cxix–cxxii and 507–29. Quoted at 520–1.

Figure 7. Master of St Severin, altarpiece of the Cologne rosary brotherhood, c.1500–10 (St Andreas, Cologne)

Mary's intercession. We need to recognize, however, that some manifestations of Mary's cult had darker connotations. In Germany, as elsewhere in Europe, a number of the most spectacular outbursts of medieval Mariolatry owed their genesis in part at least to anti-Semitism. Germany's key examples are well known. In 1519 a chapel dedicated to the Schöne Maria (Fair Virgin) was constructed in Regensburg on the site of a destroyed synagogue. Regensburg's Schöne Maria attracted thousands of pilgrims during the early 1520s, and her shrine was promoted in songs and miracle books as the site of a great Christian triumph over the Jews.[58] The story of a Jewish attack on an image of the Virgin at the Abbey of Cambron in Belgian Hennegau, said to have taken place in 1322, was also widely disseminated on the eve of the Reformation. When, in 1510, Colmar's Jews were expelled amidst accusations of ritual murder Maximilian I had the crime depicted in the local Dominican cloister as part of a campaign to stir up anti-Jewish sentiment in the city. The story was also retold in

[58] For recent discussions of this cult see Allyson Creasman, 'The Virgin Mary against the Jews: anti-Jewish polemic in the pilgrimage to the Schöne Maria of Regensburg, 1519–25', *Sixteenth Century Journal* 33, no. 4 (2002).

Figure 8. Erhard Schön, the Great Rosary, 1515 (British Museum)

two broadsheets, the first published in 1515 and the second in 1517, and in various sixteenth- and seventeenth-century miracle collections.[59] From a Christian perspective, Jewish denial of Mary's perpetual virginity and of her role as mother of the prophesied Messiah was anathema. Jews, Christians believed, hated Mary and would seize any opportunity to dishonour her image or her name. This Jewish–Christian dispute will receive only limited attention in the context of this study because its significance was eclipsed during the sixteenth century by intra-Christian clashes over Mary's status. But as Regensburg and Cambron suggest, we cannot ignore the anti-Jewish element of late medieval Marian piety.[60]

Like the shrine of the Schöne Maria in Regensburg, Nuremberg's Frauenkirche had been constructed on the site of the city's razed synagogue. The determining factor behind the expulsion of Nuremberg's Jews was the desire for urban expansion. But in chronicle accounts of the events of 1349/50 – i.e. in the city's construction of its own history – it was the desire to honour the Virgin that was presented as paramount. The events received their fullest treatment in Sigmund Meisterlin's chronicle, written in 1488. Meisterlin began by describing Nuremberg's need for a Marian church: 'it was a great lack in Nuremberg, that the empress of heaven, the God-bearer, the noble Virgin Mary had no church of her own in the city'. Not only did Mary lack a church of her own, she was also, in Meisterlin's opinion, inclined to avoid a place in which so many Jews were to be found: 'I think that the mother of the crucified one fled the murdering race that had killed her dear son, and did not want to have special relationships, where so many of them lived.' A representative of the city council, Ulrich Stromer, was accordingly induced by Mary herself to present the case before Emperor Charles IV, who expressed his willingness to sacrifice temporal advantage (the income from Jewish taxes) for the sake of honouring the virginal Mother of God. He decreed that Nuremberg's Jews should sell their houses and that on the site of the synagogue a chapel should be built and consecrated 'in honour of the highest patroness of the Roman Empire, the pure Virgin Mary'. Meisterlin claimed that Nuremberg thrived as a result: everyone who saw the beautiful, joyful market noted 'how the gentle empress of heaven had there obtained the increase of the city'.[61]

59 Klaus Schreiner, *Maria: Jungfrau, Mutter, Herrscherin* (Munich and Vienna, 1994), pp. 453–4; Koerner, *The Reformation of the Image*, 134.

60 As Heiko A. Oberman observed, 'the Mother of God and ever-Virgin Mary consistently played a most prominent role throughout the dialogues with Jews'. *The Roots of Anti-Semitism in the Age of Renaissance and Reformation*, trans. James I. Porter (Philadelphia, 1984), p. 83.

61 Sigmund Meisterlin, *Chronik der Reichstadt Nürnberg, 1488*, in *Die Chroniken der deutschen Städte vom 14. bis ins 16. Jahrhundert*, 36 vols. (Leipzig 1862–1931), vol. 3: *Die Chroniken der fränkischen Städte,* vol. 3: *Nürnberg* (Leipzig, 1864), pp. 158–61. Even in the seventeenth century the association between the expulsion of Nuremberg's Jews and the construction of the Frauenkirche was still remembered. See Schreiner, *Maria*, p. 443 and an anonymous chronicle from 1621, StadtAN, Best. F1, Nürnberger Chroniken, Nr. 127, fol. 126r.

Figure 9. Stefan Lochner / the Dombild Meister, altar of the Cologne city patrons, c.1440–45 (cathedral, Cologne)

Cologne's Jewish community was expelled in 1424. In May 1426 the city took possession of the synagogue, located on a prime site directly opposite the town hall, on the basis of unpaid ground rent. The council, the *Bürgermeister* and the pastor of St Laurenz, in whose parish the synagogue lay, determined to transform it into a chapel in honour of God and the Virgin in order 'to destroy the many great dishonours that the Jews did and showed to the same [i.e. the Virgin] and to her dear child our Lord for many years, when they lived in Cologne, especially in the synagogue'. They decreed that an altar should be erected in the chapel, on which 'such offences of the Jews may be atoned for and, from henceforth, all honour should be offered to the dear Lord and to his tender mother'. The former synagogue was given a lead roof and a spire and on 8 September 1426, the feast of Mary's birth, the new chapel was dedicated in honour of 'Maria zu Jerusalem'.[62] In the early 1440s an altarpiece of the Adoration of the Magi formerly attributed to Stefan Lochner and now given to the anonymous 'Dombild Meister' was installed in the chapel (figure 9), and there were also two richly clothed statues of the Virgin.[63] Amidst this celebration of Mary the chapel's history could not be forgotten: in 1500 two Latin panels were placed in the chapel to remind visitors that this had been the site of the Jewish cult that had been forced to make way for Christendom. The inscriptions ended with a plea for the general conversion of the Jews.[64]

62 Carl Brisch, *Geschichte der Juden in Cöln und Umgebung aus ältester Zeit bis auf die Gegenwart*, 2 vols. (Cologne, 1879 and 1882), vol. 2, pp. 41–6.

63 Klaus Militzer and Wolfgang Schmid, 'Das Inventar der Kölner Ratskapelle von 1519: Edition und Kommentar', *Wallraf-Richartz-Jahrbuch* 58 (1997), 232.

64 Brisch, *Geschichte der Juden*, vol. 2, p. 46.

Why, in Nuremberg, in Cologne, in Regensburg and in a number of other medieval German towns was Mary chosen as the patron of the chapel that replaced the local synagogue?[65] The connection between anti-Semitism and Marian devotion may have been engendered in part by typological considerations. Mary symbolized the church, and in constructing chapels in her honour on the sites of razed synagogues Christians were creating monuments to the victory of *Ecclesia* over *Synagoga*. Medieval sources, however, do not often invoke this consideration. Nor, in either Nuremberg's Frauenkirche or in the council chapel in Cologne, were there any visual reminders of the typological opposition.[66] More important was the Christian desire to atone for the Jews' denial of Mary's status as the Mother of God, for their role in Christ's death and for the dishonours that they had done to Mary and her son.[67] Jews were frequently accused of calling Mary a whore, an accusation that arose, perhaps, from Christian knowledge of medieval Jewish legends such as the *Toldoth Jeschu*, in which Jesus' conception is associated with adultery and with breaking the ritual prohibition on sex during menstruation.[68] This accusation persisted even into the era of the Reformation. In 1529, for example, an armoury guard was tried by Augsburg's magistrates for causing a disturbance on the city's streets, during which he had asked why 'poor Christians' [evangelicals] were everywhere being tormented whilst Jews, who insisted that Our Lady was no virgin but a whore, that she had had children before and after Christ's birth and that Christ was not God's son but a whore's child, were tolerated.[69] For Catholic authorities, the dedication of a chapel in Mary's honour provided an opportunity to avenge such Jewish slanders. In Nuremberg, Cologne and Regensburg the synagogue – a site that had been profaned by Jewish worship – was cleansed and made holy by Mary's presence, to the benefit of the whole community.

CATHOLIC REFORM

The first generation of evangelical reformers grew up in a religious environment that was steeped in Marian piety. Feast days and images of all kinds celebrated the key events of Mary's life, while popular devotional practices

[65] Wolfgang Glüber, '"Die Judengaßen thet man zerstören / der hymelkünigin zu eren". Synagogenzerstörung und Marienkirchenbau', in *Maria – Tochter Sion? Mariologie, Marienfrömmigkeit und Judenfeindschaft*, ed. Johannes Heil and Rainer Kampling (Paderborn, 2001); J. M. Minty, '*Judengasse* to Christian quarter: the phenomenon of the converted synagogue in the late medieval and early modern Holy Roman Empire', in *Popular Religion in Germany and Central Europe, 1400–1800*, ed. Robert W. Scribner and Trevor Johnson (London, 1996); Hedwig Röckelein, 'Marienverehrung und Judenfeindlichkeit in Mittelalter und früher Neuzeit', in *Maria in der Welt*, ed. Opitz *et al.*

[66] Glüber, 'Die Judengaßen', pp. 175–8. During the fourteenth and fifteenth centuries the motif was found chiefly in Passion and carnival plays.

[67] Creasman, 'The Virgin Mary against the Jews', 969–73.

[68] Schreiner, *Maria*, pp. 418–20. [69] See below, pp. 135–6.

such as pilgrimage and the recitation of the rosary sought to secure her intercession on behalf of mankind. But while Luther and his contemporaries were surrounded on all sides by what they would later condemn as Mariolatry, they were also exposed to the reforming ideas that played a part in shaping the religious life of the late medieval church: to the intensely personal piety of the *devotio moderna*, which left Thomas à Kempis's bestselling *Imitatio Christi* as its legacy, and to the Christian humanism of Desiderius Erasmus. Kempis's devotional text and Erasmus' writings are very Christocentric. Unlike the evangelical reformers, neither author sought to destroy Mary's cult, but they did both attempt to redress what they perceived as an imbalance in contemporary piety. Devotion should, they believed, be focused on Christ rather than on Mary, and Erasmus in particular condemned the excesses of the late medieval Marian cult. Ultimately, under pressure from the Protestant Reformation, the Catholic Church rejected Erasmus' type of reformed Marianism, and reaffirmed the value of traditional devotional practices, as we will see in chapter 4. But a number of the great humanist's criticisms of the cult lived on in the teachings of the evangelical reformers, in a form he would have doubtless found abhorrent.

The *devotio moderna* originated in the Netherlands in the late fourteenth century and spread rapidly into the Rhineland and other parts of Germany. Its founder, Geert Groote (1340–84), spent his time preaching spiritual and moral reform, and by the middle of the fifteenth century there were about one hundred houses of the Brethren and Sisters of the Common Life dedicated to implementing his ideals. Members of these communities sought to cultivate religious virtues without taking formal monastic vows. They prayed the canonical hours, studied Scripture, attended mass and spent much of their time copying religious texts. Some individuals eventually moved into the monastic fold: a monastery for regular canons was established at Windesheim in 1386, and other foundations soon followed. But whether its adherents resided in the seclusion of a monastery or out in the world, the *devotio moderna* directed them towards inner piety. Thomas à Kempis's early fifteenth-century text, the *Imitatio Christi*, contains the most important exposition of the principles of the *devotio moderna*. Kempis advocated an inward-looking spirituality that was inspired by the Scriptures and that focused entirely on Christ. The believer must, Kempis wrote, bring his or her life into conformity with that of Christ. Christ should provide a pattern for self-knowledge, self-mortification, humility and obedience. Through identification with his suffering and reliance on his virtues the individual believer would progress towards union with the divine via the Eucharist.

Despite its strongly Christocentric focus, the *devotio moderna* was by no means hostile to the cult of the Virgin. Thomas à Kempis's biography of the movement's founder records that Groote 'translated the Hours of the Blessed Virgin together with certain other Hours from Latin into the Germanic language so that simple unlearned lay people might have them in their mother tongue'. Moreover, at the Windesheim Congregation's monastery of Mount St Agnes near Zwolle, where Kempis was later to serve as canon, the first chapel and altar were consecrated in honour of Mary.[70] But in Kempis's *Imitatio* we see the implications that an intense devotional focus on Christ had for the veneration of saints. Whereas another medieval best-seller, Voragine's *Golden Legend*, had dwelt at length on the glories and miracles of the saints, Kempis's text, which was reproduced in at least 800 manuscript copies and 100 incunabula editions in the first century of its existence, devoted very little attention to them.[71] The saints were not worthless: they provided examples of virtue, and were worthy of imitation. Devout Christians could also legitimately seek their intercession: Kempis wrote that on festivals, for example, the prayers of the saints should be 'implored more fervently than ever'.[72] But the believer must remember that 'the teaching of Jesus far transcends all the teachings of the saints', and that he or she must trust and hope in God alone.[73] Voragine had devoted a whole text to telling the stories of the saints' lives, but Kempis gave no sense of them as individuals. He mentioned Mary only once, and from the vast panoply of medieval saints he named only St Francis.[74] Kempis did not condemn the accoutrements of the saints' cults – images and pilgrimages – but he emphasized that contemplation, virtuous living and devotion to Christ and to the Eucharist were of much greater significance.[75]

As a movement for spiritual renewal the *devotio moderna* had lost impetus by the beginning of the sixteenth century, but Kempis's text lived on. It was used in various translations and editions by both Protestants and Catholics, by people as diverse as Caspar Schwenckfeld, Leo Jud and Ignatius Loyola.[76] Northern Europe's greatest humanist, Desiderius Erasmus, surely knew it even though he never cited it in his copious writings. As Halkin states, the spirituality that Erasmus taught was 'inspired by the same impulses and rooted in the same tradition' as that of Thomas à Kempis.[77] Erasmus preserved, as we shall see, Kempis's Christocentric focus, but he also had a lot more to say about the Virgin Mary than the author of the *Imitatio Christi* had done. In the early stages of his career Erasmus wrote fulsome praises of the Virgin. The *Paean in Honour of the Virgin Mother* and the *Prayer of Supplication to Mary* were among his first published works (1503). Both invoked the Virgin in very traditional terms. The

[70] Max von Habsburg, 'The devotional life: Catholic and Protestant translations of Thomas à Kempis' Imitatio Christi, c.1420–c.1620', unpublished PhD thesis, University of St Andrews, 2001, pp. 34, 50.
[71] Ibid., p. 1.
[72] Thomas à Kempis, *The Imitation of Christ*, trans. Leo Sherley-Price (Harmondsworth, 1952), pp. 37–8, 49.
[73] Ibid., pp. 27, 180–2.
[74] Habsburg, 'The devotional life', pp. 50–1.
[75] Kempis, *The Imitation of Christ*, pp. 28, 186.
[76] Habsburg, 'The devotional life'.
[77] Léon-E. Halkin, *Erasmus: a critical biography*, trans. John Tonkin (Oxford, 1994), p. 4.

Paean described her as the 'singular glory of heaven, earth's surest safeguard' and as the mother of mercy. Erasmus emphasized, as later reformers were also to do, that Mary's grace came from God, but he nonetheless celebrated her as an advocate. 'Indeed, who else is there for suffering humanity to call upon with hymns and prayers than you, Mary, who alone among the heavenly host, by virtue of your merits, favour, and dignity, possess the power to appease the anger of the judge?'[78] As the *Supplication* said, Christ 'listens readily to your entreaties, and, what is more, so reveres you (since he is a most loving and dutiful son) that he never denies you anything you ask'. To traditional Marian titles such as 'star of our sea' and to allegories drawn from the Song of Songs Erasmus added typically humanist mythological comparisons, identifying Mary as 'the true Diana'.[79]

Erasmus sent a copy of the volume in which these two Marian works were published to his friend John Colet in 1504, saying that he had written them 'almost against the grain'.[80] In the *Catalogus*, a description of his works addressed to Johann von Botzheim and published in 1523, Erasmus again denigrated the *Paean* and the *Supplication*, saying that he had composed them to suit the taste of his patron, Anna van Borssele, Lady of Veere, and her young son Adolph of Burgundy, rather than to please his own judgment.[81] These prayers certainly caused him some embarrassment later on – in his 1528 *Ciceronian*, for example, he explicitly ridiculed those who portrayed Jesus' mother as Diana – but he nonetheless permitted them to be published repeatedly and included them in his *Catalogus*.[82] The Virgin remained important to him; even though he sought to relativize her significance and to eliminate what he saw as superstitious abuses of her cult.[83] He upheld the key Marian doctrines of the Catholic Church. He acknowledged that belief in Mary's perpetual virginity was not supported by scripture, but defended it because 'it has been handed down to us by the consensus of early orthodox writers'.[84] In the *Paean* and *Supplication* he had alluded to Mary's Immaculate Conception, saying that she had never been 'defiled by any stain of sin'. In 1527 and again in 1531 he cited these early works as proof of his enduring adherence to the doctrine that was by that time under attack not only from 'maculist' Dominicans but also from evangelical reformers.[85] In his 1524 *The Method of Praying to God* he defended against Luther's condemnations the practice of invoking the saints, saying that 'if Scripture neither enjoins nor forbids this practice, we should neither require

[78] *CWE*, vol. 69, pp. 20, 23. [79] *CWE*, vol. 69, pp. 44–5.
[80] *CWE*, vol. 2, p. 87. [81] *CWE*, vol. 9, p. 322.
[82] MacCulloch, 'Mary and sixteenth-century Protestants', p. 192; *CWE*, vol. 69, p. xiii.
[83] Hilmar M. Pabel, *Conversing with God: prayer in Erasmus' pastoral writings* (Toronto, 1997), pp. 69–108.
[84] *Modus Orandi Deum* (1524), *CWE*, vol. 70, p. 187.
[85] *CWE*, vol. 69, p. 27, n. 46; *CWE*, vol. 84, pp. 243–4. Léon-E. Halkin, 'La mariologie d'Erasme', *Archiv für Reformationsgeschichte* 68 (1977), especially 39–43.

it as necessary nor, since by its very nature it does not involve impiety, prohibit it as irreligious'.[86]

Erasmus' Christocentrism imposed firm limits on his Mariology.[87] He stated clearly in his *Apologia adversus monachos quosdam hispanos* of 1528: 'In Christ, not the Virgin, is found the sacred anchor of our salvation.'[88] But his Christocentrism, unlike that of later Protestant reformers, was not anti-Marian: Erasmus advocated 'salvation through Jesus, but not without his mother'.[89] In his mature works he emphasized that Mary was important, but only because of Christ. His 1523 *Liturgy of the Virgin Mother Venerated at Loreto* did not, as one might expect, celebrate the famous cult of the Holy House, the house in which the Annunciation had supposedly occurred.[90] Instead Erasmus emphasized Mary's relationship with Christ. The collect, for example, asked Mary to grant 'that those who with piety worship you in the Son and the Son in you, and venerate the Son in the Mother and the Mother because of the Son, may by heavenly protection be freed from all evils'.[91] He was glad, he reported, in the homily included in the second edition of this *Liturgy* (1525), to see crowds gather to commemorate Mary, for 'this love for the Mother is an act of piety towards the Son'.[92] His *Liturgy* and its homily comprise an implicit reproach of popular piety; of the kind of exaggerated Marian devotion displayed at pilgrimage sites such Loreto. But Erasmus was careful to separate himself, on the other hand, from Protestant iconoclasts, who sought to cleanse churches of every trace of Mary's cult. In his famous dialogue, *A Pilgrimage for Religion's Sake*, Erasmus included a letter purporting to be from Mary herself, in which she commented on the activities of the Zwinglian iconoclasts who had cast the saints out of their churches. 'Me', she says, 'you shall not eject unless at the same time you eject my Son, whom I hold in my arms. From him I will not be parted. Either you expel him along with me, or you leave us both here, unless you prefer to have a church without Christ.'[93]

Despite Erasmus' abiding attachment to Mary, he did not mince his words when it came to condemning contemporary abuses of her cult. As MacCulloch points out, Erasmus may have wished every ploughman to read his Bible, but he was repelled by the realities of late medieval lay devotion.[94] In his *Colloquies*, a collection of dialogues on religious and moral issues that he added to throughout his life, he directed his biting sarcasm at gullible devotees of the saints and at the unscrupulous clergymen who abused them. *The Shipwreck*, which was first printed in the August 1523 edition of the *Colloquies*, mocks sailors who, when a storm threatens their ship, pray to Mary using her traditional epithet

[86] *CWE*, vol. 70, pp. 186–7. See also Halkin, *Erasmus*, p. 229.
[87] Ibid., p. 230. [88] *LB*, vol. 9, col. 1087. [89] Halkin, *Erasmus*, p. 230.
[90] On the Loreto cult see Bäumer and Scheffczyk, eds., *Marienlexikon*, vol. 4, pp. 151–5.
[91] *CWE*, vol. 69, pp. 86–7. [92] *CWE*, vol. 69, p. 91. [93] *CWE*, vol. 40, p. 628.
[94] MacCulloch, 'Mary and sixteenth-century Protestants', pp. 193–4.

'Star of the Sea', and flatter her with 'many other titles the Sacred Scriptures nowhere assign to her' rather than trusting in the paternal love of God. When asked to explain Mary's connection to the sea, the traveller who witnessed the shipwreck says: 'formerly Venus was protectress of sailors, because she was believed to have been born of the sea. Since she gave up guarding them, the Virgin Mother has succeeded this mother who was not a virgin.'[95] Here, as elsewhere in his mature works, Erasmus suggests that Christian saints have replaced pagan deities, and receive, as a result, the superstitious supplications of ignorant people.

In *A Pilgrimage for Religion's Sake*, first published in February 1526, Erasmus ridiculed medieval pilgrimage practice, taking as his examples the shrine of the Virgin Mary at Walsingham and that of Thomas à Becket at Canterbury, both of which he had visited during his second stay in England (1509–14).[96] In the letter attributed to the Virgin, cited above, Mary complains that she had been 'all but exhausted by the shameless entreaties of mortals', some of whom had even 'asked of a Virgin what a modest youth would hardly dare ask of a bawd'. People, she laments, 'demanded everything from me alone, as if my Son were always a baby (because he is carved and painted as such at my bosom), still needing his mother's consent and not daring to deny a person's prayer'.[97] Here, as in his *Annotations on the Gospel of Luke* where he stated that Jesus no longer owed obedience to his mother, Erasmus undermined the whole edifice of Marian intercession: if Mary had no hold over Christ then her prayers were no more valuable than those of any other saint.[98] Moreover, for Erasmus the notion, implicit in the practice of pilgrimage, that one image or relic of the Virgin was more efficacious than another, was pure superstition. Menedemus, the dialogue's 'stay-at-home' who responds to the stories of Ogygius' pilgrimages, speaks with typically Erasmian scepticism about relics: 'O Mother most like her Son! He left us so much of his blood on earth; she left so much of her milk that it's scarcely credible a woman with only one child could have so much, even if the child had drunk none of it.' Such relics are, Menedemus fears, 'contrived for profit', and his suspicions regarding the greed of the clergy are confirmed when Ogygius reports that the custodian of the Walsingham shrine 'approached us, quite silent, but holding out a board like those used in Germany by toll collectors on bridges'.[99] Erasmus also abhorred the physicality of pilgrimage: the trust that foolish pilgrims placed in sacred objects. Ogygius is one such credulous fool, and tells his companion that when he spoke a prayer to the Virgin before her milk 'Mother and Son both seemed to nod approval . . .

[95] *CWE*, vol. 39, p. 355.
[96] On Erasmus and Walsingham see Aston, *England's Iconoclasts*, pp. 197–9.
[97] *CWE*, vol. 40, p. 625. [98] MacCulloch, 'Mary and sixteenth-century Protestants', p. 193.
[99] *CWE*, vol. 40, pp. 632–3.

the sacred milk appeared to leap up, and the Eucharistic elements gleamed somewhat more brightly.'[100]

If Christ was the anchor of man's salvation, if supplications were better directed to him than to Mary and if traditional saints' cults were of pagan origin and were suffused with superstition, how then was one supposed to venerate the Virgin? Ogygius had a concise answer to this question: 'you will admire her most acceptably if you imitate her'.[101] Erasmus gave the same response in a number of his other works: in his influential *Handbook of the Christian Soldier* (1504) he wrote 'no devotion is more pleasing to Mary than the imitation of Mary's humility', while in *The Praise of Folly* (1511) he mocked people who lit candles to Mary in broad daylight but did not 'try to imitate her in the chastity and modesty of her life, in her love for celestial things'.[102] The homily from the 1525 edition of Erasmus' *Liturgy of the Virgin Mother Venerated at Loreto* elaborated on this theme, stating that 'the cult of the most holy Virgin consists principally in four things – praise, honour, invocation, and imitation. The final one is so superior that the others without it would be unfruitful, and this one also embraces the others in itself.'[103] Mary had been co-opted into Erasmus' typically humanist programme of moral reform and religious renewal. She was not pleased, Erasmus wrote, by 'these fasts with which some honour her on certain days, fasting for one purpose only – that the next day they may drink more abundantly; nor that she is won over by songs chanted by certain people, who are completely corrupted by lust and luxury'.[104] Instead of fasting and making offerings, we should therefore strive to imitate her continence, her chastity and her modesty.[105]

Erasmus' attempts to curtail the cult of the Virgin were not well received by his fellow Catholics. Perhaps inevitably, at a time at which many of the traditions of the Catholic Church were under attack from evangelical reformers, Erasmus' criticisms of contemporary religious practice were viewed with suspicion. The Sorbonne condemned his *Colloquies* in 1526, the Spanish Inquisition subjected his writings to hostile examination, and the Italian prince and diplomat Alberto Pio de Carpi denounced him for having prepared the way for the Reformation.[106] Erasmus sought to defend himself against such censures in a number of Apologies. As well as refuting accusations that he had attacked the structure of the church and rejected the Trinity, Erasmus excused his sarcastic comments about Marian devotion. In *The Shipwreck* he had not intended, he said, to denigrate Mary, but only to condemn the superstition of those who appealed to her rather than to God. His irony, he claimed in another defence of the same *Colloquy*, had been aimed not at Mary but at the foolish

[100] *CWE*, vol. 40, p. 633. [101] *CWE*, vol. 40, p. 640.
[102] MacCulloch, 'Mary and sixteenth-century Protestants', p. 192; *CWE*, vol. 27, p. 120.
[103] *CWE*, vol. 69, p. 92. [104] *CWE*, vol. 69, p. 93.
[105] See also *CWE*, vol. 40, p. 719; Halkin, *Erasmus*, pp. 228–9. [106] Ibid., pp. 206, 212.

sailors who invoked her. The letter purporting to be from the Virgin published in *A Pilgrimage for Religion's Sake* had, Erasmus said, been intended as a joke, directed at those miscreants who condemned the veneration of the saints and destroyed their images.[107] 'I do not make fun of the Virgin', he concluded in his response to Pio, 'but of the monstrosity of human superstition.'[108]

Elsewhere, however, Erasmus' Marian message found a receptive audience. Other humanists and reforming clergy agreed that true devotion to the saints consisted of the imitation of their virtues. In the final decades of the fifteenth century German humanists had, James Weiss points out, tried to 're-orient the methods and goals of hagiography'. Sigmund Meisterlin, Jakob Wimpheling, Hieronymus Emser and Johannes Trimethius produced new editions of traditional saints' lives, all of which emphasized the importance of the saints as examples for reform and religious renewal.[109] Erasmus' arguments also struck a chord with reforming clergy such as Christoph von Stadion, bishop of Augsburg (1517–43). At the close of his first diocesan synod (1517) Stadion gave a great *Reformrede*, in which he urged his clergy to follow the examples of the saints, to live modestly and to look after the poor. For this speech, Stadion extracted passages word-for-word from Erasmus' *Handbook of the Christian Soldier*.[110] As we shall see, the notion that imitating the saints' faith and other virtues was the proper way to venerate them lived on in Lutheran teaching.

Other elements of Erasmus' message also found echoes in the writings of the Protestant reformers. In his 1519 New Testament, for example, Erasmus had revised the Vulgate's translation of Gabriel's greeting to Mary, turning her epithet from 'gratia plena' to 'gratiosa'. Like Erasmus, Luther worried that the Vulgate's version ascribed too much merit to Mary.[111] In a sermon published in 1612 a Lutheran preacher, Johannes Schuler, reminded his congregation of Erasmus' concern that the worship of saints distracted attention from the worship of Christ: 'Erasmus says, there are many who rely more on the help of the Mother of Christ or Christopher than on Christ himself.'[112] Reformed Protestants picked up on the humanist's harsh condemnations of the superstitious

[107] See in particular the *Apologia adversus monachos quosdam hispanos* (1528) (*LB*, vol. 9, cols. 1084–7); the *Apologia adversus rhapsodias Alberti Pii* (1531) (*LB*, vol. 9, cols. 1163–7, translated in *CWE*, vol. 84, pp. 105–360) and the *Declarationes as censuras Lutetiae vulgatus* (*LB*, vol. 9, col. 942).

[108] *CWE*, vol. 84, p. 254.

[109] James Michael Weiss, 'Hagiography by German humanists, 1483–1516', *Journal of Medieval and Renaissance Studies* 15, no. 2 (1985), especially 300.

[110] Peter Rummel, 'Die Augsburger Diözesansynoden. Historischer Überblick', *JbVAB* 20 (1986), 28–9.

[111] MacCulloch, 'Mary and sixteenth-century Protestants', p. 193; Heinz Bluhm, 'Luther's translation and interpretation of the Ave Maria', *Journal of English and German Philology* 51 (1952), 198; *Opera omnia Desiderii Erasmi Roterodami*, vol. 6, part V (Amsterdam, 2000), pp. 458–9.

[112] Johannes Schuler, *Etliche Christliche Predigen* (Stuttgart, 1612), p. 44.

invocation of saints: Calvin echoed Erasmus' sarcasm with regard to relics in a tract of 1544, while Bullinger restated his belief that saints' cults were of pagan origin, and that the titles traditionally given to Mary, such as 'Star of the Sea', were sacrilegious.[113] Such superficial affinities between Erasmus and the evangelical reformers, however, disguise deep differences of opinion with regard to Mary's significance. Erasmus may have undermined the medieval edifice of Marian intercession, but it was the Protestants who brought about its collapse. For Erasmus it was clear that Mary could not be thrown out of the church, lest Christ be thrown out alongside her. For the Protestants, by contrast, Christ could not be properly worshipped until his church had been cleansed of all traces of idolatrous devotion to Mary his mother.

PROTESTANT REFORMERS

> The fact of the matter is that in popular estimation the blessed Virgin has completely replaced Christ. Men have invoked her, trusted in her mercy, and sought through her to appease Christ, as though he were not a propitiator but only a terrible judge and avenger.[114]

Philip Melanchthon's criticism of the cult of the Virgin Mary in article 21 of his *Apology for the Augsburg Confession*, a statement of faith that became a normative symbol for the Lutheran Church, epitomizes Protestant concern about the nature of traditional Marian veneration.[115] Theologians had, according to Melanchthon, made Mary and the other saints into propitiators or mediators of redemption. They had invoked them as intercessors, asserting that Christians could be considered righteous on account of the saints' merits. They had sought mercy from Mary and her fellow saints rather than from Christ, the true source of all salvation. Encouraged by the theologians, the 'common people' had therefore come to venerate Mary more than Christ. Similar concerns had been voiced by Catholic reformers, but Protestant criticisms went much further than those of men such as Kempis and Erasmus. On the basis of their interpretations of Scripture, the Protestants challenged the key precepts of the medieval cult.

Reformers' attacks on the cult of the Virgin were part of a wider campaign against the invocation of saints, a practice that, according to Martin Luther, offended God and undermined true Christian piety. Belief in saintly intercession lost its *raison d'être* when Luther argued that man was saved only by

[113] MacCulloch, 'Mary and sixteenth-century Protestants', p. 194.
[114] *Die Bekenntnisschriften der evangelisch-lutherischen Kirche* (Göttingen, 1959), p. 322. Translation from Theodore G. Tappert, ed., *The Book of Concord: the confessions of the evangelical Lutheran Church* (Philadelphia, 1959), pp. 232–3.
[115] On the Augsburg Confession see Robert Kolb, *Confessing the Faith: reformers define the church, 1530–1580* (St Louis, 1991), pp. 38–42.

God's grace received through faith.[116] In the Schmalkaldic Articles, drawn up in 1536, Luther wrote that the invocation of saints 'conflicts with the chief article of the faith and blots out the recognition of Christ. It is neither commanded nor suggested in Scripture and has no basis there at all.'[117] The veneration of the saints also encouraged works righteousness, the belief that salvation could be earned through pilgrimage, the veneration of images and relics and other similar practices.[118] Inspired by the devil, the Catholic Church had promoted this veneration to increase its own profits and to divert believers from true forms of worship.[119] The clergy taught 'fairy tales' about the saints in public, and superstitious beliefs had developed around individual cults, so that St Sebastian was credited with the power to protect from plague and St Valentine to heal epilepsy.[120] Like Erasmus, Melanchthon suggested that such beliefs were 'obviously of pagan origin'. Moreover, saints' images were venerated as if they contained some magical power, a practice that Luther condemned as 'great error and idolatry'.[121]

The cult of the Virgin Mary presented the reformers with particular problems. As Luther recognized in a sermon preached in 1522 on the feast day of Mary's birth, people were especially deeply attached to her cult. This excessive Marian veneration had two consequences: an injury was done to Christ because Christians turned their hearts more towards her than towards him; and there was a social cost, because in venerating Mary they forgot their poor brethren.[122] The social cost of the cult of saints was emphasized particularly strongly in the writings of the Swiss reformer Huldrych Zwingli.[123] Above all, however, Protestant reformers were concerned to refute popular notions of Mary's intercessory power. In his 1521 *Commentary on the Magnificat* Luther complained that 'now we find those who come to her for help and comfort, as though she were a divine being, so that I fear there is now more idolatry in the world than ever before'.[124] He emphasized that Mary, like the other saints, could not serve

116 The notion of Mary as intercessor between man and God was established in the eastern Church by the end of the patristic period, and appeared in the writings of theologians in the west from the eighth century onwards. Graef, *Mary*, vol. 1, pp. 161, 167–8, 170–1.

117 Kolb, *For All the Saints*, p. 13.

118 Carol Piper Heming, *Protestants and the Cult of the Saints in German-Speaking Europe, 1517–31*, Sixteenth Century Essays and Studies 65 (Kirksville, MO, 2003), p. 17.

119 Kolb, *For All the Saints*, p. 13; *WA*, vol. 6, p. 448 (*An den Christlichen Adel deutscher Nation*, 1520).

120 *WA*, vol. 1, p. 412; vol. 56, p. 417. See also Heming, *Protestants and the Cult of the Saints*, p. 11.

121 Tappert, ed., *The Book of Concord*, p. 233; *WA*, vol. 17, part II, p. 424 (*Festpostille*, 1527).

122 *WA*, vol. 10, part III, pp. 313–14. For a discussion of this sermon see Hans Düfel, 'Die Marienverehrung im Licht des reformatorischen "sola scriptura"', in *De culto Mariano saeculo 16 [decimo sexto]. Acta congressus Mariologici-Mariani Internationalis Caesaraugustae anno 1979 celebrati* (Rome, 1985), pp. 16–19.

123 Campi, *Zwingli und Maria*, pp. 79–80.

124 *WA*, vol. 7, p. 570; Jaroslav Pelikan, ed., *Luther's Works*, 55 vols. (St Louis / Philadelphia, 1958–67), vol. 21, pp. 323–4.

as our *Fürsprecherin* [advocate/intercessor] but only as our *Fürbitterin* [one who prays for us].[125] Her prayer had no more authority than that of any other Christian, and she could offer no consolation. Criticizing the traditional Marian antiphon, *Salve Regina*, Luther wrote 'I will gladly have her pray for me, but I will not have her as my consolation and my life, and your prayer is as dear to me as hers.'[126] Zwingli, who from 1516 to 1519 had preached at the Benedictine monastery of Einsiedeln where pilgrims paid homage to a miracle-working statue of the Virgin, was even firmer in his condemnation of Mary's intercessory role. He stated in his response to Johannes Eck's *Pseudologia Zwinglii* that 'one may not call upon anyone except Christ as *Fürbitter*' for he alone is 'the true *Fürbitter* and mediator', and he warned that 'those who make the saints in heaven into *Fürbittern* do so because they do not dare to come to God; but this is against God's word, and diminishes his grace, goodness and mercy'.[127]

Alongside this doctrinal concern with intercession a number of devotional practices were singled out for attack: Luther spoke scathingly of the mindless repetition of the Hail Mary, rejecting as useless what he described as the 'babbling of lips and the rattling of rosaries'; antiphons such as the *Salve Regina* and *Regina Caeli* were condemned because they dishonoured Christ, contravening his assertion that he himself was the way, the truth and the light; and Marian pilgrimages were ridiculed as fools' works, the products of diabolic and monastic manipulation.[128] In his 1530 *Admonition to the Clergy* Luther condemned all innovations in the veneration of saints, including new cults such as that of St Anne, Mary's mother. He attacked the recent proliferation of pilgrimages, saying that there were so many Madonnas that scarcely a chapel or an altar now lacked its own pilgrimage. He also criticized the practice of hanging rosaries and other devotional objects on doors to ward off evil and misfortune.[129]

Images, which, as we saw in the Introduction, had been one of the key manifestations of Marian piety on the eve of the Reformation, also came under attack. Sometimes this was because of what they depicted and sometimes because of the ways in which they had been manipulated by profit-seeking clergy. The

125 *WA*, vol. 10, part III, p. 325.

126 *WA*, vol. 10, part III, p. 322 (1522 sermon on the feast day of Mary's birth). Sermons preached on John 2:4, Christ's reproach to Mary at Cana, provided an opportunity for Luther and his followers to reiterate this message. See for example Schimmelpfennig, *Die Geschichte der Marienverehrung*, p. 10; *WA*, vol. 21, p. 65; G. Müller and Gottfried Seebass, eds., *Andreas Osiander d. Ä: Gesamtausgabe*, 10 vols. (Gütersloh, 1975–97), vol. 1, pp. 80–1 and Beth Kreitzer, 'Reforming Mary: changing images of the Virgin Mary in Lutheran sermons of the sixteenth century', unpublished PhD thesis, Duke University, 1999, p. 208.

127 Campi, *Zwingli und Maria*, p. 92.

128 *WA*, vol. 7, p. 596; on antiphons see *WA*, vol. 10, part III, pp. 321–2 (this condemnation was echoed by other reformers: see for example Müller and Seebass, eds., *Gesamtausgabe*, vol. 1, p. 242; Kreitzer, 'Reforming Mary', pp. 58ff. and 249; Düfel, 'Die Marienverehrung im Licht des reformatorischen "sola scriptura"', 16–18); on pilgrimages see *WA*, vol. 28, pp. 677–8 and *WA Br.*, vol. 3, no. 141.

129 *WA*, vol. 30, part II, pp. 295–7.

Schutzmantelmadonna or Virgin of Mercy was singled out because in it Mary usurped Christ's mediating role (figures 6 and 7).[130] Intercessory images that showed Mary pleading with Christ and Christ supplicating a wrathful God the Father were also condemned (figure 5).[131] Luther complained of the 'disgraceful and shameful' image in which 'the son falls down before the father and shows him his wounds, and St John and Mary pray to Christ for us at the Last Judgment, and the mother shows the son her breasts, which had suckled him'.[132] Such images should be removed because they taught men to fear Christ.[133] Stories of supposedly miraculous statues of the Virgin and Child that were revealed as frauds provided additional ammunition for the reformers' attacks on Mary's cult: Melanchthon recorded that 'in one monastery we saw a statue of the blessed Virgin which was manipulated like a puppet so that it seemed to nod Yes or No to the petitioners'.[134] Variants on this story, where by means of false images priests and monks led the simple people into idolatry, appear in a number of Lutheran texts.[135]

While the Protestant reformers were unanimous in their condemnation of the invocation of saints, some, in particular Martin Luther, still had many positive things to say about Mary. All mainstream reformers upheld the Marian doctrines that related to Christ: Mary was still described as *Theotokos*, God-bearer, and belief in the virgin birth remained unchallenged. Luther also, however, defended belief in Mary's perpetual virginity, described her as sinless, provided a particular interpretation of the controversial doctrine of her Immaculate Conception and even refused to rule out the possibility of her bodily assumption into heaven. Indeed, some of Luther's statements were so traditional that his writings were cited by contemporary Catholic commentators seeking to defend Mary's cult.[136]

Of course, Luther was familiar with the teachings of the early and medieval church, in which Mary featured prominently. In the writings of Augustine, for

130 On this iconography see Herbert Immenkötter, 'Glaubensbilder der Renaissance in Deutschland', in *Das 16. Jahrhundert: europäische Renaissance*, ed. Hildegard Kuester (Regensburg, 1995), pp. 170–3.

131 On this iconography see ibid., pp. 173–4.

132 *WA*, vol. 33, pp. 83–4 (sermon on John 6).

133 See also: *WA*, vol. 10, part II, p. 434; vol. 46, p. 663; vol. 47, pp. 257, 276; vol. 51, p. 128.

134 Tappert, ed., *The Book of Concord*, p. 234.

135 *WA Tr.*, vol. 6, no. 6848. See Wolfgang Brückner, ed., *Volkserzählung und Reformation: ein Handbuch zur Tradierung und Funktion von Erzählstoffen und Erzählliteratur im Protestantismus* (Berlin, 1974), pp. 671–2. Hieronymus Rauscher, who studied in Wittenberg and later served as a deacon in Schweinfurt and then Nuremberg, listed a whole series of such deceits in his 1562 work, *Auserwählten papistischen Lügen*, Brückner, ed., *Volkserzählung*, p. 238.

136 Peter Canisius, *De Maria Virgine incomparabili* (Ingolstadt, 1577), pp. 57–8. A Spanish Franciscan friar, Pedro de Alva y Astorga, also cited Luther in his defence of the Immaculate Conception: Pedro de Alva y Astorga, *Militia Immaculatae Conceptionis Virginis Mariae contra malitiam originalis infectionis peccati* (Louvain, 1633), column 1,016. I am grateful for Dr Trevor Johnson for bringing this reference to my attention.

example, which Luther began to read early in his studies, Mary was described as a perpetual virgin, without personal sin, and as a prototype for the church.[137] Luther does not cite Augustine or other early authorities extensively in his chief writings on the Virgin, yet there can be no doubt that in the early stages of his career he was heavily influenced by traditional Marian piety.[138] In 1539 he looked back on his earlier devotion to the Virgin and wrote that 'in the time of the papacy Mary was given greater honours than the Son. I devoted myself to her.'[139] He moderated this early Marian piety – already in 1516 he was emphasizing Mary's humility over her greatness and assigning her a passive role in the story of salvation – yet remnants of medieval devotion undoubtedly remained.[140] In his 1523 tract, *That Jesus Christ Was Born a Jew*, he defended the doctrine of Mary's perpetual virginity, which had no basis in Scripture but had been widely accepted from the time of the early church.[141] This defence of Mary's perpetual virginity remained part of the currency of Lutheran devotion, even though it was not universally emphasized. For example, while Luther's German text of the Schmalkaldic Articles spoke of Mary as merely pure and holy, in the Latin translation prepared for the Book of Concord in 1580 she was once again described as *sempervirgine*.[142]

Unlike Luther, Huldrych Zwingli did not preach a great deal about the Virgin Mary, but his one surviving sermon dedicated to her, *A Sermon on the Eternally Pure Maid Mary, the Mother of Jesus Christ our Saviour* (published 1522), demonstrates that he too abided by the traditional notion of her perpetual virginity. In this sermon he stated his belief that 'according to the words of the holy Gospel a pure Virgin bore the son of God for us and she remained a pure, unscathed virgin both during and after the birth for ever'.[143] As Emidio Campi points out, according to Zwingli's interpretation Mary's virginity was important because it testified to the extraordinary nature of Christ's incarnation and removed any suspicion that he might have been tainted with original sin. As a perpetual virgin and as *Theotokos*, mother of God, Mary was a witness to both Christ's divine and human natures, an important theme in Zwingli's soteriology.[144] In Zwingli's own *Fideo ratio* of 1530 Mary's perpetual virginity

137 Graef, *Mary*, vol. 1, pp. 94–100.

138 Düfel, *Luthers Stellung*, pp. 33–69.

139 *WA*, vol. 47, p. 644.

140 *WA*, vol. 1, pp. 61, 77; Düfel, 'Die Marienverehrung im Licht des reformatorischen "sola scriptura"', 7–8.

141 *WA*, vol. 11, p. 314. For a discussion of the circumstances surrounding the production of this text see Peter Newman Brooks, 'A lily ungilded? Martin Luther, the Virgin Mary and the saints', *Journal of Religious History* 13 (1984–5), 142. Luther also asserted in later sermons that Mary was 'virgo ante partum, in partu et post partum': *WA*, vol. 49, pp. 174, 182; vol. 54, p. 207. On the doctrine of Mary's perpetual virginity in the early church see Graef, *Mary*, vol. 1, chapter 2.

142 *Die Bekenntnisschriften der evangelisch-lutherischen Kirche*, p. 414.

143 Campi, *Zwingli und Maria*, p. 49.

144 Ibid., pp. 42–4.

was emphasized (Christ was born 'from the immortal and perpetual virginity of Mary').[145] But in official Zwinglian statements of belief, as in their Lutheran equivalents, reference to Mary's perpetual virginity was often omitted. Oswald Myconius' Basle Confession of 1534, for example, described her as 'pure' and 'immaculate' in its printed version, though its manuscript version and the Reformation order based on it included the word 'eternal' after 'pure'.[146] The First Helvetic Confession of 1536 likewise described Mary as 'immaculate' (which in a Zwinglian context should not be taken as a reference to her immaculate conception), but not as a perpetual virgin.[147] There was, as these examples suggest, a certain ambiguity in the reformers' position with regard to Mary's perpetual virginity. As Diarmaid MacCulloch has argued, mainstream Protestant theologians defended this doctrine, despite its non-scriptural origins, in order to distinguish their teaching from that of more radical groups, for example the Anabaptists.[148] In 1527, for example, Johannes Oecolampadius of Basle wrote to Zwingli, in the context of a discussion of the opinions of the radical Balthasar Hubmaier, that 'the whole of Christendom' stood or fell on the recognition of the perpetual virginity of Mary, Christ's conception free from Original Sin and his true status as the son of God.[149]

While Luther, Zwingli and even Calvin defended Mary's perpetual virginity, Luther's very traditional teaching on other key medieval Marian doctrines set him apart not only from Zwingli and the other leading proponents of the Swiss and Upper German Reformations, but also from many of his own followers.[150] Luther, for example, continued to describe Mary as sinless, though he emphasized that this state was achieved through God's grace rather than through her own merit.[151] His exact position on the Immaculate Conception has been the subject of extensive debate.[152] Belief in Mary's sinlessness did not necessarily imply belief in her Immaculate Conception,[153] but Luther does seem to have held that Mary had been purified from sin by the Holy Spirit at some point before Christ's incarnation.[154] His sermon on the feast day of Mary's conception in 1520 put him firmly on the immaculist side of the medieval controversy: Mary's first conception was, he argued, normal but at her second conception, when the soul informed the body, she was purified from original sin. 'So from

145 Karl Müller, *Die Bekenntnisschriften der reformierten Kirche* (Leipzig, 1903), p. 80. On the *Fideo ratio* see Bruce Gordon, *The Swiss Reformation* (Manchester and New York, 2002), pp. 129–30.

146 Müller, *Die Bekenntnisschriften der reformierten Kirche*, p. 96.

147 Ibid., p. 103; Campi, *Zwingli und Maria*, p. 60.

148 Diarmaid MacCulloch, *Reformation: Europe's house divided, 1490–1700* (London, 2003), pp. 613–14; MacCulloch, 'Mary and sixteenth-century Protestants', pp. 211–14.

149 Tappolet, ed., *Das Marienlob der Reformatoren*, p. 246.

150 For Calvin on Mary's perpetual virginity see ibid., pp. 171–3.

151 See especially *WA*, vol. 52, p. 633 (*Hauspostille*, 1544); Kreitzer, 'Reforming Mary', pp. 73–4.

152 Düfel, *Luthers Stellung*, pp. 164–6; Campi, *Zwingli und Maria*, pp. 59–60.

153 Kreitzer, 'Reforming Mary', p. 73.

154 Ibid., p. 76.

the first moment that she began to live, she was without all sin.'[155] His later position wavered somewhat, and in sermons dating from 1539 and 1540 he stated that Mary was conceived and born in sin like all men.[156] Yet he still, in 1543, felt able to write that Mary was 'a holy virgin, who was saved and purified from Original Sin by the Holy Ghost', although he no longer specified at what point this purification took place.[157] His position on the related doctrine of the Assumption was equally ambiguous.[158] Although in his view there was no biblical evidence for Mary's bodily assumption into heaven, certain biblical passages did bear witness to the fact that the saints lived in Christ: 'The Scriptures say clearly that Abraham, Isaac, Jacob and all the faithful live, therefore it is necessary that you believe that the mother of God lives; but how this happens, that one must entrust to our own loving God.'[159]

Later Lutheran preachers and adherents of the Zwinglian Reformation were less enthusiastic about such doctrines. Beth Kreitzer's extensive study of Lutheran sermons suggests that around the middle of the sixteenth century there was a shift in attitude towards Mary, with preachers showing a greater willingness to speak of her error, weakness and even sin.[160] The doctrine of the Immaculate Conception was disregarded by Zwingli and was generally rejected by later evangelical theologians also.[161] Like the Immaculate Conception, the doctrine of the Assumption seems to have been largely ignored or condemned by later preachers, although in two sermons published in 1541 and 1542 Johannes Brenz, reformer in Württemberg and later Stuttgart, stated that 'it is most certain that Mary has reached perpetual happiness', and suggested that although we do not know how, it could have been through a bodily assumption like that of Enoch.[162] The 1564 edition of Caspar Goldtwurm's *Kirchen Calender* also indicates some abiding uncertainty about Mary's Assumption. It condemns the papist idolatry associated with the festival – the blessing of herbs – but contains a woodcut showing Mary's ascent into heaven, and states that we should know that after she had stayed a while with the Apostles she was 'finally in

155 *WA*, vol. 17, part II, p. 288 (*Festpostille*, 1527); Kreitzer, 'Reforming Mary', pp. 241–5.
156 *WA*, vol. 47, p. 860 and vol. 49, p. 173.
157 *WA*, vol. 53, p. 640. 158 Kreitzer, 'Reforming Mary', p. 253.
159 *WA*, vol. 10, part III, p. 269 (sermon on feast day of Assumption, 15 August 1522). Bullinger also seems to have been prepared to countenance the possibility that Mary's body was assumed into heaven, though he devotes little attention to it. See MacCulloch, 'Mary and sixteenth-century Protestants', p. 203.
160 Kreitzer, 'Reforming Mary', pp. 75–6.
161 Schimmelpfennig, *Die Geschichte der Marienverehrung*, pp. 19, 24–5. On Calvin see Tappolet, ed., *Das Marienlob der Reformatoren*, p. 167. For examples of Lutheran authors who rejected the doctrine see Caspar Goldtwurm, *Kirchen Calender* (Frankfurt am Main, 1564), p. 321 and Andreas Hohndorff, *Calendarium sanctorum & historiarum* (Frankfurt am Main, 1587), p. 686.
162 Quoted in Kreitzer, 'Reforming Mary', 254; see also Schimmelpfennig, *Die Geschichte der Marienverehrung*, pp. 25–7; Hohndorff, *Calendarium sanctorum & historiarum*, p. 465.

blessed and constant understanding [bekandtnuß] called away from this life, and brought to the heavenly company in great joy'.[163]

Although many evangelical reformers were firmer than Luther in their rejection of traditional Marian doctrines, Mary nonetheless continued to feature in their writings as an exemplary recipient of God's grace and as a model of faith, obedience and humility.[164] In article 21 of his *Apology for the Augsburg Confession* Melanchthon wrote that Christians should honour the saints in three ways: they should give thanks to God for the saints, because he had given them great gifts; they should strengthen their own faith through the saints' examples; and they should imitate their faith and other virtues.[165] Zwingli argued that above all, Mary and the saints are witnesses who point us towards God.[166] The saints served a useful pastoral purpose for, as the Nuremberg reformer Andreas Osiander acknowledged to his congregation in his 1547 sermon, *Of the Saints, and How They Should Be Honoured*, 'although God's word in Holy Scripture teaches us sufficiently and plentifully what we should do and not do . . . we also need because of our weak will good examples and patterns'.[167] This desire to provide the faithful with good 'patterns' prompted the production of Lutheran calendars that listed the saints' traditional feast days and enumerated their exemplary deeds. Caspar Goldtwurm's *Kirchen Calender*, which went through four editions between its initial publication in 1559 and the end of the sixteenth century, was intended, according to its preface, to strengthen the reader's belief and improve his or her way of life.[168] Focusing particularly on martyrs and confessors, it nonetheless included many of the traditional saints' days, including seven Marian festivals. In order to reinforce the new, Lutheran understanding of the Virgin it condemned the 'idolatrous' and 'heathen' practices previously associated with Candlemas and the feast of the Assumption, and focused on the details of Mary's life that could be derived from Scripture. Here, as in other evangelical texts, Mary's true significance was seen to lie in her role as an example and pattern for ordinary Christians.[169]

Grace was, of course, a key concept for the reformers. Central to all their teachings was the belief that justification came about through the bestowal of

[163] Goldtwurm, *Kirchen Calender*, p. 218.
[164] Tappolet, ed., *Das Marienlob der Reformatoren*, pp. 180–93.
[165] Kolb, 'Festivals of the saints', 613; *Die Bekenntnisschriften der evangelisch-lutherischen Kirche*, pp. 317–18.
[166] Campi, *Zwingli und Maria*, p. 93.
[167] Andreas Osiander, *Zwo Predig. Eine von den heiligen / wie man sie ehren sol. Die ander / vonn Verstorbnen / wie man fuͤr sie bitten sol* (n. p., 1547), fol. 2v.
[168] Goldtwurm, *Kirchen Calender*, fol. Biiir.
[169] Other Lutheran calendars also emphasized the value of saints as exemplars. See, for example, Hohndorff, *Calendarium sanctorum & historiarum*, which, like Goldtwurm's *Kirchen Calender*, discusses all seven of the traditional Marian feast days (dismissing entirely only Mary's Presentation and Conception). See also Schuler, *Etliche Christliche Predigen*, p. 50.

divine grace on sinful man. Man could do nothing to earn this grace: it was an unmerited gift from God. Mary's story, as told by the reformers, provided a perfect illustration. Catholic authors had tended to enumerate the exceptional merits that had made her worthy to bear God's only son. Erasmus, as we have seen, worried that too much merit was being attributed to Mary, but Luther went even further, describing her as a humble maiden, who had been chosen despite 'her insignificance, lowliness, poverty and inferiority'. She was therefore, in his words, 'the foremost example of the grace of God'. In a sermon for the feast day of the Annunciation, published in the 1544 *Hauspostille*, Luther argued that the angel's words to Mary, 'you have found grace with God', were intended to show 'what it was, that is grace, and not merit'.[170] Zwingli likewise emphasized the importance of grace over merit, attributing to Mary the statement that God had worked this wonder in her 'not according to my merit, but according to his grace'.[171]

Mary's story also demonstrated the importance of faith. In a sermon on the feast day of the Annunciation, delivered in 1522, Luther stated that 'the Virgin Mary had such a high faith, the equal of which we have not often found in the Scriptures'.[172] She believed the angel's message that she, a virgin, would bear a son and would remain 'uncorrupted'. As Zwingli argued in his 1522 sermon, human reason could never have comprehended this message. For Mary, as for every Christian, faith and understanding of the word of God came only through God's grace.[173] Mary's faith was also exemplary in that it never faltered, despite all her suffering. In times of hardship Christians should comfort themselves with the knowledge that even Mary, who was given such grace and honour by God, was poor and suffered persecution, pain and sorrow. They, like Mary, should remain constant and should learn to subjugate themselves to God's will: 'Through the example of her faith all, both rich and poor, should be strengthened.'[174] As Johannes Brenz argued in a sermon on the wedding at Cana published in 1556, Mary was a 'useful example', showing that we should take our petitions to God and that even if we receive a harsh answer we should 'persevere in faith, in prayer, and in obedience to God'.[175]Mary's humility and good conduct – for example her voluntary submission to the Law of Moses when she went to the temple to be purified after Christ's birth and her domestic labour – were also praised by the reformers.[176] This model of Mary as a humble *Hausmutter* was probably of particular relevance to women, as we will see in chapter 6.

170 *WA*, vol. 7, pp. 546, 569; *WA*, vol. 52, p. 627.
171 Campi, *Zwingli und Maria*, p. 128.
172 Kreitzer, 'Reforming Mary', p. 50.
173 Campi, *Zwingli und Maria*, p. 127.
174 Ibid., pp. 144–5.
175 Kreitzer, 'Reforming Mary', p. 200. On Mary's exemplary faith see also ibid, pp. 77–9 and 189 and *WA*, vol. 21, p. 63.
176 See for example *WA*, vol. 51, pp. 167–8.

For Luther the Magnificat and the Ave Maria, biblical texts that had been crucial to the pre-Reformation Marian cult, remained important because when interpreted correctly they taught Christians about grace, faith and humility. Luther's lengthy *Commentary on the Magnificat*, addressed to Prince John Frederick of Saxony, recommended that the text should be sung daily at vespers.[177] It must be understood, however, as a text about God rather than about Mary's wisdom or power.[178] His own interpretation served to illustrate this point: while the Vulgate spoke of Mary's 'humilitas' [humility], which might be understood as a virtue, Luther spoke of her 'Nichtigkeit' or lowliness. God had chosen Mary, a 'poor, despised, unprepossessing little maid' over rich and powerful daughters of kings, dukes and lords. God's consideration for her lowly standing was key: 'therefore the emphasis lies not on the word "humilitatem", but on the word "Respexit", because her lowliness is not to be praised, but rather God's regard for her'.[179] Once correctly translated, the Magnificat provided a lesson in humility and in trust in God. Later preachers repeated similar messages, for example Veit Dietrich in Nuremberg, who called the text a 'beautiful sermon, in which the Virgin Mary teaches us how we might come to God's grace'.[180]

Luther also advocated the retention of the Ave Maria, though he emphasized that this was no longer to be understood in the traditional sense as a prayer to Mary herself, but rather as 'pure praise and honour' (Zwingli likewise emphasized that 'the Hail Mary is not a prayer, but a greeting and a statement of praise').[181] In his *Personal Prayer Book* of 1522, which provided an evangelical alternative to traditional collections of invocations, Luther emphasized that 'we should make the Hail Mary neither a prayer nor an invocation because it is improper to interpret the words beyond what they mean in themselves and beyond the meaning given them by the Holy Spirit'. The Hail Mary did, however, serve to demonstrate God's grace and to make Christians recognize Mary's significance.[182] Again a key passage needed careful translation: Luther, like Erasmus, believed that the Vulgate's 'gratia plena' granted Mary too high a place, implying that she herself was full of grace.[183] Although he did not abandon this traditional term completely, in his *Septembertestament* of 1522 he replaced 'voll gnaden' (full of grace) with 'holdselige' (highly or well favoured). Luther defended this translation in his 1530 *Letter on Translation*,

177 *WA*, vol. 7, p. 544. See G. Müller, 'Protestant veneration of Mary: Luther's interpretation of the Magnificat', in *Humanism and Reform: the church in Europe, England, and Scotland, 1400–1643. Essays in honour of James K. Cameron*, ed. James Kirk (Oxford, 1991).

178 Kreitzer, 'Reforming Mary', p. 101. For a discussion of Luther's commentary see Düfel, 'Die Marienverehrung im Licht des reformatorischen "sola scriptura"', 10–15.

179 *WA*, vol. 7, pp. 559–61.

180 Kreitzer, 'Reforming Mary', pp. 113–14.

181 *WA*, vol. 10, part II, p. 408; Campi, *Zwingli und Maria*, p. 124.

182 *WA*, vol. 10, part II, p. 408; Pelikan, ed., *Luther's Works*, vol. 43, pp. 39–40. On Lutheran sermons on the Ave Maria see Kreitzer, 'Reforming Mary', pp. 55–64.

183 Bluhm, 'Luther's translation'.

arguing that divine grace had been bestowed on Mary, the humble recipient. His only concern was, he said in a sermon of 1539, to ensure that Mary was no longer 'invoked as one by whom grace was bestowed'.[184] In the 1544 *Hauspostille* Luther suggested a new translation, 'begnadete', which is probably, as Bluhm argues, most faithful to the Greek original.[185]

Evangelical reformers condemned the medieval cult of saints. In their view the invocation of saints, which found no support in Scripture, conflicted with the central Christian tenet of justification by faith alone and distracted attention from the true worship of Christ. The cult of the Virgin was a particular problem: through excessive veneration, Christians had made Mary into an idol, seeking from her the grace that could only be found in Christ himself. This must stop. Yet the leading reformers recognized the explosive potential of their topic. As Luther told his congregation in his 1522 sermon on the feast day of Mary's birth, 'you know, my friend, that the honour that one gives to the Mother of God is too deeply formed in the hearts of men, and also that people do not gladly hear it spoken against'.[186] The fervent Marian devotion described in the first section of this chapter could not easily be eliminated, and it is indicative of Mary's continuing importance that not only Erasmus but also both Zwingli and Luther felt the need to defend themselves from accusations that they had denigrated her honour. In his 1522 sermon Zwingli set out to exonerate himself from charges that he had preached that 'Mary was a stupid woman, like any other floozie' and had ridiculed her purity. He was concerned, he said, that his opponents had used this accusation to discredit him with the 'common man', who venerated the Virgin highly.[187] Luther likewise in his 1523 tract, *That Jesus Christ Was Born a Jew*, set out to defend himself against rumours that he had preached against the doctrine of Mary's perpetual virginity.[188] The reformers had no desire to dishonour Mary. They merely wished to moderate her veneration in accordance with their interpretations of Scripture. There was therefore a certain ambiguity in the Protestant position on Mary: reformers condemned her cult, but could not afford to denigrate the Mother of God entirely. As we shall see in chapter 2, this ambiguity facilitated the preservation of Marian images and devotion in parts of Protestant Germany.

[184] *WA*, vol. 47, p. 703. [185] *WA*, vol. 52, p. 626. [186] *WA*, vol. 10, part III, p. 313.

[187] Campi, *Zwingli und Maria*, p. 20. Zwingli had to defend himself again from similar accusations in 1531, Walter Delius, *Geschichte der Marienverehrung* (Munich and Basle, 1963), p. 230.

[188] *WA*, vol. 11, p. 314.

2. *Marian piety in Lutheran Germany*

How far were the theoretical prescriptions of the reformers reflected in the day-to-day reality of Lutheran devotional practice? Did Mary, as Luther wished, come to be regarded as a model of faith and humility? Or was her idolatrous cult, as he feared, too deeply embedded to be easily eradicated? These are partly, of course, questions about the gulf between elite and popular belief, about the Lutheran preachers and their frequently frustrated attempts to eliminate traditional forms of devotion. The fate of Marian images and liturgy also, however, sheds light on a much broader issue: the interaction between religion and society. In order to understand the realities of Protestant devotional practice we need to consider what happened when the Reformation was realized on the ground, when religion had to accommodate itself to local political, social and cultural concerns. This chapter will therefore focus for the most part on a case study. Nuremberg was, as we have seen, the first imperial free city to adopt the Lutheran faith (1525) and an important early centre of reform. Here, in the survival of medieval Marian images, of traditional liturgy and even of pre-Reformation blasphemy legislation, we have a clear illustration of Mary's continued prominence in the Lutheran Church. In theological terms, the persistence of these traditional forms was justified by the reformers' conviction that their meaning could be transformed, and that Mary could be presented as a humble *Hausmutter* rather than as a divine intercessor. Yet, as this case study demonstrates, other considerations, both political and cultural, also played a crucial role in shaping post-Reformation Marian devotion. The fate of Marian images and liturgy in and around Nuremberg shows how a particular urban context could create a unique framework of devotional understanding and practice.

THE SURVIVAL OF IMAGES OF THE VIRGIN

Figure 1 shows the interior of the Frauenkirche, the imperial chapel that stood (and stands) on Nuremberg's main market square. In 1525 the administration of this church was taken over by officials from the civic poor-relief fund, and its Catholic priests were replaced by a preacher and several deacons. When this engraving was made in 1696 the Frauenkirche had therefore been in use as a Protestant preaching hall for more than 150 years. According to Andreas Würfel, writing in 1761, on Sundays and festival days a sermon was preached there in the morning and in the evening vespers were observed with a German hymn and a Bible reading. On weekdays three services with readings and singing were celebrated in the church.[1] Yet, as Krauss's engraving indicates, there were very few visual accommodations to this transformation in use: in 1696 the Frauenkirche was still full of paintings and statues of the Virgin Mary and other saints.[2] Indeed, were it not for alignment of the pews in the foreground, facing towards the pulpit rather than towards the high altar, and the galleries, added in the late sixteenth century, the viewer could be forgiven for assuming that Krauss's engraving depicts a church that was still in use as a Catholic place of worship.

There are a number of particularly interesting survivals. The high altar, clearly visible in Krauss's engraving, had been donated in around 1522 by the local merchant Jakob Welser and his wife Ehrentraut von Thumenberg. This altarpiece survived intact and *in situ* throughout the Frauenkirche's Protestant history only to be dismembered in 1815, five years after the church was restored to Catholic use. Its survival is remarkable, given what we know of the altar's imagery. At its centre was a fifteenth-century statue of Mary as the Woman of the Apocalypse, holding the Christ Child (figure 10). This statue's history suggests that it was especially venerated on the eve of the Reformation: it was copied in 1498 (figure 11) and then set in the new Welser-Thumenberg altar about twenty-five years later. The altarpiece's painted wings showed scenes from the lives of Christ and the Virgin, including non-scriptural ones: the meeting of Mary's parents, Joachim and Anne, at the Golden Gate; the birth and presentation of the Virgin at the temple and Mary's death, assumption and coronation (figures 2 and 3). Another Welser-Thumenberg donation also deserves special mention: a stained-glass window, probably installed at about the same time as the high altar.[3] Only fragments survive today, but its original design is recorded in a preparatory drawing attributed to Hans Suess von Kulmbach and dated 1515 (figure 12).[4] It shows the Virgin Mary, without the Christ Child, sheltering

[1] Andreas Würfel, *Diptycha Cappellae B. Mariae* (Nuremberg, 1761), pp. 20–3; M. Herold, *Alt-Nürnberg in seinen Gottesdiensten: ein Beitrag zur Geschichte der Sitte und des Kultus* (Gütersloh, 1890), pp. 253–72.

[2] The evidence from Krauss's engraving can be substantiated using printed descriptions and church inventories. Heal, 'A woman like any other?', pp. 51–61.

[3] Metropolitan Museum of Art and Germanisches Nationalmuseum, eds., *Gothic and Renaissance Art*, p. 92.

[4] In 1960 four panels from the window, including the *Schutzmantelmadonna*, still survived in the Frauenkirche.

Figure 10. Virgin and Child, c.1440 and c.1522 (Frauenkirche, Nuremberg)

diminutive supplicants, male and female, lay and clerical, beneath her cloak. The donors kneel on either side of a coat of arms in the field below, presented to the Virgin by patron saints. As we have seen, Luther explicitly condemned such images of the Virgin of Mercy.[5]

Beneath the organ in Krauss's engraving hangs a panel that depicts another non-scriptural Marian iconography: the rosary. This panel survives today in

[5] Above, p. 56.

Figure 11. Adam Kraft, Pergenstorffer epitaph, 1498 (Frauenkirche, Nuremberg)

the Germanisches Nationalmuseum (figure 13).[6] It was originally intended as a retable, though by the time of Krauss's engraving the altar that it adorned had been destroyed (three of the church's altars were removed, probably in the late sixteenth century when galleries were added). The panel's iconography is very similar to that of Erhard Schön's Great Rosary, printed in around 1515 in Nuremberg (figure 8), though the central figure of the crucified Christ has been lost. A garland of fifty-five roses, representing the prayer cycle that constituted

[6] Germanisches Nationalmuseum, ed., *Veit Stoß in Nürnberg: Werke des Meisters und seiner Schule in Nürnberg und Umgebung* (Munich, 1983), pp. 149–58.

Figure 12. Hans Suess von Kulmbach, design for a stained-glass window, 1515 (Kupferstich-kabinett, Dresden)

Figure 13. Workshop of Veit Stoß, rosary panel, c.1518–19 (GNM, Nuremberg)

Figure 14. The Coronation of the Virgin, roof boss from the portal of the Frauenkirche, mid fourteenth century (Frauenkirche, Nuremberg)

the late medieval rosary, encloses a selection of male and female saints. In the Last Judgment scene depicted below Mary and John intercede before Christ. Schön's woodcut, and others like it, included written instructions for praying the rosary and announced the indulgences that would accrue from its recitation. Viewers' experiences of the Frauenkirche retable would originally have been determined by their knowledge of such devotional practices. The panel displayed on the column in front of the organ in Krauss's engraving, which depicts the Virgin of Sorrows, her breast pierced by swords, surrounded by smaller scenes, may also have served as an altarpiece originally. Contemplation of the Sorrows of the Virgin – a series of five or more events from Christ's childhood and Passion – was a popular form of Marian devotion from the fifteenth century, and was sometimes undertaken in conjunction with the recitation of the rosary.[7]

Other Marian images survived amongst the church's sculptural decoration. It is perhaps not surprising that the Virgin continued to adorn the church's exterior – the central *trumeau* of the main portal depicts the Virgin and Child, for example – since even radical iconoclasts rarely targeted façade sculpture. The interior of the west portal is adorned with a complex sculptural scheme of prophets and saints honouring the Virgin Mary and culminating in her coronation depicted on the central roof boss (figure 14).[8] Several other sculptures are visible in Krauss's engraving: a depiction of St Anne with the Virgin and Child (*Anna Selbdritt*), which survives today in the church of St Jakob; statues of the Three Kings, the Virgin and Child and various other saints between the windows of the choir; and figures of St Christopher, St Veronica, another female saint and

[7] Bäumer and Scheffczyk, eds., *Marienlexikon*, vol. 6 (1994), pp. 28–35.
[8] Adolf Essenwein, *Der Bildschmuck der Liebfrauenkirche zu Nürnberg* (Nuremberg, 1881).

the Virgin and Child on either side of the triumphal arch.[9] Only one sculpture is known to have been removed as a direct result of the Reformation: in October 1529 the city council decreed that an image of the Virgin should be taken away from the Frauenkirche because of idolatry.[10] Inventories of the church's treasure drawn up before the Reformation indicate that there were originally two freestanding sculptures of the Virgin, which were richly decorated with robes, crowns, veils, rosaries and jewels, and it seems likely that it was one of these two sculptures that was removed in 1529.[11] The other remained, but was no longer adorned in the post-Reformation period. In a detailed inventory from 1578 no robes or jewels for Marian statues are mentioned, only four 'simple Marian crowns' that were kept in boxes in the sacristy.[12]

Textiles – pluvials, altar cloths and tapestries – depicting the Virgin also survived, and are recorded in inventories dating from 1578 and 1594.[13] It seems that the liturgical vestments, some of which bore images of the Virgin stitched in pearls, were still used by Nuremberg's Lutheran clergy on feast days and at the administration of communion.[14] Silver treasures – monstrances, reliquaries and statuettes – were destroyed however. In 1466 the Frauenkirche possessed a rich collection of treasures, including various Marian reliquaries: a silver gilded monstrance containing her girdle, a silver statuette on an amethyst base containing part of her veil and a bust-length image with a clear crystal set in it also containing part of her veil.[15] Such images were alien to Lutheran teaching, like the Virgin of Mercy and rosary panel described above, but these items were more vulnerable than paintings, sculptures and textiles because of their monetary worth. In 1530 Nuremberg's council considered the possibility of melting down the gold and silver treasures that had come into its possession five years earlier when it had assumed control of local ecclesiastical property. Precise inventories were drawn up in which the values of all of the treasures in the city's main churches were recorded. Most of these treasures were then locked away in chests, and only liturgical vessels essential to the celebration of communion

[9] On the *Anna Selbdritt* see Germanisches Nationalmuseum, ed., *Veit Stoß in Nürnberg*, pp. 295–302.

[10] T. Hampe, ed., *Nürnberger Ratsverlässe über Kunst und Künstler im Zeitalter der Spätgotik und Renaissance*, 2 vols., Quellenschriften für Kunstgeschichte und Kunsttechnik des Mittelalters und der Renaissance, n. s. 11, 12 and 13 (Vienna and Leipzig, 1904), no. 1729.

[11] StaatsAN, Rep. 44e, Losungsamt, Akten, S. I. L. 130, Nr. 7a and S. I. L.131, Nr. 10.

[12] StaatsAN, Rep. 44e, Losungsamt, Akten, S. I. L.131, Nr. 14.

[13] Ibid, S. I. L.131, Nr. 14; Ibid, S. I. L.131, Nr. 15. See Heal, 'A woman like any other?', pp. 60–1 and Metzner, 'Stephan Schuler's Saalbuch', pp. 26–9.

[14] Max Hasse, 'Maria und die Heiligen im protestantischen Lübeck', *Nordelbingen: Beiträge zur Kunst- und Kulturgeschichte* 34 (1965), 72.

[15] StaatsAN, Rep. 44e, Losungsamt, Akten, S. I. L.130, Nr. 7a; other Marian relics are listed in Metzner, 'Stephan Schuler's Saalbuch,' pp. 31–6. By 1505 various new objects had been acquired including a small panel with an alabaster image of the Virgin. StaatsAN, Rep. 44e, Losungsamt, Akten, S. I. L.131, Nr. 13.

and a few other items remained at the pastors' disposal.[16] For two decades the council refrained from destroying the confiscated church treasure, but it was finally induced to liquidate its assets by the costly Second Margrave's War against Albrecht Alcibiades of Brandenburg-Kulmbach. In September 1552 plate with a total value of almost 16,000 *Gulden* was gathered in the town hall and taken to the smelter. Only a few pieces escaped destruction, amongst them a gilded silver image of the Virgin and Child and two clasps for vestments, both bearing images of the Virgin, from the Frauenkirche. The authors of the 1552 inventory stated that these clasps could not be sold in Nuremberg, presumably because of their iconography, and proposed that they should therefore be sent to Catholic Poland.[17]

The history of the furnishings of the Frauenkirche suggests that in Nuremberg no consistent attempt was made to remove images of the Virgin Mary. This is confirmed by evidence from the city's two parish churches, the Lorenzkirche and Sebalduskirche. The Lorenzkirche, for example, preserved almost all of its late medieval furnishings, despite its central role in the city's Reformation movement (figure 15).[18] It was in this church that Andreas Osiander, one of the leading Lutheran theologians of his generation, preached from 1522 to 1548.[19] Of the approximately fifteen altars that the church possessed at the end of the fifteenth century most survived the Reformation intact and *in situ*, for example the one dedicated to St John the Evangelist with an elaborate Renaissance retable, visible at the west end of the choir in Krauss's engraving.[20] Only a few altars are known to have been removed, and then not until 1542 or 1543. In July 1542 the council ordered the removal of three in the Sebalduskirche because they 'get in the way of the people hearing the word of God and in front of them the preacher cannot be seen or heard well'.[21] Although the Lorenzkirche is not mentioned in the council minutes that record this decision, it seems likely that several of its altars were removed at the same time. The chronicle of Wolfgang Lüder (1551–1624), deacon at St Sebald, records that two were destroyed during the night in October 1543.[22]

16 Carl Christensen, 'Iconoclasm and the preservation of ecclesiastical art in Reformation Nuremberg', *Archiv für Reformationsgeschichte* 61 (1970), 220. StaatsAN, Rep. 60b, Ratsbuch Nr. 15, fol. 91r.

17 StaatsAN, Rep. 44e, Losungsamt, Akten, S. I. L.131, Nr. 22, fol. 29v.

18 Heal, 'A woman like any other?', pp. 32–50.

19 On Osiander's life and work see Seebass, *Osiander*, passim.

20 Heal, 'A woman like any other?', p. 36. This retable is still in the Lorenzkirche today, complete with its relic display, as is the altar dedicated to St Deocarus (though the saint's sarcophagus was removed sometime after the Reformation). The St Bartholomew altar, the St Rochus altar, the St Anne altar and various others also survive today, complete with their depictions of saints, though not always in their original forms or locations.

21 Hampe, ed., *Nürnberger Ratsverlässe*, vol. 1, no. 2664.

22 StaatsAN, Rep. 52a, Nürnberger Handschriften, Nr. 46, fol. 434v. Walter Haas, 'Die mittelalterliche Altaranordnung in der Nürnberger Lorenzkirche', in *500 Jahre Hallenchor St Lorenz zu*

Figure 15. Johann Ulrich Krauss (after Johann Andreas Graff), interior of the Lorenzkirche, 1685 (GNM, Graphische Sammlung, Nuremberg)

Amongst the church's surviving furnishings – which included a number of Marian epitaphs – two items deserve particular mention: Adam Kraft's sacrament house and Veit Stoß's Angelic Salutation. Kraft's masterpiece, which at

Nürnberg 1477 – 1977, ed. Herbert Bauer, Gerhard Hirschmann and Georg Stolz (Nuremberg, 1977), p. 87 suggests that the Marian altar and perhaps the Conrad altar were also destroyed at this time.

almost twenty metres high dominates the east end of the choir, was commissioned in 1493 by Hans IV Imhoff, *Kirchenpfleger* (lay custodian) at St Lorenz, and completed in 1496. It was used to reserve and display the consecrated host, a practice condemned by Protestant reformers, and yet it remained undisturbed at the Reformation.[23] Veit Stoß's magnificent, double-sided limewood sculpture showing the Angelic Salutation set within a rosary hangs in the centre of the choir (figure 16). It was donated in 1518 by Anton Tucher, member of the city council and *Kirchenpfleger* at St Sebald, and provides eloquent testimony to the importance of rosary devotion on the eve of the Reformation. Krauss's engraving shows the Angelic Salutation, concealed inside a fabric covering, hanging above the high altar. For many years it was thought that this covering was an innovation of the post-Reformation period. More recent research has demonstrated, however, that it was part of the sculpture's original conception. Tucher's account book for 1519 records payments made for a 'chubert' [covering] and includes individual entries for cutting, sewing, gilding and hanging it and for purchasing cloth, brass rings and chains.[24] The cloth was drawn back only on high feast days.

Although Stoß's Angelic Salutation remained in place, it seems that after 1529 it was no longer uncovered on feast days.[25] Tradition records that it was Andreas Osiander himself who caused it to be permanently removed from view. Writing in 1756 Andreas Würfel claimed that 'because Andreas Osiander preached against this image and called the Mary a golden milk-maid a green covering was made for it'.[26] As we have seen, the green covering was part of the donor's original conception rather than an innovation of the post-Reformation period, and there is no reference to the sculpture amongst the reformer's surviving writings. Yet it is at least possible that Osiander did play some part in ensuring that it remained covered. Johannes Nas's satirical defence of the Catholic faith, *Centuria: das antipapistisch eins und hundert* (Ingolstadt, 1567), contains what is probably the earliest surviving report of the sculpture's condemnation by a Lutheran preacher. Nas records that a beautiful image of Mary in a rosary hung in the Lorenzkirche and that when it came to the attention of a Lutheran preacher 'he sighed, and lost his colour, and said several

23 The Twenty-Three Articles of Faith drawn up by Osiander in 1528 recommended that the practice of reserving the host should be abandoned. Christensen, 'Iconoclasm', p. 218. On sacrament houses see Achim Timmermann, 'Staging the Eucharist: late gothic sacrament houses in Swabia and the Upper Rhine. Architecture and iconography', unpublished PhD thesis, University of London, 1996.

24 Georg Stolz, 'Der Engelsgruß in St. Lorenz zu Nürnberg: Stiftung und Schicksal', in *Der Englische Gruß des Veit Stoß zu St Lorenz in Nürnberg*, ed. Bayerisches Landesamt für Denkmalpflege (Munich, 1983), p. 5.

25 Jörg Rasmussen, 'Der Englische Gruß', in *Veit Stoß in Nürnberg: Werke des Meisters und seiner Schule in Nürnberg und Umgebung*, ed. Germanisches Nationalmuseum (Munich, 1983), p. 203.

26 Andreas Würfel, *Diptycha Ecclesiæ Laurentianæ* (Nuremberg, 1756), p. 17.

Figure 16. Veit Stoß, Angelic Salutation, 1517–18 (Lorenzkiche, Nuremberg)

times before everyone, as often as I look at this milk-maid my heart becomes cold in my body'.[27] The designation of Mary as a milk-maid may have had a particular significance for a sixteenth-century audience: milk-maids had a reputation in the erotic sphere, which was perpetuated in contemporary prints

[27] Quoted in Jacob Grimm and Wilhelm Grimm, *Deutsches Wörterbuch*, 16 vols. (Leipzig, 1854–1954), vol. 4.1.5, cols.1986–9.

and poetry.[28] Despite this alleged attack and its permanent fabric cover, Stoß's sculpture remained an object of pride for Nuremberg's citizens, as we will see in the third section of this chapter.

Outside as well as inside Nuremberg's churches a remarkable amount of Marian imagery survived intact and *in situ*. Bob Scribner suggested that at the Reformation Germany's physical landscape was 'confessionalized', and that travellers would have been able to deduce the religion of a region's inhabitants from the presence or absence of religious monuments: 'thus, as one passed through Franconia, the sudden absence of roadside image shrines betrayed that one had passed from a Catholic into a Protestant area'.[29] Marc Forster likewise associates crucifixes and statues of saints with Catholic identity in his study of baroque southwest Germany, and argues that 'they may have had a special resonance in places where Catholics came into direct contact with Protestants'.[30] Yet these confessional contrasts should not be overstated: in Nuremberg itself, and therefore probably also in its surrounding territory, there was apparently no attempt to remove religious statues from public view.

The custom of adorning the exteriors of buildings with images of the Virgin or, much less frequently, other saints had emerged during the fourteenth century in Nuremberg and persisted up to the eve of the Reformation. These images were originally intended to secure the favour of the depicted saint for the building and its inhabitants, though records of property transactions suggest that they also came to serve a practical purpose as house signs.[31] Although it seems that no new *Hausmadonnen* were erected after 1525, the existing sculptures were allowed to remain in place. In 1855 G. W. K. Lochner published a description of Nuremberg's surviving house sculptures.[32] He counted forty showing the Virgin Mary and knew of another six that were no longer in existence. Lochner's list demonstrates the predominance of *Hausmadonnen* over other house saints, and the extent of their survival. In defiance of notions of 'confessionalized' space, the day-to-day life of Nuremberg's Lutheran citizens was conducted beneath the watchful eyes of numerous images of the Virgin Mary (figure 17).

[28] Eddy de Jongh and Ger Luijten, *Mirror of Everyday Life: Genreprints in the Netherlands 1550–1700*, trans. Michael Hoyle (Amsterdam, 1997), pp. 260–3, cat. no. 52. See also R. G. Schöller, *Der Gemeine Hirte: Viehhaltung, Weidewirtschaft und Hirtenwesen vornehmlich des mittelalterlichen Umlandes von Nürnberg*, Schriftenreihe der Altnürnberger Landschaft 18 (Nuremberg, 1973), pp. 168–9.

[29] Scribner, 'The impact of the Reformation', p. 318.

[30] Forster, *Catholic Revival*, p. 73. See also Siegfried Müller, 'Repräsentationen des Luthertums – Disziplinierung und konfessionelle Kultur in Bildern', *Zeitschrift für historische Forschung* 29 (2002), 234–6.

[31] Heal, 'A woman like any other?', p. 136. On the functions of *Hausmadonnen* see also Bernhard Schemmel, *Figuren und Reliefs an Haus und Hof in Franken* (Würzburg, 1978), pp. 11–14.

[32] G.W.K. Lochner, *Die noch vorhandenen Abzeichen Nürnberger Häuser* (Nuremberg, 1855).

Figure 17. Obstmarkt, Nuremberg (with *Hausmadonnen*), 1935

Evidence concerning the private ownership of images also testifies to Mary's continued prominence. In some Protestant areas, for example Berne, the private ownership of images of saints was strictly prohibited,[33] and in others, for example Zwinglian-influenced Augsburg, it seems to have been voluntarily abandoned, as we will see in chapter 3. Indeed, over the course of the sixteenth and early seventeenth centuries it seems that Europe's confessional divisions had a major impact on the ownership of religious imagery. Susan Foister's survey of sixteenth-century English probate inventories indicates that after the reign of Henry VIII there was a gradual shift away from the ownership of conventional devotional imagery, including representations of the Virgin Mary, to biblical subjects offering the opportunity for narrative treatment and to secular forms of imagery, most notably the portrait.[34] Philip Benedict's analysis of private collections of paintings in Metz, a provincial French city with a substantial

[33] Dupeux, Jezler and Wirth, eds., *Bildersturm*, cat. no. 100.

[34] Susan Foister, 'Paintings and other works of art in sixteenth-century English inventories', *The Burlington Magazine* 123, no. 938 (1981), 276.

Huguenot minority, indicates that in seventeenth-century France the situation was even more clear-cut. His sample of 270 household inventories from 1645–7 and 1667–72 reveals that religious paintings accounted for 61 per cent of works owned by Catholics and only 27 per cent of works owned by Protestants. The discrepancy is even more marked when Marian images are considered alone: 90 paintings of the Virgin and 12 of the Annunciation appear in Catholic hands whilst only 4 pictures of the same subjects were owned by Protestants.[35]

In Lutheran Nuremberg, however, it was apparently considered perfectly acceptable to collect and display images of the Virgin. When Lazarus Spengler, the civic secretary who played a leading role in the city's Reformation, drew up a detailed inventory of his possessions in 1529 it listed four Marian images and twenty-five rosaries.[36] Spengler was amongst the first generation of Lutheran converts, and it is therefore not entirely surprising that he still had some pre-Reformation images in his possession. But Marian images continued to appear in the much larger art collections of the mid to late sixteenth century, for example that of Willibald Imhoff (1519–80). Building on the foundations laid by his grandfather, the humanist Willibald Pirckheimer, Imhoff established one of the most valuable and extensive collections of the period. He augmented Pirckheimer's original collection of medals and antiquities and also acquired numerous sculptures and paintings, including a number of works from the estate of Albrecht Dürer. His inventory also lists paintings by Georg Pencz (with whom he was personally acquainted), Lucas Cranach, Michelangelo and Raphael.[37] The house on Egidienplatz that the family occupied from 1564, in which this magnificent collection was displayed, became a favoured residence for visiting princes: in 1570, for example, during Emperor Maximilian II's trip to Nuremberg, Duke Albrecht V of Bavaria stayed there.[38] Imhoff's Lutheran credentials are not open to question: amongst the bequests that he made before his death were several to the pastors and preachers of Nuremberg's Lutheran churches.[39] Yet he had no inhibitions about owning and even acquiring Catholic devotional imagery. The 1580 inventory lists eleven images of the Virgin. Seven, including two by Dürer, were displayed in the *Oberstube* [upper reception room], amongst a selection of other religious and profane paintings. The four remaining Marian

35 Philip Benedict, 'Towards the comparative study of the popular market for art: the ownership of paintings in seventeenth-century Metz', *Past & Present* 109 (1985), 112. For an equivalent comparison between Catholic Antwerp and Protestant Delft see Jeffrey M. Muller, 'Private collections in the Spanish Netherlands: ownership and display of paintings in domestic interiors', in *The Age of Rubens*, ed. Peter C. Sutton (Boston, 1993), p. 197.

36 Spengler's inventories can be found in the StadtAN, Rep. B14/III, Inventarbücher, Nr. 11, fols. 166r–175v.

37 The 1580 inventory is published in Horst Pohl, ed., *Willibald Imhoff, Enkel und Erbe Willibald Pirckheimers* (Nuremberg, 1992), pp. 279–339.

38 T. Hampe, 'Kunstfreunde im alten Nürnberg und ihre Sammlungen', *MVGSN* 16 (1904), 74.

39 Pohl, ed., *Willibald Imhoff*, pp. 337–8.

images were displayed in other rooms, including one of Mary and Joseph in the room occupied by visiting dignitaries.[40]

The suggestion that Nuremberg's patricians were comfortable with such relics of Catholic culture is confirmed by evidence relating to the art collection established by the city council itself.[41] In 1526 Dürer donated his *Four Apostles* to the council. These two panels were placed in the *Regimentsstube* of the *Rathaus* and were soon joined by his portraits of the emperors Charlemagne and Sigismund that had, prior to the Reformation, been displayed alongside the imperial relics.[42] During the final years of Dürer's life or shortly after his death the council also acquired various other works including his 1498 and 1500 self-portraits. The collection was augmented by paintings, both religious and profane, by other artists.[43] The council apparently had no qualms about incorporating Marian images into this collection: a Virgin and Child from the Cranach workshop that had been given to the city in 1522 by Frederick the Wise was added to the *Rathaus* display during the first half of the sixteenth century. Amongst the other sixteenth-century works that entered the collection during the later sixteenth or early seventeenth century was Martin von Heemskerck's *St Luke Painting the Virgin*. This was seen by Philipp Hainhofer, an Augsburg patrician and diplomat, hanging in the *Regimentsstube* in 1617.[44] And amongst the silverware belonging to the council that was inventoried in 1613 was a table ornament in the form of the Virgin Mary.[45]

One final example of Marian imagery deserves mention: a house altar from around 1480, which did not simply survive the Reformation but even continued to be used and renovated until at least 1620 (figure 18).[46] The carved central shrine shows the Virgin and Child surrounded by rays of sun. Two angels hold a crown above Mary's head, and two artisans kneel at her feet. The relief panels on the interiors of the two wings depict saints Lorenz and Sebald and two arms-bearers (the dove of the Holy Ghost and an angel). On the exterior of the wings is a painted Annunciation scene. The information that can be gleaned concerning the history of this small triptych provides a fascinating glimpse of the devotional concerns of Nuremberg's Lutheran citizens. A painted inscription on its console reads '1558 / Verneuert 1577/1620'. The 1620 renovation was

40 Ibid., p. 300, no. 60 and no. 66, 2.
41 On the development of this collection in the sixteenth century see Wilhelm Schwemmer, 'Aus der Geschichte der Kunstsammlungen der Stadt Nürnberg', *MVGSN* 40 (1949), 97–9.
42 GNM Inv. Nr. Gm 167 and Gm 168.
43 Schwemmer, 'Aus der Geschichte der Kunstsammlungen der Stadt Nürnberg', 99.
44 Philipp Hainhofer, *Reise-Tagebuch enthaltend Schilderungen aus Franken, Sachsen, der Mark Brandenburg und Pommers im Jahr 1617* (Stettin, 1834), p. 4. On Hainhofer see Bruno Bushart, 'Kunst und Stadtbild', in *Geschichte der Stadt Augsburg*, ed. Gottlieb, p. 383.
45 Schwemmer, 'Aus der Geschichte der Kunstsammlungen der Stadt Nürnberg', 110.
46 Germanisches Nationalmuseum, ed., *Spiegel der Seligkeit: Privates Bild und Frömmigkeit im Spätmittelalter* (Nuremberg, 2000), cat. no. 52.

Figure 18. House altar, c.1480 (restored 1558, 1577 and 1620) (GNM, Nuremberg)

particularly intrusive: the exterior was repainted; the kneeling artisans were added; and the heraldic fields were altered. The heraldry indicates that these transformations were carried out on behalf of Nuremberg's metalworkers. The house altar had become a *Zechtafel*, an image used to represent the artisinal group at communal assemblies. Nuremberg's metalworkers chose, for their *Zechtafel*, to adapt a pre-existing altarpiece and to depict representatives of their trade kneeling in prayer before the Virgin and Child.

All of the examples cited above come from Nuremberg, but similar images could still be found in many parts of the predominantly Lutheran north and east of Germany.[47] In the imperial free city of Lübeck, which adopted the Lutheran Reformation in 1530 under the moderate direction of Johannes Bugenhagen and which remained a stronghold of Lutheran orthodoxy into the eighteenth century, as much imagery survived as in Nuremberg. Apart from the melting down of

[47] Johann Michael Fritz, ed., *Die bewahrende Kraft des Luthertums: mittelalterliche Kunstwerke in evangelischen Kirchen* (Regensburg, 1997). On Silesia see Paul Knötel, *Kirchliche Bilderkunde Schlesiens* (Glatz, 1929), p. 127.

Figure 19. Altarpiece showing the death of the Virgin, 1518 (Marienkirche, Lübeck)

church treasures, which was done in 1533 to finance war with Denmark, very little changed in the city's churches.[48] Figure 19 shows, for example, a splendid carved, gilded and polychromed altarpiece of the death of the Virgin, illustrated according to the Golden Legend, which still stands in Lübeck's Marienkirche. As Max Hasse has pointed out, local guilds and corporations valued images of their patron saints highly, and as a result only a few, for which no one registered a right of possession, were removed.[49] In the Mark of Brandenburg the Lutheran Reformation introduced under Elector Joachim II in 1538–40 was equally traditionalist in visual terms. Eager to demonstrate continuity with the Roman Church, Joachim preserved as many of its images and ceremonies as possible. He continued to expand his own collection of relics, which was displayed on the high altar of Berlin Cathedral until 1598, and in 1547 acquired a number of images, including two of the Virgin Mary, which were probably intended for the cathedral.[50] New paintings from the Cranach school were also brought in. Joachim's successor, Johann Georg, stipulated in his testament that

[48] Hildegard Vogeler, *Madonnen in Lübeck: ein ikonographisches Verzeichnis der mittelalterlichen Mariendarstellungen in den Kirchen und ehemaligen Klöstern der Altstadt und des St Annen-Museums*, ed. Museum für Kunst und Kulturgeschichte der Hansestadt Lübeck (Lübeck, 1993).

[49] Hasse, 'Maria und die Heiligen', 72.

[50] Bodo Nischan, *Prince, People, and Confession: the second Reformation in Brandenburg* (Philadelphia, 1994), pp. 17–18. Nikolaus Müller, *Der Dom zu Berlin* (Berlin, 1906), pp. 46–8.

all 'church vestments, ornaments, silverware, treasures, vessels, paintings, and other church decorations' were to remain in Berlin Cathedral after his death, though this provision failed to protect them against the attacks of local Calvinists during the late sixteenth and early seventeenth centuries.[51] Many Marian images also survived in the neighbouring duchy of Pomerania.[52]

Elsewhere the survival of pre-Reformation images was less comprehensive, but still surprisingly extensive. In the duchy of Mecklenburg on the Baltic coast, which was confessionally divided during the 1530s and 1540s but moved firmly towards Lutheranism in 1549, altar retables from the fifteenth and early sixteenth centuries remained *in situ*.[53] Some were certainly Marian: in 1670, for example, the archdeacon of Parchim complained that, to his horror, there was still an image of the coronation of the Virgin in his church.[54] Elsewhere such images seem to have remained an accepted part of Lutheran devotional life. An altarpiece showing the coronation of the Virgin from the Bonifatiuskirche in Sömmerda, Thuringia, was clearly still valued in the early seventeenth century, when it was augmented by a depiction of the Last Supper and given a new baroque framing.[55] In the duchy of Württemberg in south-west Germany attitudes towards imagery were less moderate,[56] yet even there, in the Peterskirche at Weilheim an der Teck, an *Anna Selbdritt*, a Holy Kindred and a depiction of Christ as the Man of Sorrows before a rosary survived. The image of the rosary was even renewed in 1601.[57] In Pfalz-Neuburg, which from 1554 had a church order modelled on the Württemberg prototype, a number of Marian statues survived despite the extensive destruction of late medieval altarpieces.[58] And of the 269 late medieval retables that survive today from Saxony, the heartland of the Lutheran Reformation, more than half show the Virgin Mary as their central image.[59]

There is abundant evidence that old Marian images survived in various parts of Lutheran Germany, but were new ones also produced in the post-Reformation period? In Nuremberg it seems not. The few commissions that

[51] Nischan, *Prince, People, and Confession*, p. 52.

[52] Marcin Wislocki, 'Saints in Protestant theology, devotion and art in Pomerania', *Colloquia: Journal of Central European Studies* 12, nos. 1–2 (2005), 41–65.

[53] Eike Wolgast, 'Die Reformation im Herzogtum Mecklenburg und das Schicksal der Kirchenausstattungen', in *Die bewahrende Kraft des Luthertums*, ed. Fritz, pp. 64–6.

[54] Ibid., p. 67.

[55] Karl-Heinz Meissner, 'Zwischen Zerstörung und Umdeutung: Kunst-Schicksale in den Kirchen der lutherischen Reformation', *Kunst und Kirche* 4193 (1993), 280.

[56] Reinhard Lieske, *Protestantische Frömmigkeit im Spiegel der kirchlichen Kunst des Herzogtums Württemberg* (Munich and Berlin, 1973), pp. 10–11. In 1540 Duke Ulrich decreed 'das alle Bülder und gemält in den Kirchen abgethan werden sollen'.

[57] Ibid., p. 115. Martin Scharfe, 'Der Heilige in der protestantische Volksfrömmigkeit', *Hessische Blätter für Volkskunde* 60 (1969), 174.

[58] Franz Josef Merkl, 'Kunst und Konfessionalisierung – das Herzogtum Pfalz-Neuburg 1542–1650', *JbVAB* 32 (1998), 195–6.

[59] Ingo Sandner, *Spätgotische Tafelmalerei in Sachsen* (Dresden and Basle, 1993), p. 56.

entered Nuremberg's churches after 1525 were commemorative, either epitaphs or stained-glass windows, and their iconography was generally Christocentric. The same is true for Augsburg's key Lutheran church, St Anna (see chapter 3). And in Saxony, where the Cranach workshop did most to create a new and specifically Lutheran iconography, Mary was likewise marginalized. Cranach altarpieces tended to focus on the Last Supper, recommended by Luther himself as a suitable subject in 1530, or on Christ's Crucifixion.[60]

In other areas, however, there is evidence for the continued production of Marian images. In 1533 Lübeck's young Protestant congregation gave its first commission, a pulpit for the local Marienkirche. This pulpit was crowned by a sculpted image of the Annunciation. New images of the Virgin and of other patron saints adorned portals, doors, liturgical vessels, clocks and bells in Lübeck's Lutheran churches.[61] And amongst the surviving woodcuts produced there during the first half of the seventeenth century, some of which were displayed on prayer book cupboards in the Jakobikirche until the nineteenth century, are several depicting Mary. One produced by the Augsburg-trained artist Jürgen Creutzberger shows the Virgin and Child in a rosary. Its inscriptions celebrate Mary, describing her as 'Die heilige Jungfraw Maria' and citing Luke 11:27, 'blessed is the womb that carried you and the breasts that suckled you'.[62] In Flensburg (duchy of Schleswig) Mary was likewise still being depicted anew in the post-Reformation period. As patron of Flensburg's Marienkirche she featured on a number of post-Reformation commissions: a sculpture of the Virgin and Child was placed on the newly built west gable of the church in 1589; several liturgical vessels donated during the first half of the seventeenth century show her with the Christ Child; and in 1677 the stained-glass window behind the high altar was replaced with a Marian image.[63] In the duchy of Pomerania new images of the Virgin continued to be installed in Lutheran churches throughout the later sixteenth and seventeenth centuries.[64] In northern Germany, where the Reformation was firmly established and was not under immediate threat from neighbouring Catholic territories, Lutherans were apparently happy not only to assimilate old Marian images but also to produce new ones.[65]

THE PERSISTENCE OF MARIAN PIETY

In Nuremberg and in other Lutheran areas it was not only Marian images but also Marian liturgy that survived. Luther's own position on Marian feast days

[60] *WA*, vol. 31, part I, p. 415. [61] Hasse, 'Maria und die Heiligen', 79 n. 5. [62] Ibid., 77–8.

[63] Ludwig Rohling, *Die Kunstdenkmäler der Stadt Flensburg* (Munich and Berlin, 1955).

[64] Wislocki, 'Saints in Protestant theology, devotion and art in Pomerania'.

[65] There is also a limited amount of evidence for the continued production of epitaphs and altarpieces showing Mary in Lutheran Silesia. See Knötel, *Kirchliche Bilderkunde Schlesiens*, pp. 128–9.

was moderate, although he seems to have hoped for the eventual demise of all except the Annunciation and Purification. In his 1520 *Address to the Christian Nobility of the German Nation* he advocated the abolition of all feast days except for Sunday, but added that if people wished to retain Marian festivals and those of the great saints they should either be celebrated on Sundays or observed as only half-day holidays. In the past the abuse of these holy days with drinking and gambling had, he said, caused great offence to God.[66] In his 1523 tract, *Concerning the Order of Public Worship*, he likewise said that 'all the festivals of the saints are to be discontinued'. Where the saint's legend was likely to be of use it could be inserted after the Gospel reading on Sunday. Once again, Marian festivals were to some extent exempt: 'the festivals of the Purification and Annunciation of Mary may be continued, and for the time being also her Assumption and Nativity'.[67] In his *Order of Mass and Communion for the Church at Wittenberg* of the same year he stated that 'we in Wittenberg intend to observe only the Lord's days and the festivals of the Lord'. The Annunciation and Purification were, he said, to be included as feasts of Christ. But his rejection of all other feast days for the Wittenberg congregation was not intended to be binding: 'Let others act according to their own conscience or in consideration of the weakness of some.'[68]

In practice, most Lutheran churches retained at least three of the seven traditional Marian feast days: the Annunciation, the Visitation and Mary's Purification.[69] These three feast days were considered legitimate because they commemorated events recorded in Scripture, events that were of significance for Christ as well as for Mary.[70] Bugenhagen's church order for Braunschweig, drawn up in 1528, stated for example that they should be celebrated 'as long as the stories are contained in the Gospels and concern our lord Christ'.[71] Feast days that commemorated non-scriptural events – Mary's conception, her birth, her presentation in the temple and her assumption into heaven – were often abandoned.[72] Church orders reveal, however, that there was considerable variation between territories.[73] As Robert Lansemann points out, feast days, like images and ceremonies, were regarded by the reformers as matters of Christian freedom, and it is clear that some territories retained far more than Luther

66 *WA*, vol. 6, pp. 445–6.
67 *WA*, vol. 12, p. 37.
68 *WA*, vol. 12, pp. 208–9. This message was repeated in the 1528 'Unterricht der Visitatoren an die Pfarrherren', *WA*, vol. 26, pp. 222–3.
69 Zeeden, *Katholische Überlieferungen*, pp. 47–8. For further information on the celebration of Marian feast days in the Protestant Church see P. Graff, *Geschichte der Auflösung der alten gottesdienstlichen Formen in der evangelischen Kirche Deutschlands*, vol. 1: *Bis zur Eintritt der Aufklärung und des Rationalismus*, 2nd edn (Göttingen, 1937), pp. 112–26.
70 Jaroslav Pelikan, *Obedient Rebels: Catholic substance and Protestant principle in Luther's Reformation* (London, 1964), p. 86.
71 Quoted in Schimmelpfennig, *Die Geschichte der Marienverehrung*, p. 34.
72 Kreitzer, 'Reforming Mary', pp. 239–41.
73 For a complete table see Lansemann, *Die Heiligentage*, pp. 196–7.

would ideally have wished.[74] While in ducal Prussia, for example, the liturgical calendar was thoroughly purified in 1525, leaving only the Annunciation and the Purification, in Brandenburg numerous saints' feast days were retained: five Marian feasts (the usual three plus Mary's Nativity and Assumption), as well as the feasts of the Apostles, of All Saints, and of saints Katherine, Martin, Lawrence, Mary Magdalene, John the Baptist and Michael the Archangel.[75] Joachim II's 1540 church order for Brandenburg has, in fact, been described as the most Catholic of all the Protestant church orders: while its central teaching was justification by faith alone, it retained almost all of the traditional ceremonies and usages and was, as a result, the only Protestant church order to win approval from both Vienna and Wittenberg.[76]

The evidence from Nuremberg provides a good example of the kinds of concerns that might determine local attitudes towards feast days. In April 1525 Nuremberg's city council asked its preachers and provosts to discuss which pre-Reformation feast days should be retained.[77] In their response the preachers and provosts argued that since feast days had, in the past, led to 'nothing other than all evil, vice, disgrace, drinking [and] murder' their number should be severely curtailed. In addition to Sunday, the day of rest instituted by the Lord, only Easter, Ascension, Pentecost, Christmas and Circumcision should be allowed to remain. On all other traditional feast days Nuremberg's citizens should be free to work or not work, as they pleased.[78] Not satisfied with this answer the council asked whether the Annunciation and the feast days of the Twelve Apostles might not also be retained. With some reluctance the preachers and provosts eventually conceded these festivals, along with the Purification, the Visitation, St John the Baptist and St Steven.[79] These were the festivals that were named in the mandate issued by the council on 24 May 1525, prescribed in the 1533 church order and listed in Veit Dietrich's *Agendbüchlein* for rural pastors.[80] The belated addition of two extra Marian festivals – the Purification and the Visitation – is of particular interest: Nuremberg's religious authorities were apparently compelled to adopt a more moderate position with regard to

[74] Ibid., pp. 8, 46–7.

[75] Kolb, *For All the Saints*, Sehling, ed., *Die evangelischen Kirchenordnungen*, vol. 4, p. 35 (Prussia), vol. 3, pp. 86–7 (Brandenburg, 1540). See also Andreas Zieger, *Das religiöse und kirchliche Leben in Preussen und Kurland im Spiegel der evangelischen Kirchenordnungen des 16. Jahrhunderts* (Cologne and Graz, 1967), pp. 103–5.

[76] Nischan, *Prince, People, and Confession*, pp. 18–24.

[77] Seebass, *Osiander*, pp. 179–80.

[78] Gerhard Pfeiffer, ed., *Quellen zur Nürnberger Reformationsgeschichte: von der Duldung liturgischer Änderungen bis zur Ausübung des Kirchenregiments durch den Rat (Juni 1524–Juni 1525)*, Einzelarbeiten aus der Kirchengeschichte Bayerns 45 (Nuremberg, 1968), p. 236.

[79] For a record of the debate see ibid., pp. 236–9.

[80] StadtAN, Rep. A6, Sammlung der (gedruckten) Mandate, Urkunden und Verordnungen der Reichsstadt und Stadtverwaltung Nürnberg, 1219 bis Gegenwart, 1525 Mai 24; Sehling, ed., *Die evangelischen Kirchenordnungen*, vol. 11 (Bayern I, Franken), p. 204; StaatsAN, Rep. 56, Nürnberger Druckschriften, Nr. 97a (1543).

Marian liturgy than they would, of their own volition, have chosen, and the significance of this compulsion will be explored below.[81]

The feast of the Assumption, which was, as we have seen, frequently abolished, caused Nuremberg's council particular problems. The council was advised in May 1525 that although the Visitation was more firmly grounded in Scripture than the Assumption, the latter 'has had . . . much standing amongst the common folk'. Its day, 15 August, which was a harvest celebration and an important holiday, should therefore be appropriated for the celebration of the Visitation.[82] An anonymous description of the city's liturgy drawn up in 1527 reiterates that the Assumption was tolerated because of the common people's will.[83] Similarly Veit Dietrich's *Agendbüchlein*, written for pastors in Nuremberg's rural hinterland, said that the feast of the Assumption should be observed with readings and songs telling the story of the Visitation 'not because it [i.e. Assumption] has basis in Holy Scripture, but because of the common working peasant folk'.[84] This solution to the problem of the Assumption was also recommended by Luther in his 1544 *Hauspostille*.[85] The debates surrounding this festival provide a clear illustration of the early reformers' desire to proceed gradually in the matter of religious reform, making allowance where possible for what Luther described as 'the weakness of some'. Indeed, even in Zwinglian Zurich the feast of the Assumption was retained until the beginning of the 1530s.[86]

Other remnants of traditional Marian liturgy also met with a mixed fate. In general it seems that, as Luther wished, antiphons such as the *Salve Regina* and *Regina Caeli* were abandoned. According to a 1527 list of ceremonies transformed since Nuremberg's Reformation, the *Salve Regina* was 'entirely set aside' because it named 'the holiest Virgin and Mother of God as our life's sweetness, intercessor and hope' and thereby 'blasphemed most badly' against God and his mother.[87] The 1525 church order for Lutheran Prussia likewise proscribed these traditional antiphons: 'One should not sing the Salve Regina, because it belittles God.'[88] In Nuremberg the abolition of the *Salve* met with some resistance: Peter Imhoff, who had endowed its singing in the Lorenzkirche, asked the provost and city council 'on what grounds such praise and honour had

[81] A liturgical compendium produced for the Sebalduskirche in 1599 and now located in the Pierpoint Morgan Library in New York (MS M.1109) confirms that all three Marian feast days were still being celebrated in Nuremberg's churches at the end of the sixteenth century. *Antiphonae, Responsoria, Hymni, Introitus, Missae, Alleluia . . . per annum in Templo Sebaldino Choraliter cantari solent. Collecti a Joanne Schirmero, Scholae Sebaldine cantore* (Nuremberg, 1599). I am grateful to Dr Volker Schier for bringing this manuscript to my attention.

[82] Pfeiffer, ed., *Quellen*, p. 239. For equivalent justifications in other Lutheran territories see Zeeden, *Katholische Überlieferungen*, p. 48 and Graff, *Geschichte der Auflösung*, p. 126.

[83] Pfeiffer, ed., *Quellen*, p. 447.

[84] Sehling, ed., *Die evangelischen Kirchenordnungen*, vol. 11 (Bayern I, Franken), p. 204.

[85] Kreitzer, 'Reforming Mary', p. 87; *WA*, vol. 52, p. 681.

[86] Campi, *Zwingli und Maria*, pp. 77–8.

[87] Pfeiffer, ed., *Quellen*, p. 445.

[88] Sehling, ed., *Die evangelischen Kirchenordnungen*, vol. 4, p. 29.

been withdrawn and turned away from God Almighty and the Mother of God'.[89] Other Marian texts – the Magnificat and Ave Maria – were generally retained. In Nuremberg the Angelic Salutation was recited in the vernacular from the pulpit by the pastor on Sundays and on feast days after the first office and before the sermon, along with an Old Testament lesson, the Ten Commandments, the Creed, the Our Father and an admonition to the congregation. The 'song of praise of the Mother of God', the Magnificat, was also still used at vespers.[90] In some places, however, these texts were regarded with suspicion: the author of the Kurland church order of 1570 wrote that the Ave was used 'from papist habit', and stated that it should be gradually given up.[91]

Another indication of the predominantly conservative attitude of Lutheran authorities towards Marian devotion was the persistence of legislation that made blasphemy against the Virgin a punishable offence. Attacks on the Virgin had, by the eve of the Reformation, become part of the standard repertoire of offences condemned by civic authorities. If allowed to go unpunished, verbal assaults on the honour of God and of his saints would, it was believed, incur God's wrath and punishment on the whole community.[92] A fifteenth-century police ordinance from Nuremberg decreed, for example, 'that no-one should swear wickedly or severely, as by God, Our Lady or the like'.[93] This ordinance threatened offenders with the pillory, with expulsion from the city or, in extreme cases, with corporal or even capital punishment. In a decree issued on 3 March 1526, a year after the introduction of the Reformation, the council condemned blasphemy against God and against the sacrament of the altar (the body and blood of Christ), and went on to state that:

> Where someone speaks malevolently of the Virgin Mary and Mother of Christ our saviour, as though she had not borne Christ the Son of the most high (that is God) as a pure virgin, or were he to speak similar words, thus immediately harming the Virgin Mary in abuse or damage of the honour with which she is endowed by God, according to Holy Scripture, he should be punished in body, life, members or possessions, as is described above concerning blasphemy and wrong-doing.[94]

A 1529 decree that was to be proclaimed on the first Sunday in Lent from pulpits in Nuremberg's rural churches repeated the same warning with regard to Marian blasphemy, as did an ordinance against blasphemy and drinking issued

89 H. Dormeier, 'St Rochis, die Pest und die Imhoffs in Nürnberg vor und während der Reformation', *Anzeiger des Germanischen Nationalmuseums* (1985), 54.

90 Pfeiffer, ed., *Quellen*, pp. 443–5.

91 Sehling, ed., *Die evangelischen Kirchenordnungen*, vol. 5, p. 80. On Prussia and the Kurland see Zieger, *Das religiöse und kirchliche Leben.*

92 Schwerhoff, 'Blasphemie', 56.

93 Joseph Baader, ed., *Nürnberger Polizeiordnungen aus dem XIII. bis XV. Jahrhundert* (Stuttgart, 1861), p. 114. See also Schwerhoff, 'Blasphemie', 46.

94 StadtAN, Rep. A6, Sammlung der (gedruckten) Mandate, Urkunden und Verordnungen der Reichsstadt und Stadtverwaltung Nürnberg 1219 bis Gegenwart, 1526 März 3, fol. 2r.

in 1560 that was to be read out annually in the parish churches of St Sebald and St Lorenz.[95] As we shall see in chapter 3, in Augsburg edicts issued after the Reformation no longer listed Marian blasphemy as a punishable offence. In moderate Nuremberg, however, legislation continued to reflect Lutheran theologians' determined defences of Mary's honour.[96]

There may, of course, have been a significant gap between prescription and practice. Nuremberg's citizens heard from their preachers that they were not to impugn God's virginal mother, but were they in fact punished if they did so? The nature of Nuremberg's criminal sources makes it impossible to answer this question: despite Nuremberg's extensive municipal archives, the records of interrogations, trials and punishments are fragmentary for the sixteenth century.[97] The council minutes (*Ratsverlässe*) do record that in January 1525, i.e. three months before the official introduction of the Reformation, Marx Plickner, a knife-maker who had 'blasphemed much against the Virgin Mary', was imprisoned. Plickner's fellow knife-makers petitioned for his punishment to be moderated, but their case was dismissed until after carnival and Plickner was expelled from the city. At the end of March, as a result of the knife-makers' 'fluent plea', Plickner was sentenced to four weeks' imprisonment after which he was pardoned by the city.[98] Nuremberg's council was already, by this time, firmly committed to the Lutheran cause, and yet its members were still determined to castigate those who spoke ill of the Virgin. We cannot be sure, however, whether the prosecution of Marian blasphemy continued after the early stages of the Reformation.

THE CHANGING SIGNIFICANCE OF MARIAN LITURGY AND IMAGES

This deliberate preservation of images of the Virgin, of Marian feast days and of various other manifestations of Marian devotion seems odd, given the Lutheran

[95] Ibid., 1529, fol. 3v; ibid., B 31/1, fol. 100r.

[96] For a general discussion of post-Reformation attitudes to Marian blasphemy see Gerd Schwerhoff, *Zungen wie Schwerter: Blasphemie in alteuropäischen Gesellschaften 1200–1650* (Konstanz, 2005), pp. 247–9.

[97] T. Hampe, *Die Nürnberger Malefizbücher als Quellen der reichsstädtischen Sittengeschichte vom 14. bis zum 18. Jahrhundert*, ed. Gesellschaft für Fränkische Geschichte, Neujahrsblätter 17 (Bamberg, 1927). Brief summaries of cases were drawn up for the benefit of the council in the *Achtbücher* and executions were recorded in the *Halsgerichtsbücher*. I have sampled the earliest surviving *Achtbuch*, which covers the period 1578–81, and the *Halsgerichtsbuch* from 1487–1558 (StaatsAN, Nürnberger Amts- und Standbücher, Nr. 209 and Nr. 221). These compendiums are concerned almost exclusively with executions for robbery and violence: my samples revealed no prosecutions for blasphemy. Heal, 'A woman like any other?', pp. 178–9. On records of prosecutions for blasphemy in Nuremberg see also Schwerhoff, 'Blasphemie', 61–2, 96–8.

[98] Pfeiffer, ed., *Quellen*, pp. 289, 311, 445.

rejection of the cult of saints described in chapter 1. If the reformers were worried that, as Philip Melanchthon put it, the Virgin Mary had 'completely replaced Christ' in popular devotion, if they wanted to reverse this situation and refocus Christians' attention on Christ, then why did they permit so much Marian material to survive? It looks, at first sight, like another example of what Gerald Strauss, Scott Dixon and others have documented for various Protestant territories: a failure to eradicate traditional attitudes and to instill in their place a truly Lutheran belief system.[99] When considering the fate of a key religious symbol such as the Virgin Mary we need, however, a more nuanced understanding of the transition to Lutheranism. Mary's continued prominence points not to the reformers' inability to eradicate Catholic superstitions, but rather to their ability to absorb and adapt existing representations. Cultural artefacts do not, as both historians and art historians have long been aware, have fixed meanings: the significance of images and texts is defined only through a process of appropriation on the part of the audience.[100] As David Sabean observed in his study of village discourse in early modern Württemberg, 'inherited items of culture continually changed shape as they were situated in new contexts'.[101] Luther acknowledged as much in his discussion of the elevation of the host, when he distinguished between the act itself and the interpretation given to it. The symbol might be retained for the sake of the weak, but vernacular sermons would, he argued, give it a new meaning.[102] It was this possibility for transformation in meaning that sanctioned the survival of pre-Reformation liturgy and imagery. Lutheran preachers believed that their parishioners could be taught, through the power of the word, to abandon the superstitious elements of Marian veneration and to regard the Virgin not as an intercessor and protector but as a model of right belief and conduct. Of course, we still need to ask, as Strauss did, whether their optimism was justified, and the final section of this chapter will consider the issue of popular belief in more detail.

The transformation of meaning brought about by the reformers was perhaps most obvious in the case of surviving Marian liturgy.[103] Feast days were cleansed of their popish abuses, and were reinterpreted to fit with the new understanding of Mary's role as an exemplary recipient of God's grace. Where the festivals of the Purification and Assumption survived, they were stripped

[99] Dixon, *The Reformation and Rural Society*, pp. 143–93; Gerald Strauss, 'Success and failure in the German Reformation', *Past & Present* 67 (1975), 30–63.

[100] See, for example, Roger Chartier, *Cultural History: between practices and representations*, trans. Lydia G. Cochrane (Cambridge, 1988), pp. 40–1 and E. H. Gombrich, *Art and Illusion: a study in the psychology of pictorial representation* (London, 1960), pp. 154–244.

[101] David Sabean, *Power in the Blood: popular culture and village discourse in early modern Germany* (Cambridge, 1984), p. 4.

[102] *WA*, vol. 12, pp. 212–13; Pelikan, *Obedient Rebels*, p. 84.

[103] Lansemann, *Die Heiligentage*, pp. 109ff.

of the 'pagan' practices that had accompanied them in the pre-Reformation period.[104] The blessing of candles at Purification was unanimously condemned and frequently explicitly forbidden, for example in the Prussian church order of 1525.[105] In Nuremberg the provisional liturgical instructions drawn up for the Lorenzkirche and Sebalduskirche in 1524 stated that wax was no longer blessed at Purification and that all other benedictions were held to be 'fools' works'.[106] An anonymous list of ceremonies that had been transformed or abolished, produced in 1527, stated that: 'water, salt, wax, palms and *Fladen* [Easter cakes] are no longer blessed, because they have all been consecrated before through the word of God as his creations, which were made for the good of mankind'.[107] The Assumption was referred to in Nuremberg's festival ordinance issued in 1525 as the feast that 'we *until now* have called herb dedication', suggesting that the traditional blessing of herbs on this day had ceased.[108] The meaning of this unscriptural feast day was also, as we have seen, transformed because preaching on the scriptural story of the Visitation replaced traditional accounts of Mary's Assumption.

Once 'popish' rituals such as benedictions had been abandoned, Marian feast days were celebrated with sermons, hymns and prayers addressed to Christ. Sermons, as we saw in chapter 1, praised Mary as an exemplary recipient of God's grace and as a model of faith, obedience and humility. Vernacular hymns written for the surviving feast days and for general use echoed the same themes, and played, as Rebecca Wagner Oettinger has demonstrated, an important role in spreading Lutheran ideas.[109] Traditional Marian hymns were 'corrected' to eliminate all mention of Mary's mediating role. Under Luther's pen, for example, 'Sancta Maria ste uns bey, so wir sullen sterben' became 'Gott der vater wohn' uns bey'.[110] The Nuremberg cobbler and *Meistersinger* Hans Sachs likewise 'changed' and 'corrected in a Christian manner' two popular hymns, 'Maria zart' and 'Die fraw von hymmel'.[111] Wackernagel's collection of evangelical church songs contains other 'corrected' Marian hymns, as well as four versions of the *Salve Regina* where Christ's name has simply been substituted

104 For a Lutheran discussion of the pagan origins of Candlemas see Hohndorff, *Calendarium sanctorum & historiarum*, p. 73.

105 Zieger, *Das religiöse und kirchliche Leben*, p. 104. The blessing of candles was described in Goldtwurm's *Kirchen Calender* of 1559 as 'grewliche abgötterei und zäuberey', Brückner, ed., *Volkserzählung*, p. 149.

106 StadtAN, Rep. E1, Familienarchiv Spengler, Nr. 47, fol. 2r–v.

107 Pfeiffer, ed., *Quellen*, p. 444.

108 StadtAN, Rep. A6, Sammlung der (gedruckten) Mandate, Urkunden und Verordnungen der Reichsstadt und Stadtverwaltung Nürnberg, 1219 bis Gegenwart, 1525 Mai 24.

109 For a list of evangelical hymns written for Marian feast days see Schimmelpfennig, *Die Geschichte der Marienverehrung*, pp. 44–5. Rebecca Wagner Oettinger, *Music as Propaganda in the German Reformation*, St Andrews Studies in Reformation History (Aldershot, 2001).

110 Düfel, *Luthers Stellung*, p. 228. *WA*, vol. 35, p. 178.

111 Philipp Wackernagel, *Das deutsche Kirchenlied von der ältesten Zeit bis zu Anfang des XVII. Jahrhunderts*, 5 vols. (Leipzig, 1864–77), vol. 3, pp. 80, 81.

for Mary's.[112] In 1523 Sebald Heyden, rector of St Sebald, introduced this revised form of the *Salve* in Nuremberg.[113] It was, however, quickly abandoned: the danger that the majority of the populace, knowing no Latin, would fail to understand the changed text and would be strengthened in their superstitious beliefs by the antiphon's retention was apparently too great.[114] A number of other vernacular hymns reinforced the evangelical message that Mary should not be falsely invoked.[115] Where Mary was mentioned in new hymns, it was primarily in the context of Christ's incarnation. Evangelical authors focused on Gabriel's message to her, on her song of praise (the Magnificat), on her visit to Elizabeth and on her son's birth.[116] Interpretations of these scriptural events echoed those found in Lutheran sermons and treatises. In a verse rendering of the Magnificat, for example, Mary describes herself as God's 'poor servant girl, looked upon with grace'.[117] As in sermons, Mary's purity, chastity and perpetual virginity are often mentioned, and her virtues are held up for emulation.[118] A hymn telling the story of the Annunciation says, for example, that Mary wore three roses representing faith, humility and Christian love, virtues that should be imitated by all, but particularly by women.[119] Mary may have remained prominent, but through the Lutheran liturgy she was presented in a new way, as a model of piety. As Luther emphasized in a sermon on the feast of the Visitation, 'Our celebration is very different to the pope's celebration, and primarily aims to praise God and thank him, as the dear young Virgin praised and thanked him.'[120]

Images of the Virgin, just like Marian liturgy, could be reinterpreted to fit with the new, Lutheran understanding of Mary's proper role in Christian devotion. Luther's conviction that images belonged to the domain of Christian freedom, that they were neither good nor bad, unnecessary to Christian worship but matters of indifference before God, is too well known to require further elaboration.[121] For the present discussion, however, it is important to note his

[112] Ibid., vol. 3, nos. 549 and 569–72. [113] On this revised form see chapter 6, pp. 294–7.

[114] Gustav Georg Zeltner, *Kurtze Erläuterung der Nürnbergischen Schul- und Reformations-geschichte / aus dem Leben und Schriften des berühmten Sebald Heyden / Rectoris bey S. Sebald* (Nuremberg, 1732), pp. 11, 17.

[115] Wackernagel, *Das deutsche Kirchenlied*, vol. 3, no. 1023. Schimmelpfennig, *Die Geschichte der Marienverehrung*, p. 46 points out that only two hymns in Wackernagel's collection address Mary directly. On hymns that condemn trust in the Mother of God see also Kolb, *For All the Saints*, p. 144.

[116] For a comprehensive discussion see Schimmelpfennig, *Die Geschichte der Marienverehrung*, pp. 37–47, though her conclusion that 'das protestantische Kirchenlied des 16. Jahrhunderts hat . . . eine evangelisch begründete Ehrung der Gottesmutter zum Inhalt' is overstated.

[117] Wackernagel, *Das deutsche Kirchenlied*, vol. 3, no. 1043.

[118] See, for example, ibid., vol. 3, nos. 574, 895, 1353 and vol. 4, no. 297. Schimmelpfennig, *Die Geschichte der Marienverehrung*, p. 45, nn. 41–4.

[119] Wackernagel, *Das deutsche Kirchenlied*, vol. 3, no. 1139.

[120] *WA*, vol. 52, p. 682 (*Hauspostille*, 1544).

[121] S. Michalski, *The Reformation and the Visual Arts* (London, 1993), pp. 1–42.

dismissal of contemporary notions of the autonomous power of images. While Karlstadt warned 'how dangerous and harmful images are, and how *we* can be violated *by them* in an instant', Luther located agency not with the images themselves but with their viewers.[122] In a sermon preached at Wittenberg in March 1522 in response to Karlstadt's iconoclasm, Luther cited the example of the Apostle Paul who had travelled to Syracuse on a ship adorned with the figures of Castor and Pollux. He argued that Paul had tolerated these images because he wished to demonstrate 'that outward things could do no harm to faith, if only the heart does not cleave to them or put its trust in them'.[123] In Luther's opinion, Karlstadt and his supporters had reversed the natural order for the removal of images: they had taken images from before men's eyes but had left them embedded in their hearts. Reformers must instead strive to 'tear [images] from the heart by God's word . . . For when they are cast out of the heart they no longer harm the eye.'[124] Here we have an explicit denial of the agency of images: once the idols in men's hearts had been destroyed through preaching, images would no longer beguile them. The power of the word and the power of faith would triumph over the power of the image.

Luther's defence of imagery was certainly well known in Nuremberg: his key tract on the subject, *Against the Heavenly Prophets*, was printed there twice in 1525.[125] Local commentators upheld his conviction that images did not possess autonomous power. Albrecht Dürer, in the dedicatory epistle to his book, *Instruction in Measurement* (1525), wrote that a Christian was as little provoked to idolatry by the mere presence of an image as a pious man was to murder by the presence of a weapon. Only people truly lacking in understanding would ever pray to painting, wood or stone.[126] Similar sentiments were expressed in a broadsheet published in Nuremberg in around 1530 by Erhard Schön entitled *Complaint of the Poor Persecuted Idols and Church Images on their so Unfair Condemnation and Punishment*. The woodcut illustration shows the removal and destruction of images – the false idols – being directed by a man who is accompanied by women and money – the true idols or idols of the heart. In the accompanying text the images berate their attackers: 'You yourselves started with us, who are lifeless . . . You yourselves made us into idols, and now you deride us for it . . . It is you who have brought us to a point we never dreamed of reaching.' The message is clear: men project into the stone, wood or pigment what is inherent not in *it* but in *them*.[127]

[122] B. D. Mangrum and G. Scavizzi, eds., *A Reformation Debate: Karlstadt, Emser, and Eck on sacred images. Three treatises in translation* (Toronto, 1991), pp. 19 and 35–6.
[123] *WA*, vol. 10, part III, pp. 26–30. [124] *WA*, vol. 18, p. 67.
[125] Josef Benzing, *Lutherbibliographie: Verzeichnis der gedruckten Schriften Martin Luthers bis zu dessen Tod*, Bibliotheca bibliographica Aureliana 10, 16, 19 (Baden-Baden, 1966), nos. 2090, 2093.
[126] H. Rupprich, ed., *Dürer: Schriftlicher Nachlass*, 3 vols. (Berlin, 1956–70), vol. 1, p. 115.
[127] Quoted in Baxandall, *The Limewood Sculptors*, pp. 78–81.

If the fault lay with the viewers themselves rather than with the paintings and statues that surrounded them then it should be possible to transform attitudes and expectations without removing images. Idolatry could be eliminated through right teaching, and images could remain and even serve a useful purpose. To a much greater extent than either Zwingli or Calvin, Luther recognized the value of the visual in religious devotion: 'I have always condemned and punished misuse and false confidence in images . . . What, however, is not misuse I have always allowed to remain and told [people] to keep, so that it can be put to helpful and blessed use.'[128] Images, or at least visualizations, were an inevitable part of religious life: 'whether I will or not, when I hear of Christ, an image of a man hanging on a cross takes form in my heart'.[129] They could also serve as didactic tools, for, as Luther wrote in the 1529 edition of his *Personal Prayer Book*, children and simple folk were 'moved more by picture and parable . . . than by mere words or instruction'.[130] Other Lutheran reformers echoed these sentiments: Andreas Osiander, for example, wrote in a report submitted to Nuremberg's council in 1526 that images could serve as 'writing and reminders for the peasants'. And in a sermon preached in 1547 he added that images 'can be of use because they remind people or put into their thoughts a thing that they would not otherwise have thought of, or because they present models of things that we would not otherwise have understood'.[131] Images became part of the Lutheran reformers' popular pedagogy, of their attempts to reach out to the common man.[132]

According to Luther, Marian images were amongst those that could serve a useful purpose as devotional aids and didactic tools. In his 1521 *Commentary on the Magnificat* he criticized 'the masters who so depict and portray the blessed Virgin that there is found in her nothing to be despised, but only great and lofty things'. 'What are they doing', he asked, 'but contrasting us with her instead of her with God? Thus they make us timid and afraid and hide the Virgin's comfortable picture [das trostlich gnadenbild vorblenden], as the images are covered over in Lent. For they deprive us of her example, from which we might take comfort; they make an exception of her and set her above all examples.'[133] When correctly conceived, the Virgin's 'comfortable picture' could, he believed, provide consolation for all Christians. Luther also defended the survival of Marian images on the basis of their commemorative value: 'my image breakers must let me keep, wear, and look at a crucifix or a Madonna,

128 *WA*, vol. 10, part II, p. 459 (*Prayerbook*, 1522).
129 *WA*, vol. 18, p. 83; Pelikan, ed., *Luther's Works*, vol. 40, p. 99. See Hans Campenhausen, 'Die Bilderfrage in der Reformation', *Zeitschrift für Kirchengeschichte* 68 (1957), 121–3.
130 *WA*, vol. 10, part II, p. 458.
131 Müller and Seebass, eds., *Gesamtausgabe*, vol. 2, p. 287, vol. 7, pp. 898–9.
132 Scribner, *For the Sake of Simple Folk*.
133 *WA*, vol. 7, p. 569. Translation from Pelikan, ed., *Luther's Works*, vol. 21, p. 323.

yes, even an idol's image, in full accord with the strictest Mosaic law, as long as I do not worship them, but only have them as memorials'.[134] Indeed we learn from the 'Table Talk' that he himself did in fact have an image of the Virgin and Child hanging in his study.[135]

In order to be properly assimilated into Lutheran devotional life, however, pre-Reformation images had to be reinterpreted in accordance with the evangelical understanding of Mary as *Hausmutter* rather than as divine intercessor. This process of reinterpretation can be explicitly documented only in a few exceptional cases.[136] A woodcut produced by Lucas Cranach the Elder in 1509 to illustrate the Wittenberg *Heiligtumsbuch* is one such case. This woodcut showed a statue of the Virgin and Child that, according to the *Heiligtumsbuch*, contained fifty-six Marian relics. Yet in the edition of Georg Rhau's Lutheran educational text, *Hortulus Animae, Lustgarten der Seelen*, that was produced in Wittenberg in 1558, it appeared alongside a passage condemning the invocation of the saints: 'one should not call on the Virgin Mary' (figure 20). The text went on to condemn papist idolatry and to explain that although Mary was blessed above all other women and had found grace with God, she, like every other saint, had done nothing to merit this grace.[137] Even non-scriptural Marian iconographies could be reinterpreted, for example the Holy Kindred, which was based on medieval texts such as the Golden Legend. A Cranach Holy Kindred woodcut, produced in 1509 or 1510 to promote the cult of St Anne that flourished in Wittenberg on the eve of the Reformation, was reissued twice in 1518 or shortly thereafter with a text by Philip Melanchthon added beneath (figure 21).[138] Melanchthon's text explained the central importance of education to a Christian upbringing, thus reinterpreting the image in an evangelical context, focusing the attention of its audience on the educational obligation of parents (illustrated by Alpheus teaching his sons to read in the lower left-hand corner of the image).[139] The reformer clearly recognized the pedagogic potential of this traditional iconography.

[134] *WA*, vol. 18, p. 70 (*Against the Heavenly Prophets*). Translation from Pelikan, *Luther's Works*, vol. 40 (1958), p. 88.

[135] *WA Tr.*, vol. 2, no.1755 and vol. 5, no. 6364. Attempts have been made to identify this with an existing painting of the Virgin and Child by Lucas Cranach. Josef Lieball, *Martin Luthers Madonnenbild* (Stein am Rhein, 1981), pp. 77–80.

[136] For a discussion of the difficulty of proving this process of reinterpretation see Meissner, 'Zwischen Zerstörung und Umdeutung', 279.

[137] Hamburger Kunsthalle (Werner Hofmann), ed., *Luther und die Folgen für die Kunst* (Munich and Hamburg, 1983), p. 227.

[138] Gerhard Bott, ed., *Martin Luther und die Reformation in Deutschland* (Frankfurt am Main, 1983), no. 592.

[139] Hamburger Kunsthalle (Hofmann), ed., *Luther und die Folgen für die Kunst*, p. 118 and Christiane Andersson, 'Religiöse Bilder Cranachs im Dienste der Reformation', in *Humanismus und Reformation als kulturelle Kräfte in der deutschen Geschichte*, ed. L. W. Spitz (Berlin and New York, 1980).

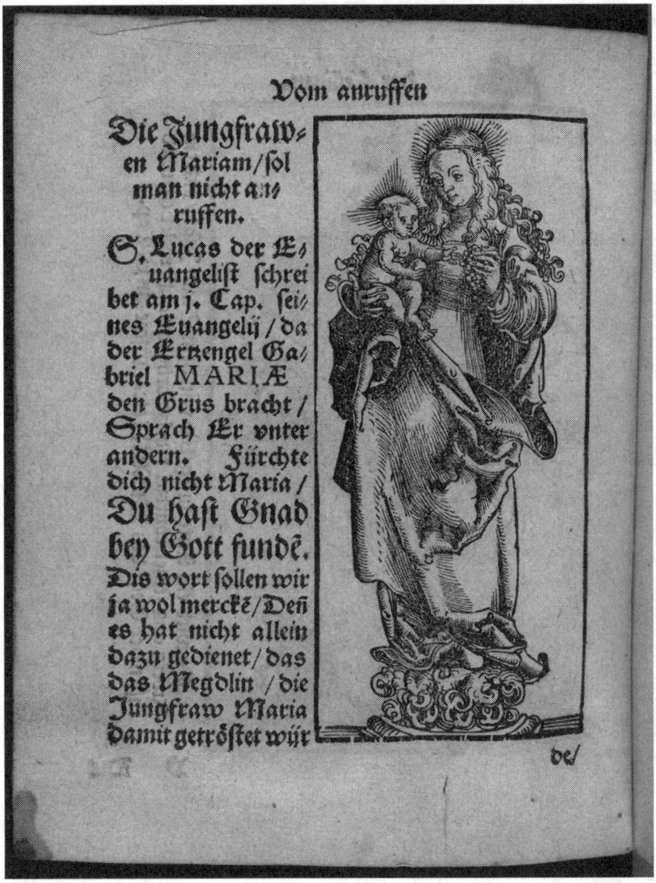
Vom anruffen

Die Jungfraw-
en Mariam/sol
man nicht an-
ruffen.

S. Lucas der E-
uangelist schrei
bet am j. Cap. sei-
nes Euangelij / da
der Ertzengel Ga-
briel MARIÆ
den Grus bracht /
Sprach Er unter
andern. Fürchte
dich nicht Maria /
Du hast Gnad
bey Gott fundē.
Dis wort sollen wir
ja wol merckē/Denn
es hat nicht allein
dazu gedienet/das
das Megdlin / die
Jungfraw Maria
damit getröstet wür
de/

Figure 20. Lucas Cranach the Elder, Virgin and Child, from Georg Rhau, *Hortulus Animae, Lustgarten der Seelen* (Wittenberg: Georg Rhau, 1558) (Hamburger Kunsthalle, Bibliothek)

These two Cranach woodcuts demonstrate that the process of reinterpretation could be facilitated by the addition of new texts.[140] Lutherans frequently added inscriptions to their own images.[141] There are twelve, for example, in the greatest visualization of Luther's doctrine of *sola fide*, Cranach's *Law and Gospel* of around 1530. These references provided the key to understanding

[140] For other examples of the evangelical revision of pre-Reformation images see Koerner, *The Reformation of the Image*, pp. 63–4.

[141] Dieter Koepplin points out that during the second half of the sixteenth century Lutheran artists always attached texts to new images, 'Reformatorische Kunst aus der zweiten Hälfte des 16. Jahrhunderts', in *Die lutherische Konfessionalisierung in Deutschland*, ed. H.-C. Rublack (Gütersloh, 1992).

Figure 21. Lucas Cranach the Elder, Holy Kindred, c.1510 (Kupferstichkabinett, Staatliche Museen zu Berlin)

the image, giving a theological commentary more complex than symbols alone could convey, and demonstrated its legitimacy, proving that it was based on the Bible.[142] Above all, they reduced the potential for misinterpretation, as in the case of Rhau's instruction that 'one should not call upon the Virgin Mary'. Other Marian images acquired similar inscriptions:[143] in 1619, for example, an image of Mary as Queen of Heaven in the Marienkirche in Zittau (Saxony) had an inscription added that said: 'Maria honoranda, non adoranda' [Mary is to be honoured but not adored or prayed to].[144] Texts were not, however, essential: even without them images could serve reformers' pedagogical purposes. In a sermon published in 1609 Johannes Schuler, pastor at Kirchheim unter Teck (Württemberg), spoke of a fresco showing St Martin dividing his

142 Sergiusz Michalski, 'Inscriptions in Protestant paintings and in Protestant churches', in *Ars Ecclesiastica: the church as a context for visual arts* (Helsinki, 1996).

143 See, for example, ibid., p. 44.

144 Meissner, 'Zwischen Zerstörung und Umdeutung', 280. For examples from Silesia see Knötel, *Kirchliche Bilderkunde Schlesiens*, p. 129.

Figure 22. Albrecht Altdorfer, Anne and Mary putting the Christ Child to bed, c.1520 (Hamburger Kunsthalle, Kupferstichkabinett)

cloak with a beggar that was painted on the vault of the choir in the local parish church. Schuler told his congregation that they should recognize God's gifts in the saints, and imitate their zeal and virtue, 'as then St Martin is put before us as an example in this parish church'.[145] As Luther argued in his response to Karlstadt's iconoclasm, the proper preaching of God's word was all that was necessary to eradicate idolatry.

On the basis of such examples we can infer that even if traditional images of the Virgin did not have new texts added to them they might still have been interpreted in a Lutheran light, provided that the right devotional context was created through proper preaching. Images that focused on Mary's human motherhood were perhaps particularly easy to assimilate. Figure 22, for example, an engraving by Albrecht Altdorfer, shows Mary and Anne putting the Christ Child in his cradle, a scene that is unusually intimate even by the standards of late medieval Holy Family depictions. In figure 23 Barthel Beham has depicted

[145] Schuler, *Etliche Christliche Predigen*, pp. 33–4.

Figure 23. Barthel Beham, Mary in a window niche, c.1529 (Hamburger Kunsthalle, Kupferstichkabinett)

Mary as a prosperous Italian wife nursing her child at a window seat.[146] In this image Beham, who a few years previously had been expelled from Nuremberg for his 'gottlos' behaviour, depicts a young woman in contemporary dress engaged in an everyday task.[147] Were it not for the vase of lilies and the glass flask, traditional symbols of Mary's purity, this intimate scene could be taken as a depiction of any mother and child. These two images were probably not intended for an exclusively Lutheran audience (Barthel Beham was by this point in the service of the duke of Bavaria), but like many of Albrecht Dürer's

[146] Hamburger Kunsthalle (Hofmann), ed., *Luther und die Folgen für die Kunst*, pp. 119 and 120.
[147] Herbert Zschelletzschky, *Die 'drei gottlosen Maler' von Nürnberg: Sebald Behan, Barthel Beham und Georg Pencz. Historische Grundlagen und ikonologische Probleme ihrer Graphik zu Reformations- und Bauernkriegzeit* (Leipzig, 1975), pp. 180–1.

Marian images they were perfectly compatible with Lutheran sentiment.[148] To an adherent of the old faith they might have referred as much to Mary's divine intercession as to her human motherhood, but in themselves they contained nothing that would have offended Lutheran sensibilities. It seems likely that paintings such as Hans Traut's epitaph for Johannes Löffelholz (figure 24) and Wolf Traut's altarpiece (figure 25), both of which survived in Nuremberg, were reinterpreted in a similar way in a Lutheran context.[149] In these images the divine was, to an extent at least, already domesticated: in Lucas Cranach's Torgau altar Mary Salome even picks nits from the hair of her son (figure 61).[150] This domesticity fitted well with the reformers' emphasis on women's role in the home (see chapter 6).

Prints and paintings of the Virgin could clearly be assimilated into Lutheran devotional life, but what about statues? Throughout the Reformation they were the most frequent targets of iconoclastic attacks since they were generally the most lifelike and most venerated of images. They could not be reinterpreted through the addition of texts, yet in many Lutheran areas they survived. Here transformations in visual presentation facilitated the process of reinterpretation. Statues of the Virgin were stripped of the symbols of veneration – clothes, jewels, crowns, candles, etc. – that had testified to their supposed supernatural power. They were no longer clothed in velvet robes and adorned with jewels, rosaries and golden crowns, as they had been in the late medieval period. Whereas Nuremberg's pre-Reformation inventories had listed many such ornaments, a detailed inventory from 1578 from the Frauenkirche mentions no robes or jewels for the surviving Madonna, only four 'simple Marian crowns' that were kept in boxes in the sacristy.[151] They were also no longer illuminated by numerous votive candles: in Lutheran Prussia, for example, it was forbidden to light candles before the images of saints displayed in churches or in homes.[152] Finally, they were no longer carried in solemn processions on holy days. A description of Nuremberg's reformed liturgy dating from 1527 records that 'public processions, in which the saints were made into intercessors and

148 Günter Vogler, *Nürnberg 1524/25: Studien zur Geschichte der reformatorischen und sozialen Bewegung in der Reichsstadt* (Berlin, 1982), p. 306. See Zschelletzschky, *Die 'drei gottlosen Maler' von Nürnberg*, p. 179, ills. 32–3 for further examples.

149 On the fate of Wolf Traut's epitaph see Corine Schleif, *Donatio et Memoria: Stifter, Stiftungen und Motivationen an Beispielen aus der Lorenzkirche in Nürnberg* (Munich, 1990), p. 114. Sometime after 1625 it was acquired by Wolf IV. Harsdörffer and moved from the disused Annenkapelle in the graveyard of the Lorenzkirche to the evangelical parish church of Artelshofen, thirty-three kilometres east of Nuremberg.

150 Max Friedländer and Jakob Rosenburg, *Die Gemälde von Lucas Cranach* (Berlin, 1932), cat. no. 18, 20. On the *Verbürgerlichung* of biblical figures see Hamburger Kunsthalle (Hofmann), ed., *Luther und die Folgen für die Kunst*, p. 248.

151 StaatsAN, Rep. 44e, Losungsamt, Akten, S. I. L.131, Nr. 14.

152 Zieger, *Das religiöse und kirchliche Leben*, p. 81.

Figure 24. Hans Traut, epitaph for Johannes Löffelholz, 1504 (Lorenzkirche, Nuremberg)

called upon', i.e. processions during which images and relics had been carried and invoked, were abolished.[153]

In the past all of these rites had served to mark the images out as particularly sacred, and to encourage idolatrous worship. They had articulated the images'

[153] On candles see Hirschmann, *Die Kirchenvisitation*, p. 258 (in 1560/1 the visitors to the parish church in Eltersdorf complained that local custodians were burning too many candles and lamps in the church on feast days). On processions see Pfeiffer, ed., *Quellen*, p. 444.

Figure 25. Wolf Traut, Holy Kindred altar from the Annenkapelle at St Lorenz, 1514 (Bayerisches Nationalmuseum, Munich)

cult status. The records of Nuremberg's 1560/1 church visitation confirm the significance accorded to visual presentation. In the village of Hüll near Betzenstein the commissioners uncovered evidence of an idolatrous cult based around two statues, one of St Martin and one of the Virgin. The local pastor complained that two men, Sebald Walther and Fritz Wintrer, had deliberately fostered this cult. They had, for example, on the past Whit Monday, crowned the statue of the Virgin, wrapped her head in old scarves and rags and placed garlands on her. She had been adorned 'like a lure, with which one attracts birds to catch'. By such means, i.e. by means of visual presentation, these 'idol-servants catch the simple people into idol sacrifice, idolatry and superstition'.[154] In another village, Rasch, a statue of the Virgin that had been worshipped by 'old wives from the countryside' was allowed to remain on condition that the veils that had covered its head were removed.[155] Much-venerated images of the Virgin often accumulated such veils and their presence provided a visual reminder of the image's miraculous status and therefore an incitement to idolatry.[156] In decreeing their forcible removal the visitors intended to demonstrate to the local population that the Madonna was no more than a block of stone or wood. With robes, jewels, rosaries, crowns, veils, garlands and candles gone, and with supplicatory processions abolished, the connection between image and traditional devotion was broken. The statues remained *in situ*, but as we shall see in the final section of this chapter, lay people gradually forgot their traditional meanings. They were still valued highly by local communities, but under the new preaching regime they represented not intercessory power but exemplary faith.

While much Marian iconography could, as we have seen, be legitimately incorporated into post-Reformation devotional life, it is clear that even in moderate Lutheran areas the wholesale preservation of ecclesiastical art was not a foregone conclusion. Sergiusz Michalski points, for example, to the extensive iconoclasm that occurred during the 1520s on the Baltic coast.[157] Carl Christensen's research suggests that even in Nuremberg iconoclasm was a serious threat during the early years of the Reformation. After initial incidents of stone throwing in 1523 adherents of the old faith certainly feared the escalation of iconoclastic violence. During the autumn of 1524 in particular, there were signs of more radical influences at work amongst Nuremberg's evangelicals: the writings of the painter Hans Greiffenberger; the dissemination of the ideas of Karlstadt and Müntzer; and the teachings of men such as Martin Reinhart and Hans Denck.

154 Hirschmann, *Die Kirchenvisitation*, p. 134.

155 StaatsAN, Reichsstadt Nürnberg, Kirchen und Ortschaften auf d. Lande, Nr. 454, fols. 32r, 47r.

156 On the practice of covering *Gnadenbilder* in veils see R. C. Trexler, 'Der Heiligen neue Kleider: eine analytische Skizze zur Be- und Entkleidung von Statuen', in *Gepeinigt, begehrt, vergessen: Symbolik und Sozialbezug des Körpers im späten Mittelalter und in der frühen Neuzeit*, ed. Klaus Schreiner and N. Schnitzler (Munich, 1992), p. 368.

157 Michalski, *The Reformation and the Visual Arts*, pp. 86ff.

The decisive intervention of Nuremberg's civic authorities – in particular their use of censorship and the expulsion of foreign preachers – prevented the escalation of such radical activity.[158] In 1526 Zwingli's writings were proscribed, alongside those of Karlstadt, Oecolampadius and their followers, and surveillance and disciplinary action served to discourage further iconoclasm.[159]

The council's determination to protect religious art cannot be explained solely in terms of theological conviction, since many of the images that were preserved depicted themes that had been explicitly condemned by Luther and by local reformers.[160] Luther, for example, criticized iconographies such as the *Schutzmantelmadonna* that showed Mary usurping Christ's mediating role, and Nuremberg's leading reformer, Andreas Osiander, was adamant in his prescription that only images showing biblical stories or true events from the lives of model Christians should be allowed to remain on display. He denounced what he described as 'fabricated legends', non-scriptural stories about the saints.[161] In his first years as preacher at the Lorenzkirche he advised the council to remove side altars and their retables, as well as images of the saints and of other subjects that were without biblical foundation.[162] He also, as we have seen, initially advocated the abolition of all feast days except the Annunciation. Yet in 1600 Nuremberg's churches still contained paintings and statues of the Virgin of Mercy, of Mary's Assumption and Coronation, of the Madonna of the Rosary and of other non-scriptural subjects, and various Marian festivals were still being celebrated. The city council's reluctance to follow the recommendations of its leading theologian indicates that its decisions with regard to Marian art and liturgy were influenced by something other than straightforward religious ideology.

In Nuremberg the fate of ecclesiastical art was shaped by the council's determination to preserve order and by the desire of influential citizens to protect objects donated to the church by themselves and by their families. Given that Nuremberg's Reformation was predominantly patrician-led it is scarcely surprising to find that iconoclasm, along with any other expression of revolutionary sentiment, was firmly suppressed. Most of the images that filled Nuremberg's churches on the eve of the Reformation had been donated by patricians who either sat on or had close connections to the city council, and it was the city council that was making the crucial decisions on religious imagery during the 1520s.[163] Veit Stoß's Angelic Salutation, for example, to which Andreas Osiander is said to have objected, had been donated to the Lorenzkirche by

158 Vogler, *Nürnberg 1524/25*, chapters 4 and 5. 159 Christensen, 'Iconoclasm'.

160 See, for example, Schuler, *Etliche Christliche Predigen*, pp. 53, 61.

161 For another example from the Kurland see Zieger, *Das religiöse und kirchliche Leben*, p. 82.

162 Gottfried Seebass, 'Mittelalterliche Kunstwerke in evangelisch gewordenen Kirchen Nürnbergs', in *Die bewahrende Kraft des Luthertums*, ed. Fritz, pp. 38, 40.

163 Key donors to the Lorenzkirche, for example, included members of the Imhoff, Tucher, Kreß and Loeffelholz families. Schleif, *Donatio et Memoria*.

Anton II Tucher in 1518. Tucher was the city's treasurer, a key figure in the years preceding the implementation of the Reformation, and the magnificent and prominently positioned rosary sculpture testified to his family's wealth and prestige.[164] As Corine Schleif has pointed out, in post-Reformation Nuremberg the notion that ecclesiastical furnishings served as monuments to the families who had donated them seems to have enjoyed particular currency.[165] Respect for private property was, of course, equally important elsewhere: even in Zurich, for example, those who had donated images were invited to reclaim them before the official cleansing of the city's churches began.[166] As a result, religious art went into patrician homes. There is a crucial difference, however, between merely preserving patrician property, as Zurich's council was determined to do, and actually keeping religious images on display in the ecclesiastical domain, as Nuremberg's council did. Nuremberg's determination to leave images *in situ* suggests that there was a broader dimension to its political circumspection.

An incident that took place in the city of Breslau in Silesia at the eastern edge of the Holy Roman Empire can, I think, help us understand why the secular authorities in places such as Nuremberg proceeded as cautiously as possible with regard to the removal of medieval art and abolition of traditional liturgy. Breslau's council, against the wishes of its archbishop, adopted the Lutheran Reformation in 1523. In 1526 Silesia, along with Hungary and Bohemia, became part of the Habsburg monarchy when King Louis II was killed fighting the Ottoman Turks at the Battle of Mohácsz. In 1527 Emperor Charles V, brother of Silesia's new Habsburg ruler Archduke Ferdinand of Austria, sent out an anxious inquiry regarding Breslau's religious affiliation. In its reply the city council assured the emperor that no religious change had occurred in Breslau, and pointed to the fact that the city's churches were still full of images as evidence of its supposed adherence to the old faith.[167]

Nuremberg may well have been engaged in a similar process of dissimulation. Economic interests, historic memories and fresh political experience combined to make the city loyal to its imperial overlord despite its religious transgression.

[164] Even in the nineteenth century this sculpture was regarded as family property. When the civic authorities needed money to restore it after it had fallen in 1826 it was to the Tuchers that they first turned. Wilhelm Schwemmer, 'Das Mäzenatentum der Nürnberger Patrizierfamilie Tucher vom 14.–18. Jahrhundert', *MVGSN* 51 (1962), 27. On Anton II's activity during the years preceding the official introduction of the Reformation see Ludwig Grote, *Die Tucher: Bildnis einer Patrizierfamilie* (Munich, 1961), pp. 78–84.

[165] Schleif, *Donatio et Memoria*, p. 236.

[166] Charles Garside, *Zwingli and the Arts* (New Haven, 1966), pp. 151, 156.

[167] S. Michalski, 'Die Ausbreitung des reformatorischen Bildersturms 1521–1537', in *Bildersturm: Wahnsinn oder Gottes Wille?*, ed. Dupeux, Jezler and Wirth, p. 50. On the survival of pre-Reformation Marian altarpieces in Lutheran Silesia see Knötel, *Kirchliche Bilderkunde Schlesiens*. On Habsburg attempts to intimidate Lutheran Breslau and to recatholicize the whole of Silesia see H. Schöffler, *Deutsches Geistesleben zwischen Reformation und Aufklärung*, 2nd edn (Frankfurt am Main, 1956), pp. 3–25.

Like other free cities, Nuremberg depended on imperial assistance for the maintenance of its long-distance trade routes and for the perpetuation of the commercial privileges that allowed it to prosper from these trade routes. It also, however, enjoyed an especially privileged status as the city in which each German emperor was, according to Charles IV's Golden Bull, to hold his first Diet, and from 1424 it was the repository of the imperial regalia. Under Charles V the Empire's agencies of central government – the governing council and chamber court – were both situated in Nuremberg, and the Imperial Diet met there in the winter of 1522/3 and again in 1524. In Strauss's words: 'Diet and emperor made of Nuremberg something like the capital of the Empire.' [168] Nuremberg's *Kaisertreue* [loyalty to the emperor] has been widely acknowledged. Heinrich Schmidt, for example, writes of the city's 'political quietism', and points out that respect for the emperor played an important role in shaping Nuremberg's political decisions during the 1520s and beyond. Nuremberg was reluctant to join an evangelical alliance because of its concern about trade relations with Catholic neighbours, because of its desire to distance itself from the 'Sakramentsschwärmerei' (in this case 'Zwinglian' cities such as Strasbourg and Ulm), because of its hope that the emperor would eventually tolerate Lutherans and because of its 'basic world view in which loyalty to the emperor became a theological precept'. Nuremberg's loyalty to its 'natural' or 'legitimate' master, the emperor, was frequently professed in council correspondence, and the city's ultimate refusal to join the Schmalkaldic League was determined largely by this sense of obedience.[169] This refusal ultimately cost the city its position in the forefront of the Reformation movement.[170] It may have spared it from the most traumatic events of the Schmalkaldic War (1546–7), yet it did not enable it to entirely escape Charles's wrath. The emperor was not happy when he learned of the spread of evangelical teaching there: he threatened to withdraw the city's privileges and there was even the possibility that he would use military force against it.[171] Given this situation, it is scarcely surprising that the city council proceeded as cautiously as possible with regard to reform, and it seems likely that in Nuremberg, as in Breslau, the preservation of pre-Reformation images was intended to demonstrate religious moderation.

[168] Strauss, *Nuremberg*, p. 163. On Lutheran church interiors and dissimulation see Koerner, *The Reformation of the Image*, p. 68. On Nuremberg's relationship with its emperor see Baron, 'Religion and politics', 405–27 and 614–33; E. Franz, *Nürnberg, Kaiser und Reich. Studien zur reichsstädtischen Außenpolitik* (Munich, 1930); Bräutigam, 'Nürnberg'; Heinrich Richard Schmidt, *Reichsstädte, Reich und Reformation: korporative Religionspolitik 1521–1529/30*, Veröffentlichungen des Instituts für Europäische Geschichte Mainz 122 (Stuttgart, 1986).

[169] Schmidt, *Reichsstädte, Reich und Reformation*, pp. 53, 173, 237, 317–20.

[170] On Nuremberg's ongoing concern about its relationship with the emperor and on the impact that this had on its religious stance see Gerhard Pfeiffer, 'Nürnberg und das Augsburger Bekenntnis 1530–1561', *Zeitschrift für bayerische Kirchengeschichte* 49 (1980), 2–19. Pfeiffer points out that other evangelical territories regarded Nuremberg's church politics as 'dubious' (11).

[171] Dixon, *The Reformation in Germany*, pp. 106ff.

It is difficult to prove that Nuremberg's political conservatism helped determine its attitude towards Marian imagery and devotion yet this may be surmised from the fact that the council – the city's *political* body – pushed local preachers and provosts – its *religious* advisors – to agree to the preservation of more paintings, sculptures and feast days than they would, of their own volition, have countenanced. The fact that the furnishings of cloister churches and chapels suffered a different fate to the furnishings of churches in which Lutheran services were held also supports the hypothesis that the council's decision to preserve pre-Reformation imagery in the latter was, to an extent at least, determined by its preoccupation with public display and imperial identity. Most cloister churches and private chapels were given into the council's keeping soon after the religious colloquy of March 1525. Between 1526 and 1528 many of these now disused ecclesiastical buildings were closed. There was very little plundering and the council kept the churches under its supervision. In the right circumstances, however, it was ready to permit the dispersal of imagery. Of the eight altars that originally stood in the Augustinerkirche only three survive, two because they were sold during the second half of the sixteenth century. Of the fourteen altars belonging to the Carmelite cloister hardly anything remains, apart from Veit Stoß's Marian altar, which was returned to the sculptor's heirs in 1543 and then sold to the bishop of Bamberg.[172] The contrast between the arbitrary fate of these images and the careful preservation of the altarpieces, paintings and sculptures that filled the parish churches and the Frauenkirche is immediately apparent. The images in the disused cloister churches could be disposed of because they were no longer contributing to a public display of moderation.

The same concern to present a façade of continuity helped determine the preservation of Marian liturgy. As we have seen, Nuremberg's preachers and provosts were pushed to concede the retention of more pre-Reformation festivals than they had initially wished. Furthermore the liturgy of the Sebalduskirche and Lorenzkirche, the city's two parish churches, retained more of its pre-Reformation elements than the liturgy of the Spitalkirche.[173] An entry in the account book of the Frauenkirche for the year 1536 mentions a payment 'to the cantor who sings the *Salve*', despite the assertion of the anonymous author of a 1527 list of transformed ceremonies that this antiphon had been 'entirely set aside' in Nuremberg.[174] This account entry does not necessarily demonstrate that the antiphon itself was still being performed: by the eighteenth century

[172] Seebass, 'Mittelalterliche Kunstwerke', pp. 42–8.

[173] I am grateful to Dr Volker Schier for bringing this to my attention. As the emperor passed through Nuremberg en route to Regensburg in 1541, the council planned to welcome him with a solemn *Te Deum* in St Sebald. Pfeiffer, 'Nürnberg und das Augsburger Bekenntnis 1530–1561', 12–3.

[174] Staatsarchiv Nürnberg, Rep. 44e Losungsamt, Akten, S. I. L. 113, Nr. 11.

the term *Salve* had come to refer to the service of evening prayer held at the Frauenkirche an hour before sunset, and no longer indicated an invocation of Mary.[175] Whether the *Salve* survived in its original form or merely in name in 1536, it seems possible that the Frauenkirche was protected especially carefully because of its imperial connection: it had been founded by Charles IV, and still bore many reminders of its illustrious past, including the imperial eagle on its west façade and from 1509 an automated clock that commemorated the 1356 Golden Bull. Even in the eighteenth century it was referred to by local chroniclers as the *Kaiserkapelle*.[176] Here and elsewhere in Nuremberg, it seems likely that the preservation of Marian images and liturgy exceeded the bounds of legitimate Lutheran tolerance partly because of a desire to avoid alienating the Catholic emperor.

One final explanation for the preservation of medieval images deserves mention. In his study of the psychological significance of images from late antiquity to the Renaissance, Hans Belting argues that the sixteenth century marked the beginning of what he terms the 'era of art'. During this period the old notion of the image as a revelation of the divine was replaced by an obsession with the image as aesthetic object: 'the new presence *of* the work succeeds the former presence of the sacred *in* the work'. Because of the converging effects of Reformation criticism of images and Renaissance emphasis on collecting 'the cult of the work of art . . . replaces the cult of the holy image'. Belting carefully avoids suggesting that the evangelical reformers were themselves responsible for this change of consciousness. Rather they were, in this respect, 'the children of their time'. Criticism of religious imagery moved in sync with the emergence of purely aesthetic evaluation: 'as images fell from favour, they began to be justified as art'.[177]

Belting has been rightly criticized for his teleology. Olivier Christin points out, for example, that 'the victory of aesthetic judgment . . . does not emerge except in terms of a long and complex struggle, which is far from over at the start of the seventeenth century'.[178] It is impossible to designate the Reformation, or any other historical event, as the decisive turning point, the moment at which the image was desacralized and secularized. On the one hand, religious commissions and pious gifts had never been incompatible with the quest

175 Zeltner, *Kurtze Erläuterung*, p. 17.

176 Christoph Gottlieb von Murr, *Beschreibung der vornehmsten Merkwürdigkeiten in des H. R. Reichs freyen Stadt Nürnberg und auf der hohen Schule zu Altdorf* (Nuremberg, 1778), p. 136.

177 Hans Belting, *Likeness and Presence: a history of the image before the era of art*, trans. Edmund Jephcott (Chicago and London, 1994), pp. 16, 459, 470, 490.

178 Olivier Christin, 'Christian worship to art worship: notes on the transformation of the status of the image (15th–18th centuries)' (transcript of paper presented at the Deutsch-Britisch-Französischer Göttinger Sommerkurs at the Max-Planck-Institut für Geschichte, 16 September 1999), p. 7.

for artistic quality and aesthetic pleasure, as numerous late medieval examples demonstrate. On the other hand, even during what Belting describes as the 'era of art' the religious use of images survived alongside the practices of collecting. Yet Luther, at least, seems to have hoped for the kind of transition Belting claims to have observed: 'If the common man knows that it is no service to God to put up images he will abandon the practice without your force, and have them painted on the wall or use them in other ways only for pleasure or decoration, which is no sin.'[179]

Belting's thesis goes some way towards accounting for the survival of pre-Reformation imagery in sixteenth-century Nuremberg. As Joseph Koerner has argued, in some Lutheran areas 'church pictures escaped the charge of superstition by being categorized as art'.[180] Seebass has demonstrated that awareness of the aesthetic merits of Nuremberg's pre-Reformation imagery played a role in determining the city council's decisions on religious art during the second half of the sixteenth century. During this period the council sold or gave as gifts several of the finest retables from the disused cloister churches and chapels in its possession.[181] Aesthetic awareness may, indeed, have had an impact earlier than Seebass suggested. In 1538 an English Catholic, Thomas Goldwell, wrote to his father describing his travels through southern Germany. On his way from Ingolstadt to Innsbruck Goldwell passed through three towns, Windsheim, Markt Erlbach and Nuremberg, 'wherein were few other than heretics'. Goldwell reported to his father that: 'in all these towns are goodly churches full of images, which they regard as ornaments of the church and memorials that such holy men have been before us'.[182] His comment suggests that in Nuremberg and, to a certain extent at least, elsewhere in southern Germany, a decade after the Reformation ecclesiastical imagery had come to assume an aesthetic and commemorative function. It beautified local churches and served to remind viewers either of the piety of its donors or of the virtues of the saints it depicted (it is unclear from Goldwell's phrasing – 'memorials that such holy men have been before us' – whether he intends to refer to the images' patrons or to the figures represented).

Christin qualifies Belting's thesis by pointing out that during the sixteenth century aesthetic discourse was imposed only locally and in certain circles.[183] Given this qualification it seems important to emphasize that Nuremberg's patriciate was uniquely well positioned to become one such circle. Nuremberg was

179 *WA*, vol. 10, part II, p. 34 (*Von beiderlei Gestalt*).
180 Koerner, *The Reformation of the Image*, p. 61.
181 Seebass, 'Mittelalterliche Kunstwerke', pp. 46–7.
182 James Gardner, ed., *Letters and Papers, Foreign and Domestic, of the Reign of Henry VIII*, vol. 13, part I (London, 1892), no. 935, 5 May 1538. I am very grateful to Dr Peter Marshall for bringing this letter to my attention.
183 Christin, 'Christian worship to art worship', p. 19.

the crossroads at which Belting's 'Reformation criticism of images' and his 'Renaissance emphasis on collecting' converged. It is perhaps hardly surprising that the city that produced Albrecht Dürer, and that basked in his reflected glory, was precocious with regard to the emergence of a predominantly aesthetic mode of viewing.[184] Nuremberg was home to several of the leading humanists of the period, in particular Conrad Celtis (1459–1508) and Willibald Pirckheimer (1470–1530), who aspired to turn Germany into Europe's principal cultural centre through their own literary endeavours and through their patronage of art and letters. There is no doubt that these men were preoccupied by the artistic merit of the paintings and sculptures that surrounded them, from Pirckheimer, whose 1531 household inventory listed five paintings 'for the adornment' of his *Saal*, to his grandson Willibald Imhoff, who built up Nuremberg's first true private art collection. The treatment afforded to Veit Stoß's Angelic Salutation perhaps provides the best proof of local patrician pride in Nuremberg's artistic heritage. Kept permanently covered after 1529, the sculpture nonetheless remained in place and was well maintained: it was cleaned in 1590 and regilded in 1612. In 1614 a poem was written in its honour and it was lowered and removed from its covering several times during the seventeenth century for the benefit of visiting Catholic dignitaries.[185] Nuremberg's religious images remained in place into the seventeenth century partly because local citizens were proud of their artistic heritage.

POPULAR BELIEF

In order to account for the extensive survival of Marian imagery and liturgy in Nuremberg and in other Lutheran territories it is necessary, as we have seen, to consider the ways in which theological precept interacted with local political and cultural circumstance. But what were the implications of this survival for popular belief and religious experience? The reformers hoped to change the common perception of Mary, turning her from a divine intercessor into a humble *Hausmutter*. In attempting to convince people to attach new meanings to old images and festivals they were, however, playing a dangerous game: they were privileging the art of intellectual persuasion over custom with all its tenacity. As Robert Kolb has pointed out, into the seventeenth century any treatment of saints, whether verbal or visual, carried with it the danger of arousing old associations. Particularly in a city like Nuremberg, where there were so many manifest reminders of pre-Reformation cults, could those old associations possibly have been eliminated? Could the reformers really retain

[184] On Dürer's cult see Paul Münch, 'Changing German perceptions of the historical role of Albrecht Dürer', in *Dürer and his Culture*, ed. Dagmar Eichberger and Charles Zika (Cambridge, 1998).

[185] Germanisches Nationalmuseum, ed., *Veit Stoß in Nürnberg*, p. 203.

Mary as a model, and yet break the habit of generations and stop people from praying to her?[186] Ever since the 1970s, when Gerald Strauss argued that in general the reformers' aims were realized to only a limited degree, there has been general pessimism about their level of success in transforming traditional beliefs and practices. Only in large urban centres such as Strasbourg, it seems, did their pedagogical efforts bear any real fruit.[187]

Evidence from Nuremberg confirms, to an extent at least, the importance of this perceived urban–rural distinction. Within the city of Nuremberg itself evangelical reformers do indeed seem to have successfully transformed popular belief with regard to Marian devotion. A hymn from the *Enchiridion*, a collection of hymns and psalms published in Nuremberg in 1527, suggests that in the early stages of the Reformation it was still necessary to broadcast an anti-idolatry message: the author complains that Christians had made 'golden idols' in defiance of biblical prohibitions and had put their trust in them rather than in God.[188] We know of only one occasion, however, on which the authorities found it necessary to compel adherence to those prohibitions: in 1529 the city council was forced to remove one statue of the Virgin from the Frauenkirche because of idolatry.[189] After the initial stages of the Reformation the subject was, it seems, rarely mentioned.[190] During and after the 1543 Imperial Diet, which was held in Nuremberg, Veit Dietrich, preacher at the parish church of St Sebald, felt obliged to report some abuses to the city council, but idolatry did not feature amongst them. In a sermon preached later the same year during a severe outbreak of plague Dietrich did remind his congregation of the dangers of turning to the saints, but he located this abuse firmly in the past: 'We all know what idolatry there *was* in the time of the papacy.'[191] Evidence from artisan household inventories also suggests that Mariolatry was essentially dead by the mid sixteenth century. Although about half of the householders whose possessions were inventoried in 1530 still owned rosaries, a sample of seventy inventories for the period 1550–60 revealed only one solitary set of prayer beads.[192] Local patricians may have kept Marian paintings in their private collections but by the mid century the majority of Nuremberg's citizens had abandoned their 'papist playthings'.

[186] Kolb, *For All the Saints*, p. 18.

[187] Gerald Strauss, *Luther's House of Learning* (Baltimore, 1978); James Kittelson, 'Successes and failures in the German Reformation', *Archiv für Reformationsgeschichte* 73 (1982); Strauss, 'Success and failure'.

[188] Wackernagel, *Das deutsche Kirchenlied*, vol. 3, no. 601.

[189] Hampe, ed., *Nürnberger Ratsverlässe*, vol. 1, no. 1729.

[190] Robert Kolb's study of sermons preached on saints' feast days suggests that at least by the second half of the sixteenth century the veneration of the saints was causing relatively little concern amongst Lutheran theologians. Kolb, 'Festivals of the saints'.

[191] My italics. Klaus, *Veit Dietrich*, pp. 221–2.

[192] StadtAN, Rep. B14/III, Inventarbücher, Nr. 8 and Nr. 12 (fol. 87r).

It comes as no surprise to find that the pace of religious change was significantly slower in the countryside, where the progress of Lutheran indoctrination varied according to the degree of central supervision and the ability of local pastors.[193] Around Nuremberg the reformers' difficulties were compounded by the disruption of the Second Margrave's War (1552–5), which destroyed some of the good practices that had been introduced over the preceding three decades and slowed the further extension of the Reformation.[194] In 1560–1 Nuremberg's city council sent out a commission, led by two theologians, to visit the parishes of its rural territory. The commissioners in charge of this visitation toured fifty-seven parishes and examined local pastors and members of their congregations for knowledge of the catechism, frequency of attendance at communion and morality of lifestyle in general.[195] Their records contain the usual litany of complaints: ignorance and the persistence of superstitious and improper beliefs and practices, from apotropaic magic to blasphemy and failure to attend communion. They also uncovered a number of individual cases of the misuse of Marian formulae and of image worship. Stefan Rummer's wife, from the village of Rasch near Altdorf, was accused, for example, of having repeatedly participated in a pilgrimage to the parish church in Trautmannshofen in the Upper Palatinate that took place annually on the feast day of Mary's birth. She was said to have offered veils to the image of the Virgin that formed the focal point of this pilgrimage and, according to the commissioners, she believed that she had successfully brought up a daughter through doing this. Although the woman denied having offered veils, she admitted that she had twice pledged her seven-year-old daughter before the miraculous image.[196]

The commissioners also found evidence of four image cults within Nuremberg's own territory. The statues of the Virgin and St Martin that stood in the church at Hüll near Betzenstein were, according to the local pastor, the subjects of 'very horrifying, terrible, idolatrous abuses' involving pilgrimage, processions and offerings of money, votive candles and human hair. A local resident, the wife of Fritz Linberger, had, for example, made an offering to the Madonna at Hüll: 'she took a wax [candle], as thick as she is, and offered it to Our Lady in the name of the Father, Jesus and the Holy Ghost, so that our God would confer grace on her birth'. In the village of Rasch rural women burnt candles and genuflected before an image of the Virgin located behind the church, before

193 Roth estimates that in Upper and Middle Franconia, i.e. the area covering Rothenburg, Brandenburg-Ansbach, Eichstätt, Nuremberg, Bamberg and Brandenburg-Kulmbach, there were eighteen evangelical churches that continued to attract pilgrims in the post-Reformation period, eleven of which had Marian images. Elisabeth Roth, 'Wallfahrten zu evangelischen Landkirchen in Franken', *Jahrbuch für Volkskunde*, n. s. 2 (1979), 152.

194 Hirschmann, *Die Kirchenvisitation*, p. 19.

195 Gerhard Hirschmann, 'The second Nürnberg church visitation', in *The Social History of the Reformation*, ed. L. P. Buck and J. W. Zophy (Columbus, OH, 1972), p. 375.

196 Hirschmann, *Die Kirchenvisitation*, pp. 183, 190–1.

going into the church to sing psalms. In Tennelohe a richly clothed image of the Virgin formed the focus of parishioners' idolatry. And in the neighbouring village of Eltersdorf, where the parish folk were apparently still obsessed with idolatry, another Madonna, decorated with (amongst other things) a veil, occupied a privileged place on the church's altar.[197]

The pilgrimage to Hüll proved to be a persistent problem. Its custodian had already, in 1535, been told by the council to keep the church closed during the week, to reject offerings from pilgrims and to stop celebrating mass, but local pastors failed to prevent Catholics from surrounding areas from visiting the cult images.[198] In 1560/1 the commissioners decreed that the image of the Virgin should be removed and replaced with a crucifix.[199] This decree was apparently not put into effect. Right up to the beginning of the twentieth century, when the Madonna was forcibly transferred to the church of St Aposteln in Viernheim (*Landkreis* Heppenheim/Bergstraße) against the wishes of Hüll's residents, it continued to form a focal point for pilgrimage and prayer. The cult was maintained in part by visiting Catholics, yet there can be little doubt that the grace-giving image also continued to command the devotion of local Lutherans. Indeed even in 1978 the evangelical pastor at Hüll travelled with his congregation to Viernheim to visit their beloved statue in its new home![200] In Rasch the Madonna itself was allowed to remain in place but the commissioners in charge of the visitation decreed that the veils that had adorned it were to be removed early in the morning, while the congregation was absent.[201] It is unclear whether this action was sufficient to break the Lutheran congregation's idolatrous habits: parish records reveal that until the 1820s the evangelical church retained a Marian image that was visited by Catholics from the neighbouring Upper Palatinate.[202] In Tennelohe the commissioners apparently took possession of the Marian image whilst in Eltersdorf they oversaw its removal from altar to sacristy, i.e. from a prominent and privileged position to a place accessible only to church officials.[203] It seems that in both of these communities the image cults were successfully eradicated.

What are we to make of these cases? It is inevitably problematic to base conclusions solely upon records of prosecutions. The cases that were prosecuted were the cases that reached the attention of the authorities. There may have been other cults that went unnoticed. Bearing in mind this proviso, four

197 On these four cults see ibid., pp. 131–2, 141 (Hüll), p. 182 (Rasch) and pp. 245, 256, 258–9 (Tennenlohe and Eltersdorf). On the Hüll cult see also Elisabeth Roth, *Volkskultur in Franken*, vol. 1: *Kult und Kunst* (Bamberg and Würzburg, 1990), p. 257. On the Rasch cult see also H. Dannenbauer, 'Die Nürnberger Landgeistlichen bis zur zweiten Nürnberger Kirchenvisitation', *Zeitschrift für bayerische Kirchengeschichte* 4 (1927), 236–7.

198 Roth, 'Wallfahrten', 142.

199 Hirschmann, *Die Kirchenvisitation*, p. 144.

200 Roth, *Volkskultur in Franken*, pp. 256–7.

201 Hirschmann, *Die Kirchenvisitation*, p. 197.

202 Roth, *Volkskultur in Franken*, pp. 257–8.

203 Hirschmann, *Die Kirchenvisitation*, pp. 256, 258–9.

localized cults and a few individual idolaters constitute a relatively small total in a rural hinterland the size of Nuremberg's. Various extenuating circumstances may also be invoked to account for the persistence of these particular cults. Hüll and Tennelohe were filial churches – churches without their own pastors to hold weekly services and direct the sustained efforts necessary to eradicate deeply held beliefs. Hüll and Rasch were also on the very edge of Nuremberg's territory, Hüll next to the Catholic bishopric of Bamberg and Rasch next to the only relatively recently Protestantized Upper Palatinate. As Elisabeth Roth points out, the extent to which a cult site continued to attract devotees after the Reformation depended to a great extent on the confessional structure of the surrounding area.[204] The testimony of local residents concerning the cult at Hüll certainly indicates that it was maintained in part at least through contact with neighbouring communities. One parishioner reported to the visitors that the local pastor no longer wished to hold services in Hüll because 'the bishop's [people] and other people make pilgrimages there and . . . do idolatry'.[205] Nineteenth-century evidence from Hüll and Rasch confirms that both cults survived partly because of the peregrinations of nearby Catholics.[206]

Within the evangelical community various groups seem to have been particularly susceptible to the charge of idolatry. Firstly, and most conspicuously, women: almost all of the individuals accused were female and several of the cults were, according to the men conducting the visitation, maintained only by women. In Tennelohe and Eltersdorf it was women who visited the 'idolatrous statues' and 'held them in higher esteem than God' and in Rasch it was 'old wives from the countryside' who made offerings before the Madonna behind the church before attending the evangelical services.[207] The notion that superstition was a female prerogative was deeply ingrained in the reformers' minds, and its significance will be explored further in chapter 6. Alongside women the elderly were singled out. Elisabeth Roth argues that 'the main caesura for the gradual stopping of pilgrimage to evangelical churches is the second half of the sixteenth century, when the generation died out for whom this practice had since childhood been a matter of course'.[208] This is confirmed by the commissioners' report on Tennelohe, where it was especially the elderly parishioners who persisted in their idolatry.[209] Finally, accusations were levelled at the ignorant, the 'simple people' as the pastor at Hüll described those who had been seduced into idolatry there. In Eltersdorf too, the authorities believed that ignorance was the root of the problem: 'in this parish . . . the parishioners did not

[204] Roth, 'Wallfahrten', 136. [205] Hirschmann, *Die Kirchenvisitation*, p. 139.
[206] Roth, *Volkskultur in Franken*, pp. 256–8.
[207] Hirschmann, *Die Kirchenvisitation*, pp. 245, 182.
[208] Roth, *Volkskultur in Franken*, p. 269. [209] Hirschmann, *Die Kirchenvisitation*, p. 256.

do well in the general questioning; moreover they still do all kinds of idolatry and are obsessed with this'.[210]

Whether or not the nature of Marian devotion was successfully transformed within a particular community appears to have depended upon the extent of educational provision and upon geographical location. This was not simply a case of urban success and rural failure. The formation of clear confessional identities, with all its attendant changes in belief and practice, may have happened most easily in the cities.[211] But even in Nuremberg's rural hinterland, in areas that were under the supervision of a competent Lutheran pastor and that were effectively isolated from the subversive influence of Catholicism, the 'superstitious' practices that had characterized popular devotion to the Virgin in the late medieval period did die out. Reform was not immediate: it did not take full effect until the demise of the generation that had been brought up in the traditions of the pre-Reformation church. Moreover, the gradual cessation of practices labelled as superstitious cannot be taken as conclusive evidence of a transformation in belief. The fact that people stopped going on pilgrimage and making offerings to Marian images does not necessarily mean that they no longer had recourse to the Virgin in their prayers. Given, however, that for the vast majority of the population behaviour is the only indication that we have of belief, we must at least allow for the possibility that changes in religious practice genuinely reflected a revised understanding of the role of the saints.

Although scholars have acknowledged that Mary retained considerable theological significance for many Protestant reformers, her importance in the visual and liturgical culture of the Lutheran Church has been largely overlooked. Because of the survival of traditional images, feast days and liturgy she remained prominent in Nuremberg and in many other parts of Lutheran Germany, as this chapter has shown. The survival of Marian images and festivals might suit the political and cultural concerns of local secular authorities: in the delicate world of sixteenth-century German politics, behaviour with regard to images of the saints and liturgy was one of the criteria by which religious identity was judged, and in Nuremberg the city council used this criterion to its own advantage, in order to demonstrate its moderation for the benefit of outside observers. There was also undoubtedly a general reluctance to remove images that testified to the wealth and status of local patricians and to the talent of local artists. These secular objectives were not necessarily, however, at odds with those of the religious reformers. Lutheran theologians preferred, where possible, to rework old, established symbols rather than abolish them. Mary was therefore stripped of

210 Ibid., pp. 134, 305–6.

211 Thomas A. Brady, 'Settlements: the Holy Roman Empire', in *Handbook of European History, 1400–1600: late Middle Ages, Renaissance, and Reformation*, ed. Thomas A. Brady, Heiko A. Oberman and James D. Tracy (Leiden and New York, 1994–5), p. 361.

her salvific power, but was instead exalted as a model of right belief and conduct. The reformers' optimism about their ability to transform the meaning of such a powerful symbol was not always entirely justified: in Nuremberg, as elsewhere, visitation records reveal the persistence of some idolatrous practices. But in the city itself and in much of its territory Luther's conviction that the cult of saints would die out under the new evangelical regime appears to have been largely vindicated. Nuremberg apparently assimilated numerous potentially controversial remnants of Catholic culture with relative ease. Elsewhere, as we shall see in the next chapter, this was not to be the case: other Protestants were much less comfortable with the Marian legacy left to them by the pre-Reformation church.

3. *Confessional frictions and the status of the Virgin*

While in Nuremberg and in other parts of Lutheran Germany Mary remained prominent in the visual and devotional culture of the post-Reformation church, elsewhere her images and feast days were largely eliminated. In Augsburg, for example, as we shall see in this chapter, most manifestations of Mary's cult disappeared during the early stages of the Reformation, and until well into the seventeenth century she was spurned by local Protestants. A similar pattern emerged in other south German cities such as Strasbourg and Ulm, as well as in the Swiss cities of Zurich, Berne and Basle.[1] It comes as no surprise to find that there was diversity in Protestant devotional practice, given that right from the start the evangelical movement lacked unity. The reformers shared common ground in their emphasis on justification by faith, in their reliance on Scripture and in their rejection of Rome's authority, but beyond this there was little consensus. The irreconcilable split arose, of course, over the definition of the sacraments, especially the Eucharist, but other issues also caused controversy. For this study, the differences between Lutheran and Reformed attitudes towards the saints and their images, which are symptomatic of more profound disagreements over the pace of religious reform and over the role of externals in religious devotion, are of particular significance. As this chapter will demonstrate, however, attitudes towards the Virgin Mary owed as much to local political and ecclesiastical circumstances as to doctrinal norms. Devotional practice was influenced by external factors, producing ecologies of understanding that varied according to place and not just according to confession. In Augsburg, for example, Mary disappeared not only from the city's Zwinglian but also from its Lutheran milieu. In this biconfessional city after 1548 the Catholic appropriation of Mary (see chapter 4) left little space for Nuremberg's type of revalued Lutheran Virgin. As we shall see in the final section of this

[1] Wandel, *Voracious Idols*; H. R. Guggisberg, *Basle in the Sixteenth Century* (St Louis, MO, 1982); Franz-Josef Sladeczek, 'Bern 1528 – Zwischen Zerstörung und Erhaltung', in *Bildersturm*, ed. Dupeux, Jezler and Wirth; Martin Nestler, *Ulm. Geschichte einer Stadt* (Erfurt, 2003).

chapter, patterns of Marian piety indicate that during the age of confessionalism Lutheran worship could be shaped by its exposure to the more militant creeds of Counter-Reformation Catholicism and Calvinist Protestantism.

MARY IN A BICONFESSIONAL CITY

Slower than Nuremberg to decide in favour of the Reformation, Augsburg nonetheless came to surpass the Franconian city in the radical nature of its religious and political affiliations. Augsburg's initial Reformation owed more to the theology of the Swiss reformers than to Wittenberg (see below). In keeping with its more venturous religious stance, Augsburg joined the Schmalkaldic League, but when this Protestant military alliance was defeated by Charles V in 1547 the city's devotional and political life underwent an abrupt transformation. The Catholic cult was renewed, and all churches confiscated by the Protestants in 1534 and in 1537 were returned to Catholic use. Augsburg's constitution was emasculated: the guilds were abolished, and henceforth the city's elite Catholic minority enjoyed disproportionate political representation. The 1548 settlement provided the basis for a kind of co-existence of Catholicism and Protestantism within the city, and the Religious Peace of Augsburg confirmed a form of legal parity between the two confessions throughout the Reich in 1555. The terms of this peace finally compelled Augsburg's evangelicals to abandon Zwinglianism and to adhere to the Lutheran Reformation, though in practice the influence of reformed Protestantism extended well beyond 1555. During the second half of the sixteenth century the renewal of Catholicism, heralded by the arrival of the Jesuits, led to the gradual hardening of confessional boundaries, a process that reached its apogee during the traumatic era of the Thirty Years War.

Augsburg's leading Protestant reformers had initially sought a theological 'middle way' that would permit reconciliation with Lutheran Saxony, but their attitudes towards imagery and liturgy ultimately marked them out as reformed. Their determination to eliminate idolatry was reflected in the council's decisions concerning ecclesiastical art and traditional feast days. In a decree of 17 January 1537 the council stated that the papist mass and ceremonies should be abolished and that all 'misused carved, cast and painted images' should be removed 'because all hopeless, godless superstition, against the honour and command of God, has flowed and sprung from the praying-to and venerating of idols and images'. There was still an element of circumspection: all images were to be removed, unbroken, in an orderly fashion, and were to be carefully preserved until the summoning of a council or national assembly.[2] As in Nuremberg, the political elite was afraid of the reaction that extensive iconoclasm would provoke from the city's imperial overlord. In his account of the iconoclasm that

[2] Quoted in Roth, *Augsburgs Reformationsgeschichte*, vol. 2, p. 360.

had taken place in the Barfüßerkirche in 1529 the Augsburg chronicler Jörg Breu wrote, for example, that when the idols were removed 'it was feared that the Emperor might come and conquer the city because of the great evil, that the pious saints had been killed [erschlagen] and destroyed'.[3] Such fears did not, however, prove a sufficient deterrent: a Zwinglian-inspired desire for an entirely new start, for the obliteration of all 'papist horrors', prevailed.[4]

On 18 January representatives of the council arrived to cleanse the cathedral of its images. The civic official charged with carrying out the council's commission, Alexander Bestler, a friend of the Zwinglian preacher Michael Keller,[5] spent two days in the cathedral working behind locked doors and with the protection of an armed guard.[6] Breu reported that 'on that afternoon the *Vogt* together with others from the council, as well as carpenters, builders [and] smiths, who were necessary to this work, came into the church of Our Lady and closed the church doors and then smashed and destroyed altars, sculptures, paintings and everything that had served the idols and idolatry'.[7] There can be little doubt that Bestler went to his work 'mit Lust und Liebe',[8] although in keeping with the council's original instructions some images were in fact hidden in the crypt rather than destroyed. A cathedral canon, Eberhard von Hürnheim, reported to Duke Ludwig of Bavaria: 'on Thursday after lunch they closed our church and destroyed the panels and pictures' and 'laid all of the same in the crypt and made them inaccessible with planks. Then afterwards they took away from us what else belonged to us in the way of vestments, books, chalices and so on and had it shut away.'[9] Having completed their work in the cathedral, Bestler's team moved on and 'cleansed' the churches of SS Ulrich and Afra, Heilig Kreuz, St Moritz and St Georg.[10] In March 1537, in a final attempt to exclude images from the devotional life of Augsburg's citizens, the council instructed the guards at the city gates to ensure that no one left the town to hear mass, to honour images or to seek out other such ceremonies and abuses.[11]

[3] *Chroniken*, vol. 29, p. 44. On the council's concerns about the implications of religious reform for its relationship with the emperor see Broadhead, 'Politics and expediency'.

[4] Jörg Rasmussen, 'Bildersturm und Restauration', in *Welt im Umbruch: Augsburg zwischen Renaissance und Barock*, ed. Städtische Kunstsammlung Augsburg and Zentralinstitut für Kunstgeschichte Munich (Augsburg, 1981), vol. 1, p. 96.

[5] Roth, *Augsburgs Reformationsgeschichte*, vol. 2, p. 319.

[6] Whilst it was not unusual for such measures to be undertaken in relative secrecy, it seems that in Augsburg the authorities were concerned with preventing the escalation of iconoclastic violence rather with deterring the intervention of iconophiles. Rasmussen, 'Bildersturm und Restauration', p. 99.

[7] *Chroniken*, vol. 29, p. 76. [8] Roth, *Augsburgs Reformationsgeschichte*, vol. 2, p. 319.

[9] *Chroniken*, vol. 29, p. 76 n.3. Some of the pictures and panels shut away in 1537 were restored in 1548 when the cathedral was returned to Catholic use.

[10] Bushart, 'Kunst und Stadtbild', p. 370.

[11] StadtAA, Reichsstadt, Geh. Ratsbücher, Nr. 3, fol. 231r.

As a result of the officially sponsored iconoclasm that took place in 1537 much less Marian imagery survived in Augsburg than in Nuremberg. It is very difficult to reconstruct exactly what was destroyed during the 'cleansing' of the city's churches, but evidence relating to the cathedral, the best-documented building, suggests that images of the Virgin were neither more nor less vulnerable than other iconographies.[12] Subject matter sometimes influenced the iconoclasts' decisions: crucifixes fared particularly badly, probably because of the Zwinglian conviction that viewers identified them with Christ, eliding image and prototype, and that it was, in any case, disrespectful to depict God in base wood.[13] In other churches crucifixes had already been attacked by iconoclasts working without state sponsorship: in 1529, at the instigation of the preacher Michael Keller, a crucifix was dismantled in the Barfüßerkirche and in 1531 a crucifix was amongst the images destroyed at Heilig Kreuz.[14] In general, however, images of saints were not singled out unless they had been associated with particular pre-Reformation devotions, for example the fourteen-metre high wall painting of St Christopher in the cathedral that Martin Bucer preached against in 1537.[15] Location seems usually to have been more important than subject matter: the most spectacular incident of Marian iconoclasm – the destruction of Hans Holbein's painting of the Virgin and Child that had adorned the altar in the cathedral's east choir (see chapter 4) – was probably as much a result of the prominent position of this particular image as of its potentially idolatrous subject matter.[16] Sculptures and paintings inside ecclesiastical buildings, especially those placed on altars, were much more likely to be targeted than images that adorned façades.[17] The sculpture on the cathedral's south portal, for example, survived undisturbed even though it depicted numerous apocryphal scenes from the life of the Virgin. Medium also seems to have been a decisive factor in determining the fate of individual images. As Jörg Rasmussen points out, very few carved images were allowed to remain, whereas some panel paintings and almost all of the city's stained glass (including various Marian panels) survived. There was apparently a perceived hierarchy of danger: the more lifelike the image, the more likely it was to provoke idolatrous worship.

Yet even if, as this evidence suggests, images of the Virgin were not specifically targeted by local iconoclasts very few remained on display in Augsburg's

[12] Heal, 'A woman like any other?', ch. 1.

[13] Rasmussen, 'Bildersturm und Restauration', pp. 101–2.

[14] Roth, *Augsburgs Reformationsgeschichte*, vol. 1, p. 305 and vol. 2, p. 66.

[15] Ibid., vol. 2, p. 328.

[16] The pattern of the survival and destruction of Marian and other imagery in Augsburg parallels that described by Lee Wandel in her study of iconoclasm in Strasbourg. Wandel, *Voracious Idols*, p. 122. See also Dupeux, Jezler and Wirth, eds., *Bildersturm*, p. 88 and cat. no. 48.

[17] On the destruction of images that served as para-liturgical props see Scribner, 'The image and the Reformation', pp. 543–4. For comparative material relating to English iconoclasm see Aston, *England's Iconoclasts*, pp. 401–8.

Protestant churches. When Bestler's team had finished their work, the interiors of the 'cleansed' buildings undoubtedly looked more like the thoroughly stripped churches of Zwinglian Zurich, Strasbourg and Basle than the still richly furnished churches of Lutheran Nuremberg. It was not until Lutheran sensibilities prevailed over Zwinglian in the wake of the Religious Peace of Augsburg (1555) that a somewhat more tolerant attitude with regard to imagery began to emerge.[18] Painted epitaphs with Christological themes were commissioned for the city's Protestant churches during the 1560s and 1570s.[19] By the mid seventeenth century, when the evangelical church of Heilig Kreuz was rebuilt following the destruction of the Thirty Years War (consecrated 1653), Protestantism within the city was no longer synonymous with bare walls: this church was richly adorned with paintings, most of them showing narrative scenes from Christ's life.[20] Yet Marian images made only a very cautious reappearance. Michel de Montaigne travelled through Augsburg in 1580 and recorded in his diary that an image of Mary with the Christ Child and other children and saints hung above the door at Heilig Kreuz. The image was, according to Montaigne, accompanied by one of the texts beloved of Lutheran artists: 'Let the children come unto me' (Mark 10:13).[21] From Montaigne's description it seems likely that this was a pre-Reformation image of the Holy Kindred that had been given an evangelical interpretation by the addition of a biblical text. Such tolerance and even reuse of traditional Marian iconographies was, however, much less common in Augsburg than in Nuremberg.

Although surviving church inventories do not permit a full reconstruction of the furnishings of Augsburg's churches before and after the Reformation, the evidence that can be assembled suggests that between the 1530s and the later seventeenth century the churches that were under Protestant control contained very few images of the Virgin.[22] In St Anna, for example, a stronghold of Lutheranism, it seems that Marian images survived only when civic politics prevented their removal. This former Carmelite cloister was the institutional

[18] On appearance of Augsburg's Protestant churches to 1629 see Freya Strecker, 'Bilderstreit, Konfessionalisierung und Repräsentation: zur Ausstattung protestantischer Kirchen in Augsburg zwischen Reformation und Restitutionsedikt', in *Wolfgang Musculus*, ed. Dellsperger, Freudenberger and Weber, pp. 263ff. Strecker argues that the relatively meagre furnishings of Augsburg's churches from the mid sixteenth century to 1629 were a result of the lack of interest in patronage. Potential patrons were aware that local preachers and citizens were not favourably disposed towards images (pp. 277–8).

[19] Bushart, 'Kunst und Stadtbild', pp. 370–1.

[20] Bernd von Hagen and Angelika Wegener-Hüssen, *Stadt Augsburg*, Denkmäler in Bayern 7/83 (Munich, 1994), pp. 226–30.

[21] Michel de Montaigne, *Montaigne's Travel Journal*, trans. Donald M. Frame (San Francisco, 1983), p. 39.

[22] For an equivalent example from another south German biconfessional city see August Gebessler, *Stadt und Landkreis Dinkelsbühl*, Bayerische Kunstdenkmale 15 (Munich, 1962), pp. 28ff. on the Spitalkirche in Dinkelsbühl.

centre of Augsburg's Reformation movement. The prior Johannes Frosch sheltered Luther during his 1518 meeting with Cardinal Cajetan, and the cloister became a focus for evangelical preaching under Urbanus Rhegius and Stephen Agricola. The church was closed from 1534 to 1545, but it remained in Protestant hands after Charles V's 1548 *Restitutionsvertrag* and continued to play a key role in opposing the Catholic authorities until its temporary surrender to the Jesuits in 1631.[23] The appearance of the church was gradually transformed, probably starting in around 1545.[24] In 1552 galleries were mentioned for the first time and in 1553 payments were made for the construction of a communion table.[25] Most of the medieval furnishings must have been removed during this time, since very few are mentioned in the church inventories produced during the seventeenth century or in the first detailed description of the interior of the church dating from 1788.[26]

In keeping with Lutheran emphasis on the commemorative function of art, epitaphs were the most important, indeed perhaps even the only, genre of image to enter St Anna during the second half of the sixteenth century.[27] All depicted narrative or allegorical scenes, and many had extensive inscriptions to clarify and reinforce their meaning. From the mid sixteenth century to the late seventeenth century it seems that the only Marian images on display in St Anna were those located in the Fugger Chapel: a roof boss showing the Virgin and Child and one of the two painted organ wings, which depicted Mary's Assumption into heaven.[28] The Fugger Chapel was the property of the most powerful Catholic family in the city and, as such, could not be violated. Only in 1581 was the chapel finally opened up: its grille was removed and its altar enclosed within

[23] See W. Schiller, *Die St Annakirche in Augsburg: ein Beitrag zur Augsburger Kirchengeschichte* (Augsburg, 1938), pp. 53–60 and 67–9 and Andreas Hahn, 'Die St-Anna-Kirche in Augsburg', in '. . . *wider Laster und Sünde*', ed. Kirmeier, Jahn and Brockhoff (Cologne, 1997), pp. 73–4. St Anna was held by the Jesuits 1631–2, then again from the expulsion of the Swedes to 1649.

[24] Freya Strecker suggests that St Anna was amongst the churches 'cleansed' under the direction of the city council in 1537, *Augsburger Altäre zwischen Reformation (1537) und 1635: Bildkritik, Repräsentation und Konfessionalisierung*, Kunstgeschichte 61 (Münster, 1998), p. 43. There is, however, no concrete evidence to support this hypothesis. Indeed it seems unlikely that St Anna would have been targeted at this stage given that it had already been closed for three years. Furthermore the city council offered St Anna and the Dominican church to Charles V for the celebration of mass after his triumphal entry into the city in 1548. The council's choice of church may well have been determined by the fact that in St Anna and in the Dominican church the furnishings of the pre-Reformation period had remained largely undisturbed. Rasmussen, 'Bildersturm und Restauration', pp. 103–4.

[25] Strecker, *Augsburger Altäre*, pp. 45–6. An altar was in use again by 1565.

[26] StadtAA, E. W. A., Nr. 666 (1668, 1684, 1689 and 1695); Paul von Stetten, *Beschreibung der Reichs-Stadt Augsburg, nach ihrer Lage* (Augsburg, 1788), pp. 159–63.

[27] Kirmeier, Jahn and Brockhoff, eds., '. . . *wider Laster und Sünde*', p. 222. Hahn, 'Die St-Anna-Kirche', pp. 79–80.

[28] On the altar wings see Andrew Morrall, *Jörg Breu the Elder: art, culture, and belief in Reformation Augsburg*, Histories of Vision (Aldershot, 2001), pp. 103–31. Bruno Bushart, *Die Fuggerkapelle bei St Anna in Augsburg* (Munich, 1994), 240–59, 89–90.

railings.[29] During the second half of the seventeenth century, however, St Anna began to acquire significant number of paintings again, as inventories from 1668, 1684, 1689 and 1695 demonstrate. Like the paintings that entered Heilig Kreuz and the Ulrichskirche at around the same time, they tended to depict typically evangelical themes: Protestant preachers, Old Testament scenes and illustrations of Christ's life and Passion.[30] The 1695 inventory is the first to list a Marian image, a panel of the Mother of God given by one Frau Merz.[31] A second Marian image entered the church between 1695 and 1722 as a donation of Christian von Stetten.[32] This panel, which shows the Virgin and Child with St John, remains in St Anna today and is attributed to a member of Cranach's circle.[33] In general, between the 1530s and the late seventeenth century Marian imagery seems to have been confined to the city's Catholic churches. When Marian images appeared in an evangelical context they certainly attracted surprised comment in a way those in Nuremberg's churches did not: in 1684, for example, a local Jesuit commented that he 'saw with astonishment' a statue of Mary standing in the evangelical preaching house of St Ulrich.[34]

It seems that Augsburg's Protestants were equally reluctant to countenance the display of Marian images in the domestic sphere, though the evidence provided by household inventories does not permit absolute certainty on this point. Whereas in Nuremberg it is clear that local patricians, and even the city council itself, readily assimilated paintings of the Virgin into their art collections during the later part of the sixteenth century, in biconfessional Augsburg the private ownership of images of the Virgin appears to have been largely confined to Catholics. This reflects the pattern identified by Susan Foister for England during the second half of the sixteenth century and by Philip Benedict for

[29] Strecker, *Augsburger Altäre*, p. 46. The Fuggers stopped using the chapel for burials after 1538 and transferred the mass that they had endowed to the Dominican church, yet their permission was still required before either the chapel or its organ could be used during Protestant services. Schiller, *Die St Annakirche*, p. 46.

[30] StadtAA, E. W. A., Nr. 666, 'Verzeichnuß was der Mesner bey St: Anna in verwahrung hat. beschrieben den 8 September A° 1668'. Ibid., 'Verzaichnuß waß der mesner bey St: A: in verwahrung hat: beschriben Im Monat April A. 1684'. Ibid., 'Verzaichnuß waß der Mesner bey St. Anna, in der verwahrung hat. beschriben Im Monat October Ao 1689'. Ibid., 'Inventarium des Innerlichen Kirchen Schmucks, bücher, vnd anderer sachen, bey St: Anna . . . Ao. 1695 dz 10 Decembris'.

[31] On the Merz family, merchants, see Wolfgang Reinhard, ed., *Augsburger Eliten des 16. Jahrhunderts: Prosopographie wirtschaftlicher und politischer Führungsgruppen 1500–1620* (Berlin, 1996), pp. 804–7.

[32] On the von Stettens, a predominantly Protestant family of merchants and patricians, see ibid., pp. 1349–57.

[33] Kirmeier, Jahn and Brockhoff, eds., '. . . *wider Laster und Sünde*', p. 159.

[34] StadtAA, E. W. A., Nr. 941, Tom. I, Nr. 6, fol. 1v. I am grateful to Prof. Duane Corpis for bringing this reference to my attention. On the Catholic cloister and evangelical preaching house of St Ulrich see Warmbrunn, *Zwei Konfessionen in einer Stadt*, pp. 230–8.

seventeenth-century Metz: painting ownership varied according to confession, with Catholics continuing to own devotional images of saints while Protestants showed a preference for Old Testament and Christological scenes.[35] In Augsburg, however, the significance of this pattern should not be overstated. The number of surviving inventories is too small to permit a significant statistical analysis. The Augsburg inventories also tend to contain many generic references to 'painted panels', amongst which there may or may not have been further images of the Virgin. Moreover, even by the end of the sixteenth century it is rare to be able to determine with absolute certainty the religious affiliations of the images' owners.

Despite these provisos, there is sufficient evidence to suggest that while Augsburg's Catholics continued to own Marian images, local Protestants were considerably less comfortable than their Nuremberg counterparts with such remnants of the Catholic past. Of sixty-eight surviving Augsburg inventories, most dating from the second half of the sixteenth century, forty-five mention images, rosaries or both.[36] Marian images appear in only six of those forty-five, and in four of the six cases the owner is known to have been an adherent of the old faith. Conrad Peutinger, eminent humanist and civic secretary from 1495 to 1534, built up a spectacular collection of art objects and books. An inventory of this collection drawn up in 1600 lists twelve images of the Virgin.[37] Raymund Fugger (1582) had a painted house altar showing Our Lady with the Christ Child and an angel and a small 'wasserfarb' (probably *tempera*) *Vesperbild* or *pietà*.[38] Paul Welser (1615) had nine images of the Virgin including two *Vesperbilder*.[39] Octavian Secundus Fugger (1601), an eminent collector with close connections to the Jesuit order and an ardent venerator of the Virgin (see chapter 4), had over seventy Marian images of various types. The remaining Marian images belonged to two local residents whose confessions cannot be determined with certainty, although in both cases circumstances suggest Catholic affinities. The inventory of one Anton Weyssen (1584), possibly to be identified with Anton I Weiß, lists two images of the Virgin, one showing the rosary. Weyssen's confession is impossible to determine, but his ownership of a collection of sermons by a Catholic preacher, Johannes Wild, may indicate Catholic sympathies.[40]

[35] Benedict, 'Towards the comparative study of the popular market for art'.

[36] StadtAA, Reichsstadt, Spreng'sche Notariatsakten; StadtAA, Reichsstadt, Schuld-, Klag-, und Apellationsakten; StadtAA, Schätze, Nr. 165, Augsburger Pflegschaftsbuch von 1501–1542.

[37] I am grateful to Dr Hans-Jörg Kunast for allowing me access to a transcript of Peutinger's 1597 inventory.

[38] StadtAA, Reichsstadt, 100/2, Spreng'sche Notariatsakten 1581–93, 1582 Nr. 46½, no folio numbers. On Raymund's inheritance from his father, Raymund Fugger the Elder, see Norbert Lieb, *Die Fugger und die Kunst im Zeitalter der hohen Renaissance* (Munich, 1958), p. 51.

[39] SStBA, 2^0 Cod. Aug. 88, Paul v. Welser, Inventar 1615, fols. 17r, 41r–42r.

[40] StadtAA, Reichsstadt, 100/2, Spreng'sche Notariatsakten 1581–93, 1584 Nr. 2. On Weiß see Reinhard, ed., *Augsburger Eliten*, p. 1392.

Maria Meuting (1586), who was married to Christoph II Rehlinger, had gilded panel with an image of Mary. Again, her confession cannot be determined, but the Rehlingers are known to have been a predominantly Catholic family.[41]

I have found only one clear-cut case of a Protestant owning an image of the Virgin. An inventory of the property of the Protestant *Ratsdiener* (council administrator) and copious chronicler Paul Hector Mair, drawn up in 1579–80 after his execution for embezzling municipal funds, mentions a gilded wooden image of the Virgin. This image, probably a statuette, was not on display but was kept in a chest containing silverware.[42] When they owned religious images, Protestants seem, in general, to have favoured those depicting scenes from Christ's life and Passion or from the Old Testament. Marxen Walther (1574), a member of a prominent Protestant family, owned three crucifixes.[43] David Haug (1575), whose ownership of Lutheran books suggests Protestant sympathies, owned a painted panel showing the Flood.[44] Victor Röhlin (1577), who owned a Lutheran bible, had a large painted panel of Samson.[45] And amongst the paintings belonging to the Protestant Paul Vöhlin (1579) were six panels showing the Creation of Man and a panel showing the Crucifixion.[46] The persistence of crucifixes and Crucifixion scenes amongst the religious imagery owned by Augsburg's Protestants merits particular mention. This persistence surely reflects the predominantly Lutheran, as opposed to Zwinglian, sympathies of Augsburg's Protestant community after 1555, as adherents of the more radical Protestant sects would not have tolerated such 'images of devotion and veneration'.[47]

Evidence concerning the ownership of rosaries underlines, however, the need to avoid assuming that confessional considerations were always paramount in shaping collecting habits. Rosaries were certainly confessionally charged in Augsburg, as in other Protestant cities. In Bern, for example, the city council introduced a fine of ten *Gulden* for anyone found carrying one in 1529.[48] In Augsburg in the same year Georg Zeindelweber, an armoury guard with

41 StadtAA, Reichsstadt, 100/2, Spreng'sche Notariatsakten 1581–93, 1586, 20. Reinhard, ed., *Augsburger Eliten*, p. 1013. Katarina Sieh-Burens, *Oligarchie, Konfession und Politik im 16. Jahrhundert: zur sozialen Verflechtung der Augsburger Bürgermeister und Stadtpfleger 1518–1618*, Schriften der Philosophischen Fakultäten der Universität Augsburg 29 (Munich, 1986), p. 189.

42 StadtAA, Reichsstadt, Strafamt, Urgichten 400–401 (1579–80), Rechnung u^{e}ber weylund Paul Hector Mairs Verlassenschafft, 59. I am grateful to Dr Benedikt Mauer for bringing this document to my attention.

43 StadtAA, Reichsstadt, 100/1, Spreng'sche Notariatsakten 1567–80, 1574 Nr. 76¼, fols. 9r, 11r.

44 Ibid, 1575 Nr. 77½, no folio numbers.

45 Ibid, 1577 Nr. 16¼, no folio numbers.

46 StadtAA, Reichsstadt, 100/1, Spreng'sche Notariatsakten 1567–80, 1579 Nr. 37½, fols. 6r–v, 10r, 13r, 14r, 18v, 21r and 29r. On Vöhlin's confession see Reinhard, ed., *Augsburger Eliten*, 1339.

47 Benedict, 'Towards the comparative study of the popular market for art', 110–12. Crucifixion scenes are conspicuously lacking amongst the religious images owned by Benedict's French Calvinists.

48 Delius, *Geschichte der Marienverehrung*, p. 230.

evangelical sympathies, was hauled before the local magistrates for his part in a confrontation that had begun when he asked a fellow citizen, Hainrich Meckenloher, why he was carrying a rosary. Meckenloher replied that he carried it so that Berthold Aichelin, the imperial official responsible for the arrest and execution of many south German Anabaptists, did not catch him.[49] Given such deliberate uses of rosaries as symbols of loyalty to the old faith, it is somewhat surprising to find them listed in Protestant inventories later in the century. Marxen Walther (1574) and Mattheß Manlich (1576) both owned rosaries, and Paul Vöhlin (1579) had thirteen. Vöhlin's inventory in particular warns us against assuming a simple, confessionally defined pattern of ownership. Vöhlin had a substantial collection of art objects: in addition to ninety pictures, his inventory lists silverware and many other treasures, for example a chain with jewels and an *Agnus Dei* that he apparently wore, a ruby ring with the face of a pope, a carved cornelian showing the Three Kings and various precious crosses.[50] We can only suppose that this Protestant patrician valued his collection of rosaries and Catholic jewels for its aesthetic merit and financial worth rather than for its religious associations.

Just as Mary more or less disappeared from the visual culture of Augsburg's Protestant church, so her role in its liturgical life was also dramatically reduced. Whereas in Lutheran Nuremberg, as we have seen, three Marian festivals continued to be celebrated, in Augsburg the Annunciation (interpreted as a festival of Christ) was the only one to survive the council's radical purging of the cycle of traditional feast days. On 3 July 1537 it was decreed that from henceforth only Sundays, Easter, Pentecost, Christmas, New Year, the Ascension and the Annunciation would be observed.[51] With regard to Marian liturgy, as with regard to Marian images, Augsburg's stance reflected that of the Swiss reformers. Augsburg's Lutheran preachers had produced early drafts for the city's evangelical church ordinance that had retained Marian and other feast days in line with the liturgical calendar observed in Wittenberg and Nuremberg. But the city's Upper German theologians, who ultimately prevailed over the Lutherans on this point as on all others, looked not to Wittenberg and Nuremberg but to Switzerland and Strasbourg.[52]

Of the traditional Marian festivals Zwingli had sought to keep only 'the day *annunciationis Marie*, that is: the Annunciation of Mary'.[53] In 1527 Berne

49 StadtAA, Reichsstadt, Strafamt, Urgichten, Nr. 7, 15. Juni 1529 (Georg Zeindelweber, Zeugwart).

50 StadtAA, Reichsstadt, 100/1, Spreng'sche Notariatsakten 1567–80, 1579 Nr. 37½, fols. 38r–58r.

51 StadAA, Reichstadt, Ratsbücher, Nr. 16, fol. 126v. Enshrined in the *Feiertagsordnung*, Sehling, ed., *Die evangelischen Kirchenordnungen*, vol. 12 (Bayern II, Schwaben), p. 84.

52 Gottfried Seebass, 'Die Augsburger Kirchenordnung von 1537 in ihrem historischen und theologischen Zusammenhang', in *Die Augsburger Kirchenordnung von 1537 und ihr Umfeld*, ed. Reinhard Schwarz (Gütersloh, 1988), p. 44.

53 Campi, *Zwingli und Maria*, p. 79.

decreed the survival of only one Marian festival, the Annunciation.[54] Strasbourg did the same at Bucer's instigation in 1534.[55] Zurich maintained a more moderate position for a while: its council issued a decree on 28 March 1526 that reduced the number of feast days, but the Purification and the Assumption survived alongside the Annunciation. These Marian festivals even enjoyed the same status as the key Christological feasts, in that their eves were to be properly observed.[56] This ordinance was renewed in 1530,[57] according to the synod out of consideration for Zurich's neighbours and for the weak.[58] A sudden transformation of the calendar, in particular the removal of Marian feasts, would, it was thought, cause too much unrest.[59] Zurich's Marian festivals were purified, as Nuremberg's had been. The chronicle of Gerold Edlibach recorded that: 'in the year of our Lord 1524 Candlemas, the laudable feast of the most worthy Mother of God, the Virgin Mary, was no longer celebrated, neither with singing, reading and the holding of mass as before, nor with the consecration of candles and lights, nor with a procession around the church. All of this was given up and dismissed.'[60] Eventually, however, Zurich's anomalous position on this matter attracted unfavourable attention, and in 1535 the council issued a revised ordinance limiting the celebration of feast days to Sundays and festivals of the Lord.[61] By the time of Augsburg's Reformation there was therefore a broad consensus that Mary was scarcely to be commemorated at all during the liturgical year, a consensus to which Augsburg's Protestant magistrates were apparently happy to conform.

Given the determination with which Augsburg's Protestants rejected images of the Virgin and Marian feast days it comes as no surprise to learn that they also repudiated the traditional notion that blasphemy against the Virgin was a criminal offence. Imperial legislation had already, in 1495/7, included Mary alongside Christ in its decree against blasphemy and swearing.[62] Charles V's 1532 legal code, the *Carolina*, again stated that blasphemers, including those who dishonoured God's 'holy mother the Virgin Mary', should be punished. This decree was repeated in the police ordinance that was issued by Charles V

54 Lansemann, *Die Heiligentage*, p. 46. Tappolet, ed., *Das Marienlob der Reformatoren*, p. 258.
55 Lansemann, *Die Heiligentage*, p. 45.
56 Emil Egli, *Actensammlung zur Geschichte der Zürcher Reformation in den Jahren 1519–1533* (Zurich, 1879), p. 946.
57 Ibid., p. 1656. 58 Ibid., p. 1604. 59 Campi, *Zwingli und Maria*, p. 78.
60 Ibid., p. 78, n. 209.
61 J. J. Hottinger and H. H. Vögeli, eds., *Heinrich Bullingers Reformationsgeschichte*, vol. 1 (Frauenfeld, 1838), pp. 328–9. MacCulloch, 'Mary and sixteenth-century Protestants', p. 202.
62 Gerd Schwerhoff, 'Fehltritt oder Provokation? Theologisch-rechtliche Deutung und sozialen Praxis der Gotteslästerung im 15. und 16. Jahrhundert', in *Der Fehltritt: Vergehen und Versehen in der Vormoderne*, ed. Peter van Moos (Cologne, 2001), p. 407 and Schwerhoff, 'Blasphemie', 58.

in 1548 and renewed in 1577.[63] This concern to defend Mary's honour was also reflected in the blasphemy legislation issued by Catholic magistrates. In Lucerne, for example, in 1561 a decree threatened those who damaged the honour of God or of the Virgin Mary with a fine.[64] As we saw in chapter 2, in some Lutheran areas Marian blasphemy remained a punishable offence long after the Reformation (above pp. 87–8), and even some reformed territories showed an initial reluctance to break with tradition. In December 1526, for example, Zurich's council warned its citizens and subjects that they should not swear 'by God, his respected mother and the saints', on pain of punishment.[65] Mary and the saints did, however, disappear from Zurich's later blasphemy legislation.[66]

Augsburg's pre-Reformation legislation had, like that of other imperial territories, prescribed punishments for those who impugned Mary's honour. Two decrees issued by the council in 1520 and 1524 declared, for example, that it was inappropriate and against 'Christian order' to blaspheme against 'God's mother, the immaculate Virgin Mary'.[67] In Augsburg, however, the discipline ordinance issued by the Protestant city council in 1537 omitted all mention of the Virgin Mary and the saints and focused exclusively on offences against God.[68] Its formulation on blasphemy was repeated in police ordinances issued in 1553, 1580 and 1590.[69] From the formal institution of the Reformation in 1537 until 1607 Mary did not feature in the council's decrees on blasphemy.[70] Her absence from legislation produced between 1548 and 1607 perhaps reflects the biconfessional council's regard for the delicate religious balance within the city.[71] The council pursued its politics of pacification, and had no interest in drawing

63 Richard van Dülmen, 'Wider die Ehre Gottes: Unglaube und Gotteslästerung in der Frühen Neuzeit', *Historische Anthropologie. Kultur. Gesellschaft. Alltag* 2, no. 1 (1994), 35. Stadtarchiv Augsburg, Literalien 1576–1579, 9/11 1577. Schwerhoff suggests that the imperial legislation on Marian blasphemy did not cause controversy because Protestants recognized the need to defend Mary's honour. Schwerhoff, *Zungen wie Schwerter*, p. 247.

64 Francisca Loetz, *Mit Gott handeln: von den Zürcher Gotteslästern der frühen Neuzeit zu einer Kulturgeschichte des Religiösen*, Veröffentlichungen des Max-Planck-Instituts für Geschichte 177 (Göttingen, 2002), pp. 510, 518.

65 Egli, *Actensammlung*, p. 1077. Basle's 1529 Reformation order also forbade blasphemy against Mary. Schwerhoff, *Zungen wie Schwerter*, p. 247.

66 Loetz, *Mit Gott handeln*, p. 493.

67 StadtAA, Reichsstadt, Ratserlasse, 1507–1599, 1520 11/2, 1524 17/1. Two subsequent decrees, 1526 21/10 and 1528 8/3, contained only prohibitions on blasphemy against God and the saints.

68 StadtAA, Reichsstadt, Ratserlasse, 1507–1599, 1537 14/8, fol. 3r. This ordinance played a key role in the institutionalization of the Reformation, transferring control over marriage and morals from the ecclesiastical to the civic authorities. Roper, *The Holy Household*, p. 56.

69 StadtAA, Reichsstadt, Schätze, Nr. ad 36/3, fol. 3v on blasphemy; StadtAA, Reichsstadt, Schätze, Nr. ad 36/7 (21. Oct. A[nn]o 90), fol. 18r.

70 StadtAA, Reichsstadt, Schätze, Nr. ad 36/7 (17. Nouembris Anno 1607).

71 On the composition of the council see Warmbrunn, *Zwei Konfessionen in einer Stadt*, pp. 106–14 and ch. 4, especially pp. 132–7 and 162–75.

public attention to religious confrontations. Mary's reappearance in 1607 might perhaps reflect the council's increasing concern to prevent Protestant attacks on the Catholic cult in light of the imperial ban imposed on Donauwörth in 1607 for Protestant disturbances there.[72] As we shall see when we consider records of prosecutions (below, pp. 134–9), Augsburg's Catholic leaders did not, however, make much effort to enforce proper respect for the Virgin until their hegemony was assured during the 1630s.[73]

THE IMPACT OF REFORMED PROTESTANTISM

Why were Augsburg's Protestants apparently less comfortable than Nuremberg's with the Marian legacy left to them by the late medieval church? Their initial determination to abolish all reminders of Mary's cult must be attributed to the more radical nature of their Reformation movement, to the fact that during the 1520s adherents of the new faith in Augsburg moved away from Luther and towards the teaching and practices of the Swiss and Upper German cities.[74] Zwingli's own attitude towards the Virgin Mary was, as we have seen, not that dissimilar to Luther's, and other key Swiss and Upper German reformers also continued to accord her considerable respect. Johannes Oecolampadius (1482–1531), reformer in Basle, adopted a position very similar to Luther's, describing Mary as a model of faith, humility, chastity and maternal love and mercy. In his 1526 tract, *On the Invocation of Saints*, for example, he emphasized that Mary was to be praised but was not to be called our life, our sweetness or our hope, titles that properly belonged only to God.[75] Martin Bucer, reformer in Strasbourg, was very firm in his condemnation of saints' cults, but even he maintained that Mary should be praised and honoured.[76] In 1558 Heinrich Bullinger, Zwingli's successor in Zurich, preached a sermon on Mary in which he defended Mary's perpetual virginity and praised her as 'the most excellent creature, most pleasing to God'.[77]

Yet when religious reform was actually implemented in Zurich, Basle, Strasbourg and elsewhere in Switzerland and Upper Germany very few manifestations of Marian devotion survived. Augsburg was by no means atypical in this respect. The reformers may have continued to honour Mary, but because of their determination to remove images and abolish ceremonies very few reminders of her cult remained. In Zurich, for example, considerable attention was devoted

[72] On Augsburg's reaction to the Donauwörth incident see Leonhard Lenk, *Augsburger Bürgertum im Späthumanismus und Frühbarock (1580–1700)* (Augsburg, 1968), pp. 21–2 and Roeck, *Als wollt die Welt schier brechen*, pp. 165–6, 169.

[73] The next decree against Marian blasphemy dates from 10 July 1638. StadtAA, Reichsstadt, Anschläge und Dekrete, 1490–1649, Nr. 1–86, Nr. 70.

[74] Immenkötter, 'Kirche', p. 396. [75] Delius, *Geschichte der Marienverehrung*, pp. 230–1.

[76] Ibid., pp. 232–3. [77] Tappolet, ed., *Das Marienlob der Reformatoren*, p. 275.

to the intercession of saints and to the question of images during the disputations that marked the official beginning of the Reformation (1523–4). Zwingli was more vehement than Luther in his denunciation of the invocation of saints, writing in article 20 of his *Schlußreden* that 'reliance upon the intercession of saints obscures, denies and rejects the healing suffering of Christ'.[78] He was also firm in his assertion that images must be eliminated, telling Zurich's pastors and preachers in his *Short Christian Introduction* that 'clearly, the images and paintings which we have in the churches have caused the risk of idolatry. Therefore they should not be left there, nor in your chambers, nor in the marketplace, nor anywhere where one does them honour.'[79] Zwingli believed that images had the power to turn men from God, a position that was most clearly formulated in his *Brief Reply Given to Valentin Compar* (1524/5). He credited images with much greater agency than Luther did: if they remained, idolatry would inevitably result. The practical consequence of this conviction was the cleansing of churches that occurred in Zurich in the summer of 1524. Again at the Bern disputation of 1528 Zwingli, supported by Bucer and Wolfgang Capito, condemned the intercession of saints and the veneration of images, and the removal of the city's images followed immediately after.[80]

Bucer, who had preached against the cult of saints and its visual manifestations during the Zurich disputation, wrote in 1530 what Rasmussen describes as '*the* theory of the image hostility of the Upper German observance'.[81] In *Das einigerlei Bild bei dem Gotgläubigen* he, like most other Reformed theologians, took the Old Testament prohibition on images as his starting point, arguing that the veneration of images was detrimental to true belief and to the love of God. He countered Luther's assertion that images were a matter of Christian freedom, neither good nor bad, by pointing out that where they were venerated they harmed belief. He did not trust the power of words to overcome the power of images. Images must be removed from before men's eyes, because the ignorant would inevitably venerate them if they remained: 'One can pursue the word as seriously as one wishes, but so long as images are tolerated in the churches they will be prayed to and honoured by many simple people on account of habit, the public encouragement of the malicious and the secrets of the devil.' The weak in faith must be strengthened in their belief in the word through the force of physical example.[82] Bucer's tract was written and published in Strasbourg in order to justify what was already a *fait accompli* in that city: after initial

[78] Huldrych Zwingli, *Huldreich Zwinglis sämtliche Werke*, Corpus Reformatorum (Leipzig, 1904–), vol. 2, p. 190.

[79] Melchior Schuler and Johannes Schulthess, eds., *Huldreich Zwinglis Werke*, vol. 1 (Zurich, 1828), p. 561.

[80] Heming, *Protestants and the Cult of the Saints*, pp. 86–7.

[81] Rasmussen, 'Bildersturm und Restauration', p. 101.

[82] Robert Stupperich, ed., *Martin Bucers deutsche Schriften, Martini Buceri opera omnia*, ser. 1, vol. 4: *Zur auswärtigen Wirksamkeit 1528–1533* (Gütersloh, 1975), pp. 166–74, especially 171.

unauthorized incidents of iconoclasm in 1524, the council had encouraged the removal of offensive images, and the stripping of the city's churches had been completed in 1529–30.[83]

Similar messages were heard, with similar effect, in Augsburg. For Michael Keller, Zwinglian preacher at the Barfüßerkirche, the medieval cult of saints, in particular the cult of the Virgin, was anathema. In his writings he mocked the debate between the Franciscans and Dominicans over Mary's Immaculate Conception, describing both as heretics. For him Mary was 'a woman like another ordinary woman' (ain frau wie ain andere schlechte frau). In his sermons, according to the chronicler Sender, he referred to images of the saints as idols and said that those who had, in the past, removed their hats, knelt or prayed before such images 'had blasphemed against God through such works and sinned more than if they had committed a mortal sin'.[84] Such sentiments found concrete expression in the destruction of a crucifix in the Franciscan Barfüßerkirche, masterminded by Keller in 1529. While Augsburg's leading Lutheran, Johannes Forster, defended images in churches citing both Wittenberg and Nuremberg as examples of evangelical communities where they had been permitted to survive, Keller's iconophobic message was reiterated by Wolfgang Musculus and Bonifacius Wolfart, who arrived from Strasbourg in 1531 to bolster the Reformed cause. Bucer himself was also summoned by Augsburg's council in 1534 to help standardize the organization of the city's fledgling Protestant Church.[85] Both Musculus, who became Augsburg's most prominent preacher and a trusted advisor to the council, and Bucer sought a doctrinal 'middle way' that would permit reconciliation with Lutheran Saxony.[86] Bucer initially preached moderation with regard to images in opposition to Keller and Wolfart, recognizing that iconoclasm would prejudice any agreement with Wittenberg. By June 1537, however, he found himself compelled to defend the removal of images that had occurred in January of that year.[87]

The iconophobic convictions of Keller and Wolfart were reflected in the rhetoric of the city council's instructions for reform. In May 1533, for example, Augsburg's council sent a delegation to the supposedly reform-minded bishop, Christoph von Stadion, in an attempt to reach an understanding that would allow

[83] Frank Muller, 'Der Bildersturm in Strassburg 1524–1530', in *Bildersturm*, ed. Dupeux, Jezler and Wirth.

[84] Roth, *Augsburgs Reformationsgeschichte*, vol. 1, p. 305. *Chroniken*, vol. 23, pp. 215–16.

[85] Immenkötter, 'Kirche', p. 399; Gottfried Seebass, 'Martin Bucer und die Reichsstadt Augsburg', in *Martin Bucer and Sixteenth Century Europe. Actes du colloque de Strasbourg (28–31 août 1991)*, ed. Christian Krieger and Marc Lienhard (Leiden, 1993).

[86] Rudolf Dellsperger, 'Wolfgang Musculus (1497–1563): Leben und Werk', in *Wolfgang Musculus*, ed. Dellsperger, Freudenberger and Weber (Berlin, 1997); James Thomas Ford, 'Unter dem Schein der Concordien und Confession: Wolfgang Musculus and the confessional identity of Augsburg, 1531–1548', in *Wolfgang Musculus*, ed. Dellsperger, Freudenberger and Weber.

[87] W. Germann, *D. Johann Forster der Hennebergische Reformator* (Meiningen, 1894), pp. 199–203. Also Seebass, 'Die Augsburger Kirchenordnung', p. 46.

the division amongst the city's preachers to be amicably settled. They presented him with a written document detailing the 'errors' of papal belief. Amongst these errors was the following complaint: 'in the previously identified places and elsewhere, the images and pilgrimages will be shown and maintained at the risk of veneration, against the Old and New Testament'.[88] By 1537 the rhetoric had grown stronger: 'all hopeless, godless superstition, against the honour and command of God, has flowed and sprung from the praying-to and venerating of idols and images'.[89] The cleansing of the city's churches followed, supervised, as we have seen, by Bestler, a friend of the Zwinglian preacher Michael Keller. The removal of religious images and the purification of the traditional cycle of feast days thus symbolized the triumph of the Upper German over the Lutheran faction within Augsburg, of Wolfgang Musculus over Johannes Forster (who left the city in 1538). For hostile observers Augsburg was now marked out as Zwinglian. Johannes Cochlaeus, for example, taunted Musculus, saying 'the churches of Augsburg, chiefly through your ranting and raving, have retained hardly more Catholic services and altars than in Zurich where Zwingli has wreaked havoc'.[90] In these circumstances it is hardly surprising that very few manifestations of the pre-Reformation cult of the Virgin remained.

For a decade Augsburg remained one of the most important centres of reformed Protestantism in southern Germany, until Charles V compelled the renewal of the city's Catholic cult in the wake of his 1547 victory over the Schmalkaldic League. The attempts of Charles and of Augsburg's bishop, Cardinal Otto Truchseß von Waldburg, to enforce the Interim of 1548 were never wholly successful, thanks to the resistance of the city's evangelical preachers and its predominantly evangelical population. Charles was finally forced to abandon the Interim in 1552, and the Religious Peace of Augsburg of 1555 prescribed a lasting confessional compromise. Article 27 of this peace exempted imperial free cities from the principle of 'cuius regio, eius religio', stating that in cities in which both Catholicism and the Augsburg Confession had previously been practised, members of both confessions should be allowed to continue to worship freely. The designation of Lutheranism and Catholicism as the two legitimate confessions of the Empire was of great significance: reformed Protestantism received no recognition in 1555, and the citizens of Augsburg and of other south German cities were therefore compelled to abandon the Swiss tradition and follow Luther's Reformation.

In accordance with the terms of the 1555 peace, Augsburg's city council sought to shore up the Augsburg Confession within the city against local evangelicals' still perceptible tendencies towards reformed Protestantism. The council appointed ministers loyal to the Augsburg Confession, reprimanded any who

[88] *Chroniken*, vol. 23, p. 349. [89] Roth, *Augsburgs Reformationsgeschichte*, vol. 2, p. 360.
[90] Quoted in Ford, 'Unter dem Schein der Concordien und Confession', pp. 120–1.

subsequently deviated and in 1578 compelled the adoption of the Formula of Concord.[91] From 1559 the council also held up Luther's *Large Catechism* as the norm for preaching (though his *Small Catechism* did not replace that of the local Augsburger Johann Meckart for teaching purposes until 1632).[92] Given these decisive moves towards Lutheranism, it is scarcely surprising that a more lenient attitude towards religious art emerged during the second half of the sixteenth century, as demonstrated by the numerous epitaphs in St Anna and by the richly decorated interiors of Heilig Kreuz and St Ulrich. Yet Mary, as we have seen, did not reappear. Although Augsburg's Protestants now adhered to a creed that credited her with considerable importance as a model of right belief and conduct (see chapter 2), she never became part of their visual or liturgical culture.

MARY AS A CONFESSIONAL MARKER

The continued reluctance of Augsburg's evangelicals to condone any displays of Marian piety even during the later sixteenth and early seventeenth centuries must be attributed in large part to the increasingly tense confessional situation in the Swabian city in the decades around 1600. The *Restitutionsvertrag* of 1548 and the Peace of Augsburg established the lasting co-existence of Catholicism and Lutheranism. Legal parity was prescribed, and there was no longer an immediate danger that one confession might be able to force the other from the city.[93] For much of the time Catholic and Lutheran citizens lived side by side in relative harmony, adopting a pragmatic attitude towards confessional diversity. Mixed marriages remained common until the 1580s, for example, and Protestant parents sent their children to the Jesuit school because, unlike its Protestant counterpart, it was free.[94] Yet ultimately, as Heinz Schilling has argued, the mid sixteenth century witnessed the creation of a political and legal system of co-existence rather than a religious and ideological one.[95] From 1548, when the Catholic cult was forcibly renewed in conjunction with constitutional reform that shifted the balance of political power towards an elite Catholic minority, the city's Protestants had to work hard to defend their confessional integrity.[96] This was especially true during the final decades of the sixteenth century, when inflammatory preaching became more common, and when public manifestations of Catholic piety such as processions and pilgrimages were

[91] On Augsburg and the Formula of Concord see Matthias Simon, *Evangelische Kirchengeschichte Bayerns*, 2nd edn (Nuremberg, 1952), pp. 334–5. Augsburg's clergy signed, but the council would not subscribe to the Book of Concord because of its Catholic members.
[92] Immenkötter, 'Kirche', pp. 402–4.
[93] Warmbrunn, *Zwei Konfessionen in einer Stadt*, p. 124.
[94] Immenkötter, 'Kirche', p. 405.
[95] H. Schilling, *Religion, Political Culture and the Emergence of Early Modern Society: essays in German and Dutch history* (Leiden, 1992), p. 211.
[96] Warmbrunn, *Zwei Konfessionen in einer Stadt*, pp. 76, 121.

firmly re-established, thanks largely to the activities of the Jesuits.[97] A better understanding of differences in belief combined with the renewal of external ceremonies fomented confessional conflict, and the vehemence with which Augsburg's evangelicals resisted the implementation of the Gregorian calendar reform in 1583–4 demonstrates the extent to which they felt the need to defend their religious and political autonomy.[98]

The situation of Augsburg's evangelicals was very different from that of their Nuremberg counterparts. Thanks to Nuremberg's refusal to join the Schmalkaldic League, the imposition of the Interim there in 1548 was not accompanied by constitutional change, and the council continued to be run by an evangelical oligarchy.[99] From the 1590s the bishops of Bamberg and Eichstätt made sporadic attempts to recover ecclesiastical goods secularized by Nuremberg's city council, and to convert Nuremberg subjects resident within their territories. And Nuremberg, like every other evangelical *Reichsstadt*, was threatened by plans for recatholicization formulated at the Regensburg *Kurfürstenkonvent* of 1631.[100] None of this, however, compares to the traumas faced by Augsburg's Protestants: the Interim and *Verfassungsänderung* of 1548; the determination of the city's bishops, especially Cardinal Otto Truchseß von Waldburg and Heinrich V von Knöringen, to establish the Counter-Reformation; the preaching activity of Peter Canisius and subsequent Jesuits; the founding of a Jesuit college in 1579; and finally the upheavals of the Thirty Years War, culminating in the early 1630s with the establishment of a purely Catholic regime (1629 to 1632), subsequent Swedish occupation, and then the successful Habsburg/Bavarian siege of 1634–5.[101] From the second half of the sixteenth century onwards, Augsburg's Protestants were confronted with militant Counter-Reformation Catholicism on a daily basis, in a way that Nuremberg's were not. Their legal parity might have been assured, but their devotional lives were decisively shaped by the presence of a powerful competing confession.

Mary played an important part in Augsburg's Counter-Reformation cult, as we shall see in chapter 4. Otto Truchseß von Waldburg, Peter Canisius and his fellow Jesuits and members of prominent Catholic families such as the Fuggers all actively promoted Marian piety. Marian images and liturgy reappeared in

97 Hoffmann, 'Konfessionell motivierte und gewandelte Konflikte'.

98 Immenkötter, 'Kirche', pp. 405–6.

99 On Nuremberg's adoption of the Interim see Simon, *Evangelische Kirchengeschichte Bayerns*, pp. 254–5. The Ansbach 'Actuarium' formed the basis for the city's 'Interimsordnung', which altered as little of the liturgy as possible.

100 Karl Braun, *Nürnberg und die Versuche zur Wiederherstellung der alten Kirche im Zeitalter der Gegenreformation, 1555–1648*, Einzelarbeiten aus der Kirchengeschichte Bayerns 1 (Nuremberg, 1925).

101 For an evangelical print commemorating Gustavus Adolphus' arrival in Augsburg in 1632 see Oskar Planer, *Verzeichnis der Gustav Adolf Sammlung mit besonderer Rücksicht auf die Schlacht am 6./16. November 1632* (Leipzig, 1916), p. 124. Here Mary is depicted as the Woman of the Apocalypse, and represents the true Christian Church.

the city's Catholic churches, and devotional practices such as processions and pilgrimages that invoked the Virgin's aid were re-established. The Virgin celebrated in these images and rituals was not, of course, the humble *Hausmutter* of the Lutheran tradition, but the powerful intercessor of the Counter-Reformation. Her cult also had political import, since it bound Augsburg's renewed Catholicism not only to the Roman Church but also, much more immediately, to the Wittelsbach court in nearby Bavaria where Marian devotion was central to state-sponsored piety.[102] Not surprisingly, this Catholic appropriation of Mary made her unpalatable to evangelicals. In the preface to the printed version of his sermon on the Ave Maria Christoff Mollen, a native Augsburger who served as evangelical *Kirchendiener* in Gernsbach near Strasbourg, told his overlord Ludwig von Fleckenstein of his concern about the 'great abuse of the invocation of the dead saints'. This problem was greatest in areas of Catholic renewal: 'the people are above all instructed in and driven to such error and horror in the places where the papacy is newly founded and built up again by the Jesuits'. In such areas, he complained, poor people were refused alms by Catholics if they refused to acknowledge Mary as well as Christ, and to pray the Hail Mary alongside the Our Father. In the sermon itself he lamented that before children knew the Our Father they could recite the Hail Mary fluently. The Hail Mary, in the form that it was currently used, was, Mollen argued, a papist invention. The Jesuits, inspired by the devil, had added an intercessory invocation: 'Holy Mary, Mother of God, pray for us poor sinners.' Mollen cited the exorcism performed by Peter Canisius at Altötting (see chapter 4), and claimed that the devil had, at this exorcism, taught the Jesuits how to pray the Hail Mary and had 'also in addition praised the Mother of God most highly and given her powerful titles'.[103] The papists had also, Mollen argued, encouraged people to venerate and to put their trust in images of Christ and the saints. Once Mary was perceived as a weapon in the campaign for Catholic reconquest, as she was by Mollen, there was little chance that she would be welcomed back into evangelical devotion.

Augsburg's criminal records suggest that it was not only evangelical preachers who identified Mary with the enemy's cause: she could also serve as a confessional marker in confrontations between laypeople. As Francisca Loetz observed in her study of blasphemy in Zurich, differences of opinion with regard to Mary were by no means the exclusive preserve of theologians.[104] Augsburg is an excellent place to explore such popular conflicts because the city's archive contains an unusually complete set of *Urgichten*, trial records,

[102] On the connections with Bavaria that arose from the Catholic majority in the city government see Lenk, *Augsburger Bürgertum*, p. 21.

[103] Christoph Mollen, *Ein Predig von dem Ave Maria, vnd von anrüfung der heyligen* (Strasbourg, 1575), especially fol. Aiiv.

[104] Loetz, *Mit Gott handeln*, p. 427.

covering the period from the late fifteenth to the late seventeenth century. Each record contains a transcript of the questions posed to the suspect by the presiding patrician magistrates and of the answers given, and many also include supplementary material such as the testimony of witnesses, letters of intercession and a verdict. Penalties imposed are recorded in the city's *Strafbücher* (punishment books). As a source the *Urgichten* are hardly, of course, problem free: testimony was inevitably shaped by the circumstances of the trial. Moreover, the records are so copious that within the confines of this study it has proved impossible to search them all for references to Mary.[105] Nonetheless, the narratives that emerge from a few particularly interesting cases offer us considerable insight into local perceptions of the Virgin.

On a Friday evening in June 1529 – i.e. during a period when reformed ideas had taken root in Augsburg but had not yet won official recognition – a confrontation occurred on one of the city's streets.[106] As we saw above (pp. 124–5), an armoury guard, Georg Zeindelweber, accosted a fellow citizen, Hainrich Meckenloher, and asked him why he was carrying a rosary. Meckenloher replied that he was carrying it so that Berthold Aichelin, the *Bundesprofosen* (imperial official) responsible for the persecution of Anabaptists in the region, did not catch him.[107] The rosary served, for him, as a practical demonstration of religious allegiance. During the ensuing exchange Zeindelweber at first concealed his aversion to such Mariolatry with a discussion of Jewish blasphemy. When goaded by Meckenloher he eventually, however, cried out that Mary was a whore, adding 'she is not God's mother, she is the devil's mother, because God had no mother'. During his interrogation he moderated this provocative statement, putting himself back within the bounds of doctrinal orthodoxy. He denied that Mary was God's mother, pointing out that 'if he did have a mother, the mother must be older than the Almighty God', but he conceded, as he had in fact done during the initial altercation, that Mary was Christ's mother.[108] Zeindelweber's offensive comments about the Virgin owed more to long-established Christian stereotypes of Jewish belief than to Reformed theology, but the final challenge that he issued to Meckenloher, in which he invoked the power of the Gospel over that of the devil, certainly suggests his exposure to and sympathy with evangelical teaching. Even though in 1529 the long process of confessional indoctrination had barely begun, the heated exchange of views between the two artisans indicates that they were already aware that Marian devotion

[105] I would like to thank Dr Carl Hoffmann for his insight into the sixteenth-century records. For the period from 1629 to the arrival of the Swedes in April 1632 and for August 1634 to 1648 I have used the *Strafbücher* to check all blasphemy cases.

[106] StadtAA, Reichsstadt, Strafamt, Urgichten, Nr. 7, 15. Juni 1529 (Georg Zeindelweber, Zeugwart).

[107] On Aichelin see Roth, *Augsburgs Reformationsgeschichte*, vol. 2, pp. 402 and 16 n. 15.

[108] Unfortunately the *Strafbuch* for 1529, which would have recorded the punishment inflicted on Zeindelweber, no longer survives.

might mark a boundary of belief within Christianity as well as between Christians and Jews. Both Zeindelweber and Meckenloher read Marian devotion, in this case manifested by the wearing of a rosary, as a sign of loyalty to the Catholic faith.

For the city council, which in 1529 was still trying to steer a precarious middle course between popular pressure for reform and loyalty to the emperor, one important issue seems to have been the threat that such conflict presented to public order and civic harmony. In addition to pursuing the issue of Zeindelweber's Marian blasphemy, the magistrates also reprimanded Meckenloher, the accuser, for his role in bringing public attention to the conflict: '*Haubtman* Scheitlin says . . . he punished Meckenloher because he saw that Meckenloher had been to everyone and reported on the events.' He also told him that 'he was not doing the *Bürgermeister* any favours by bringing the events into disrepute'.[109] An entry in the council minutes records that as the trial began Meckenloher was again admonished to keep silent about Zeindelweber's comments.[110] This desire to stifle religious conflict also emerges clearly in records of trials conducted after the institution of biconfessionality,[111] but from the 1530s into the early seventeenth century the council showed little concern for Marian blasphemy *per se*. Indeed, as we have seen, the offence was omitted from the discipline ordinance issued in 1537 and from police ordinances of 1553 and 1580. It was not until the periods of Catholic hegemony during the Thirty Years War that the issue of Marian decorum once again emerged in cases of religious conflict.

In October 1630, a year and a half after the promulgation of Ferdinand II's *Restitutionsedikt*, Martin Haller, a 53-year-old weaver, was interrogated by Augsburg's magistrates.[112] He had, according to his accusers, disrupted a Catholic baptism and had failed to have his own children properly baptized. He was also found to be in possession of two scurrilous songs, one describing the emperor as a tyrant, the bishop of Augsburg as godless and the clergy as fools and a nest of vipers,[113] and a mock confession, purporting to record what those who converted from the Protestant to the Catholic faith were required to pray. Pressed, in his second interrogation, for details as to where he obtained the songs and confession Haller claimed that he did not know who had written them nor where they had come from (though the council subsequently identified

109 On Augsburg's *Hauptleute*, the officials who stood at the top of the city's military organization, see Kiessling, *Bürgerliche Gesellschaft*, p. 116.

110 StadtAA, Reichsstadt, Geh. Ratsbücher Nr. 2, fol. 315v.

111 Hoffmann, 'Konfessionell motivierte und gewandelte Konflikte'.

112 StadtAA, Reichsstadt, Strafamt, Urgichten Sammlung, K 212 (1630 August bis 1631 Dezember), Urgicht des Martin Haller, Burgers zu Augsburg.

113 On this case see Alexander J. Fisher, *Music and Religious Identity in Counter-Reformation Augsburg, 1580–1630*, St Andrews Studies in Reformation History (Aldershot, 2004), pp. 54–60 and 309–14.

Barbara Magenbuech as the source of the songs, which had been given to her by her soldier son). As punishment for his attacks on the Catholic establishment Haller was put in the stocks then expelled from the city.[114] The contents of the confession, a copy of which is preserved in Haller's *Urgicht*, offer an insight into what Augsburg's evangelicals saw as the distinguishing characteristics of Catholic piety: belief in the authority of the church, regardless of whether or not it was based on Scripture; the invocation of saints; belief in purgatory; the administration of seven sacraments, with communion in only one kind; and worship of the Virgin Mary. Article 5 reads: 'we believe in the holy Virgin Mary, [and] that she is to be prayed to more highly than the Son of God himself'. For local Protestants such as Haller Marian veneration was a misguided Catholic practice in which no evangelical would willingly engage.

Pilgrimage was one of the most public manifestations of Augsburg's renewed Marian cult, and a case from September 1631 suggests that it provoked the contempt of opponents of the Catholic regime. According to the magistrates, three butchers' sons, Hanns Tenn, Hanns Burckhart and Mattheus Kauffinger, had ridden to the Lechfeld the previous Sunday, where they had mocked churchgoers who were en route to the shrine of Maria Hilf.[115] They were accused of having cried out insulting names and made disgraceful gestures. They had also apparently shouted obscene words at four women, provoking the magistrates to ask whether they thought that the Catholic practice of pilgrimage involved fornication, and had nearly knocked over a priest. The accused denied all of this, claiming that their laughter and ridicule had been directed at one of their number, Mattheus Kauffinger, whose horse had lost a shoe. The *Strafbuch* suggests, however, that they failed to convince the presiding magistrates: they were imprisoned on bread and water for several days. Whatever the truth of the case, the young men's *Urgicht* testifies to the inflammatory potential of Marian pilgrimage

In August 1636 Abraham Raiffinger, a 36-year-old painter, was brought before the city's magistrates for his Marian blasphemy and disruptive behaviour.[116] The insults for which he was punished had taken place during two separate episodes, the first on the feast of Mary Magdalene (22 July) and the second on the feast of the Virgin Mary's Assumption (15 August). On 22 July Raiffinger had appeared at the house of the accusers, Georg Böhem and his wife, at about eight in the morning carrying a carved and painted bust-length image of a fool, decorated with bells. At the house a young woman from Lechhausen, who was described by Raiffinger as a 'peasant person', demanded to know what he was carrying. He asked her 'whether she was Catholic, and didn't recognize it'

[114] He was allowed to re-enter only in May 1632 after the arrival of Gustavus Adolphus' armies.

[115] StadtAA, Reichsstadt, Strafamt, Urgichtensammlung K212; and Strafamt, Nr. 105 (Strafbuch 1615–32), pp. 728.

[116] StadtAA, Reichsstadt, Strafamt, Urgichten, Nr. 322, August 1636 (Abraham Raiffinger, Kunstmaler).

and announced 'it is Our Lady'. Shocked, the girl retorted 'oh no, it is a wild, gawping fool, Our Lady looks more beautiful'. On the feast day of the Assumption, a major Catholic holiday, Raiffinger again appeared at the Böhem house, this time drunk. Various insults passed between Raiffinger and the Böhem couple, with Böhem's wife casting slurs on Raiffinger's marital status. In response Raiffinger thrust his buttocks in the wife's face and demanded 'she should kiss him there on account of Our Lady'. A brawl ensued, during which Böhem's wife made reference to the incident of 22 July, saying that Raiffinger was 'such a careless person that he even compared our dear Lady to a fool's head'.

When questioned, Raiffinger claimed that on the 15 August he had arrived at the Böhem house on business, and the wife had 'jumped out on him like a cat'. She and her husband had, he said, begun the fight. He denied having asked her to kiss his behind for the Virgin Mary's sake, but admitted the incident with the fool's head, claiming that the comment about the Virgin Mary had 'not been intended badly' and that 'the people themselves had merely laughed about it'. When questioned about the inspiration for his comments he told the magistrates that he had heard 'our dear Lady's beauty praised by a Catholic priest' in Memmingen, and that the priest had said, amongst other things, that 'she has such a beautiful forehead, like a sow's loo'. He was, however, unable to identify either the church in which the sermon occurred or the priest who had delivered it.

Raiffinger's case again demonstrates the extent to which Marian devotion was confessionalized in Augsburg. Raiffinger told the peasant girl from Lechhausen, whether in jest or as a deliberate insult, that she should recognize his fool's head as an image of Mary because she was Catholic. And the girl, Regina Mayrin, immediately labelled him as a Protestant on account of his comments. She told the magistrates that 'she . . . and her sister (as they were both Catholic) were frightened in their hearts by such horrifying speech and wondered, even though they were simple folk, that the Lutherans were allowed to speak so'. On hearing about this insult, and about Raiffinger's indecent behaviour on 15 August, the magistrates asked Raiffinger whether his preachers and his religion taught him 'such horrifying blasphemy and dishonour'. They also forced him to admit that the 'priest' in biconfessional Memmingen, whom he had taken for a Catholic on account of his surplice, might in fact have been a Protestant preacher. This blasphemy against the Virgin could only, in their view, have been perpetrated by a Protestant. Raiffinger's wife and child submitted supplications asking for him to be pardoned on account of his 'fitting veneration of all the saints', in particular of the Virgin Mary, but the magistrates obviously regarded this as mere subterfuge. They described Raiffinger as a 'tremendous enemy of Mary' [ein gwaltiger Mariaefeindt] and stated that his description of a 'shameful fool's image' as Our Lady could not be taken as a joke but must be 'exemplarily punished' because otherwise similar scandals and dishonours would be perpetrated by other careless people. After a public declaration of his crimes against the Virgin he was placed in the stocks and was then expelled from the city.

Blasphemy had always been a matter of concern for magistrates, whether Protestant or Catholic. If blasphemers were allowed to impugn God's honour the whole community might suffer divine punishment.[117] Early modern authorities also, of course, perceived a close relationship between religious and social conformity, and all of the Augsburg blasphemers discussed above threatened civic order while they defied confessional norms. While it is likely that in biconfessional Augsburg Marian blasphemy continued throughout the sixteenth century, it is impossible to be sure since it reached the attention of the magistrates only before the Reformation and in the immediate aftermath of the Edict of Restitution (1629). The cases that are recorded in the *Urgichten* indicate a shift in the significance of Marian blasphemy over the course of this period. There was, as we have seen, a clear confessional element in Zeindelweber's 1529 confrontation with Meckenloher, but during his interrogation Zeindelweber acknowledged that if the accusations against him were proved he deserved death. He also maintained that his words had been spoken in anger, an assertion that was likely to win him some leniency.[118] In 1629 Raiffinger, by contrast, said merely that his comments about the Virgin had been intended as a joke. His trial and that of the three Protestant butchers who had mocked Marian pilgrims suggest that by the 1630s Marian devotion had become an object of ridicule for evangelical artisans.

In Augsburg from the second half of the sixteenth century the many visible manifestations of the Virgin's renewed cult – images, pilgrimages and feast days – made her into a powerful symbol of Catholic confessional identity. This Catholic appropriation left no space for Nuremberg's type of revalued Virgin: while Mary was a champion of the Catholic cause, local evangelicals could not comfortably assimilate her into their devotional lives. As one of the most obvious symbols of Catholic devotion Mary became, for some evangelicals such as Raiffinger, an object of contempt. Of course, one should be wary of drawing too firm conclusions on the basis of a limited number of cases. As has been frequently pointed out in recent literature, for the majority of ordinary people the process of confessional indoctrination was a very slow one. Certainly not every citizen had such a strong sense of Mary's confessional connotations as these evangelical troublemakers and the Catholic magistrates who interrogated them. Bernd Roeck's study of baptism books indicates, for example, that even in the 1630s a significant proportion (11.4 per cent) of the girls baptized at the Barfüßerkirche, Augsburg's most frequented evangelical church, were still

117 Dülmen, 'Wider die Ehre Gottes', p. 36.
118 Schwerhoff, 'Fehltritt oder Provokation?', p. 413.

named Maria. Unlike Calvin, Augsburg's reformers made no attempt to prevent children from being given traditional saints' names, but given its Catholic connotations, Maria might well have fallen from favour with Protestant parents. The name did indeed remain more popular amongst Catholics: it was given to 18.1 per cent of girls baptized in the Catholic cathedral in 1632 and 1648. We must, of course, bear in mind that for all parents family traditions might well outweigh confessional concerns when choosing names (especially, Roeck suggests, girls' names).[119] But the fact that generations of local Protestants continued to favour the name Maria does warn us against assuming that the relationship between religious rhetoric and day-to-day reality was entirely clear cut.

THE SIGNIFICANCE OF CONFESSIONAL CONFLICT

Our ability to access popular perceptions of the Virgin is inevitably limited by the availability of relevant source material. Nuremberg's 1560–1 visitation records provide valuable information about popular practice in the city's rural hinterland, but there was no equivalent evangelical church visitation in Augsburg. Conversely, the Augsburg interrogation records discussed above have no counterpart in Nuremberg. There all that survive are brief summaries of criminal cases drawn up for the benefit of the council in the *Achtbücher*, and accounts of executions entered into the *Halsgerichtsbücher*. These compendiums are concerned almost exclusively with robbery and violence, and it seems that religious discord does not feature at all.[120] It is therefore difficult to compare artisans' attitudes in the two cities. However, given what we know of the survival of Marian imagery, liturgy and blasphemy legislation in Nuremberg it is hard to conceive of local artisans showing as much disrespect for the Mother of God as Zeindelweber, Haller, the butchers' sons and Raiffinger did in Augsburg. Indeed when the Marian *Zechtafel* [guild panel] discussed in chapter 2 (figure 18) was renovated by members of Nuremberg's metalworkers' guild in 1620 they added representatives of their profession kneeling at Mary's feet. It seems that in Nuremberg local evangelicals assimilated the Marian legacy left to them by the pre-Reformation church much more successfully than in Augsburg. In Augsburg the immediate juxtaposition of Protestant and Catholic led to what Marc Forster has described as a 'mania for differentiation', and the polarization of opinion on Mary was one manifestation of this.[121] The Catholic appropriation of her cult alienated local Protestants from all things Marian.

[119] Roeck, *Eine Stadt in Krieg und Frieden*, pp. 858–64.

[120] I have sampled the earliest surviving *Achtbuch*, which covers the period 1578–81, and the *Halsgerichtsbuch* from 1487–1558. StaatsAN, Rep. 52b, Nürnberger Amts- und Standbücher Nr. 209 and Nr. 221. See Hampe, *Die Nürnberger Malefizbücher*.

[121] Marc Forster, *The Counter-Reformation in the Villages: religion and reform in the bishopric of Speyer, 1560–1720* (Ithaca and London, 1992), p. 225.

A comparison of Mary's status and role in these two evangelical churches demonstrates the extent to which Protestant piety was shaped not only by theological precept but also by local environment. During the second half of the sixteenth century Protestants in both cities professed their loyalty to the Augsburg Confession.[122] Yet in one Mary remained an important part of visual and devotional culture, while in the other she was almost entirely rejected. In the early stages of the Reformation this difference was due to the influence of Zwinglian and Reformed preaching in Augsburg, but after 1555 Marian piety responded to external forces, in particular to the cultural polemic of the Counter-Reformation. The final section of this chapter will suggest that Lutheran worship also inflected in response to the presence of later, more radical Protestant creeds, in particular Calvinism. Whereas exposure to Counter-Reformation Catholicism encouraged the rejection of Mary, during the Second Reformation Lutherans confronted by Calvinist invective sometimes went to the opposite extreme, manifesting an attachment to Marian images and devotions that was even stronger than that seen in places such as Nuremberg and Lübeck.

Calvinism was established within the Holy Roman Empire largely by princely fiat. During the second half of the sixteenth century there were very few urban Reformations, such as those that had brought Lutheranism and Zwinglianism into many areas during the 1520s and 1530s. The introduction of Calvinism was rarely supported by popular opinion, though free presbyteries and synods similar to those found in France and the Netherlands did develop in the duchies of Jülich-Cleves and in East Friesland (especially at Emden), while the imperial free city of Bremen adopted the Reformed faith in 1581. It was, though, the conversion of Elector Frederick III of the Palatinate in around 1560 that first established Calvinism in Germany. Although the Electorate was twice temporarily returned to Lutheranism in 1576–83 and 1583–1610, Heidelberg nonetheless emerged as the political and theological focus of the Reformed faith within the Empire, the German Geneva. The Rhine-Palatinate remained key until the defeat of Elector Frederick V at the Battle of the White Mountain in 1620. Other important princely conversions included Johann VI of Nassau-Dillenburg (1578), Johann Georg of Anhalt (1596), Moritz of Hesse-Kassel (1605), Simon VI of Lippe-Detmold (1605) and Johann Sigismund of Brandenburg (1613).[123] By 1620 there were twenty-eight Calvinist states within the Empire. Although, as Henry Cohn points out, Reformed territories occupied only a small proportion of the

[122] On Nuremberg and the Augsburg Confession see Pfeiffer, 'Nürnberg und das Augsburger Bekenntnis 1530–1561'.

[123] For a complete list see J. F. Gerhard Goeters, 'Genesis, Formen und Hauptthemen des reformierten Bekenntnisses in Deutschland: eine Übersicht', in *Die reformierte Konfessionalisierung in Deutschland – das Problem der 'zweiten Reformation'*, ed. H. Schilling (Gütersloh, 1986).

Empire's total land mass, from a Lutheran perspective the advance of Calvinism was undoubtedly alarming.[124] Indeed electoral Saxony, the heartland of the Lutheran Reformation, itself fell under the influence of crypto-Calvinists from 1571 to 1574, and moved again towards Calvinism during the reign of Elector Christian I (1586–91), though without ever firmly embracing it.

As a primarily princely Reformation, Germany's so-called 'Second Reformation' does not occupy a central place in this study. Nonetheless, a number of preliminary remarks can and should be made concerning the role of Marian images and liturgy in Lutheran resistance to Reformed Protestantism. The adoption of Calvinism entailed, of course, certain shifts in doctrine, above all with regard to the Eucharist. It also required, crucially, the reform of Christian life. Germany's Calvinist theologians were convinced of the need to eliminate what they perceived to be old papal superstitions, which had been left untouched by the Lutheran Reformation: the exorcism rite in baptism; the presence of crucifixes and images; and the use of a church calendar that still contained feast days of the Virgin and other saints. These rituals and symbols confused simple Christians, blurring the boundary between Catholicism and Protestantism and providing a means by which the papists might lure people back to the false religion. Christoph Pezel's Nassau confession of 1578, for example, asserted the need for a continuation of the Wittenberg Reformation by means of a further 'Reformation', 'emendation' or 'improvement'. The challenge of the Counter-Reformation, in particular the activities of the Jesuits, necessitated, it argued, the abolition of all superstitious ceremonies.[125] The institution of Calvinism therefore entailed the purging of traditional feast days and liturgy as well as extensive iconoclasm.[126] Theodosius Fabricius of Göttingen recorded in his *Historia Certaminis Sacramentarii* (Magdeburg, 1593) that when Heidelberg was reformed in 1563 the Calvinists removed pictures from churches, abolished auricular confession, deleted exorcism from the baptism ceremony, eliminated numerous festivals and discarded altars and baptismal fonts. Johann Olearius of Halle, a Lutheran who witnessed the introduction of Calvinism in Anhalt, likewise commented on the elimination of altars, candles, vestments and the like.[127]

The Lutheran attachment to images and ceremonies grew stronger as a result of such attacks. Luther himself had seen the preservation of ecclesiastical imagery and music as one way to distinguish his church from those of more

[124] Henry J. Cohn, 'The territorial princes in Germany's Second Reformation, 1559–1622', in *International Calvinism, 1541–1715*, ed. Menna Prestwich (Oxford, 1985), p. 138 and map 2.

[125] Carl Andresen and Adolf Martin Ritter, eds, *Handbuch der Dogmen- und Theologiegeschichte*, 3 vols. 2nd edn (Göttingen 1998–9), vol. 2, p. 295.

[126] On Brandenburg see Nischan, *Prince, People, and Confession*, ch. 5.

[127] Bodo Nischan, *Lutherans and Calvinists in the Age of Confessionalization* (Aldershot, 1999), p. 146.

radical reformers, writing in his preface to the 1524 Wittenberg hymn book: 'Nor am I of the opinion that the Gospel should destroy and blight all the arts, as some of the pseudo-religious [abergeystlichen] claim. But I would like to see all the arts, especially music, used in the service of Him who gave and made them.'[128] By 1525, having seen the destruction wrought by 'fanatics' before and during the peasants' revolt, Luther had adopted an even more conservative attitude towards imagery. As Joseph Koerner argues, images became 'a badge of evangelical victory'. Their presence in churches 'signalled the return to order'. Religious images could be a sign of right belief, a way of marking boundaries between Lutherans and 'Sacramentarians'.[129] For Lutheran churches exposed to the threat of Calvinism the need to defend the ecclesiastical arts took on a new urgency. The preface to the church order produced for the duchy of Prussia in 1568, for example, marks out the Lutheran position from that of the Calvinists, saying that the authors could not agree with 'the wretched Calvinists and enthusiasts, who themselves think that one cannot be evangelical if one does not attack all paintings, pull down all images, abolish all ceremonies and rudely, immodestly, without discipline and order let everything become confused like senseless cattle'.[130] As Bodo Nischan has demonstrated, by the late Reformation liturgy and ritual had become 'marks of confessional identity' for Lutherans confronted by Reformed Protestantism.[131] In Brandenburg, for example, 'liturgical traditionalism' was seen as a mark of genuine Lutheranism in the face of the growth of crypto-Calvinist and Calvinist sentiment during the 1570s. Here adherents of the Augsburg Confession argued that Calvinists would be kept at bay by the retention of old ceremonies.[132]

In response to Calvinist iconoclasm, Lutheran theologians reworked traditional defences of images. Jacob Heilbrunner, for example, in his 1595 refutation of Calvinist teaching, argued that images should have been allowed to remain in the churches of the Palatinate. He, like Luther, denied images' agency: 'an idol is nothing in the world because of itself it can do no damage'. Where the word of God was correctly preached images would do no harm. He also criticized the Calvinists' division of the first commandment of the Decalogue into two, which emphasized the prohibition on images by making it into a separate injunction, and pointed out that images were not prohibited in the Gospel.[133]

128 Quoted in Pelikan, ed., *Luther's Works*, vol. 53, p. 316. *WA*, vol. 35, p. 475.

129 Strecker, 'Bilderstreit, Konfessionalisierung und Repräsentation', pp. 248–9. See also Koerner, *The Reformation of the Image*, p. 159 and on later Lutheran attitudes to images Thomas Kaufmann, 'Die Bilderfrage im frühneuzeitlichen Luthertum', in *Macht und Ohnmacht der Bilder*, ed. Blickle *et al.*

130 Sehling, ed., *Die evangelischen Kirchenordnungen*, vol. 4, p. 73.

131 Nischan, *Lutherans and Calvinists*, p. 144.

132 Nischan, *Prince, People, and Confession*, pp. 3, 48.

133 Jacob Heilbrunner, *Synopsis Doctrinae Calvinianae*, vol. 2: *Widerholte Erzehlung der Caluinischen Irrthumb* (Laugingen, 1595), pp. 202, 360.

In Brandenburg, where Lutheranism was well established before the arrival of Calvinism, a Lutheran provost, Simon Gedicke, dedicated a detailed defence of images and altars to Margrave Johann Georg.[134] Gedicke's pleas on behalf of images had no effect however: in 1615, acting as regent for Johann Sigismund, Johann Georg ordered the removal of all artwork and liturgical paraphernalia from Berlin Cathedral. At this point the Lutheran defence of images moved from the realm of theory to that of practice: the stripping of the cathedral provoked a major riot in Berlin itself, and there was similar if less violent resistance to iconoclasm in other Markish towns.[135] At the level of the political elite, opposition to the imposition of Calvinism was often a product of the desire to prevent the consolidation of princely authority,[136] but for the majority of the population the threat that the new confession posed to images and traditional rites was undoubtedly key. Calvinism had a greater impact on popular religion than any other confession, and events such as the 1615 riot in Berlin testify to the extent of Lutheran attachment to images and liturgy.[137] Whether they were, as the Calvinists supposed, still mired in superstition, or whether they had successfully reconciled elements of pre-Reformation practice with evangelical belief, Lutherans were prepared to defend what they saw as an essential part of their devotional lives.

Nischan is undoubtedly correct to argue that for both Lutherans and Calvinists the key 'litmus test of confessional loyalty' was the Lord's Supper and the manner in which it was celebrated.[138] But Mary also played a role in the delineation of confessional boundaries. Calvin himself had some positive things to say about Mary: he defended her perpetual virginity and, like Luther and Zwingli, described her as a model of belief. But any invocation of her would, he believed, detract from the honour due to God and to Christ. Commenting on John 2:4, Calvin explained Jesus' reasons for calling Mary 'woman' and not 'mother' at Cana: 'Christ spoke thus to his mother . . . so that the false honour of the mother would not obscure his divine fame.' He argued that through giving Mary names such as 'Queen of Heaven', 'hope', 'life', 'salvation of the world' Catholics robbed Christ of the honour due to him.[139] Mary's devotional role was also circumscribed by the Calvinist hatred of anything that smacked of idolatry,

[134] Simon Gedicke, *Von Bildern und Altarn / In den Evangelischen Kirchen Augspurgischer Confession* (Magdeburg, 1597). See also Simon Gedicke, *Calviniana Religio oder Calvinisterey* (Leipzig, 1615), pp. 496–521.

[135] Nischan, *Prince, People, and Confession*, pp. 185–93.

[136] Cohn, 'The territorial princes', 156–7; Schilling, *Religion, Political Culture and the Emergence of Early Modern Society*, pp. 285–8.

[137] Richard van Dülmen, 'Volksfrömmigkeit und konfessionelles Christentum im 16. und 17. Jahrhundert', in *Volksreligiosität in der modernen Sozialgeschichte*, ed. Wolfgang Schieder, *Geschichte und Gesellschaft* 11, special issue (Göttingen, 1986).

[138] Nischan, *Lutherans and Calvinists*, p. 157.

[139] Tappolet, ed., *Das Marienlob der Reformatoren*, p. 195; Delius, *Geschichte der Marienverehrung*, pp. 233–4.

a sin that was much more broadly defined in this church than in the Lutheran. According to the 1563 Heidelberg Catechism, which was widely adopted both in Germany and abroad, to commit idolatry was 'to imagine or possess something in which to put one's trust in place of or beside the one true God who has revealed himself in his Word'.[140] Images, especially those of the Virgin Mary, could do nothing but harm, distracting Christians from their proper focus on God and on his Word. Martin Füssel, a Reformed superintendent from Anhalt, told Brandenburg's Lutherans, for example, that 'paintings of the Virgin Mary are like papal concubines or adulterer's whores': they 'mislead and seduce the common man' and lead him to false worship.[141]

As MacCulloch has argued, from the 1520s onwards mainstream evangelicals defended certain key Marian doctrines, for example her perpetual virginity, in order to distance themselves from the teachings of more radical Protestant sects.[142] During the late sixteenth century Marian imagery, rather than Marian doctrine, seems to have come to serve a similar purpose, this time distinguishing not mainstream reformers from Anabaptists and the like but Lutherans from Calvinists. As Calvinists attacked Mary, so Lutherans intensified their defence of her. Several incidents that occurred in Danzig, a German community beyond the imperial frontier where Calvinism grew rapidly during the final decades of the sixteenth century, indicate the significance that Mary might take on for Lutherans under threat.[143] In the winter of 1589–90 a preacher at the church of St Bartholomew came into conflict with the Lutheran church fathers because he preached 'often and hard' against images. This conflict reached a climax when the Lutheran church fathers, in a final bid to get rid of this Calvinist interloper, placed a statue of the Virgin Mary on the high altar. Driven to despair, the preacher told the council that he could no longer stand such behaviour and wished to retire to another quieter parish (which he was permitted to do).[144] It is possible, at least, that the immediate threat of Calvinism even encouraged some Lutherans to maintain or revive traditions that had been abandoned elsewhere. In Danzig we know, for example, that the Lutheran clergy at St Marien kept the high altar, which showed the Coronation of the Virgin, open and richly illuminated with candles on feast days during the period of Calvinist dominance.[145]

[140] Translated in full in David Freedberg, *Iconoclasm and Painting in the Revolt of the Netherlands, 1566–1609*, Outstanding Theses in Fine Arts from British Universities (New York, 1988). For a discussion of the catechism see Goeters, 'Genesis, Formen und Hauptthemen', pp. 52–6.

[141] Quoted in Nischan, *Prince, People, and Confession*, p. 146.

[142] MacCulloch, *Reformation*, pp. 613–14.

[143] On Danzig see Michael G. Müller, 'Zur Frage der zweiten Reformation in Danzig, Elbig und Thorn', in *Die reformierte Konfessionalisierung in Deutschland*, ed. H. Schilling.

[144] Christoph Hartknoch, *Preussische Kirchen-Historia* (Frankfurt am Main and Leipzig, 1686), pp. 756–7.

[145] Katarzyna Cieslak, 'Die "zweite Reformation" in Danzig und die Kirchenkunst', in *Historische Bildkunde: Probleme – Wege – Beispiele*, ed. B. Tolkenmitt and R. Wohlfeil, *Zeitschrift für historische Forschung*, supplementary volume 12 (Berlin, 1991), p. 167.

These Danzig cases provide particularly compelling evidence of Lutherans' attachment to Marian images, but it seems likely that there were similar conflicts in other areas where Calvinists proselytized against Lutheran idolatry. In Brandenburg the Lutheran provost Simon Gedicke defended the presence of images of Christ, the Virgin and the Apostles in churches, saying that they were intended not as true portraits but as 'exemplars . . . and a commemoration of the stories of Christ, Mary and the Apostles'.[146] Images of the Virgin were probably amongst those removed from Berlin Cathedral in 1615 and transferred to the elector's palace chapel where Johann Sigismund's wife, Anna, continued to worship according to the Lutheran rite.[147] In territorial cities such as Amberg (Upper Palatinate) and Lemgo (Lippe), where Lutheran magistrates held out against the imposition of a court-sponsored Calvinist Reformation, it is possible that Marian images were protected in similar ways. In Amberg, for example, a beautiful image of the Virgin Mary was amongst the treasures that the city council removed from the parish church of St Martin for safekeeping in the late sixteenth century. This image was returned to the church, along with the other treasures, when the Catholic cult was restored in 1621.[148] The Palatinate's initial Lutheran Reformation had been less image-friendly than Brandenburg's, but some Marian images certainly remained in place and survived at least the first outbreaks of Calvinist iconoclasm during the reign of Friedrich III (1559–76).[149] A church visitation sent out by the Lutheran elector Ludwig VI in 1579 found, for example, a *Gnadenbild* showing Mary surrounded by rays of sun in Pappenberg (which was eventually burned by Calvinist enthusiasts in the 1610s) and other Marian images in Lintach near Amberg and Kastl near Kemnath.[150]

The different attitudes towards Marian images and devotion that have been outlined in chapters 2 and 3 of course owed a good deal to the theological divisions within Protestantism. Nuremberg was a staunchly Lutheran city, and its council and citizens accordingly adopted a very moderate stance with regard to images and liturgy. Augsburg was heavily influenced by Zwinglianism, and was therefore much less tolerant of such remnants of pre-Reformation devotion. The diversity within Lutheran practice revealed by comparing Nuremberg and Augsburg in the decades after 1555 can only, however, be explained by

[146] Gedicke, *Calviniana Religio*, p. 497.

[147] Nischan, *Prince, People, and Confession*, p. 148.

[148] Feliz Mader, *Stadt Amberg*, Die Kunstdenkmäler des Königreichs Bayern 2: Regierungsbezirk Oberpfalz und Regensburg 16 (Munich, 1909), pp. 64ff. On Amberg see also Arno Herzig, *Der Zwang zum wahren Glauben: Rekatholisierung vom 16. bis zum 18. Jahrhundert* (Göttingen, 2000), p. 108.

[149] H. Rott, 'Kirchen- und Bildersturm bei der Einführung der Reformation in der Pfalz', *Neues Archiv für die Geschichte der Stadt Heidelberg und der rheinischen Pfalz* 6, no. 4 (1905).

[150] J. B. Götz, *Die religiösen Wirren in der Oberpfalz von 1576 bis 1620*, Reformationsgeschichtliche Studien und Texte 66 (Münster in Westfalen, 1937), pp. 55–6, 346.

reference to local circumstance. By the late sixteenth century Lutherans across the German-speaking world were involved in what Tilemann Hesshusen described as a two-front war with Jesuits and Calvinists.[151] As Nischan has shown, in this war externals counted. Lutherans sought to define and distinguish themselves both from the Roman Church and from other Protestant churches through their use of liturgy and images. In cities such as Nuremberg and Lübeck, where adherents of the Augsburg Confession were never under immediate threat from militant Counter-Reformation Catholicism, Marian images and feast days could be comfortably assimilated into post-Reformation devotional life. They were retained, and in northern Germany even continued to be produced, but they were stripped of their idolatrous associations. Their continued presence helped ease the transition from the old faith to the new and demonstrated for the benefit of outside observers the moderate nature of these cities' reformations. The evidence from Danzig suggests that the radicalism of the Calvinist reformers sometimes made Lutherans even more conservative, leading them to honour Marian images with candles in a way that would have been unacceptable in Nuremberg. In Augsburg, by contrast, despite the relatively secure legal status of the Augsburg Confession there was an ever-present threat of recatholicization. Because of the city's biconfessional status, attitudes towards the Virgin were highly polarized. Mary was thoroughly appropriated by Augsburg's militant Catholics, as we shall see in chapter 4, and by the era of the Thirty Years War she had become a marker, a litmus test for confessional allegiance. In this religiously divided city Mary was so closely identified with the Catholic cause that there was no space left for Nuremberg's type of revalued Lutheran Virgin.

151 Nischan, *Lutherans and Calvinists*, p. 145.

4. *The Counter-Reformation cult*

In his 1577 text, *De Maria Virgine incomparabili*, Peter Canisius, Germany's leading Jesuit, wrote that Catholics should 'revere and imitate the most sacred Virgin at home and in public', in defiance of those who abused 'the most excellent mother of the Lord' and fabricated lies about her.[1] For post-Tridentine Catholics the veneration of saints was a valuable devotional exercise in itself. The twenty-fifth session of the Council of Trent (3–4 December 1563) affirmed its importance, stating that 'it is a good and beneficial thing to invoke [the saints] and to have recourse to their prayers and helpful assistance to obtain blessings from God'.[2] In areas where Catholic reformers were confronted by purified Protestant piety the promotion of saints' cults also, however, served a polemical purpose. Canisius' 800-page defence of Catholic teaching on Mary was part of a larger project, never completed, dedicated to refuting the works of the gnesio-Lutheran Flaccius Illyricus and his followers.[3] Canisius, who was active in Germany and Austria for most of his life, was acutely aware of the perilous state of Catholicism within the Empire, and of the need to halt the advance of evangelical teaching. Mary's cult provided, it seemed, an antidote to Protestantism, an opportunity to strengthen Catholic identity. Mary was, of course, a key symbol of the universal post-Tridentine church, but her cult was also important because it had, as this chapter will demonstrate, strong local resonances. In Augsburg, for example, the renewal of Marian liturgy and the reintroduction of Marian images served both to re-establish the city's connection with its own pre-Reformation past and to bind its Catholic cult to a wider Counter-Reformation present, embodied in particular by the state-sponsored piety of the nearby Bavarian court. The revival of Marian pilgrimage and the popularity of Marian sodalities in Augsburg and elsewhere in southern Germany suggest that in Mary the Jesuits had chosen the right weapon for

[1] Canisius, *De Maria Virgine incomparabili*, preface.
[2] Norman P. Tanner, ed., *Decrees of the Ecumenical Councils*, 2 vols. (Washington, DC, 1990), vol. 2, p. 774.
[3] John W. O'Malley, *The First Jesuits* (Cambridge, MA, 1993), p. 270.

their campaign of reconquest. Mary became, as Canisius wished, an emblem of Catholic allegiance, a rallying point for the Catholic cause.

THE RENEWAL OF MARIAN PIETY IN A BICONFESSIONAL CITY

Augsburg's confessional history offers an ideal opportunity to explore the process of Catholic renewal. As we saw in chapter 3, by the end of 1537 the city's religious life had been thoroughly purified at the behest of Zwinglian-influenced reformers. Liturgy had been simplified, traditional saints' festivals had been eliminated and local churches had been stripped of their altars and images. The majority of the city's population was, it seems, sympathetic towards the Reformation cause, and little attempt was made to perpetuate Catholic practices. When the Catholic cult was forcibly restored in 1548 its chief proponents were therefore faced with a difficult task. Although a number of the city's wealthy patricians – in particular members of the Fugger family – had remained loyal, Catholicism otherwise enjoyed little support. In 1548, for example, the papal nuncio reported that only three or four women had attended a Sunday mass celebrated in the cathedral and that only about twenty people had assembled to hear one of the bishop's sermons.[4]

Otto Truchseß von Waldburg, the zealous reforming bishop who had succeeded the moderate Christoph von Stadion in 1543, was determined to rectify this situation.[5] In 1559 he secured the appointment of a new cathedral preacher, Peter Canisius. Canisius had already had more than a decade's experience of strengthening the Catholic Church in Upper Germany, and between 1559 and 1567 through his sermons, his literary works and his spectacular individual conversion successes he instilled a new sense of self-confidence amongst Augsburg's Catholics.[6] Thanks to the efforts of Canisius and subsequent reformers the proportion of Catholics rose from around 10 per cent of Augsburg's population in the 1560s to around 27 per cent at the beginning of the Thirty Years War. It is important to bear in mind that this campaign of recatholicization was dependent on persuasion, not coercion. Augsburg was, of course, officially biconfessional: Catholic leaders could not *enforce* religious conformity as they could, for example, in Bavaria. At least until 1629 the city council itself was resolutely neutral in its religious policies. It followed what one author has described

[4] Rasmussen, 'Bildersturm und Restauration', p. 113 n. 102. For a report on Otto's preaching activity see *Chroniken*, vol. 33, pp. 55–7.

[5] On Otto's reforming activity see F. Zoepfl, 'Die Durchführung des Tridentinums im Bistum Augsburg', in *Das Weltkonzil von Trient: sein Werden und Wirken*, ed. Georg Schreiber (Freiburg, 1951), pp. 135–51.

[6] Peter Rummel, 'Petrus Canisius und Otto Kardinal Truchsess von Waldburg', in *Petrus Canisius – Reformer der Kirche. Festschrift zum 400. Todestag des zweiten Apostels Deutschlands*, ed. Julius Oswald and Peter Rummel, *JbVAB* 30 (Augsburg, 1996), 52–5.

as the 'politics of pacification', attempting to treat Protestant and Catholic citizens alike and urging moderation on local preachers.[7] Catholic leaders therefore needed to rely on the carrot rather than the stick in their attempts to recover lost souls.

In this campaign of persuasion Mary played an important role. Both Bishop Otto Truchseß and Canisius were themselves deeply devoted to Mary. Truchseß's favourite pilgrimage was to Loreto near Ancona on Italy's Adriatic coast. The Holy House in which Mary had received Gabriel's greeting had, according to legend, been carried by angels from Palestine via Dalmatia to Loreto in the 1290s. Truchseß visited this shrine repeatedly, always bearing costly gifts for the 'Virgo Lauretana', and in 1554 he had a chapel built there in Mary's honour.[8] Canisius also visited Loreto several times.[9] He was probably responsible for the first German printing of the Litany of Loreto, a series of forty-nine invocations of the Virgin Mary, in Dillingen in 1558, and promoted its use throughout his career.[10] In 1561 Otto had the Loretan Litany printed 'for the use and convenience of his diocese', and it was also included in his *Preces ecclesiae in processionibus* printed by Sebald Mayer in Dillingen in 1566.[11] In 1562 Truchseß laid the foundation stone for the first Jesuit church in Rome, Santa Maria Annunciata, and he subsequently became protector of the Jesuits' Marian congregation in that city.[12] In 1571 he induced the pope to approve the wider use of the Marian Office in German translation, a version of which Canisius had appended to his *Hortulus animae. Der seelen Garten*, published in Dillingen in 1563. Truchseß also, in 1571, had another version of the vernacular Office published in Dillingen. In the following year he helped Canisius to obtain certain references for his great work, *De Maria Virgine incomparabile*.[13] This work was the culmination of Canisius' Mariology, and has been described as 'the classic defence of the whole of Catholic teaching on Mary against Protestantism'.[14]

In Augsburg Truchseß, Canisius and their fellow Catholic reformers were presented with a *tabula rasa* with regard to Marian devotion. At the behest of

[7] Hoffmann, 'Konfessionell motivierte und gewandelte Konflikte', p. 120.

[8] F. Zoepfl, *Das Bistum Augsburg und seine Bischöfe im Reformationsjahrhundert* (Augsburg, 1969), pp. 277–8.

[9] Walter Pötzl, 'Loreto in Bayern', *Jahrbuch für Volkskunde* 2 (1979), 196.

[10] Fisher, *Music and Religious Identity*, pp. 258–9. On the Loreto Litany see Graef, *Mary*, vol. 1, p. 232 and Walter Pötzl, *Loreto – Madonna und Heiliges Haus: die Wallfahrt auf dem Kobel. Ein Beitrag zur europäischen Kult- und Kulturgeschichte*, Beiträge zur Heimatkunde des Landkreises Augsburg 15 (Augsburg, 2000), p. 76.

[11] Pötzl, 'Loreto in Bayern', 196.

[12] Theodor Rolle, 'Die Anfänge der marianischen Kongregationen in Augsburg', *JbVAB* 23 (1989), 29.

[13] Zoepfl, *Das Bistum Augsburg*, p. 408.

[14] Peter Canisius, *Maria, die unvergleichliche Jungfrau und hochheilige Gottesgebärerin*, trans. Carl Telch (Warnsdorf, 1933), p. 17.

the Protestants, Marian festivals had been abolished, images of the Virgin had been concealed or destroyed and confraternities dedicated to her had been disbanded. After 1548 the cult of the Virgin was gradually re-established, thanks to the efforts of Truchseß and subsequent bishops, of Canisius and his fellow Jesuits and of lay patrons, in particular the Fuggers.[15] This was achieved partly, as we shall see, by renewing traditional expressions of devotion such as the pre-Reformation cycle of Marian feast days. Yet, in Augsburg, to a greater extent than in some other parts of Germany, the Marian piety that flourished during the later sixteenth and seventeenth centuries also served a new, polemical purpose. In a biconfessional context public processions invoking the Virgin, pilgrimage shrines that reproduced Italian cults, sodalities whose members swore to defend Mary's honour, and altarpieces that represented her as Augsburg's protectress necessarily constituted a challenge to Protestant devotional culture. While the humble *Hausmutter* described in Luther's writings could be reconciled with Protestant piety, the powerful intercessor celebrated in post-Tridentine Augsburg was entirely alien to evangelical sensibilities. Moreover, in Augsburg Marian piety had political connotations, since it reflected the state-sponsored Marianism of the nearby Bavarian court. Devotion to the Virgin therefore became a means of displaying confessional allegiance, a boundary marker between the two confessions.

The reintroduction of the traditional cycle of Marian feast days provided the structural framework for the revival of Marian devotion within Augsburg's Catholic churches. The liturgical calendar of the new missal commissioned by Otto Truchseß in 1555 mandated the observance of all seven Marian festivals, as well as of those honouring Mary's husband, Joseph, and father, Joachim.[16] The 1555 missal also contained a number of special masses that could be celebrated in honour of Mary: 'De sancta marie ad niues'; 'De septem gaudiis beate marie virginis'; 'De septem doloribus/seu compassione beatissime marie virginis'; 'De pietate beate marie virginis' and 'De tota geneologica beatissime anne matris marie'. Truchseß's liturgical calendar was soon modified, however. It was during this period that the Roman Church began its attempts to standardize Catholic liturgy and to reform the medieval calendar by suppressing many of the feasts that had proliferated unchecked during previous centuries.[17] Although rites that were more than two hundred years old, such as Augsburg's, were exempted from the Council of Trent's mandate concerning the universal

[15] On Canisius' Marian preaching in Augsburg see Peter Canisius, *Beati Petri Canisii, Societatis Iesu, epistulae et acta*, ed. Otto Braunsberger, 8 vols. (Freiburg im Breisgau, 1896–1923), vol. 2, p. 839.

[16] ABA, Fr. 34; Hoeynck, *Geschichte der kirchlichen Liturgie*, pp. 337–9.

[17] J. Harper, *The Forms and Orders of Western Liturgy from the Tenth to the Eighteenth Century: a historical introduction and guide for students and musicians* (Oxford, 1991), pp. 156–7.

adoption of the Roman pattern of liturgical observance, the city's post-Tridentine calendar nonetheless reflected the Catholic reformers' concerns.[18] The synod that Truchseß summoned to Dillingen in 1567 after his return from Trent produced a calendar that omitted, for example, the festivals of Mary's Visitation, Presentation and Conception and of Joseph and Joachim. The Ritual printed in Dillingen in 1580 also omitted the feast day of Mary's mother, Anne, which was reinstated only in the early 1620s when it was prescribed by Pope Gregory XV.[19]

The dialogue between the desire for universal liturgical reform and local attachment to traditional observances was an ongoing one, in Augsburg as elsewhere. In 1597 Bishop Johann Otto von Gemmingen promulgated a decision to compel the adoption of the Roman rite, though it was only under his successor, Heinrich von Knöringen, that real progress was made towards this goal.[20] Knöringen was a former student of the Jesuit university in Dillingen and an ardent advocate of the Counter-Reformation, and his 1610 synod insisted on the full implementation of the Roman rite, though Augsburg's *Sanctorale* remained that proclaimed in 1567.[21] Heinrich was reluctant, at this stage, to eliminate local saints such as Ulrich and Afra. He did, however, actively promote the celebration of feast days that were of particular significance to the Counter-Reformation church.[22] In 1605 Heinrich issued a decree that expanded the observance of the feasts of the Virgin Mary, the Guardian Angels and St Michael. This decree emphasized the importance of the Virgin's intercession in troubled times, and stated the bishop's desire that 'by the ancient example of the Catholic Church and by the customs of our ancestors the festal days of the Virgin Mary be observed with more ardent piety, reverence and sanctity . . .' Mary's Nativity, in particular, should be observed with greater solemnity. The militant tone of this document is unmistakable: St Michael the Archangel is described, for example, as the 'commander designated by God of the church militant, and strongest defender of the Roman Empire'.[23] In September 1629 Heinrich mandated the celebration of the feast of the Conception of the Virgin throughout his diocese, in a context that made the political overtones of Mary's cult even more explicit. This feast had been reinstated in the aftermath of the Edict of Restitution at the behest of Emperor Ferdinand II, who wished to see it celebrated 'out of particular devotion, and because he attributed the happy

[18] Hoeynck, *Geschichte der kirchlichen Liturgie*, p. 290.

[19] Bayerische Staatsbibliothek München, Res/Liturg. 1459c. It also authorized the use of German formulae at the administration of the sacraments and gave a number of German songs that could be sung by the congregation at various times of the liturgical year. On the reinstatement of the feast day see Hoeynck, *Geschichte der kirchlichen Liturgie*, p. 326.

[20] Ibid., pp. 293–5.

[21] Fisher, *Music and Religious Identity*, pp. 93–4 and Hoeynck, *Geschichte der kirchlichen Liturgie*, pp. 306–9.

[22] Fisher, *Music and Religious Identity*, p. 95.

[23] Quoted in ibid., pp. 95–6.

success of his arms and his victories besides God especially to the intercession of the Holy Virgin'.[24] In 1638, accordance with the wishes of Duke Maximilian I of Bavaria, Heinrich also mandated the celebration of the feast days of the Visitation and Presentation in the Bavarian part of his diocese. He was, he told Maximilian, glad to do so, because the cathedral in Augsburg 'was built and dedicated to the honour of the same (Our Dear Lady), and the patrimony of our foundation belongs to her in particular'.[25]

The Marian feast days that survived the Tridentine-inspired reform of 1567 – the Purification (2 February), the Annunciation (25 March), the Assumption (15 August) and the Nativity (8 September) – were observed with proper solemnity. According to the *Rituale*, a text containing instructions for ecclesiastical ceremonies, published in Dillingen in 1580, the bishop's subjects were to go to church both before and after lunch on feast days, to attend mass and to hear the word of God and a discourse on the catechism.[26] The blessing of candles at Purification and herbs at Assumption probably continued – the 1580 *Rituale* contains benediction formulae for both of these rituals – though it is possible that by the second half of the sixteenth century the blessing of herbs was primarily a rural rite.[27] A decree of 1593 suggests that in the eyes of the church such rituals were still subject to abuse. In this year Augsburg's bishop instructed his priests to abstain from benedictions not recognized by the church, not to place herbs, candles and other objects to be blessed beneath the altar cloth and to follow the times and methods of blessing that were officially prescribed.[28] The Catholic Church's struggle against the misuse of Marian artefacts, such as blessed wax, and devotional formulae continued into the seventeenth century.

By the early seventeenth century some Marian feast days were marked by elaborate festivities, which had a very public character. In 1602, for example, on the Assumption of the Virgin, a Jesuit chronicler reported:

> the Marian Congregation from our church, after the well-attended sermon, betook themselves with the whole people and the retinues of the chief princes to the cathedral of the Blessed Virgin with rejoicing and song, for the sake of the indulgences that had been granted by the Pope; they persevered in their prayers for four hours, and finally left the way they came in order and with music.[29]

Such festivities of course served the devotional needs of Augsburg's Catholic community, but they were also intended to make a public statement about the importance of Marian piety. The group of devotees processing through Augsburg's streets from St Salvator to the cathedral 'with rejoicing and song' would certainly have attracted the attention of local Protestants going about their daily

[24] Stetten, *Geschichte*, vol. 2, p. 155. [25] Hoeynck, *Geschichte der kirchlichen Liturgie*, p. 327.
[26] Marquard von Berg, *Ritus Ecclesiastici Augustensis Episcopatus* (Dillingen, 1580), pp. 32–3.
[27] See chapter 5. [28] J. A. Steiner, ed., *Acta Selecta Ecclesiae Augustanae* (n.p., 1785), p. 146.
[29] Quoted in Fisher, *Music and Religious Identity*, p. 158.

business. The significance of Marian feast days was further reinforced during the 1630s, when Augsburg's Catholic city council demonstrated its willingness to punish those who failed to observe them. In 1636, for example, three weavers and a cooper were imprisoned briefly because they had worked on the festival of Mary's Nativity.[30]

Public professions of devotion to the Virgin were not confined to prescribed Marian feast days. Indeed, Marianism suffused most aspects of Augsburg's renewed Catholic cult. From the 1560s onwards processions were gradually reintroduced. The first were confined to ecclesiastical territory: in 1563, for example, Otto Truchseß decreed that processions with litanies were to be held in the city's Catholic churches every Tuesday.[31] As Catholic confidence grew, processions once again moved back into the public domain, winding their way through the city's streets as they had done in the pre-Reformation period. On 12 August 1566 Truchseß ordered that a public *Bittprozession* – an intercessory procession – should be held on the first Sunday in every month for as long as the danger from the Turks persisted.[32] In 1587 Bishop Marquard von Berg decreed that in order to avert signs of God's wrath – plague, rising prices and war – four processions should be held every year. These processions, which could go either around the church or to a specified destination 'nach gelegenheit' [as the opportunity presented itself],[33] should be accompanied by masses, the first in honour of the Trinity, the second 'in memory of the God-bearer and holy Virgin Mary, who has this bishopric under her special protection', the third in honour of St Ulrich and the fourth for peace.[34] It was not until the turn of the century, however, that public processions truly regained their pre-Reformation prominence. In 1598 Bishop Johann Otto boasted that he had restored the processions that had been suppressed for many years for fear of the Lutheran populace.[35] In April of the same year the cathedral chapter, after seventy years of trepidation, held a procession that went from the cathedral to SS Ulrich and Afra in order to express thanks for victories won during the Hungarian War.

Such processions were, as Alexander Fisher has argued, a statement of Catholic confidence: 'no other phenomenon symbolized the consolidation of the Counter-Reformation in the city of Augsburg by 1600 more effectively'.[36] Some, especially those that took place on Good Friday and on the feast of Corpus Christi, involved hundreds of participants, both clerical and lay. They also, of course, fulfilled an important spiritual function, invoking the protection

30 StadtAA, Reichsstadt Strafamt, Nr. 106 (Strafbuch 1633–53), pp. 180–1 and Strafamt Urgichten, K217 (1636 Januar bis 1637 Mai).
31 Fisher, *Music and Religious Identity*, p. 232.
32 Lenk, *Augsburger Bürgertum*, pp. 43, 45; Hoeynck, *Geschichte der kirchlichen Liturgie*, p. 181.
33 Fisher, *Music and Religious Identity*, p. 229.
34 StadtAA, Reichsstadt, K. W. A., B. 10^2–14.
35 Hoeynck, *Geschichte der kirchlichen Liturgie*, p. 182.
36 Fisher, *Music and Religious Identity*, p. 226.

of God, Christ, Mary and the saints. As we have seen, Bishop Otto Truchseß von Waldburg was a keen promoter of the Litany of Loreto, and such supplicatory litanies constituted an important part of processional practice. In 1598, for example, the Jesuits' Marian congregation participated in the procession and sang 'a beautiful litany . . . of Our Lady'.[37] This Marian congregation also played a prominent role in the annual civic Corpus Christi procession that was restored at the beginning of the seventeenth century.[38] The processions also, however, had a polemical purpose. As Canisius' successor, the Jesuit cathedral preacher Rosephius, stated, processions with crucifixes, images of saints and singing were intended to impress people who did not hear Catholic sermons or debates, and to lead them back to the church.[39] It is difficult to say whether or not they achieved this objective, but they certainly commanded the attention of local Protestants. In 1607 Melchior Volcius, Lutheran pastor at St Anna, published two sermons condemning Catholic processions in Augsburg. He complained that when the processions of flagellants passed by on Good Friday Lutherans flocked to see them, so that 'it seems that our people are often more than those going in the procession'.[40]

Marian piety was also central to the pilgrimage practice that was renewed during the later sixteenth century. Initially the most popular destination for Augsburg's post-Tridentine pilgrims was the nearby shrine of Andechs in Bavaria. This twelfth-century site was not primarily Marian – the most important relics were three miraculous hosts – but pilgrims nonetheless invoked Mary's protection as they marched, most probably using the Litany of Loreto, and Marian antiphons such as the *Regina Caeli* were sung at stations along the route.[41] Approximately 130 kilometres away was the great Marian shrine of Altötting, which since the 1490s had been one of the most popular pilgrimage destinations in Germany. From the 1520s the spread of reformed teaching resulted in a precipitous decline in pilgrimage to Altötting, but the shrine flourished again from the final decades of the sixteenth century.[42]

Peter Canisius was closely involved in Altötting's revival. In 1570 Canisius performed an exorcism on Anna von Bernhausen, lady-in-waiting to Mark and Sybilla Fugger, in the chapel at Altötting. The dramatic events that took place during this exorcism were publicized via the writings of the provost of Altötting's collegiate church, Martin Eisengrein (1535–78). During

[37] ABA, Hs 34 (Anweisungen über die Abhaltung verschiedener Feierlichkeiten in der Augsburger Domkirche 1582–1603), fol. 14r.
[38] ABA, Hs 34, fol. 23r. On the Corpus Christi procession see Wolfgang Wallenta, 'Grundzüge katholischer Konfessionalisierung in Augsburg 1548–1648', *JbVAB* 33 (1999), 223.
[39] Ibid., 224. [40] Quoted in Fisher, *Music and Religious Identity*, p. 238.
[41] Ibid., pp. 258–9 and 269–70.
[42] Phil Soergel, *Wondrous in his Saints: Counter-Reformation propaganda in Bavaria* (Berkeley and London, 1993), p. 72.

the exorcism the demon tortured the young woman, responding to Canisius' attempts to banish him by levitating her body and sending her into fits. In Eisengrein's account Mary's intercession is central to Canisius' eventual triumph. The exorcism began with the recitation of the Loretan Litany. At one point an image of the Virgin was placed on Anna's head causing the demon to cry out: 'let me go, you whore!'[43] When Anna subsequently fell unconscious Mary appeared to her and told her that the devil would torture her five more times and would then flee. In the final stages of the exorcism the demon, which had blasphemed repeatedly against the Virgin, began to praise Mary in eulogistic terms. Performing a ritual of submission, he kissed the floor seven times and when asked by Canisius why he had done so replied: 'I had to do it in order to honour the Mother of God because I had blasphemed against her.'[44] The forces of evil surrendered to an authority greater than their own. Eisengrein's apologetic text, *Vnser liebe Fraw zu Alten Oetting*, which recounts the history of the shrine as well as telling the story of Canisius' exorcism and of other contemporary miracles, was first published in 1571 and became a best-seller, giving rise to a polemical exhange with Protestant authors that lasted for over four years. In the wake of its publication the shrine flourished once again, attracting many more pilgrims from Augsburg as well as from elsewhere in southern Germany.[45]

Augsburg's wealthy pilgrims might also choose to travel to Marian shrines even further afield: Augsburg's Corpus Christi brotherhood, re-established in 1604, visited Einsiedeln in Switzerland 1607 and 1614.[46] It is two local shrines, however, that demonstrate the central importance of Marian piety to the devotional life of Augsburg's Catholic citizens. Both were early manifestations of cults that originated in Italy but that later became crucial to Counter-Reformation piety north of the Alps. The Holy House at Loreto had formed an important focal point for pilgrimage since the late thirteenth century. It contained a carved Madonna attributed to St Luke.[47] The story of the miraculous journey of the Holy House was disseminated via Latin texts during the late fifteenth century, and was certainly known in Bavaria at this time. The first Loreto chapel in German-speaking lands was founded in 1589 by Archduke Ferdinand II in Hall in the Tyrol, and the first Loreto chapel north of the Alps was built in 1602 on the Kobel hill just outside Augsburg.[48] Devotion to the Virgin of Loreto was certainly significant in Augsburg before this date. As we

43 M. Eisengrein, *Vnser liebe Fraw zu Alten Oetting* (Ingolstadt, 1571), p. 280.

44 Ibid., p. 287.

45 Ibid., pp. 273–90. On this case see Soergel, *Wondrous in his Saints*, pp. 105–26 and 131–40. Lyndal Roper, *Oedipus and the Devil: witchcraft, sexuality and religion in early modern Europe* (London and New York, 1994), pp. 171–98.

46 Fisher, *Music and Religious Identity*, p. 274.

47 Pötzl, *Loreto*, p. 124.

48 Pötzl, 'Loreto in Bayern', 194–5, 197 and 210. On later (post-1620) copies in the Habsburg territories see Franz Matsche, 'Gegenreformatorische Architekturpolitik: Casa-Santa-Kopien und Habsburger Loreto-Kult nach 1620', *Jahrbuch für Volkskunde*, n.s. 1 (1978).

have seen, both Peter Canisius and Bishop Otto Truchseß von Waldburg visited the Italian shrine on a number of occasions, and encouraged the use of the Loretan Litany as a supplicatory prayer. Members of the Fugger family went on pilgrimage to Loreto in 1570 to seek assistance for a possessed maidservant, and as early as 1582 Anton Fugger owned a copy of the Madonna of Loreto, for which he built a chapel in the garden of his castle in Hainhofen. This Madonna passed, via Anton's evangelical successor in Hainhofen, Wolfgang Paller, to Karl Langenmantel, Lord of Westheim. The Loreto chapel that he subsequently constructed to house it on the Kobel hill was a family endeavour: plans for an exact architectural copy of the Holy House were brought from Italy by Wolfgang Heinrich Langenmantel, *Domherr* in Regensburg, and Karl was assisted in his project by his two brothers-in-law, Mathäus and Markus Welser, as well as by *Bürgermeister* Paul Welser.

It is likely that the Fuggers' and Langenmantels' devotion to the Virgin of Loreto was fostered by members of the Jesuit order. The Fuggers were the Jesuits' greatest lay supporters in Augsburg. Ursula von Lichtenstein, wife of Georg Fugger and mother of Anton, was one of Canisius' most celebrated converts. She travelled to Rome via Loreto in 1569.[49] Members of the Langenmantel family also had close connections to the order. Karl's son, Paul, became a Jesuit, and Wolfgang Heinrich Langenmantel, who studied at the *Collegium Germanicum* in Rome during the 1590s and according to tradition supplied the plans for the chapel on the Kobel, was related by marriage to Peter Canisius.[50] In 1554 the Jesuit order had taken over the pastoral care of the pilgrimage shrine at Loreto, and individual Jesuits sought to promote its popularity wherever they went. In his 1577 text, *De Maria Virgine incomparabili* Canisius described Loreto as the most important Marian pilgrimage place of his time.[51] Wilhelm von Gumppenberg, the author of the monumental *Atlas Marianus* (first published in Ingolstadt in 1655) who worked as a missionary in Bavaria, the Tyrol and Switzerland for thirty years, was a keen advocate of the cult. From 1632, when he first visited Loreto, to his death in 1675, seventeen Holy House chapels were established in the region that is now Bavaria.[52] These chapels disseminated devotion to the Virgin of Loreto amongst those who could never hope to afford to make the pilgrimage to Italy. The chapel on the Kobel hill, for example, was of considerable importance for local Catholics, especially during the traumatic period of the Thirty Years War. Already in 1613 the Kobel chapel was a pilgrimage site – an inn and a stable were built there in that year – but in 1634 the shrine and four houses near it were burned at the behest of the Swedish troops. After the defeat of the Swedes the chapel was restored, the Madonna itself (which had been moved to Schloß Hainhofen for protection)

[49] Pötzl, *Loreto*, pp. 130–3. [50] Ibid., p. 143.
[51] Ibid., p. 64. [52] Pötzl, 'Loreto in Bayern'.

was returned, and the pilgrimage flourished again from 1637 to 1646. Indeed, in 1641 an external pulpit was added in order to cater to the needs of the large numbers of visitors. Partly, at least, as a result of the great influence that the Jesuits enjoyed amongst Augsburg's Catholics, the Kobel became a key local pilgrimage site.[53]

In 1602, the same year that the Kobel Loreto chapel was founded, Regina Imhof of Untermeitingen, the widow of Augsburg's *Bürgermeister*, obtained permission from Bishop Heinrich von Knöringen to construct a church dedicated to 'Maria Hilf' on the Lechfeld, an area of meadow just outside Augsburg on the main road south towards Italy. The church was founded, as Alexandra Kohlberger points out, for a mixture of religious and economic reasons – a pilgrimage site on the road to the frequently visited shrine at Andechs and on a major trade route would inevitably bring financial gain. Be that as it may, Regina's choice of architectural model and dedication for the chapel testify to the Italianate and specifically Counter-Reformation interests of Augsburg's Catholic patrons. It was modelled on Santa Maria Rotunda – the Pantheon – in Rome, which Regina's son had visited on a pilgrimage. The original chapel was a simple, windowless round building with a cupola and a lantern on top, which was extended soon after its construction.[54] An outside pulpit and altar were added to accommodate the large number of pilgrims, and the chapel was dedicated to 'Maria Hilf'. This dedication had an important historical pedigree: at the Battle of Lepanto in 1571, when the Holy League crushed the Ottoman fleet, the victors' flagship bore a banner on which was inscribed the beginning of the traditional Marian antiphon *Santa Maria succurre miseris* [Holy Mary, help of the wretched]. In thanks for the victory of the Holy League Pope Pius V officially added the invocation 'Mary aid of Christians', which was already present in some Marian litanies, to the most commonly used litany, that of Loreto.[55] The dedication 'Maria Hilf', taken from the Litany of Loreto, was therefore an invocation of Mary's aid against enemies of the Catholic faith. The antiphon used at Lepanto, *Santa Maria succurre miseris*, is inscribed beneath the Lechfeld chapel's grace-giving image in an engraving of 1618 by Daniel Manasser (figure 26).[56] This chapel of 'Maria Hilf' was an early example of what became a classic Counter-Reformation dedication. Further afield, in Innsbruck a painting of the Virgin and Child by Lucas Cranach the Elder, given to Archduke Leopold V by Johann Georg I of Saxony, was venerated under the same dedication during the Thirty Years War. A copy of the Cranach painting

[53] Pötzl, *Loreto*, pp. 149ff.

[54] Bernhard Schütz, *Die kirchliche Barockarchitektur in Bayern und Oberschwaben 1580–1780* (Munich, 2000), p. 94.

[55] Pötzl, *Loreto*, p. 76.

[56] Alexandra Kohlberger, *Maria Hilf auf dem Lechfeld: 400 Jahre Wallfahrt* (Augsburg, 2003), p. 65.

Figure 26. Daniel Manasser, the miraculous image at Klosterlechfeld, 1618 (SStBA)

was the focus of a popular pilgrimage in Passau, and a great church dedicated to 'Maria Hilf' was begun there in 1624.[57] The popularity of the Passau shrine

[57] Ludwig Dorn, 'Das Mirakelbuch der Wallfahrt Maria Hilf in Speiden', *JbVAB* 20 (1986).

increased after 1633, when Mary was credited with preserving the city from destruction by Swedish troops. It is striking how 'Maria Hilf' dedications and pilgrimages proliferated in southern Germany during and after the Thirty Years War.[58]

What attracted pilgrims was Mary's intercessory power, the power to mediate grace and to generate miracles. In the Lechfeld chapel the grace-giving image, which is attributed to the Augsburg sculptor Christoph Murmann, shows Christ as judge of the world (figure 26). Archangel Michael kneels on his left, with a raised arm and scales, ready to judge sins. Mary kneels opposite, interceding with her son. The text in the banderol before her, taken from 1 Kings 2:20 (the story of Bathsheba and Solomon), emphasizes Mary's intercessory power: the son will not reject his mother's pleas.[59] Christ will grant whatever Mary asks. In gratitude for Mary's intercession, pilgrims gave *ex votos*, which might take the form of either money or objects to adorn the Madonna and her shrine. The Lechfeld Madonna, for example, like the more famous pilgrimage images at Altötting and Loreto, was clothed in splendid robes donated by devotees.[60] Whereas Lutheran authorities had discouraged the adornment of images in order to demonstrate their mundane nature, at Catholic shrines gifts of robes, crowns and rosaries continued to emphasize images' perceived role in mediating between man and God.

Pilgrimage to the Lechfeld chapel, which had already begun in 1604, was interrupted during the Thirty Years War but flourished again thereafter. It seems likely that for the majority of visitors the fact that the Lechfeld chapel imitated Santa Maria Rotunda and that the Kobel chapel reproduced the proportions of the Holy House at Loreto was largely irrelevant. Pilgrims were interested above all in the miraculous images of the Madonna that the two chapels contained. Indeed, when the Kobel Madonna was temporarily removed from its chapel during the Thirty Years War no further miracles were reported at the shrine until its return.[61] Pilgrimage was primarily a quest for immediate spiritual and material solace, for the intercession of the Virgin mediated through her grace-giving image. Yet in biconfessional Augsburg it also constituted a conscious statement of Catholic identity.[62] No Augsburg shrines had such explicitly polemical foundation legends as, for example, Neukirchen and Weissenregen in Bavaria, which housed Marian images that had supposedly survived attacks by Hussite and Calvinist iconoclasts.[63] Yet in travelling to the Kobel and Lechfeld shrines

[58] Soergel, *Wondrous in his Saints*, p. 219; Benno Hubensteiner, *Vom Geist des Barock: Kultur und Frömmigkeit im alten Bayern* (Munich, 1978), pp. 86–7; Herzig, *Der Zwang zum wahren Glauben*, pp. 93–5.

[59] For an illustration of the carved image see Kohlberger, *Maria Hilf*, p. 28.

[60] Pötzl, *Loreto*, p. 129; Kohlberger, *Maria Hilf*, p. 68.

[61] Pötzl, *Loreto*, p. 150.

[62] See Freitag, *Volks- und Elitenfrömmigkeit*, especially pp. 86–8.

[63] Soergel, *Wondrous in his Saints*, pp. 221–2.

Augsburg's Catholics were nonetheless making public statements about their allegiance to Roman Catholicism. As the 1631 case of Protestant butchers' sons mocking pilgrims en route to the Lechfeld chapel demonstrates, their journeys were undertaken in defiance of Protestant polemic and abuse.

Central to devotional activity focused on the Virgin were the Jesuits' Marian sodalities. They played an important role in both processions and pilgrimages, and have been described as 'the Counter-Reformation leaven of a recatholicized community'.[64] Confraternities had long provided a forum for expressing devotion to the Virgin and other saints. Augsburg's greatest brotherhood, dedicated to St Ulrich, had been founded in 1440 in honour of the city's patron saint, and the Carmelite brotherhood dedicated to St Anne also flourished during the fifteenth century.[65] In Augsburg, however, the Reformation brought the activities of all of the city's brotherhoods to an abrupt end. Some reappeared after the restoration of the Catholic cult: a manuscript from 1617 mentions eighteen that were either established or re-established from 1574 onwards, including a rosary brotherhood at the Dominican church (1574).[66] By the early seventeenth century, however, it was the Jesuits' Marian sodalities that were dominant. The city's first Marian sodality, its members drawn from amongst the students of the Jesuit college, was founded in 1589. It grew rapidly and in 1609 a second *Congregatio minor* was established for younger students. Two German-speaking congregations followed in 1613 and 1623, the first for citizens and the second for journeymen. As Louis Châtellier has argued, the Jesuits had great ambitions for these sodalities. Whereas medieval confraternities had been concerned above all with the salvation of their members, Marian sodalities were intended to transform Christian society in its entirety.[67] *Sodales* were to reform their fellow Catholics and to halt the spread of Protestantism through their exemplary behaviour.

Accordingly, the activities prescribed for Augsburg's *sodales* were both private and public. They were expected to strive for personal holiness, and they were also expected to proselytize. Members confessed weekly, received communion monthly and were required to regulate their lives, for example by refraining from swearing.[68] They were also prescribed spiritual exercises,

[64] Trevor Johnson, 'The recatholicization of the Upper Palatinate', unpublished PhD dissertation, University of Cambridge (1992), p. 166.

[65] Kiessling, *Bürgerliche Gesellschaft*, 292–3.

[66] SStBA, 2^0 Cod Aug 346, De initiis et progressu omnium Fraternitatum, quæ in alma hac Vrbe Augustana fuerunt diuersis temporibus erectæ a Christi fidelibus, narratio MDCXVII.

[67] Louis Châtellier, *The Europe of the Devout: the Catholic Reformation and the formation of a new society*, trans. Jean Birrell (Cambridge, 1989).

[68] Theodor Rolle, *Heiligkeitsstreben und Apostolat: Geschichte der Marianischen Kongregation am Jesuitenkolleg St Salvator und am Gymnasium der Benediktiner bei St Stephan in Augsburg 1589–1989* (Augsburg, 1989).

for example the daily recitation of the Loretan Litany, and were encouraged to form an intensely personal bond with the Holy Mother of God. Father Matthäus Rader, president of the Marian congregation in 1599, wrote in a hymn to the Virgin that when a young *sodale* came before her he sought neither worldly glory nor goods but rather pleaded for a good, crime-free mind, a chaste body, a decent manner, a pure heart, a breast conscious of guilt and, above all, a carefree and holy end.[69] *Sodales* were also, however, expected to provide public testimony to the Virgin's power. In the oath of consecration, which probably originated in Cologne and was in use in Augsburg from 1589, each new member elected Mary as his patroness and intercessor. He pledged himself to her, asking her to take him as her servant forever. He also promised not to allow those subordinate to him to undertake anything that would impugn her honour, a significant undertaking in a society shaped by patriarchal privilege.[70] As we have seen, the *sodales* participated in public processions, singing litanies invoking the Virgin. They also encouraged pilgrimage to Marian shrines. In 1637, for example, it was the *sodales* from the college of St Salvator who were the first to return to the Loreto shrine on the Kobel after the disruptions of the Swedish occupation.[71] Such activities served to promote Mary's significance as a focal point for confessional identity amongst Augsburg's Catholics.

THE ROLE OF MARIAN IMAGES

In the renewal of Augsburg's Marian cult during the later sixteenth and seventeenth centuries images played a crucial role. In 1547, when Catholicism was forcibly reintroduced in a number of the city's churches, conditions were hardly propitious for the commissioning of new artworks. The initial restoration of the cathedral, for example, was limited to the reinstallation of pre-Reformation furnishings that had survived the iconoclasm of the 1530s and to the replacement of objects that were essential to the basic functioning of the building as a Catholic place of worship, such as a crucifix, sacrament house and font.[72] As Catholic confidence grew, however, both clerical and lay patrons (most notably members of the Fugger family) began to commission new altarpieces, many of which showed the Virgin Mary. Even before Trent's dictum that 'images of Christ, the virgin mother of God, and the other saints should be set up and kept, particularly in churches' (1563), Augsburg's cathedral chapter had instructed Christoph Amberger to paint a replacement for the chief Marian altarpiece

[69] Quoted in Rolle, 'Die Anfänge der marianischen Kongregationen', 35.

[70] Quoted in Rolle, *Heiligkeitsstreben und Apostolat*, p. 108: '. . . Firmiterque statuo ac propono, me nunquam Te derelictorum, neque contra Te aliquid unquam dictorum aut factorem, neque permissurum, ut a meis subditis aliquid contra Tuum honorem unqual agatur . . .'

[71] Pötzl, *Loreto*, p. 150.

[72] Hildebrand Dussler, 'Die Restaurierung des Augsburger Domes von 1547/48', *JbVAB* 5 (1971).

destroyed by the iconoclasts. During the later decades of the sixteenth century, Marian panels were also installed on the altars of many of Augsburg's other Catholic churches. These images were intended to honour Mary: as the Council of Trent affirmed, the worship given to an image was passed to its prototype. In the context of biconfessional Augsburg they also, however, served a polemical purpose. They presented Mary as patroness of the local Catholic cause, and they also, through their subject matter and Italianate style, evoked the Catholic Church's universal struggle for renewal and reconquest.

The first Marian images commissioned by members of Augsburg's clerical elite in the aftermath of the Reformation were archaic in tone. There is little sign of a distinctively Counter-Reformation visual aesthetic or piety in Christoph Amberger's painted panel for the altar of the east choir of the cathedral (1554, figure 27), in the stone retable showing the Nativity commissioned by Ulrich Sigmayr for the Katharinenkapelle in the cathedral cloister (1564) or in Paulus Mayr's carved wooden altarpiece for the high altar of the Benedictine abbey church of SS Ulrich and Afra (1571, figure 30).[73] Amberger's panel perhaps provides the best opportunity to explore the significance of this visual archaism. The panel originally concealed and protected one of the cathedral chapter's prize possessions, a magnificent silver retable completed between 1506 and 1508 by the local artist Jörg Seld. This silver retable had, from 1510, been covered by a panel painted by Hans Holbein the Elder. Holbein's panel was destroyed in 1537, but the silver retable that it concealed had already been taken to Dillingen for safekeeping and thus escaped the predations of the iconoclasts.[74] When it was brought back to the cathedral in 1548 it required a new protective covering. In April 1552 the cathedral chapter expressed to the city council their fear that it would be damaged during the Holy Week celebrations.[75] For the duration of these celebrations they requested the assistance of 'various employees' to prevent attacks on the retable. The chapter probably commissioned a replacement for Holbein's panel from Amberger sometime between 1548 and 1552.[76]

The similarities between Holbein's original design, preserved in a drawing attributed to the artist himself (figure 28), and Amberger's replacement panel are immediately apparent. In both cases the composition is divided into three fields,

[73] For an illustration of Sigmayr's retable see Strecker, *Augsburger Altäre*, ill. 56.

[74] Jörg Breu, a local artist with marked Protestant sympathies, wrote in his chronicle: 'on the first of August those in Our Lady's Cathedral removed the silver panel from the choir and took it to their idol in Dillingen', *Chroniken*, vol. 29, p. 61. On Breu see P. F. Cuneo, 'Propriety, property, and politics: Jörg Breu the Elder and issues of iconoclasm in Reformation Augsburg', *German History* 14, no. 1 (1996) and Morrall, *Jörg Breu the Elder*. Seld's silver retable was melted down in 1636 to buy corn for the poor of the diocese. Amberger's panel probably remained *in situ* for some time thereafter. In 1681 a new high altarpiece, painted by Johann Heinrich Schönfeld and showing the Assumption of the Virgin, was installed. Alfred Schröder, 'Das Augsburger Dombild', *Münchner Jahrbuch der bildenden Kunst*, n.s. 7 (1930), 119–20.

[75] StadtAA, Reichsstadt, Ratsbücher, Nr. 26, fol. 44v.

[76] Strecker, *Augsburger Altäre*, pp. 178–9.

Figure 27. Christoph Amberger, panel for the east choir altar of Augsburg Cathedral, 1554 (cathedral, Augsburg)

showing the Virgin and Child surrounded by music-making angels, flanked by saints Ulrich and Afra. Beneath are half-length figures of the saints connected with the Afra legend, including a portrait of Emperor Maximilian as St Afer. As Freya Strecker points out, the Amberger panel is a significantly revised version

Figure 28. Hans Holbein the Elder, design for a panel for the east choir altar of Augsburg Cathedral, 1508 (Muzeum Narodowe, Gdańsk)

of the lost Holbein rather than a direct copy.[77] Whereas Holbein's visual stage is truncated by a brocade curtain, Amberger's figures are placed against 'real'

[77] Ibid., pp. 185–8.

backgrounds. Mary is enthroned before a column-lined space that recedes into darkness and sky is visible behind the saints on the side panels. The complex painted tracery arches above the main figures in the Holbein panel have been replaced with simple arcades, the central one of which has been enlarged at the expense of the crucifixion above. The Virgin is raised above the other figures by the stone plinth upon which her throne rests. Rather than a cloth above Mary's head Amberger depicts a gloriole of blue and white light, edged with cloud within which angels' faces appear. In the centre hovers the dove of the Holy Ghost. In the panel's painted superstructure Amberger, like Holbein, depicted the crucifixion. He omitted, however, the angel collecting blood from Christ's wound in a chalice and incorporated instead Adam's skull and two panels bearing the Decalogue beneath the cross and God the Father above at the panel's apex.

The differences between the two panels may be attributed partly to changes in taste. They also, however, serve to alter the panel's theological message, and to place greater emphasis on the Virgin Mary. In Holbein's version the angel collecting blood from Christ's side and the two incense-bearing angels behind the Virgin's throne draw out the Eucharistic significance of events depicted. Amberger's version, by contrast, focuses on the redeeming effects of Christ's incarnation and crucifixion and Mary's role in the story of salvation. In the superstructure the age of grace, represented by the crucifixion, is opposed to the age of law, represented by Adam's skull and the Decalogue, in a manner reminiscent of Protestant iconography.[78] Mary's prominence has been increased in the Amberger panel: she is raised above the other figures and set against a background that immediately catches the viewer's attention. It is she, rather than the Christ Child or saints, who makes eye contact with viewer. The central axis of the panel, which leads from God the Father via the crucified Christ, Adam's skull, the Decalogue and the Holy Ghost to Mary, emphasizes her central role in the narrative of mankind's redemption as well as the mediation of the church that she embodies.

Amberger had originally proposed greater deviation from the Holbein design. A preparatory drawing shows two moveable wings with saints Ulrich and Afra, and includes Emperor Charles V and his wife alongside Maximilian in the predella (figure 29).[79] Ultimately, however, his patrons, the cathedral chapter, rejected these innovations. They requested instead what is essentially an updated version of the lost panel, which despite its stylistic innovations and modified theological message follows closely the form and basic content of Holbein's original. This traditionalism is perhaps not entirely unexpected, given the

[78] Ibid., p. 185.

[79] Freya Strecker points out that, given the proportions of the wings in Amberger's drawing, they cannot have been intended to cover the whole panel. They would rather, perhaps, have functioned as shutters covering the middle part of the panel. Ibid., pp. 184–5.

Figure 29. Christoph Amberger, design for a panel for the east choir altar of Augsburg Cathedral, c.1548–52 (British Museum)

relatively early date of the Amberger panel and the fact that throughout Germany cathedral chapters represented, as Marc Forster has argued, 'a force for continuity'.[80] More surprisingly, the desire to evoke pre-Reformation forms is still clear in Paulus Mayr's carved retable for the high altar of SS Ulrich and Afra, created during the post-Tridentine era (figure 30). This retable was commissioned in 1571 by Jakob Köplin (1548–1600), the abbot responsible for restoring the Benedictine monastery following its decimation during the 1530s. Mayr's elaborate winged retable with corpus, predella and elaborate tracery superstructure renounces the Renaissance style that was, by that time, prevalent in Augsburg and draws instead upon the altar forms of the late gothic period. It resembles closely earlier works such as Michel Erhart's altarpiece from the abbey church at Blaubeuren (1493/4).[81] Its carved central shrine shows the Virgin and Child standing on a crescent moon flanked by saints. Further half-length figures of saints appear in the predella and on the interiors of the painted wings are depictions of the Annunciation, Nativity, Adoration and Presentation. It is possible that, as in the cathedral, deliberate reference was being made to an image that had been destroyed by iconoclasts. This hypothesis cannot, however, be confirmed as no information survives concerning the appearance of the church's pre-Reformation altar.

Bruno Bushart and Jörg Rasmussen have suggested that during the second half of the sixteenth century the commissions given by Augsburg's Catholics were characterized by deliberate caution.[82] The close adherence of Amberger's panel to the lost Holbein original and the archaic style of Mayr's altarpiece could, according to their interpretation, be read as conciliatory, as an attempt to recreate a shared visual culture that had been destroyed at the Reformation. While it is true that these two altarpieces are not openly polemical in comparison to later images, they are certainly not conciliatory either. As Christian Hecht has pointed out, old iconographies and forms could be inflammatory when viewed in the new context of the Reformation.[83] Augsburg's Protestants had decisively rejected the cult of the Virgin. The placing of Marian altarpieces on the high altars of two of the city's key churches must therefore be read as a provocative rather than as a placatory act. Indeed, both images embodied the very elements of Marian piety to which Protestants most objected. Amberger's panel, as we have seen, modified Holbein's original design in ways that emphasized Mary's key role in the story of salvation and the mediation of the church that she represented – both themes unique to Catholic piety. The design of Mayr's retable

[80] Forster, 'With and without confessionalization', 329.
[81] Baxandall, *The Limewood Sculptors*, plates 18–22.
[82] Bushart, 'Kunst und Stadtbild', p. 370; Rasmussen, 'Bildersturm und Restauration', p. 106.
[83] Christian Hecht, *Katholischen Bildertheologie im Zeitalter von Gegenreformation und Barock* (Berlin, 1997), p. 407.

Figure 30. Paulus Mayr, altarpiece from the high altar of SS Ulrich and Afra, Augsburg, 1570–1 (SS Ulrich and Afra, Augsburg)

highlights Mary's importance. She stands, crowned, on a plinth that raises her above the two female saints on either side of her. Two angels hold a cloth-of-honour behind her and a diminutive figure representing the altar's donor, Jakob Köplin, kneels at her feet. Perhaps because of its archaic style Mayr's retable was displaced only one generation later in order to make way for Hans Degler's St Narcissus or Adoration of the Shepherds altar (consecrated 1604).[84] Yet in its new location it became a focal point for a type of Marian veneration that was entirely alien to Protestant sensibilities. At some point during the late sixteenth or seventeenth century it acquired a reputation as a *Gnadenbild*, a grace-giving image. Romano Kistler, writing in 1712 on the occasion of the monastery's seven hundredth anniversary, commented that: 'this image of Mary was already held in great honour long ago, but since a few years ago the Mother of God shines there with so many and such great favours and miracles that she is still today deservedly called "Mary of Comfort"'.[85]

The archaic form and content of the Amberger and Mayr retables was not a sop to Protestant sensibilities. Rather, it served the interests of Augsburg's recently restored Catholic clergy. By invoking the pre-Reformation cult of the Virgin the images made provocative allusion to a united Christian past under Rome and emphasized the historical continuity of the Catholic faith. As Jeffrey Chipps Smith has argued in relation to post-Reformation commissions in Augsburg, Münster and elsewhere, such 'physical renovation was a conscious effort to use art to mend the historical continuum of the Catholic Church that had been torn by the Reformation'.[86] The cathedral chapter's decision to include Emperor Maximilian I in the 1554 panel but not, as Amberger had originally proposed, the current emperor Charles V, testifies to this historicizing tendency. Augsburg's golden age under Maximilian I was surely a better spiritual reference point than its turbulent and confessionally divided present under Charles V. Moreover, the altarpieces' archaic forms recommended them to Catholic reformers, who were concerned to ensure that only legitimate images were reintroduced into local churches. As Freya Strecker has pointed out, their deliberate references to pre-Reformation images accorded well with the decrees of Augsburg's diocesan synods. The Dillingen synod of November 1548, for example, entrusted the deans of the *Landkapitel* with ensuring that in the churches under their supervision no new images were introduced without the approval of the bishop or his vicar.[87] Both Amberger in his 1554 version of Holbein's lost panel and Mayr in his 1571 recreation of a gothic retable invoked

[84] Jeffrey Chipps Smith, *German Sculpture of the Later Renaissance, c.1520–1580: art in an age of uncertainty* (Princeton, NJ, 1994), pp. 112–15. On the renovation of SS Ulrich and Afra see Bushart, 'Kunst und Stadtbild', p. 382.

[85] R. Kistler, *Basilika, dass ist die herrliche kirchendes Frey-Reichsklosters St Ulrich und Afra in Augsburg* (Augsburg, 1712), p. 42.

[86] Jeffrey Chipps Smith, *The Northern Renaissance*, Art and Ideas (London, 2004), p. 376.

[87] Strecker, *Augsburger Altäre*, pp. 95, 185.

Figure 31. Anonymous ('A.C.'), silhouette of Augsburg with saints, c.1566 (Städtische Kunstsammlungen, Augsburg)

images that were old and therefore, according to the synodal criteria, free from suspicion.

The Marian altarpieces commissioned in Augsburg during the later sixteenth and early seventeenth centuries were more modern and more distinctively Counter-Reformation in both content and style. Painted, in many cases, by artists associated with the Wittelsbach court in nearby Bavaria, they glorified the Virgin, and invoked her as protectress, even sovereign, of the Catholic cause. One important precursor for these painted altarpieces was an engraving commissioned by Bishop Otto Truchseß von Waldburg in 1566, possibly for distribution to participants in the imperial Diet that met in Augsburg in that year (figure 31). It bears the coats of arms of Otto Truchseß and of the imperial cloister of SS Ulrich and Afra, and shows the Virgin and Child amidst a company of local saints. Beneath the heavenly gathering is a depiction of Augsburg, based on a 1563 cityscape by Hans Rogel. With open-handed gestures Mary and the two most prominent saints, Ulrich and Afra, recommend the city to the Christ Child, and the Latin inscription asks Christ to guide supplicants to live for God.[88] The idea of depicting a city under the protection of Mary and

[88] Anja Schmidt, *Augsburger Ansichten: die Darstellung der Stadt in der Druckgraphik des 15. bis 18. Jahrhunderts*, Schwäbische Geschichtsquellen und Forschungen 19 (Augsburg, 2000), pp. 52–3.

the saints was not new – there are certainly earlier Italian examples – but it seems to have gained some currency in Counter-Reformation Augsburg. Mary appears above Augsburg's cityscape on the dedicatory page of a 1601 collection of lives of local saints and on the title page of a 1693 edition of Augsburg's diocesan decrees, as well as on three altarpieces commissioned by members of the Fugger family that deserve examination.[89]

In 1584/5 Christoph Schwarz, at the instigation of either Philipp Eduard or Octavian Secundus Fugger, produced a painting of the Virgin to adorn one of the side altars in the Jesuit church of St Salvator (figure 32).[90] Schwarz was court painter to Duke Wilhelm V in Munich and had already, in 1581, painted a Marian altarpiece for the Jesuit college in that town.[91] Both altarpieces show the Virgin and Child surrounded by music-making angels and enthroned on banks of clouds. In both Mary's foot rests on a sickle moon, identifying her as the Woman of the Apocalypse and probably also, given the Jesuit context of the paintings, alluding to her Immaculate Conception. Christ holds a rose, a symbol of Mary's virtue, of love and of his own sacrificial death. Above, angels support Christ's monogram adorned, in keeping with Jesuit tradition, with a cross and nails. The differences between the two altarpieces are, however, more revealing than their mutual affinities. Figure 33 shows Schwarz's original design for the Augsburg altarpiece: it is, like the Munich painting, an intimate depiction of the Virgin and Child accompanied by a few angels.[92] Yet the altarpiece as eventually executed, presumably with amendments proposed by its patron or by an advisor, shows Mary presiding over many more of the angelic host. God the Father and the dove of the Holy Ghost are depicted above. Mary has a crown of stars, bringing her more closely into line with Counter-Reformation visions of the *Immaculata*, and beneath her a diminutive figure of St John confirms her identity as the woman of Revelation 12:1. Most importantly the landscape beneath her incorporates not, as in the Munich painting, depictions of scenes from Christ's life (the Flight into Egypt and the Massacre of the Innocents), but rather a prospect of the city of Augsburg. Here, once again, Mary is designated as the city's special patroness.[93]

This proclamation was repeated in two other paintings commissioned by Octavian Secundus Fugger. In 1583 Octavian acquired the chapel to the west of the Simpertuskapelle in the Benedictine church of SS Ulrich and Afra as a burial chapel. He determined to consecrate its altar in honour of Mary and of saints Francis and Benedict. Schwarz produced a design for a retable for

[89] Städtische Kunstsammlungen Augsburg, ed., *Welt im Umbruch*, vol. 3, p. 393; *Decreta synodalia dioeces. August* (Augsburg: Simon Utzschneider, 1693).

[90] Reinhold Baumstark, ed., *Rom in Bayern: Kunst und Spiritualität der ersten Jesuiten. Katalog zur Ausstellung des Bayerischen Nationalmuseums München, 30. April bis 20. Juli 1997* (Munich, 1997), cat. no. 153.

[91] Strecker, *Augsburger Altäre*, pp. 305, 308, especially n. 56. Germanisches Nationalmuseum, ed., *Die Gemälde des 16. Jahrhunderts*, pp. 465–9.

[92] Baumstark, ed., *Rom in Bayern*, cat. no. 152.

[93] Strecker, *Augsburger Altäre*, pp. 308–10.

Figure 32. Christoph Schwarz, Mary in Glory, panel from the Jesuit church of St Salvator, Augsburg, c.1584 (Bayerische Staatsgemäldesammlungen, Munich)

this altar in 1585 but when the artist died in 1592 the painting was apparently still not complete. The altarpiece was finally executed by Schwarz's successor as Bavarian court painter, Peter Candid.[94] Like Schwarz's altarpiece for the

[94] Norbert Lieb, *Octavian Secundus Fugger (1549–1600) und die Kunst* (Tübingen, 1980), pp. 26–7.

Figure 33. Christoph Schwarz, design for Mary in Glory from the Jesuit church of St Salvator, Augsburg, c.1584 (Nationalmuseum, Stockholm)

Jesuit church, Candid's painting shows Mary, her foot resting on a sickle moon, seated on a bank of cloud and surrounded by music-making angels (figure 34). Beneath her kneel saints Benedict and Francis, their hands clasped in prayer, and between them, much more conspicuous than in Schwarz's painting, is a representation of the city of Augsburg. Octavian also commissioned another Marian painting that was begun by Schwarz and completed by Candid (figure 35).

Figure 34. Peter Candid, Virgin and Child with saints Benedict and Francis, c.1591–2 (SS Ulrich and Afra, Augsburg)

It originally hung in his house chapel, but was moved to the Georgskapelle in SS Ulrich and Afra in 1629.[95] Mary is again shown seated on a bank of cloud and surrounded by music-making angels. This time she is crowned and holds a

[95] Brigitte Volk-Knüttel, 'Candid nach Schwarz', *Münchner Jahrbuch der bildenden Kunst*, 3rd ser. 39 (1988), 113.

Figure 35. Peter Candid (after Christoph Schwarz), Virgin and Child with saints Ulrich and Afra, completed 1595 (SS Ulrich and Afra, Augsburg)

sceptre in her right hand: she shares in her son's sovereignty, symbolized by the orb that he holds in his left hand. In the earthly sphere below kneel saints Ulrich and Afra and Augsburg is visible between them. With both hands, St Ulrich appears to commend both the panel's viewer and the painted city of Augsburg to the mercy of Mary and her son.

Other altarpieces commissioned in Augsburg during the late sixteenth and early seventeenth centuries invoked and celebrated Mary's status and power, though without explicit reference to her patronage of the city. The Assumption and Coronation of the Virgin were especially popular themes. In 1596, for example, Philipp Eduard Fugger commissioned Hans von Aachen to paint a Coronation of the Virgin for his burial chapel, the Bartholomäuskapelle in SS Ulrich and Afra.[96] In 1611 Marx Fugger commissioned a monumental (465 by 285 cm) altarpiece from Hans Rottenhammer showing the Coronation of the Virgin above a company of saints, many of them Franciscan (figure 36).[97] Completed in 1614, this altarpiece was installed in the Franciscan cloister church (now the parish church of St Maximilian), which had been endowed by members of the Fugger family. In 1627 Peter Paul Rubens, at the behest of Ottheinrich Fugger, completed a painting of the Assumption for the Catholic church of Heilig Kreuz (figure 37).[98] In the same year Matthias Kager completed an altarpiece showing the Coronation of the Virgin for the high altar of St Georg (figure 38).[99] In the early 1630s the Dominican church of St Magdalena acquired, again at the expense of the Fuggers, a monumental high altarpiece showing Mary's Assumption, painted by the Italian artist Giovanni Lanfranco (figure 39).[100] Interest in such scenes continued throughout the seventeenth century. In 1681, for example, a new high altarpiece showing the Assumption was installed in Augsburg's cathedral.[101]

Other altarpieces focused on Mary's mediatory role, or showed her as the central figure amidst a company of saints. The lost high altarpiece of the Capuchin church, the design of which is preserved in an engraving dating from 1607 (figure 40), depicts the Virgin of the Immaculate Conception raised into heaven to kneel in prayer before the Trinity. The Apostles, the four Latin fathers of the church and saints Dominic and Francis are gathered below.[102] Again, this altarpiece was a donation of the Fuggers, given to the cloister that they had founded in 1602. In 1620 Rottenhammer produced another Marian altarpiece for the cathedral.[103] Matthias Kager painted two further Marian altarpieces, one showing Mary with saints Margaret, Cosmas and Damian for the hospital

[96] Städtische Kunstsammlungen Augsburg, ed., *Welt im Umbruch*, vol. 2, cat. no. 443.

[97] Bruno Bushart, 'Die Hochaltarblätter des Barock in Augsburg', *JbVAB* 25 (1991), 206–7; Christina Thon, ed., *Augsburger Barock* (Augsburg, 1968), cat. no. 141; Harry Schlichtenmaier, 'Studien zum Werk Hans Rottenhammers des Älteren (1564–1625) Maler und Zeichner mit Werkkatalog', PhD dissertation, Eberhard-Karls-Universität (1988), G I Nr. 72.

[98] Bushart, 'Die Hochaltarblätter des Barock', p. 202. Ottheinrich had served in the Bavarian and Spanish armies during the Thirty Years War and may have known Rubens through Isabella, governess of the southern Netherlands. Konrad Renger, *Peter Paul Rubens: Altäre für Bayern* (Munich, 1991), p. 10.

[99] Bushart, 'Die Hochaltarblätter des Barock', pp. 208–9, ill. 35; Susanne Netzer, *Johann Matthias Kager: Stadtmaler von Augsburg (1575–1634)*, Neue Schriftenreihe des Stadtarchivs München 113 (Munich, 1980), G 36.

[100] Bushart, 'Die Hochaltarblätter des Barock', pp. 209–12; Bushart, 'Kunst und Stadtbild', pp. 381–2.

[101] Bushart, 'Die Hochaltarblätter des Barock', p. 201.

[102] Ibid., p. 225, ill. 41.

[103] Karl Kosel, 'Ein vergessener Altar im Augsburger Dom und sein Gemälde', *JbVAB* 21 (1987).

Figure 36. Hans Rottenhammer, Coronation of the Virgin with saints, 1614 (St Maximilian, Augsburg)

church of St Margareth,[104] the other showing St Moritz and the martyrs of the Theban legion pleading before Mary. This second monumental altarpiece was a Fugger commission, produced for the high altar of the collegiate church of St Moritz when the church's choir area was remodelled in around 1630.[105] By the period of Catholic ascendancy following the 1629 Edict of Restitution, most

104 Bushart, 'Die Hochaltarblätter des Barock', p. 208 and ill. 34; Netzer, *Johann Matthias Kager*, G29.

105 Bushart, 'Die Hochaltarblätter des Barock', p. 197 and ill. 17. The altarpiece was destroyed in 1944.

Figure 37. Peter Paul Rubens, Assumption of the Virgin, 1627 (Heilig Kreuzkirche, Augsburg)

of Augsburg's Catholic churches had at least one new Marian altarpiece. Mary also featured prominently on other ecclesiastical furnishings, for example the painted wings of the two organs commissioned by the Fuggers for SS Ulrich and Afra (1608) and for the Dominican church (1614).[106]

Most of these late sixteenth- and seventeenth-century Marian images depict the apotheosis of the Virgin. Mary is transported to the heavenly sphere floating on clouds, with angels, saints and sometimes the city of Augsburg itself ranged beneath her. She is often shown being crowned by the Trinity or ven-

[106] Bushart, 'Kunst und Stadtbild', p. 382.

Figure 38. Johann Matthias Kager, Coronation of the Virgin, 1627 (St Georg, Augsburg)

erated by lesser saints. Although narrative scenes from Mary's life were still produced, for example Rottenhammer's 1608 Annunciation for SS Ulrich and Afra, in general Augsburg's Marian altarpieces no longer focused on her role in the story of salvation, but rather on her glory, veneration and invocation.[107] Themes such as the Assumption and Coronation of the Virgin had, of course,

[107] Schlichtenmaier, 'Studien zum Werk Hans Rottenhammers', G I 69; Bushart, 'Kunst und Stadtbild', p. 381.

Figure 39. Giovanni Lanfranco, Assumption of the Virgin, c.1631 (Christkönigskirche, München-Neuhausen)

Figure 40. Raphael Sadeler II (after Cosmas Piazza), engraving of the former altarpiece of the Kapuzinerkirche in Augsburg, 1607 (Albertina, Vienna)

been popular before the Reformation and even survived, as we have seen, in some Lutheran areas. Yet in the context of Counter-Reformation Augsburg the emphasis that newly commissioned Marian paintings placed on the Virgin's apotheosis indicates their patrons' commitment to a characteristically Catholic and Tridentine form of Marian piety. These images show Mary emphatically as a divine intercessor rather than as the humble human mother of the Lutheran tradition. The Assumption and Coronation may also have appealed to Augsburg's patrons because they depicted not only Mary's own exaltation but also the triumph of the church that she embodied.

Between Amberger's 1554 panel (figure 27) and the altarpieces of Schwarz, Candid, Hans von Aachen, Kager and Rottenhammer there are differences of style as well as of content. In art historical terms, the stylistic shift is from Renaissance to mannerist or early baroque. In the later panels increasingly dramatic compositions give a strong impression of movement. The bold use of colour and the strong tonal contrasts reinforce this dynamism, and the expressive gestures of the participants heighten the emotional impact of the images. Such visual devices, generally considered characteristic of baroque art, are most obvious in the altarpieces of the two non-German artists, Giovanni Lanfranco and Peter Paul Rubens (figures 39 and 37), but the influence of the new modes of artistic expression is also apparent in the compositions of Rottenhammer and Kager. These images no longer seek, as Amberger's and Mayr's had done, to restore the visual continuum that had been interrupted by the iconoclasts by looking back to pre-Reformation forms. Instead, they turn to the forms and techniques characteristic of contemporary Italian art.

Was this stylistic shift driven, as Alexander Fisher suggests in relation to Augsburg's Counter-Reformation music, 'more by changes in taste than confessional politics'?[108] Or was the arrival of baroque painting in Augsburg another deliberate statement of Catholic identity? We cannot dismiss the importance of aesthetic fashion: by the mid seventeenth century, for example, local Protestants seem to have shared Catholics' taste for the baroque. In 1665 Johann Heinrich Schönefeld's paintings of Christ carrying the cross and the descent from the cross were installed in the evangelical church of Heilig Kreuz in Augsburg. These paintings were, as Tilmann Breuer argues, important attempts to create 'a monumental, Protestant church painting in Germany', which incorporated baroque emotionalism in its use of light and composition.[109] Initially, however, confessional politics had certainly played an important role in establishing the new artistic style within the city. The patrons of the altarpieces produced from the 1580s onwards were leading members of Augsburg's Catholic elite, and the artists they chose to commission were associated with the nearby Catholic

[108] Fisher, *Music and Religious Identity*, p. 20.
[109] Tilman Breuer, *Die Stadt Augsburg* (Munich, 1958), p. 32.

Wittelsbach court and, in the case of Rubens and Lanfranco, with Italy and the southern Netherlands.[110] Some of these artists might, perhaps, have been willing to work for Protestant patrons had the opportunity arisen – Rubens of course worked for the English court – but in general they were closely identified with the Catholic cause. Kager, for example, whose career in Augsburg flourished with the support of the Fuggers until the arrival of the Swedes in 1632, was described by the local Protestant Hainhofer as a 'great papist, who did not wish the evangelicals well'.[111] In the work of these artists Catholic content and baroque style are inseparable: the message of Mary's apotheosis is reinforced by the dynamic and dramatic use of composition and colour.

The issue of audience is of crucial importance for understanding the significance of these Marian images. It is tempting to regard them, as much other baroque art has been regarded, as confrontational propaganda.[112] But the Marian images that entered the city's Catholic churches during this period were intended not to win over apostates but to strengthen the confessional fervour of men and women who were already loyal adherents of the old faith. The images certainly tended to emphasize the Marian doctrines that were most fiercely disputed by Protestant reformers: Mary's Immaculate Conception, her Assumption, her Coronation and her intercession. Yet it would be a mistake to assume, on the basis of their subject matter, that they were aimed at the Catholics' confessional opponents. All of these images were painted for churches where they would have been seen primarily, if not exclusively, by Catholic congregations. Protestants might well have known about them: Catholic processions and plays certainly attracted a cross-confessional audience, and it is possible to imagine that the installation of monumental new altarpieces might likewise have provided an entertaining spectacle for all comers. The Marian iconography of Rottenhammer, Kager and their fellow artists did not, however, form part of the evangelicals' day-to-day visual environment. In Augsburg the images that were most accessible to all – those that adorned the city's streets – were much more neutral in confessional terms. When the appearance of the city was transformed during the late sixteenth and early seventeenth centuries by a series of civic commissions, the figurative decoration of the new fountains, monuments and façades focused not on potentially divisive religious themes but on Augsburg's imperial origins and loyalty to empire and emperor.[113]

110 On Rubens's work for Duke Maximilian I see Renger, *Peter Paul Rubens*, p. 9.

111 Netzer, *Johann Matthias Kager*, p. 37.

112 Reinhard, 'Was ist katholische Konfessionalisierung?', p. 429.

113 Städtische Kunstsammlungen Augsburg, ed., *Welt im Umbruch*, vol. 1, p. 12. Even those few images that did depict spiritual subjects emphasized their civic rather than their confessional significance. Hans Reichle's 1603 St Michael for the façade of the Weberhaus, for example, had a particular local meaning since the eve of this saint's feast day was celebrated as the founding day of the city. Perhaps to reinforce the sculpture's import for the whole community, it was given an inscription composed by a Protestant. Ibid., pp. 18–20.

Figure 41. House altar from the Fugger house on Weinmarkt, between 1564 and 1570 (Markuskirche, Fuggerei, Augsburg)

Within Catholic homes, smaller Marian images also served to strengthen Catholic faith and identity. Figure 41, for example, shows a triptych of the Coronation of the Virgin that was produced for the chapel of Markus Fugger's house on the Weinmarkt. The chapel and its altar were consecrated in 1570, and it seems likely that the triptych was completed in the same year. Markus's wife, Sibylla von Eberstein, had converted from Lutheranism to Catholicism under the guidance of Peter Canisius in 1561, and had subsequently returned the rest of her family to the Catholic fold.[114] Although the triptych's style is archaic, its content reflects its patrons' Catholic credentials and Jesuit connections. The depiction of St Michael on the interior of the left wing indicates a concern with judgment and salvation, and hence with the intercessory power of the Queen of Heaven. The *Anna Selbdritt* on the interior of the right panel may be intended

[114] Bernhard Duhr, *Geschichte der Jesuiten in den Ländern deutscher Zunge im XVI. Jahrhundert* (Freiburg im Breisgau, 1907), p. 82. See also Anne Conrad, 'Stifterinnen und Lehrerinnen: der Anteil von Frauen am jesuitischen Bildungswesen', in *Petrus Canisius SJ (1521–1597): Humanist und Europäer*, ed. R. Berndt (Berlin, 2000), pp. 214–16.

as a reference to Mary's Immaculate Conception. And on the exterior of the wings Christ's monogram is represented in the form used above all by the Jesuits, incorporating a cross and nails.[115] This image served no propagandistic purpose, but formed a focus for the prayers and pious devotions of Markus, Sybilla and members of their household.

As we saw in chapter 3, evidence from domestic inventories suggests that in post-Reformation Augsburg the ownership of Marian images was largely confined to members of the Catholic elite. Whereas in Nuremberg prints and paintings of the Virgin had been incorporated into Protestant art collections, in Augsburg equivalent images were displayed primarily, if not exclusively, in the homes of Catholic patricians such as Conrad Peutinger, Raymund Fugger and Paul Welser. An inventory of the possessions of Octavian Secundus Fugger, drawn up in 1600/1, provides a uniquely rich record of the importance that Marian imagery had for one of these Catholic patricians. Octavian Secundus, whom we have already met as patron of two or possibly three altarpieces, was a religious zealot. In 1583, in the written undertaking for his burial chapel in SS Ulrich and Afra, Octavian spoke of the 'love and desire that I have and bear towards the true Christian Catholic religion'. He had studied in Rome and Antwerp and although his desire to become a Jesuit was frustrated by familial obligations he maintained a close connection to members of the movement throughout his lifetime.[116]

There was a Fugger family tradition of collecting: Octavian had inherited the kernel of his collection of secular and profane paintings, wall hangings, sculptures, silverwork, coins and medals from his grandfather and father (Raymund I and Georg Fugger). The images that filled his home were undoubtedly valued for their aesthetic merits as well as for their religious significance, but the preponderance of Marian depictions demonstrates Octavian's deep personal commitment to the Virgin. The inventory lists over seventy Marian images: paintings, prints, sculptures, gilded panels and treasures such as a 'black gem, in which Our Lady is carved'.[117] Only two can be securely identified with surviving objects: the large panel painted by Peter Candid that from 1629 hung in the Georgskapelle of SS Ulrich and Afra (figure 35) and a small (15.5 cm by 11.2 cm) gold relief showing the Virgin and Child with a sceptre and orb surrounded by music-making angels.[118] This gold relief, which has a companion panel showing Christ carrying the cross, copies the central composition of the large painted panel, omitting saints Ulrich and Afra and the city of Augsburg.[119]

115 Strecker, *Augsburger Altäre*, pp. 249–72.
116 Quoted in Lieb, *Octavian Secundus Fugger*, p. 174. Lieb has published the parts of the inventory that deal with art objects: ibid., pp. 232–310.
117 Ibid., p. 244, no. 69.
118 Ibid., p. 274, no. 1011; Volk-Knüttel, 'Candid nach Schwarz', 113.
119 Baumstark, ed., *Rom in Bayern*, cat. no. 154.

Its precious material and exquisite workmanship suggest that it was as much a *Kunstkammerstück* as an object of devotion.

The greatest concentration of Marian images was in the cell-like meditation room adjoining Octavian's study. The inventory mentions fourteen, ranging from a splendid-sounding house altar with 'histories' carved out of silver, a painted image of Mary and Christ in the centre and relics surrounded by pearls around it, to a coloured plaster roundel showing the Virgin. On the desk stood an ivory crucifix and behind it a large wooden panel showing the Virgin and Child with St Catherine and St John that was described as an 'ancient work of art'. There was also a carved image of the Virgin holding the Christ Child on her arm and a print showing the *Immaculata* trampling a dragon beneath her feet. The room contained a number of Marian iconographies that were particularly intimate and well suited to pious contemplation: a painted panel showing the sleeping Christ Child with Mary, Joseph and John the Baptist; a landscape showing Mary nursing her son; a small silver panel showing Mary, Joseph and the Christ Child and a painting of the Virgin and Child by Lucas Cranach. Next door, in the study itself, was a panel with a print showing Our Lady in the Sun above the city of Rome. A number of Octavian's images bear witness to his connection with Marian pilgrimage sites. In 1586 in gratitude for a recovery from illness Octavian had made a pilgrimage to the shrine at Altötting, and he owned a print of the Altötting Madonna and a written description of her miracles. Marian shrines further afield were also commemorated in Octavian's collection. In the same room in the Augsburg house was a panel with a coloured print of Our Lady of Montserrat and amongst his treasures were two silver pilgrimage signs showing Our Lady of Loreto.[120]

The evidence concerning Octavian Secundus' religious life illustrates the central part that Marian piety might play in constituting Catholic identity. Octavian went on pilgrimage to Altötting, and had mementoes from the Marian shrines at Montserrat (Catalonia) and Loreto, though we do not know whether he had visited these sites himself. For his burial chapel in SS Ulrich and Afra he donated a magnificent altarpiece showing the Virgin and Child with saints Benedict and Francis and the city of Augsburg (figure 34), and he may also have commissioned Christoph Schwarz to paint a Marian altarpiece for the Jesuit church of St Salvator (figure 32). For his house chapel he commissioned another painting of the Virgin and Child, this time with Augsburg's chief patron saints and cityscape (figure 35). In his residences in Augsburg, Oberkirchberg, Deisenhausen and Bobingen he had numerous Marian images, and these images were particularly densely displayed in the cell-like meditation room in the Augsburg house where he probably undertook many of his personal religious observances. Octavian

[120] Lieb, *Octavian Secundus Fugger*, pp. 174, 251–4, 271, 286–7, 301, 310. On the private use of pilgrimage signs see Germanisches Nationalmuseum, ed., *Spiegel der Seligkeit*, pp. 131–6.

was also, as his ownership of two rosary images and numerous sets of prayer beads suggests, a great advocate of rosary devotion. Indeed, Octavian not only owned numerous rosaries himself, he also promoted their use by others. In 1590 he gave more than one hundred simple rosaries as gifts to the schoolchildren of Oberkirchberg.[121]

While no other sixteenth- or early seventeenth-century inventories contain so many detailed descriptions of Marian images as Octavian's, other records do indicate that Augsburg's wealthy Catholics shared at least this aspect of his Marian zeal. Conrad Peutinger, for example, had twenty rosaries and Paul Welser had fifty-nine. Apollonia Rehlinger, whose possessions were inventoried in 1584, had thirty-five, and Maria Meuting had thirty-three as well as the gilded panel with an image of Mary mentioned in chapter 3. Many other inventories list smaller numbers of sets of prayer beads.[122] Some of the more valuable sets of beads were undoubtedly family heirlooms or collectors' pieces – in both Nuremberg and Augsburg wealthy Protestants kept their most precious rosaries – but their extensive presence in Augsburg's domestic inventories demonstrates the importance of rosary devotion within the city's Catholic milieu. Augsburg's rosary brotherhood was, as we have seen, re-established at the city's Dominican church in 1574, and the recitation of the rosary was one of the most important types of Marian piety during this period.[123] Inventory evidence confirms that for Augsburg's Catholics, from Octavian with his splendid collection of images to an artisan with his modest set of prayer beads, Mary played a key role in private devotion as well as in public worship.

BAVARIA AND BEYOND

Marian piety – expressed through liturgy, pilgrimage, sodalities and images – played a central part in the renewal of Augsburg's Catholic cult. The Marian piety of Augsburg's Catholic citizens cannot, however, be properly understood without reference to the religious life of nearby Bavaria. The Fuggers were key proponents of Counter-Reformation Marianism: one of their servants was exorcised by Canisius at Altötting in 1570; they helped to bring Loreto devotion to Augsburg; and the magnificent altarpieces that they commissioned for Augsburg's Catholic churches unashamedly celebrated Mary's apotheosis. And the Fuggers were closely linked to the Catholic court of the Wittelsbachs in Munich, both because of their banking and trading interests and because of their common religious and cultural concerns. In his will Anton Fugger, son of Canisius'

[121] Lieb, *Octavian Secundus Fugger*, p. 124.

[122] I am grateful to Dr Hans-Jörg Kunast for allowing me access to a transcription of Peutinger's inventory. SStBA, 2^0 Cod. Aug. 88 (Welser); StadtAA, Reichsstadt, 100/2, J. Spreng'sche Notariatsakten, 1581–93, 1584, 2 (Rehlinger) and 1586, 20 (Meuting).

[123] Fisher, *Music and Religious Identity*, p. 213.

celebrated convert Ursula von Lichtenstein, specified that his sons should finish their education either at this court or with the Habsburgs in Vienna. Such links helped shape Augsburg's Catholic cult, most notably in 1579 when the Fuggers and Jesuits joined forces with Duke Wilhelm V of Bavaria to compel Augsburg's council and cathedral chapter to accede to the establishment of a Jesuit church and college in the city.[124] They also had a decisive impact on Marian piety within the biconfessional city. Almost all of the Marian altarpieces commissioned by the Fuggers, for example, were painted by artists trained or active at the Bavarian court.[125] These altarpieces, and other manifestations of Marian piety, must therefore be viewed against the backdrop of Bavarian Marianism. They must be seen not only as manifestations of personal piety, but also as deliberate statements of *Religionspolitik*, politics dictated by religious affiliation. Augsburg's Marian cult demonstrated its Catholic citizens' allegiance to the Counter-Reformation culture of Bavaria and southern Europe.

Bavaria was the heartland of the German Counter-Reformation and a cornerstone of Catholic Europe, especially during the traumatic period of the Thirty Years War. It is well known that under Duke Maximilian I (ruled 1598–1651) devotion to the Virgin became a state programme, but even before the seventeenth century Bavaria's Wittelsbach rulers had promoted Mary's cult through their personal expressions of piety. Albrecht V (1550–79), whose reign witnessed the beginnings of the Bavarian Counter-Reformation, pledged himself to the Virgin of Altötting in 1571 and was also a devotee of the Virgin of Loreto.[126] The Litany of Loreto was adopted in the ducal household following Canisius' high-profile exorcism at Altötting in 1570.[127] Albrecht's Marian piety was also expressed visually: in 1560 he commissioned his court artist, Hans Mielich, to produce a monumental altarpiece for the high altar of the Liebfrauenmünster in Ingolstadt. The altarpiece, completed in 1572 in time for the centennial of the University of Ingolstadt, depicts on its front side scenes from the life of the Virgin. Its central panel shows the duke and his family gathered beneath the protective cloak of the Virgin.[128] Canisius' great work, *De Maria Virgine incomparabili*, was dedicated to Albrecht, and in 1578 the duke rewarded the Jesuit's labours with a gift of fifty *Gulden*.[129] Albrecht's son, Wilhelm V (1579–98), perpetuated this ducal devotion to Mary. He inscribed his name in blood in the membership book of the recently created brotherhood of the Altötting Madonna;[130] in 1581 he dedicated the city of Munich to the

[124] Strecker, *Augsburger Altäre*, pp. 247–8, 271–2, 297–8. [125] Above, pp. 171–84.
[126] Hütl, *Marianische Wallfahrten*, p. 102. Pötzl, 'Loreto in Bayern', 196.
[127] Fisher, *Music and Religious Identity*, p. 259.
[128] Smith, *The Northern Renaissance*, pp. 376–8; Baumstark, ed., *Rom in Bayern*, p. 65; Hecht, *Katholische Bildertheologie*, pp. 405–8.
[129] Helmut Dotterweich, *Der junge Maximilian: Jugend und Erziehung des bayerischen Herzogs und späteren Kurfürsten Maximilian I. von 1573 bis 1593* (Munich, 1962), p. 73.
[130] Soergel, *Wondrous in his Saints*, p. 164.

Virgin of Altötting; and he also went on pilgrimage to Tuntenhausen, the greatest Marian pilgrimage site within the bishopric of Freising, to Altötting and to Loreto.[131] In the Munich *Residenz* a light burned day and night before a copy of the Loreto Madonna.[132]

It was under Duke (from 1623 Elector) Maximilian I that Bavarian Marianism reached its apogee. Maximilian had been brought up amidst the Marian piety of the Jesuits at the behest of his father, Wilhelm V.[133] At the age of eight he had apparently learned by heart the Office of the Blessed Virgin and prayed it regularly. On Saturdays he and his siblings prayed the Loretan Litany, and they also regularly recited the *Corona quinquegenaria*, a fifty-verse rhymed Marian prayer. In 1584 the heir to the Bavarian throne entered Munich's Marian sodality, and was named *General-Praefekt* of all of Germany's Marian sodalities.[134] Maximilian's first act as duke of Bavaria was an official pilgrimage to the Marian shrine at Altötting. He also favoured other Marian shrines, for example Tuntenhausen, to which he donated a high altar dedicated to 'Virgo potens' and a statue of Mary as 'Patrona Bavariae'.[135] But it was Altötting that remained central to his piety throughout his life. He donated two canonries for the collegial foundation there, as well as a costly silver tabernacle and other ornaments for the statue of the Madonna. In secret he dedicated himself to the Virgin of Altötting, signing with his own blood a document that was sealed, hidden in the silver tabernacle in the chapel and found again only after his death: 'Into your hands I, Maximilian, chief among sinners, dedicate and devote myself to you, Virgin Mary, with this blood and signature as witness.'[136] After his death his heart and that of his first wife were placed side by side in the chapel at Altötting, a custom that all dukes and kings of Bavaria observed until the death of Ludwig III, the last king of Bavaria (1921).

Maximilian promoted Marian piety partly through his own patronage. During his rebuilding of the Munich *Residenz* (1600–7) he constructed two new chapels, both of which were dedicated to Mary (*Maria Immaculata* and *Maria Verkündigung*). The larger chapel, the *Hofkapelle*, had an altar painting by Hans Werle of Mary as queen of the saints, its ceiling showed the symbols of the Loretan Litany and on the rear upper gallery was an inscription: 'For the Virgin and Queen of the world . . . conceived through a miracle in order to conceive through a miracle, the most abject Duke Maximilian has built this

[131] Hütl, *Marianische Wallfahrten*, pp. 105–6; Dotterweich, *Der junge Maximilian*, p. 73; Georg Schwaiger, 'Maria Patrona Bavariae', in *Bavaria Sancta: Zeugen christlichen Glaubens in Bayern*, ed. Georg Schwaiger (Regensburg, 1970), pp. 30–1.

[132] Pötzl, 'Loreto in Bayern', 197. [133] Hütl, *Marianische Wallfahrten*, pp. 108–9.

[134] Dotterweich, *Der junge Maximilian*, pp. 71–2.

[135] Schwaiger, 'Maria Patrona Bavariae', p. 32; Herbert Glaser, ed., *Wittelsbach und Bayern*, 6 vols. (Munich, 1980), vol. 2, part II, p. 70; Schütz, *Die kirchliche Barockarchitektur*, p. 62 and ill. 77.

[136] Quoted in Hubensteiner, *Vom Geist des Barock*, p. 117.

chapel' (1601).[137] In 1632, the year of the Swedish occupation of Munich, Maximilian had scenes from the life of the Virgin added to the rich marble inlay on the walls of the smaller chapel, the 'Geheime Kammerkapelle' or 'Reiche Kapelle'.[138] In 1615/16 Maximilian had Hans Krumper's statue of the Virgin and Child placed on the outside of the *Residenz*. Mary has the key attributes of the Apocalyptic Woman: a crown of stars, and a moon beneath her feet. Her plinth bears the title accorded to her by Maximilian, 'Patrona Boiariae',[139] and in a cartouche above is the beginning of a Marian antiphon, *Sub tuum praesidium confugimus, sub quo secure laetique degimus*.[140] The notion that Bavaria was under Mary's special protection was also expressed in an engraving designed by the Augsburg artist Matthias Kager for Matthäus Rader's *Bavaria Sancta* of 1615 (figure 42), commissioned by Maximilian. Here the Archangel Michael, another key figure in Munich's Counter-Reformation, presents a map of the territory to Mary and the Christ Child. The city of Munich is depicted beneath.[141] Maximilian's son, Ferdinand Maria (born 1636), was the first Wittelsbach to be given Mary's name alongside his male name.[142] Alongside these acts of patronage and personal devotion Maximilian did all he could to promote the Virgin's cult throughout his territories. Whenever the Ave bell was rung, Maximilian's subjects were expected to kneel down and pray, wherever they were.[143] He also introduced three new Marian feast days (Mary's Presentation, Visitation and Immaculate Conception), and decreed that all his subjects must own a rosary. His devotion to the Mother of God even extended to the coinage: from 1623 Maximilian issued 'Marientaler' or 'Frauentaler' bearing images of the Virgin.[144]

Under Maximilian 'pietas Mariana' shaped Bavaria's political profile as well as its devotional life. Maximilian promoted Mary not only as patron of Bavaria, but also as champion of the Catholic cause in an era of increasing confessional tension. When possible, Maximilian chose to undertake important political actions on Marian feast days. His troops set out to occupy the biconfessional

[137] Schwaiger, 'Maria Patrona Bavariae', p. 31.

[138] Gärten und Seen Bayerische Verwaltung der staatlichen Schlösser, *Residenz München: amtlicher Führer* (Munich, 1937), pp. 106–10.

[139] Hütl, *Marianische Wallfahrten*, p. 115. There was no formal moment at which Bavaria was dedicated to the Virgin. A gold coin from 1610 already shows her above a silhouette of the city with the inscription 'Sub tuum praesidium'. Dieter Albrecht, *Maximilian I. von Bayern 1573–1651* (Munich, 1998), p. 294.

[140] Albrecht, *Maximilian I.*, p. 295. 'We take refuge in your protection, under which we live in security and joy.'

[141] Baumstark, ed., *Rom in Bayern*, no. 126.

[142] Hubensteiner, *Vom Geist des Barock*, p. 118.

[143] Hütl, *Marianische Wallfahrten*, p. 109 and n. 412. The practice of kneeling down to pray three Ave Marias when the bell was rung in the evening originated in Rome, and spread through parts of Germany during the Middle Ages. Janssen, *Das Erzbistum Köln*, p. 483.

[144] Hubensteiner, *Vom Geist des Barock*, p. 118; Hütl, *Marianische Wallfahrten*, p. 114; Albrecht, *Maximilian I.*, p. 294.

RELIGIO PRINCIPVM, TVTELA REGNORVM.
Parua sed alma Dei præsignat dextera BOIAM,
Propinat totum VIRGO parénsq DEVM.
Tutatur MICHAËL cælesti milite campos;
INDIGETES seruant oppida, BOIA times!

Figure 42. Raphael Sadeler I (after Matthias Kager), Archangel Michael and Virgin and Child with a map of Bavaria, engraving from Matthäus Rader, *Bavaria Sancta* (Munich, 1615) (Staatliche Graphische Sammlung, Munich)

city of Donauwörth on 8 December 1607, the feast day of Mary's Conception. His alliance with the imperial general Count Bucquoy in 1620 and his invasion of the Upper Palatinate in 1621 took place on 8 September, the feast day of Mary's Nativity.[145] During the Thirty Years War the name of Mary became the battle cry of the Bavarian army, and its soldiers fought under banners depicting the Virgin. The first great victory at the White Mountain near Prague (1620) was ascribed to her intercession, and in thanks Maximilian and Emperor Ferdinand II had a Marian chapel built on the battlefield.[146] The Bavarian–imperial triumph was attributed in particular to a miraculous image of the Adoration of the Shepherds, which had been damaged by iconoclasts and rescued from the Bohemian town of Strakonice by the Spanish Carmelite friar Dominicus a Jesu Maria. Dominicus carried this image into the heart of the battle and it was then taken to Rome where it was installed in the church of Santa Maria della Vittoria in 1622.[147]

Two monuments in Munich itself also testify to Maximilian's public invocation of Mary during the period of the Thirty Years War. In 1620 a new high altar was installed in the Frauenkirche, Munich's cathedral. Like many of the retables commissioned for Augsburg's churches during the late sixteenth and seventeenth centuries, this altar depicted the Assumption and Coronation of the Virgin. At twenty-five metres high, it dominated the choir area, and its central painted panel was the work of the Bavarian court artist Peter Candid. A prominent inscription on the reverse of the altar, facing the choir gallery, recorded the altar's dedication to God and to the Virgin, 'the best and greatest patron of Bavaria . . . the special protector of princes . . . the victorious helper'. The altar was, according to this inscription, built by Maximilian after his return from Bohemia 'in grateful remembrance' of his victory. In fact, however, it was probably almost entirely complete by the time of the battle, having been requested by the cathedral chapter in 1617. The inscription therefore records Maximilian's rededication in the light of the momentous events in Bohemia.[148] In 1638, in thanks for Munich's preservation from destruction by Swedish troops,

145 Kraus, *Maximilian I.*, pp. 75, 115; Hubensteiner, *Vom Geist des Barock*, pp. 117–18.

146 Glaser, ed., *Wittelsbach und Bayern*, vol. 2, part II, p. 566.

147 Olivier Chaline, *La Bataille de la Montagne Blanche (8 Novembre 1620): un mystique chez les guerriers* (Paris, 1999), pp. 271–4, 304–17, 511–22; Matsche, 'Gegenreformatorische Architekturpolitik', 98–100. On Dominicus see T. Johnson, '"Victoria a Deo missa?" Living saints on the battlefields of the central European Counter-Reformation', in *Confessional Sanctity (c.1500–c.1800)*, ed. Jürgen Beyer *et al.* (Mainz, 2003), pp. 323–28. For a 1622 print from Augsburg commemorating the role of the miraculous image see Renger, *Peter Paul Rubens*, p. 71.

148 The altar was destroyed in 1858. Brigitte Volk-Knüttel, 'Der Hochaltar der Münchner Frauenkirche von 1620 und seine Gemälde von Peter Candid', in *Monachium sacrum. Festschrift zur 500-Jahr-Feier der Metropolitankirche zu Unserer Lieben Frau in München*, ed. Georg Schwaiger (Munich, 1994), especially pp. 219–20. In 1623 Bishop Veit Adam von Gepeckh commissioned an altarpiece showing the Apocalyptic Woman for Freising Cathedral. This altarpiece was also closely connected with Bavaria's invocation of Mary during the Thirty Years War. Renger, *Peter Paul Rubens*, pp. 67–80.

Maximilian erected a *Mariensäule* [Marian column] on the city's Schrannenplatz. Figure 43 shows the consecration of its statue of the Virgin and Child on a crescent moon, which took place in the presence of the bishop of Freising, Maximilian, members of the cathedral chapter and other dignitaries on 7 November, the day on which a procession was held each year to commemorate the Battle of the White Mountain.[149] At the consecration, Maximilian supposedly made a special plea to Mary, in elegant Latin perhaps composed by the Jesuit Jakob Balde: 'Rem, Regem, Regimen, Regionem, Religionem conserva Bavaris Virgo Maria tuis.'[150] The original inscription, written on a bronze plaque on the base of the column, also invoked Mary's powerful protection of Bavaria.[151] This magnificent public monument, conspicuously positioned right in the middle of Munich, testified to Mary's religious and political significance for the Bavarian state.

For the Austrian Habsburgs, as much as for their Wittelsbach neighbours, Mary served as a symbol of Catholic renewal and reconquest. They, like the Bavarian Duke Maximilian I, could invoke a family tradition of Marian veneration. Charles V (1519–56) was deeply devoted to the Virgin, who seems for him to have provided a source of comfort during the religious upheavals of the Reformation. In 1541, for example, after Protestant and Catholic theologians failed to formulate a religious compromise at the Diet of Regensburg, he went on pilgrimage from there to Altötting. He also visited Montserrat many times during the course of his reign. Indeed in 1543 Bucer was provoked to complain in a letter to Calvin that the emperor fought openly against Christ, praying the rosary lying on the ground and focusing his eyes on an image of Mary. The armour that Charles wore at the Battle of Mühlberg was adorned with an image of the Madonna standing on a sickle moon, and Charles eventually died, according to contemporary reports, with a cross and a picture of Mary in his hands. Ferdinand I, who succeeded his brother as Holy Roman Emperor (1556–64), maintained this Habsburg devotion, issuing, as Duke Maximilian was later to do in Bavaria, coins bearing the Virgin's image.[152]

It was above all under Emperors Ferdinand II (1619–37) and Ferdinand III (1637–57) that devotion to the Virgin became a key element, alongside devotion to the Eucharist and the cross, of the *pietas Austriaca*, the 'dynastic political

[149] Volk-Knüttel, 'Der Hochaltar der Münchener Frauenkirche', p. 200; Albrecht, *Maximilian I.*, p. 295.

[150] Albrecht, *Maximilian I.*, p. 296. Châtellier gives the following translation: 'keep under your protection, o Holy Virgin, as its patron, your Bavaria, its property, its institutions, its lands and its religion', *The Europe of the Devout*, p. 115.

[151] Schwaiger, 'Maria Patrona Bavariae', p. 33. 'Boicae Dominae benignissimae, Protectrici potentissimae'.

[152] Johann Janssen, *Geschichte des deutschen Volkes seit Ausgang des Mittelalters* (Freiburg im Breisgau, 1894), vol. 8, p. 306 n. 2; Coreth, *Pietas Austriaca*, pp. 48–9; Werner Thomas and Luc Duerloo, eds., *Albert and Isabella, 1598–1621: essays* (Brussels, 1998), p. 171, n. 29.

Figure 43. The consecration of Munich's *Mariensäule* [Marian pillar] on 7 November 1638 (Staatliche Graphische Sammlung, Munich)

myth' that ascribed faith and Christian merit to Austria's ruling house.[153] The Marian zeal of the Austrian Habsburgs was undoubtedly inspired in part by their knowledge of the devotion of their Bavarian neighbours, transmitted in particular through Maria of Bavaria, daughter of Duke Albrecht V, wife of Archduke Charles of Inner Austria and mother of Ferdinand II. Once again, this zeal comprised both acts of personal piety and public professions of faith. Ferdinand II's Jesuit confessor and biographer, Guillaume Lamormaini, described his master's devotion to Mary: 'he revered her as a vassal his protector and loved her as a child his mother'.[154] We have already encountered Ferdinand II as a keen proponent of Mary's cult. He built, with Duke Maximilian I, a chapel dedicated to the Virgin on the site of the Battle of the White Mountain, and in 1629, the year of the Edict of Restitution, he promoted the celebration of the feast of the Immaculate Conception in thanks for the preservation of his lands and of the Catholic religion.

As these acts suggest, Ferdinand's devotion, like that of Maximilian, had a political dimension. In 1598, at age twenty, he had pledged in the presence of the Virgin of Loreto to expel sectarian preachers from Steiermark, Kärnten and Krain. After the defeat of the Bohemian Protestants Ferdinand vowed to do the same in Bohemia. This time his vow was made at Mariazell, a shrine located in northern Styria near the border with Lower Austria, which was actively promoted by the Habsburgs and their clergy (in particular Cardinal Melchior Khlesl).[155] Like Duke Maximilian I, Ferdinand recognized Mary as 'Generalissima' of his armies during the Thirty Years War, and images of the Virgin adorned Austrian banners as well as those of the Catholic League. Ferdinand II's son, Ferdinand III, went a step further, placing all his territories under Mary's protection after Vienna had been threatened by the Swedes in 1645. During a splendid ceremony on 18 March 1647, Ferdinand entrusted and consecrated himself, his dynasty, his subjects, his armies and his lands to God and the Virgin, as ruler and patroness of Austria. The *Mariensäule* erected to commemorate his vow was similar in form to the one that had adorned Munich's Marienplatz since 1638, but it depicted Mary as the *Immaculata*, crowned with stars and trampling a serpent representing heresy beneath her feet. The Austrian Habsburgs, like their Spanish cousins, were keen proponents of the Immaculate Conception. Indeed, Ferdinand III himself had petitioned the pope to promote this still-controversial doctrine. The tradition of Habsburg Marianism was continued in the later seventeenth century by Leopold I (1658–1705), who repeated Ferdinand's ceremony of consecration in 1693 at the height of the Turkish war.[156]

153 Evans, *The Making of the Habsburg Monarchy*, p. 73. On the Habsburgs' devotion to the Virgin of Loreto see Matsche, 'Gegenreformatorische Architekturpolitik', 91–8.

154 Coreth, *Pietas Austriaca*, p. 52.

155 On Mariazell see Bäumer and Scheffczyk, eds., *Marienlexikon*, vol. 4, pp. 309–11.

156 Coreth, *Pietas Austriaca*, pp. 53–8 and Regina Pörtner, *The Counter-Reformation in Central Europe: Styria 1580–1630*, Oxford Historical Monographs (Oxford, 2001), p. 242. On the *Immaculata* and heresy see Canisius, *De Maria Virgine incomparabili*, pp. 599–600.

Such examples of the polemical use of the cult of the Virgin during the era of the Counter-Reformation could be multiplied.[157] To the north-west of Bavaria, for example, lay the duchy of Pfalz-Neuburg, which had been Protestant since the 1540s. Count Palatine Wolfgang Wilhelm (1614–53) converted to Catholicism in 1613 on the eve of his marriage to the daughter of Duke Wilhelm V of Bavaria, with the aim of gaining access to Bavarian, imperial and Spanish support in his campaign to acquire the Rhenish duchies of Jülich, Berg and Cleves. Within Pfalz-Neuburg Wolfgang Wilhelm used Marian piety as part of his campaign of recatholicization. A portrait painted in around 1650 shows him as the scourge of the evangelical faith, trampling the Augsburg Confession underfoot. On the table beside him are a carved wooden statue of the Virgin and Child and a plan of the Hofkirche in Neuburg.[158] During his reign the Hofkirche, which had been begun in 1607 as an evangelical church, was handed over to the Jesuits, dedicated to Mariä Himmelfahrt and became the mother church of the Counter-Reformation in Pfalz-Neuburg. The magnificent stucco decoration of this church, designed by a Jesuit in close consultation with Wolfgang Wilhelm and executed between 1616 and 1619, testifies to the triumph of Counter-Reformation Catholicism in this formerly evangelical territory. Mary is central to its iconographic programme, which begins in the entrance hall with a relief showing Wolfgang Wilhelm and his wife dedicating the city of Neuburg to the Virgin (figure 44). Further reliefs throughout the church depict the emblems of the Loretan Litany and other Marian symbols, as well as Mary's birth and Assumption. She is shown as queen of the angels, patriarchs, prophets, evangelists and relatives of Christ, and her monogram, MRA, appears repeatedly.[159]

In his exuberant decorative programme for the Hofkirche of Mariä Himmelfahrt, as in his more sober portrait of around 1650, Wolfgang Wilhelm demonstrated his commitment to the cult of the Virgin as a symbol of Catholic renewal and reconquest, just as his fellow Counter-Reformation princes had done in Bavaria and Austria. It was not only secular princes who recognized the

[157] On Catholic cities' invocations of Mary before and during the Thirty Years War see Klaus Graf, 'Maria als Stadtpatronin in deutschen Städten des Mittelalters und der frühen Neuzeit', in *Frömmigkeit im Mittelalter: politisch-soziale Kontexte, Visuelle Praxis, körperliche Ausdrucksformen*, ed. Klaus Schreiner (Munich, 2002), p. 140.

[158] Horst H. Stierhof, *Das biblisch gemäl: die Kapelle im Ottheinrichsbau des Schlosses Neuburg an der Donau*, Forschungen zur Kunst- und Kulturgeschichte 3 (Munich, 1993), pp. 114–15.

[159] Pötzl, *Loreto*, p. 86; Jeffrey Chipps Smith, 'The art of salvation in Bavaria', in *The Jesuits: cultures, sciences and the arts 1540–1773*, ed. John W. O'Malley (Toronto, 1999), pp. 582–8. The programme of St Andreas in Düsseldorf, the capital of the duchy of Berg acquired by Wolfgang Wilhelm in 1614, was modelled on that of the Neuburg Hofkirche. Jeffrey Chipps Smith, *Sensuous Worship: Jesuits and the art of the early Catholic Reformation in Germany* (Princeton, NJ, 2002), pp. 145–58. Wolfgang Wilhelm also promoted the doctrine of the Immaculate Conception. Karl-Heinz Tekath, 'Die Unbefleckte Empfängnis Mariens – Hauptpatronin des Erzbistums Köln', in *Bistumspatrone in Deutschland: Festschrift für Jakob Torsy zum 9. Juni / 28. Juli 1983*, ed. August Leidl (Munich and Zurich, 1983), p. 61. On Marian devotion in late seventeenth-century Neuburg see Johnson, '"Victoria a Deo missa?"', p. 332.

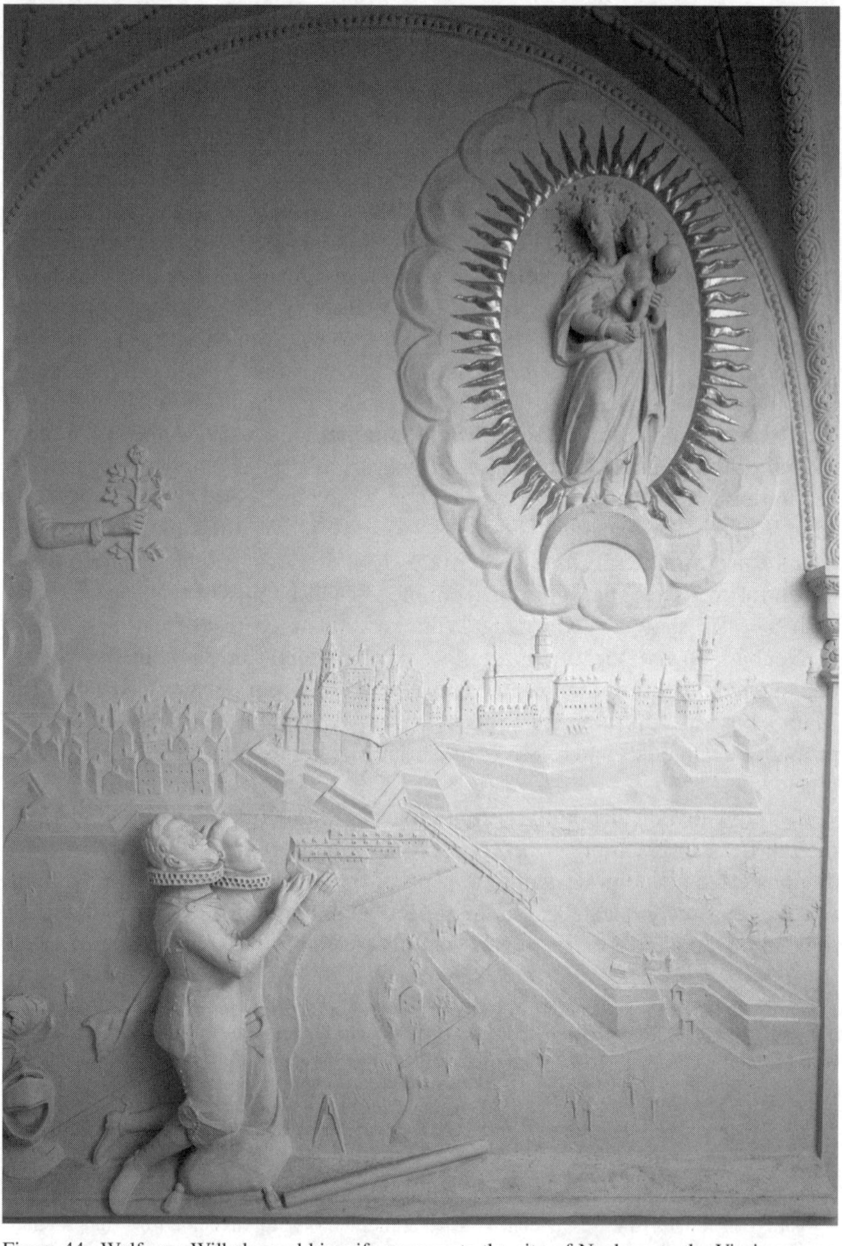

Figure 44. Wolfgang Wilhelm and his wife consecrate the city of Neuburg to the Virgin, stucco decoration from the Hofkirche in Neuburg, 1616–19

value of Marian veneration, however. In Würzburg, for example, Julius Echter von Mespelbrunn, who reigned as bishop from 1573 to 1617, promoted Marian piety as part of his campaign to restore Catholicism within his diocese.[160] In 1575 a Marian congregation was established for the benefit of the students of the newly founded University of Würzburg. Julius placed his fortified residence on the Marienburg under Mary's protection, adorning its tower with an image of the Virgin as Queen of Heaven. In his determination to promote Mary's cult Julius also erected splendid early baroque pilgrimage churches at places such as Maria-Buchen and Dettelbach.[161]

MARY TRIUMPHANT

How did Mary come to constitute such a key part of Catholic identity in Augsburg and in much of the rest of southern Germany? In each of the territories that we have considered much of the credit for the renewal of festivals, processions and pilgrimages, for the foundation of sodalities and for the fostering of Marian piety amongst local elites must go to the Jesuits. In Augsburg, in Bavaria, in Austria and in Pfalz-Neuburg the Society of Jesus enjoyed the support of leading members of the political elite, and its representatives therefore played an important role in shaping Catholic culture. In Augsburg the Fugger family had, for many years, been closely involved with the society. Between 1560 and 1564 Peter Canisius had converted all of the family's evangelical wives and one evangelical husband to Catholicism.[162] As cathedral preacher Canisius went on to win back many more souls for the Catholic Church, and Fugger support remained vital to the Jesuit endeavour within the city. Fugger funds facilitated the establishment of Augsburg's Jesuit college, and individual members of the family, for example Octavian Secundus Fugger, maintained close personal connections to the Jesuit fathers.

In Bavaria the Jesuits flourished under the patronage of the Wittelsbach dukes. Wilhelm IV summoned members of the order to the theological faculty of his university at Ingolstadt, Albrecht V founded colleges for them in Ingolstadt and Munich, and Wilhelm V financed the construction of their splendid church and college of St Michael in Munich. The Jesuits served as confessors to both Wilhelm and his son, Maximilian I. Maximilian I studied in Ingolstadt from 1587 to 1591, where he spent time with the Jesuits. As duke and later elector of Bavaria he founded numerous colleges for them, and after 1623 entrusted them

160 On Echter see Frank Kleinehagenbrock, 'Würzburg als gegenreformatorisches Zentrum', *Würzburger Diözesan-Geschichtsblätter* 67 (2005), 70–5.

161 Hütl, *Marianische Wallfahrten*, pp. 54–8.

162 Martha Schad, *Die Frauen des Hauses Fugger von der Lilie (15.–17. Jahrhundert). Augsburg – Ortenburg – Trient* (Tübingen, 1989), p. 29.

with the recatholicization of the Upper Palatinate.[163] For the Austrian Habsburgs the Jesuits were equally important. Ferdinand II, like his cousin Maximilian, had studied in Ingolstadt. There he joined the Jesuits' Marian sodality.[164] Ferdinand, again like Maximilian, chose Jesuit fathers for his confessors, and members of the order were amongst his most influential advisors. He bestowed lavish gifts on the order, and its members played an important role in the recatholicization of Inner Austria.[165] In Pfalz-Neuburg Wolfgang Wilhelm gave them his Hofkirche, and entrusted them with the reconversion of his territory.[166]

In all of these territories the Jesuits comprised the vanguard of the Counter-Reformation movement and dictated the style of Catholic religious life. In each area the prominent role ascribed to Marian piety was therefore largely a product of their promotion of Mary's cult. Ignatius Loyola, founder of the Society of Jesus, was deeply devoted to the Virgin. In 1522 he visited Mary's shrine at Montserrat, and kept a vigil before the statue there. Loyola had a vision of the Virgin and Child during his stay at Montserrat, and Marian piety remained important to him throughout his life.[167] In Loyola's *Spiritual Exercises* Mary appears as a mediator between man and God, and she came to be seen as the society's special patron.[168] The Jesuits fostered Marian piety wherever they went. They founded Marian sodalities, and promoted Marian pilgrimage cults, for example that of the Virgin of Loreto.[169] They also disseminated Marian images. The miraculous icon of the Virgin housed at Santa Maria Maggiore in Rome, for example, was promoted by Francis Borgia, general of the society from 1565 to 1572, as a devotional image and as a tool for missionary work. The Jesuits installed copies of this image in their colleges and novitiates in places such as Cracow and Ingolstadt, and even carried them as far afield as Brazil and China as part of their missionary campaigns. In 1599 Matteo Ricci gave a copy to Emperor Wan-Li.[170] Wherever they went the Jesuits also defended key Marian doctrines such as the Immaculate Conception and Assumption.[171]

Jesuit drama emphasizes the important role that members of the society ascribed to the Virgin. In Dillingen in 1617, for example, the consecration of

163 Baumstark, ed., *Rom in Bayern*, p. 55 and Dotterweich, *Der junge Maximilian*, p. 98.

164 Coreth, *Pietas Austriaca*, pp. 51–2.

165 Pörtner, *The Counter-Reformation in Central Europe*, pp. 113–14 and 195–222.

166 Duhr, *Geschichte der Jesuiten im XVI. Jahrhundert*, pp. 486–9.

167 Michael A. Mullett, *The Catholic Reformation* (London and New York, 1999), pp. 78–9 and 93.

168 Bäumer and Scheffczyk, eds., *Marienlexikon*, vol. 3, pp. 373–7.

169 The 1672 edition of the *Atlas Marianus*, composed by the Jesuit Wilhelm von Gumppenberg, recorded over 300 Marian pilgrimage sites in Germany. Ludwig Dorn, 'Aus dem Atlas Marianus: die Marienwallfahrten des Bistums Augsburg im Jahre 1672', *JbVAB* 11 (1977), 69–70.

170 Steven F. Ostrow, *Art and Spirituality in Counter-Reformation Rome: the Sistine and Pauline Chapels in S. Maria Maggiore* (Cambridge, 1996), p. 127.

171 In 1593 the defence of the doctrine of the Immaculate Conception was made into a general duty of the order. Beissel, *Geschichte der Verehrung Marias im 16. und 17. Jahrhundert*, p. 226.

the Jesuits' *Studienkirche* of Mariä Himmelfahrt was marked by the elaborate staging of a play entitled *Deiparae Virginis triumphus*. Lasting three days and involving a cast of over three hundred people this was surely one of the greatest Marian spectacles of the early modern period. In the opening scenes allegorical figures tell how heaven, earth and all created things should honour and serve Mary. The sun and other heavenly bodies pay homage to her, angels praise her and the world thanks her for her role in its salvation. Later scenes depict some of Mary's emblems and prefigurations, such as Moses' burning bush and Gideon's fleece, and enumerate her virtues. Some of the Jesuits' favourite Marian doctrines are incorporated: in act 3, for example, the Apostles and Archangel Michael testify to Mary's bodily assumption into heaven. Like most Jesuit dramas, the Dillingen play comments on contemporary events by analogy rather than directly. Hellish spirits try to demean the Virgin through their foremost tools, the heretics. The heretics who feature in the play are not, however, Protestants, but Jews, Turks and Byzantine iconoclasts. One, the iconoclast Emperor Copronymus (a nickname meaning 'the dung-named' for Constantine V, who reigned 741–75), who had decreed that none of his subjects should worship the Virgin, receives harsh punishment: he is consumed by heavenly fire and his body is thrown into hell. The fourth and fifth acts depict Mary's military victories, but again deal largely with remote rather than recent historical events. The Byzantine emperor Andronicus triumphs over an army led by his upstart grandson by calling on Mary's help; Emperor Heraclius (reigned 610–41) wins his struggle against the Persian king thanks to Mary's intervention; and in Italy Narses, general for Emperor Justinian I, defeats Totila, king of the Goths, with Mary's assistance. Of the early modern victories ascribed to Mary's intercession only Lepanto features: in the final act Don John of Austria defeats the Turks, burns their ship and places Mary's image in a triumphal wagon to which Turkish prisoners are harnessed.[172]

No other surviving plays of the period promote Marian piety in such spectacular fashion, but Mary did certainly feature in other dramas. In 1627 *Cultus imaginum vindicatus* was performed in Amberg in the Upper Palatinate. The main part of the play concerns John of Damascus (c.657–c.749), who wrote in defence of the cult of images during a period of imperial iconoclasm. As punishment John's hand was, according to the play, cut off, but was miraculously restored to him by Mary. In brief asides the play also depicts the divine punishment meted out on those who attack images of the saints. Two Jews, for example, who stabbed and mocked a Marian image became lame and blind as a result.[173] Staged shortly after the expulsion of Calvinist clergy by Maximilian I

[172] SStBA, 4° Bild 1–25. This is a shortened, printed German translation of the original Latin text.

[173] German programme reprinted in E. M. Szarota, *Das Jesuitendrama im deutschen Sprachgebiet*, 6 vols. (Munich, 1979–87), vol. 2, pp. 443–58.

of Bavaria, this play clearly dealt with themes that were of particular relevance to the Jesuits' campaign in the Upper Palatinate: the veneration of images and saints.[174] A play, *Hungaria*, performed in Augsburg in 1664 again emphasized Mary's role as vanquisher of heretics. It tells the story of Ludwig I, king of Hungary and Poland, who with the help of the Virgin defeated a Turkish army of 80,000 led by Amurath in 1363. The timing was apposite: in the same year Habsburg troops inflicted a major defeat on the Ottoman army at the Battle of Szentgotthárd. The play also records that Ludwig, in thanks for this victory, gave splendid gifts to the Madonna at Mariazell, and left his spurs, dagger and royal standard at her shrine.[175] The shrine at Mariazell was one of the key pilgrimage sites of Counter-Reformation Austria, so again the play had obvious relevance to the Jesuits' contemporary mission.[176] There were certainly many other Jesuit plays that promoted Marian piety, though in many cases no more than their names survive.[177] Such plays were performed in Latin before a limited audience, and their propaganda value should therefore not be overstated. The surviving texts do, however, demonstrate Mary's perceived importance for the Jesuits' campaign of recatholicization.

The polemical tone of the Jesuits' Marianism, as expressed in sodalities, pilgrimages, plays and other texts, cannot be denied. Canisius, for example, described Mary not as the humble human mother who had been successfully assimilated into Lutheran teaching, but rather as 'conqueror of devils and triumphant over demons and also heretics'.[178] This image of Mary vanquishing the enemies of the Catholic faith was not a new one. She had been invoked as 'alone destroyer of all heresies' during the Middle Ages, and an altarpiece from 1512 from the shrine of Mariazell shows her presiding over Ludwig I of Hungary's 1363 victory over the Turks.[179] It certainly, however, became more significant in the aftermath of the Reformation, when Mary was celebrated as the victor of the battles of Lepanto and the White Mountain, and as the figurehead of the church triumphant. Devotion to this militant Virgin was a way of delineating Catholic belief and practice. Canisius had urged that Catholics should venerate Mary fervently in defiance of Protestant criticism, and in Augsburg and in other areas where Catholic leaders had to counter evangelical teaching, the elite took such prescriptions very much to heart.[180]

174 Johnson, 'The recatholicization of the Upper Palatinate', p. 134.

175 SStBA, 4^0 Aug. 524 Gymnasium St Salvator (Jesuiten). Dissertationen, Schulkomödien, Sing- und Fastnachtspiele.

176 Pörtner, *The Counter-Reformation in Central Europe*, pp. 241–2. On Mariazell see also Bäumer and Scheffczyk, eds., *Marienlexikon*, vol. 4, pp. 309–11.

177 Jean-Marie Valentin, *Le théâtre des Jésuites dans les pays de langue allemande: répertoire chronologique des pièces représentées et des documents conservés (1555–1773)*, 2 vols. (Stuttgart, 1983–4).

178 Dotterweich, *Der junge Maximilian*, p. 73.

179 Coreth, *Pietas Austriaca*, p. 47; Gottfried Biedermann, *Katalog – Alte Galerie am Landesmuseum Joanneum. Mittelalterliche Kunst* (Graz, 1982), cat. no. 50.

180 On Pfalz-Neuburg see Merkl, 'Kunst und Konfessionalisierung', 210.

They commissioned images and participated in processions and other rituals that celebrated Mary's exceptional status and intercessory power rather than simply her faith and virtue. Even below the level of the elite Mary sometimes served as a confessional marker, as the conflicts that took place on Augsburg's streets suggest. For local artisans any manifestation of Marian piety – wearing a rosary, going on pilgrimage, defending Marian images – might be read as a sign of allegiance to the Catholic cause. Thus at both an elite and a popular level Marian piety advanced the cause of confessional politics by making visible an important boundary between Protestant and Catholic belief.

On Germany's confessional front line, however, Mary was important not only because of her status as a universal symbol of the Catholic Church but also because of her popular appeal. Historians such as Jean Delumeau and John Bossy have argued that the attempt to suppress popular religious culture was an essential part of the Counter-Reformation, but evidence concerning Marian piety indicates the opposite.[181] As R. Po-Chia Hsia has argued, the Counter-Reformation was successful in southern Germany in part at least because of the Catholic Church's ability to subsume rather than suppress the populace's desire for magical ritual and healing.[182] It is certainly true that some popular Marian rituals attracted the ire of reformers: during the 1610s, for example, several peasants were tried by Augsburg's magistrates for engaging in magical rituals involving Marian and other sacred formulae and images.[183] In general, however, Marian piety represented a triumphant synthesis between official and popular religiosity, between international Tridentine and local traditional Catholicism. Marian images and devotion proved an effective part of the Jesuits' 'conversion strategy' because they appealed to everyone from emperors and dukes to artisans and peasants.[184] In seventeenth-century Munich, for example, where Marian piety was elevated to a state programme, local citizens displayed their own Marian zeal. An entry from the 1672 edition of Gumppenberg's *Atlas Marianus* speaks of the great devotion that Munich's population showed to the Virgin. Many of the city's houses were, Gumppenberg suggests, adorned with Marian images with lights burning before them.[185]

The flourishing of Marian pilgrimage sites, especially during and after the crisis of the Thirty Years War, provides the best evidence for the popular appeal of Marian piety.[186] In Augsburg the Kobel Loreto chapel and the shrine of Maria Hilf chapel on the Lechfeld attracted numerous pilgrims, as did Altötting and

[181] See, for example, John Bossy, 'The Counter-Reformation and the people of Catholic Europe', *Past & Present* 47 (1970).

[182] R. Po-Chia Hsia, *Social Discipline in the Reformation: central Europe 1550–1750* (London and New York, 1989), p. 151.

[183] Roeck, *Eine Stadt in Krieg und Frieden*, vol. 1, pp. 93, 102. StadtAA, Reichsstadt, Strafamt, Urgichten, Nr. 235, 19. März 1612 (Anna Maria Stengler).

[184] Johnson, 'The recatholicization of the Upper Palatinate', p. 112.

[185] Wilhelm Gumppenberg, *Atlas Marianus* (Munich, 1672), pp. 941–2. See also Steiner, 'Der gottselige Fürst', pp. 258–9.

[186] Forster, *Catholic Revival*, p. 84.

Figure 45. Votive triptych of Andreas von Ettling, 1586 (Tuntenhausen, Upper Bavaria)

Tuntenhausen in Bavaria. These shrines might have been promoted by Jesuits and by other members of the Catholic elite, but pilgrims went there of their own volition. As Philip Soergel argues, these shrines were seen to have 'the ability to address situations in which human justice, economics, and medicine proved inadequate'.[187] Figure 45, for example, shows an *ex voto* given to the Madonna of Tuntenhausen by the knight Andreas von Ettling in 1586. As the small images on the wings and the inscription on the central panel record, while fighting during the Cologne War Andreas received a head wound that no medical procedure could cure. He, like many others, sought and found succour in prayer to the Virgin who, he believed, miraculously healed his wound.[188] Another *ex voto*, this time from Munich, demonstrates that it was not only Duke Maximilian I and Emperor Ferdinand II who invoked Mary during the

[187] Soergel, *Wondrous in his Saints*, p. 102.
[188] Glaser, ed., *Wittelsbach und Bayern*, vol. 2, part II, no. 104.

Figure 46. Design for an engraving showing hostages from Munich in prayer before the Virgin and Child, 1635 (Städtische Kunstsammlungen, Augsburg)

military crises of the Thirty Years War (figure 46).[189] The original painted image was commissioned from Matthias Kager to commemorate the release in 1635 of a number of Munich citizens and priests who had been taken hostage by the Swedes in 1632. The hostages kneel in front of a silhouette of Munich, adoring the Virgin of the Immaculate Conception who is enthroned on clouds above with her cloak spread out in a gesture of protection. One of the lay hostages holds an inscription that records the vow they made to the Virgin after their capture. As these *ex votos* demonstrate, in this era of confessional strife Mary was seen not only as the champion of the universal Catholic Church but also as the attentive advocate of individual causes.

In Augsburg and in many other areas of southern Germany the renewal of Marian liturgy and pilgrimage and the reinstatement of Marian images helped to mend the devotional continuum that had been interrupted by the Reformation. Christoph Amberger's panel for the high altar of Augsburg Cathedral (figure 27) and Paulus Mayr's retable for SS Ulrich and Afra (figure 30), both modelled on pre-Reformation images, provide the best evidence of the clerical elite's desire to demonstrate historicity. Where there had been a hiatus in Catholic practice, Mary's cult could link the post-Reformation Catholic Church to its late medieval predecessor. As Philip Soergel suggests in his study of early modern Bavarian pilgrimage shrines, 'the basic presuppositions and mental perceptions that people had about the saints and their intercession remained those common to the Middle Ages'.[190]

But in southern Germany Mary's cult was about much more than just historical continuity. In Augsburg and elsewhere the Mary celebrated at the feasts of the Immaculate Conception and Assumption and the Mary invoked in litanies and processions was increasingly the Mary of the Counter-Reformation. She was the protector of the Catholic cause. Peter Canisius invoked this Virgin during the exorcism he performed at Altötting; Augsburg's *sodales* pledged themselves to her service. Her apotheosis was depicted with the drama and emotionalism characteristic of baroque art on altarpieces commissioned by the Fuggers and their fellow Catholics from artists such as Rubens, Lanfranco and Kager. This Counter-Reformation Mary was the victor of the battles of Lepanto and the White Mountain, the patroness of Bavaria and later of Austria also. She was the Mary promoted by members of the Society of Jesus as the personification of their campaign against heresy. She was a symbol of the church militant and the church triumphant in an age of confessional strife, and devotion to her was therefore a mark of political as well as religious commitment.

[189] For an illustration of the original *ex voto* see ibid., vol. 2, part I, ill. 204. On the printed copy see Städtische Kunstsammlungen Augsburg, ed., *Welt im Umbruch*, vol. 2, p. 406, cat. no. 21.
[190] Soergel, *Wondrous in his Saints*, p. 3.

5. *Catholic pluralism and Cologne*

In Augsburg Marian devotion became a focal point for confessional identity and a means by which local Catholics distinguished themselves from their Protestant neighbours. Mary's cult, celebrated in images, liturgy, processions, pilgrimages and sodalities, served, to use Wolfgang Reinhard's terminology of confessionalization, as an *Unterscheidungsritus*, a rite of differentiation.[1] In Augsburg, as in Wittelsbach Bavaria, in Habsburg Austria and in other territories where members of the Society of Jesus dictated the style of religious life, Marian veneration was politicized as *demonstratio catholica*. Given the success of the Jesuit campaign to promote Marian pilgrimages and sodalities in such areas it is not surprising that the cult of the Virgin has been seen by historians as an important element in the post-Tridentine attempt to bring unity and discipline to Catholic practice and piety.[2] But the strength of Jesuit rhetoric and the prominence of state-sponsored Marianism in Bavaria should not blind us to the existence of significant variations in Marian devotion. While in the south the Jesuits' militant Marianism dominated, in Cologne and the Rhineland the situation was more complex. Cologne was an important centre of Catholic reform – Germany's first Jesuit community was established there in 1544 – but the city's Marian piety was less uniformly Counter-Reformation in tone than that of Augsburg or Bavaria. Cologne had a long history of civic devotion to the Virgin, which survived the Reformation era intact. At a parochial level traditional practices such as the clothing of Marian statues and the holding of elaborate processions continued despite the attempts of diocesan synods to introduce reforms. And Cologne's traditional Marian brotherhoods survived alongside Jesuit sodalities. In Augsburg and in Bavaria the Jesuits had created a distinct confessional culture amongst the elite, within which Mary was celebrated as the protector of the Catholic cause. In Cologne the weight of

[1] Reinhard, 'Was ist katholische Konfessionalisierung?', p. 430.

[2] See, for example, Gérald Chaix, 'Von der Christlichkeit zur Katholizität: Köln zwischen Traditionen und Modernität (1500–1648)', in *Frühe Neuzeit – Frühe Moderne? Forschungen zur Vielschichtigkeit von Übergangsprozessen*, ed. Rudolf Vierhaus (Göttingen, 1992), p. 242.

ecclesiastical tradition resulted in much greater diversity, and local Marian piety did not become so uniformly polemical. The study of Marian devotion thus highlights the importance of regional variation within German Catholicism, and the heterogeneity of Marian practice warns us not to overestimate the unifying power of the post-Tridentine church.

CATHOLIC CONTEXTS

With its numerous ecclesiastical institutions, its famous pilgrimage sites and its abundance of religious and semi-religious personnel, Cologne fully deserved its medieval epithet of 'holy'.[3] The city had a population of around 40,000 and occupied a key strategic position in the north-west of the Empire. It was by far the most important free city to remain loyal to the Catholic Church, though its confessional conservatism was by no means a foregone conclusion. Here, as in Germany's other major cities, there were plenty of Protestant influences at work. Evangelical demands featured amongst the articles presented to the city council by representatives of the *Gaffeln* (the guild groupings through which the council was elected) during a civic uprising in 1525.[4] Council minutes and *Turmbücher* (interrogation records) demonstrate that from the 1520s onwards local citizens were deliberately flaunting the taboos of the old church. In 1529 two evangelicals, Adolf Clarenbach and Peter Fliesteden, were executed, in 1543 two priests who had been distributing communion in both kinds fled the city, and in 1565 and 1595 groups of Anabaptists were arrested and expelled.[5]

From 1565 native Protestant rebellion was strengthened by an influx of refugees from the Netherlands. Between 1565 and 1570/1, when the council banished the Netherlanders for the first time, Heinz Schilling calculates that their numbers reached 2,000. Calvinist immigrants established a church organization that allowed at least some of their members to survive the first wave of persecution and in 1575 we find the first mention of a Lutheran congregation in Cologne. During the 1580s these groups were augmented by refugees from Antwerp.[6] During the period of its greatest flourishing around 1600 Cologne's German-speaking Reformed community comprised around 1,000 members while its

[3] See Introduction, p. 19. [4] Scribner, 'Why was there no Reformation in Cologne?', 235–6.

[5] H. K. Hesse, *Adolf Clarenbach: ein Beitrag zur Geschichte des Evangeliums im westen Deutschland*, Theologische Arbeiten aus dem wissenschaftlichen Prediger-Verein der Rheinprovinz, n.s. 25 (Neuwied am Rhein, 1929); L. Ennen, *Geschichte der Stadt Köln*, 5 vols. (Cologne, 1880), vol. 4, pp. 447–52; W. Herborn, 'Die Protestanten in Schilderung und Urteil des Kölner Chronisten Hermann von Weinsberg', in *Niederland und Nordwestdeutschland*, ed. W. Ehbrecht and H. Schilling (Cologne, 1983), p. 152.

[6] Heinz Schilling, *Niederländische Exulanten im 16. Jahrhundert: ihre Stellung im Sozialgefüge und im religiösen Leben deutscher und englischer Städte*, Schriften des Vereins für Reformationsgeschichte 187 (Gütersloh, 1972), pp. 59, 110, 114. See also Herborn, 'Die Protestanten', p. 151.

French-speaking equivalent had around 800. In 1590 the papal nuncio Ottavio Mirto Frangipani estimated the city's total Protestant population at 4,000 souls, and in 1623 the pastor of the church of St Maria Lyskirchen complained that a third of his parishioners were adherents of the Protestant faith. The parish of St Maria Lyskirchen was, as Rebekka von Mallinckrodt points out, exceptional in that it was located close to the city's harbour and contained a large number of traders who had close contact with people and ideas from outside Cologne. Yet the overall number of Protestants was sufficiently great for Cologne to be regarded as a missionary territory by the Catholic party, and the clandestine nature of the city's heretical communities ensured that concern about the 'Protestant danger' remained high.[7]

There were also two moments during the sixteenth century when external circumstances – the sympathies of two of Cologne's archbishops for the Protestant cause – threatened the confessional stability of the city. Opposed to Rome's financial exploitation of the church placed in his care, to the unchristian lifestyle of many of its clergy and to the abuses and superstitions that were rife in its teaching and ceremonies, Archbishop-Elector Hermann von Wied (ruled 1515–47) initially favoured an Erasmian-type reform. At a provincial synod held in 1536 he outlined his plans for the implementation of this reform. The statutes of this synod, which sought to regulate the training and conduct of the clergy, to reform the administration of the sacraments and to renew preaching and teaching, were published in 1538, but met with opposition from the city of Cologne and from other territories within the diocese.[8] Disillusioned with his chances of pushing through such a reform programme, Hermann gradually transferred his allegiance to the evangelical party. In 1542 he appointed Martin Bucer as court preacher at Bonn and in 1543, at his instigation, Philip Melanchthon produced a plan for the reform of the archdiocese that was closely based on the Nuremberg–Brandenburg church order. Despite the willingness of Hermann's provincial diet (*Landtag*) to support this reform, Cologne's civic and ecclesiastical authorities eventually, in 1546, managed to depose the archbishop. His fate was sealed by the opposition of the pope and emperor, for whom the prospect of an evangelical majority in the Empire's electoral college was a major concern. Hermann died shortly afterwards, leaving the way clear for the Catholic party's chosen candidate as his successor, Adolf von Schauenburg.[9]

[7] Mallinckrodt, *Struktur und kollektiver Eigensinn*, pp. 91–2.

[8] J. F. Gerhard Goeters, 'Die Reformation in Kurköln', in *Kurköln. Land unter dem Krummstab: Essays und Dokumente*, ed. Nordrhein-Westfälischen Hauptstaatsarchiv Düsseldorf (Kevelaer, 1985), pp. 191–2.

[9] August Franzen, *Bischof und Reformation: Erzbischof Hermann von Wied in Köln vor der Entscheidung zwischen Reform und Reformation*, 2nd edn (Münster, 1971); Ennen, *Geschichte*, vol. 4, pp. 375–568; Marijn de Kroon, 'Bucer und die Kölner Reformation', in *Martin Bucer and Sixteenth Century Europe. Actes du colloque de Strasbourg (28–31 août 1991)*, ed. Christian Krieger and Marc Lienhard (Leiden, 1993).

During the 1580s Archbishop-Elector Gebhard Truchseß von Waldburg, nephew of Augsburg's Bishop Otto Truchseß, tried once again to introduce a synodal Reformation. His attempt appears to have been as much a product of personal circumstance as of religious conviction. Gebhard, who numbered amongst his friends Protestants such as Count Adolf von Neuenar and Count Hermann von Solms, took as a mistress Agnes von Mansfeld, a canoness from the collegiate foundation in Gerresheim near Düsseldorf. The brother of this eminent lady, reluctant to tolerate her concubinage to an archbishop, tried to persuade Gebhard to convert. In 1582 Gebhard duly prepared to initiate a formal break with Rome and to implement a plan whereby the bishopric would be secularized and opened to the Augsburg Confession.[10] On 2 February 1583 he celebrated his wedding to Agnes in Bonn with great ceremony. This precipitated an imperial crisis. According to the *reservatum ecclesiasticum*, a clause of the Peace of Augsburg that never received the assent of the Protestant Estates, ecclesiastical rulers, unlike their secular counterparts, had no *ius reformandi* (right to reform the church). As far as the Catholic Church was concerned, any ecclesiastical prince, such as the archbishop-elector of Cologne, who converted to Protestantism, had therefore to resign his offices and benefices. Gebhard was deposed by the pope in 1583, but his deposition precipitated a war that lasted until 1589. Gebhard and his Protestant allies were eventually forced to surrender only after the intervention of Bavarian and Spanish troops.[11] At this moment Cologne's strategic importance sealed its confessional fate: the Catholic party within the Empire could not afford to let this key territory and its electoral vote fall to the Protestants, while the Spanish feared that Protestant success in Cologne would sever their crucial military route from northern Italy to the rebellious Dutch Republic. The Catholic orthodoxy of the archbishopric was preserved and Gebhard was replaced by Ernst von Bayern of the house of Wittelsbach.[12] Members of the Wittelsbach family retained the electorate of Cologne from this time until 1761, though not always without a struggle.

That the city of Cologne remained 'Romae ecclesiae fidelis filia', as its civic seal stated, despite a significant Protestant presence within its walls and despite the attempts of two of its ecclesiastical overlords to secularize the territory, is remarkable.[13] Why was this city so firm in its opposition to the Protestant Reformation, unlike so many others within Germany? In an article first published in 1975 Bob Scribner drew attention to the importance of the council's implacable attitude. Censorship and suppression prevented isolated incidents of religious defiance from developing into fully fledged evangelical movements:

[10] Ennen, *Geschichte*, vol. 5, pp. 529–40. [11] Ibid., pp. 41–223.

[12] Konrad Repgen, 'Der Bischof zwischen Reformation, katholischer Reform und Konfessionsbildung (1515–1650)', in *Der Bischof in seiner Zeit: Bischofstypus und Bischofsideal im Spiegel der Kölner Kirche*, ed. P. Berglar (Cologne, 1986), p. 269.

[13] Enderle, 'Die katholischen Reichsstädte', 231. See also Militzer, 'Collen eyn kroyn'.

local Protestants never obtained a proper corporate or institutional foothold within the city and so never had more than a limited opportunity for public proclamation.[14] The council's attitude was determined above all, Scribner argued, by economic and political considerations. The protection of trade routes necessitated the maintenance of good relations with the Spanish Netherlands in particular. Moreover, the city of Cologne had no rural hinterland and was surrounded by powerful territorial princes: the electors of Trier, Mainz and the Palatinate, the landgrave of Hesse and the duke of Berg. Cologne's archbishop-elector posed the greatest threat to the city's political independence. In 1475 Cologne had finally rid itself of the archbishop's lordship but plenty of potential remained for conflict over issues such as customs and tariffs. The council's determination to resist archiepiscopal claims to power and to avoid being subsumed into a secularized and hereditary electorate intensified its dependence upon imperial support.[15] Cologne's particular political circumstances and economic interests made its dependence even greater than that of cities such as Nuremberg and Augsburg.

While Scribner's analysis of economic and political concerns remains important, recent scholarship has drawn attention to other issues. Manfred Groten, for example, emphasizes the significance of the structure of Cologne's polity and suggests that the city's loyalty to Rome was more a product of inflexibility than of conscious decision. The fragmented nature of the city's religious life, in particular the large number of parishes, discouraged the emergence of communal pressure for reform.[16] In addition to economic and political determinants, Scribner also emphasized the socio-cultural forces within the city that were opposed to Protestant innovations: the university was a bulwark of Catholic orthodoxy and the city's cathedral chapter and papal nuncio also reinforced its attachment to the old faith.[17] Catholic historiography, for example the work of Franz Bosbach, goes further, highlighting the role of Catholic reform rather than mere resistance to religious innovation. Bosbach argues that the grounds for economically motivated anticlericalism had been removed by 1525 at the latest, when the council obliged the clergy to share in the burdens of civic life, and that the theological and spiritual constitution of the city was not receptive to Protestant teaching.[18]

It is certainly true that Catholic reformers such as the secular priest Johannes Gropper and members of the Carthusian and Carmelite orders had made significant efforts to reform Cologne's clerical body, to intensify local pastoral activity and to produce propaganda to counter the invective of the Protestants

[14] Scribner, 'Why was there no Reformation in Cologne?', 234.
[15] Ibid., 221–2. [16] Groten, 'Die nächste Generation'.
[17] Scribner, 'Why was there no Reformation in Cologne?', 225–33.
[18] Franz Bosbach, 'Die katholische Reform in der Stadt Köln', *Römische Quartalschrift für christliche Altertumskunde und Kirchengeschichte* 84 (1989).

during the first half of the sixteenth century.[19] It would be a mistake to assume, however, that they had purged the church of all significant abuses. As we have seen, Hermann von Wied's attempts to implement Catholic reform foundered in part because of opposition from the city of Cologne, and both episcopal visitations and papal nuncios certainly found plenty to complain of during the later decades of the sixteenth century. We should not overstate the role of Catholic reform in preventing Protestant Reformation, but we should, as Gérald Chaix has argued, nonetheless pay attention to the forms of religious life in the city: to the power of holy Cologne's 'sacred capital' and to the density of its religious institutions. Chaix argues for Cologne's transformation from a 'Christian city' into a 'Catholic metropolis' following the periodization for confessionalization advocated by Heinz Schilling.[20] The study of religious practice demonstrates that although Chaix is correct to postulate a developing sense of Catholic identity over the course of the sixteenth century, the nature and pace of Cologne's Catholic reform was very different to Augsburg's.[21] When the Jesuits arrived in Augsburg the devotional slate had been wiped clean for them by the Protestant Reformation. In Cologne, by contrast, the number and strength of competing ecclesiastical institutions made it much more difficult for them to dictate the nature of the city's devotional life. Cologne's rich and largely uninterrupted ecclesiastical heritage had, as we shall see, a profound impact on the expression of Marian piety in the city.

Cologne has been described by Hansgeorg Molitor as 'a perfect example of untridentine reform'. It was, according to Molitor's strict definition, 'untridentine' because the decrees of the Council of Trent were not promulgated there until 1662, and even then were not made fully binding.[22] Formal Tridentine reform depended upon the willingness and ability of bishops and archbishops to impose the council's decrees via synods. In Augsburg, for example, Cardinal Otto Truchseß von Waldburg was a persistent promoter of the Council of Trent, published the Tridentine decrees in 1566 and held a reforming synod in Dillingen the following year. Although even Otto never, as Molitor points out, promulgated the decrees in their entirety, the statutes of his 1567 synod refer to them extensively.[23] The effectiveness of many of Otto's reforms may have

[19] On the Carthusians see Werner Schäfke, ed., *Die Kölner Kartause um 1500. Aufsatzband* (Cologne, 1991).

[20] Chaix, 'De la cité chrétienne à la métropole catholique'.

[21] Walter Ziegler compares the Rhineland and Bavaria, pointing out that in the Rhineland confessionalization was late starting and was less clearly influenced by Rome. Ziegler, 'Typen der Konfessionalisierung'.

[22] Hansgeorg Molitor, 'Gegenreformation und kirchliche Erneuerung im niederen Erzstift Köln zwischen 1583 und 1688', in *Kurköln*, ed. Nordrhein-Westfälischen Hauptstaatsarchiv Düsseldorf, p. 203.

[23] Hansgeorg Molitor, 'Die untridentinische Reform: Anfänge katholischer Erneuerung in der Reichskirche', in *Ecclesia Militans: Studien zur Konzilien- und Reformationsgeschichte;*

been limited, but as we saw in chapter 4, his commitment to Romanization and his close alliance with the Jesuits had a profound impact on local piety. During the sixteenth century Cologne's archbishops, by contrast, did not provide suitable conduits for the transmission of either the law or the spirit of the post-Tridentine church. As Konrad Repgen has pointed out, of the nine who ruled between the beginning of the Lutheran Reformation and the Peace of Westphalia none, except Adolf von Schauenberg (1547–56), matched up to the normative ideal promulgated by Trent. For all of them spiritual lordship came a poor second to territorial and dynastic concerns, though Salentin von Isenburg (1567–77) did at least undertake a thorough visitation of the monasteries, cloisters and parishes of much of the archbishopric in 1569–70 before resigning his post in order to perpetuate his family line.[24]

When, in the aftermath of the confusion that accompanied Gebhard Truchseß's rule, Cologne was allied to Bavaria by the election of Archbishop Ernst von Bayern the pace of Tridentine reform began to pick up. It was above all his successor, Ferdinand von Bayern, son of Wilhelm V of Bavaria and brother of Maximilian I, who did for Cologne what Otto Truchseß had done for Augsburg half a century earlier. Ferdinand was elected *Koadjutor* in 1595 and ruled as archbishop from 1612 to 1650. He was a pluralist himself, was never consecrated as a priest or bishop and did not promulgate the Tridentine decrees in a one-off legislative act.[25] Yet he made important steps towards the realization of the reforms of Trent, in particular through his 1598 diocesan synod and through his ecclesiastical council (*Congregatio ecclesiastica*), set up in 1601.[26] Ferdinand was exemplary in his participation in visitations and public rituals. He also reformed pastoral care and unified the diocese's liturgy with a new *Agende* (1614), breviary (1618) and missal (1626), all of which brought Cologne's practice more closely in line with that of Rome.[27] Ferdinand, who like Duke Maximilian of Bavaria and Ferdinand II of Habsburg had spent time with the Jesuits in Ingolstadt and had chosen members of the order as advisors and confessors, promoted not only the rules and regulations but also the devotional practices of the post-Tridentine church.[28] Not surprisingly, given his Wittelsbach heritage, his close ties to the Jesuits and his strongly anti-heretical stance, he was a keen proponent of Mary's cult.

Remigius Bäumer zum 70. Geburtstag gewidmet, ed. Walter Brandmüller, Herbert Immenkötter and Erwin Iserloh (Paderborn, 1988), p. 419.

[24] Repgen, 'Der Bischof', p. 250. On Schauenberg see Hans Foerster, *Reformbestrebungen Adolfs III. von Schaumburg (1547–56) in der Kölner Kirchenprovinz*, Reformationsgeschichtliche Studien und Texte 45/46 (Münster, 1925). See also Weiler, *Die kirchliche Reform*.

[25] Repgen, 'Der Bischof', p. 284. [26] Weiler, *Die kirchliche Reform*, pp. 46–68.

[27] Ibid., pp. 122–33.

[28] Ibid., pp. 153–4; *Die Jesuitenkirche St Mariae Himmelfahrt in Köln: Dokumentation und Beiträge zum Abschluss ihrer Wiederherstellung 1980, Beiträge zu den Bau- und Kunstdenkmälern im Rheinland* (Düsseldorf, 1982), pp. 142–3.

If Cologne's archbishops failed to provide the impetus for ecclesiastical or spiritual reform until the seventeenth century, what of the city's other possible motors of religious transformation? In 1584 a papal nunciature was established in Cologne, and the permanent presence of a curial official strengthened the city's link to Rome. Giovanni Francesco Bonomi (1584–7), who was part of the reforming circle around Milan's saintly archbishop Charles Borromeo, worked to reform Cologne's cathedral chapter, to abolish concubinage and pluralism and to prevent Protestant immigration to the city. His successor, Ottavio Mirto Frangipani, struggled hard to reform the administration and finances of the archdiocese, and, like Cologne's other nuncios, conducted visitations of ecclesiastical institutions whenever possible. The nuncios' impact on local piety was, however, limited by the extent of their territorial responsibility (the provinces of Cologne, Mainz and Trier, the bishoprics of Basle, Strasbourg, Osnabrück, Paderborn and Luttich, Luxemburg and the remaining Belgian provinces and Jülich-Kleve) and by their inevitable involvement in regional and imperial legal and political disputes.[29] Only when political circumstances were favourable, for example under Ferdinand von Bayern, could the nuncios hope to engage in effective reform. In Cologne it seems likely that they made their greatest impact on devotional life through the religious orders that they introduced to the city. The Reformed Franciscans (Observants) came to Cologne under Frangipani, while Antonio Albergati (1610–21) brought the Discalced Carmelites and the Capuchins, who were, next to the Jesuits, the most successful pioneers of the Catholic restoration.[30]

In southern Germany, as we have seen, the Jesuits were probably the greatest disseminators of Counter-Reformation Catholicism, and played a central role in the reformulation of Mary's cult. Cologne was home to Germany's first Jesuit community. In 1543 Peter Canisius, who had been based at Cologne University since 1536, joined the society and invited Peter Faber to come to strengthen Catholic opposition to the reform measures proposed by Archbishop Hermann von Wied. Canisius and Faber set up house with a small group of companions, but the Jesuits found it very hard to get established in Cologne and ultimately played a less significant role in the reform of the city and bishopric than they did in Augsburg.[31] Until Ferdinand's incumbency they enjoyed little influence with Cologne's archbishops.[32] And while the city's reform-minded circle of clerics – Johannes Gropper and the leaders of the Dominican, Carmelite and

[29] Wolfgang Reinhard, 'Katholische Reform und Gegenreformation in der Kölner Nuntiatur 1584–1621', *Römische Quartalschrift für christliche Altertumskunde und Kirchengeschichte* 66 (1971), 15.

[30] Ibid.; Weiler, *Die kirchliche Reform*, pp. 6–34. On the Capuchins see *Die Jesuitenkirche St Mariae Himmelfahrt*, p. 144.

[31] Mallinckrodt, *Struktur und kollektiver Eigensinn*, p. 139.

[32] Weiler, *Die kirchliche Reform*, p. 153.

Carthusian orders – welcomed them, they were treated with suspicion by the city council, which was reluctant to grant another religious order legal and financial privileges within the city.[33] With the support of the Carthusians in particular, in 1556 Cologne's Jesuits did manage to establish a school, the *Gymnasium Tricoronatum*, under the leadership of Johann Rethius, a local *Bürgermeister*'s son, but their financial position remained insecure. Only in 1582, thanks to the intervention of the emperor and Catholic princes, did they finally acquire a church and cloister of their own.[34] Even in 1589 the council forbade the Jesuits' street catechism for fear that it would lead to tumult and the formation of secret conventicles, and it was only really under Archbishop Ferdinand von Bayern that the order was able to make its presence felt in and around Cologne.[35]

As we shall see, the Jesuits and other reformed Catholic and Counter-Reformation orders did eventually have a considerable impact on the religious lives of Cologne's citizens. But the study of Marian images, liturgy and confraternities shows that here the Tridentine vanguard did not manage to shape the Catholic cult as quickly and as fully as it had done in southern Germany. This was partly a result of the Jesuits' insecure situation within the Catholic metropolis. In Augsburg, by contrast, Bishop Otto Truchseß von Waldburg had worked closely with members of the society and the Fugger family had provided them with financial assistance, while in Bavaria the Wittelsbach dukes had given them their full support. Perhaps more importantly, however, the strength and continuity of Cologne's 'sacred capital' made the city's devotional life less susceptible to Counter-Reformation pressure. Cologne's confessional situation was not clear-cut: there was a strong Protestant presence within the city, and the city's archbishops twice threatened its confessional stability. During the mid sixteenth century there was a crisis of religious patronage and confraternity life. Yet despite this the city as a whole, unlike Nuremberg and Augsburg, retained its Catholic religious allegiance and local devotional traditions were never fully destroyed. The forces of the Counter-Reformation were not presented, as they had been in Augsburg, with a *tabula rasa*. The cult of the Virgin, as promoted by the Jesuits and their fellow reformers, had to engage with and accommodate local traditions, which continued to flourish under the supervision of the city council and in the city's parishes. As a result, forces of the Counter-Reformation never established a monopoly over Marian imagery and devotion.

[33] In 1544 the Jesuits were allowed to enter the city only on condition that they lived individually and did not try to establish a 'Konventikel'. They acquired their own house in 1563. Wolfgang Rosen, 'Rat, Bürger und geistliche Institutionen: zur Amortisationsgesetzgebung im frühneuzeitlichen Köln', in *Köln als Kommunikationszentrum*, ed. Mölich and Schwerhoff.

[34] Duhr, *Geschichte der Jesuiten im XVI. Jahrhundert*, pp. 35–6, 38–9, 42.

[35] Gerd Schwerhoff, *Köln im Kreuzverhör: Kriminalität, Herrschaft und Gesellschaft in einer frühneuzeitlichen Stadt* (Bonn, 1991), pp. 252–3; *Die Jesuitenkirche St Mariae Himmelfahrt*, p. 147.

THE STRENGTH OF LOCAL MARIAN TRADITION

Mary had long been celebrated as one of the patron saints of 'holy' Cologne. A thirteenth-century chronicle by Gottfried Hagen described her protecting the city against its archbishops, while the *Cronica van der hilliger Stat van Coellen*, printed by Johannes Koelhoff in 1499, stated that Cologne and the Virgin were sisters because Marcus Agrippa had founded the city at the moment at which Mary was born.[36] This notion of a primordial bond with the Mother of God was long lived: an engraving from 1658 showing the *Gottestracht*, the greatest of Cologne's civic processions, also carries an inscription recording that Cologne was founded at the time of Mary's birth.[37] But Mary was not the only patron of Cologne. Indeed, the city was protected by a veritable host of saints, thanks to the plethora of relics and churches within its walls. Of these the most important were the Three Kings, whose relics had arrived in Cologne in 1164, St Gereon and his companions from the Theban Legion, and St Ursula and her 11,000 virgins. In Hagen's chronicle, for example, it is not only Mary, but also St Ursula, the Three Kings and St Gereon who intercede on behalf of the city. Their relics were an important focus for local, regional and even international pilgrimage, and their presence fostered the city's conception of itself as the 'holy' and 'true daughter of the Roman Church'.

Visual representations of the city of Cologne also invoked the protection of this plurality of patrons. An illustration from Koelhoff's 1499 chronicle shows a saintly archbishop, the Three Kings, St Ursula and four of her companions manning the city walls against Archbishop Engelbert, who besieged Cologne in 1265.[38] A wing panel from a lost altarpiece, attributed to the Master of the Glorification of the Virgin and dated to 1493, shows St Anne and the Virgin and Child with saints Christopher, Gereon and Peter in front of Cologne (figure 47). In the post-Reformation period Cologne's local saints remained important. While in images of divine intercession produced in Augsburg Mary presides over Ulrich, Afra and other figures (figures 31, 34, 35), in paintings and prints from Cologne her position is less prominent.[39] In an engraving of 1589 it is Ursula, not Mary, who stands in front of a representation of the city's key

[36] Militzer, 'Collen eyn kroyn', 18–19; Janssen, *Das Erzbistum Köln*, pp. 484–5.

[37] Uta Scholten, 'Die Stadt als Kultraum: Prozessionen im Köln des 17. Jahrhunderts', in *Kunstgeschichtliche Studien. Hugo Borger zum 70. Geburtstag*, ed. Klaus Gereon Beuckers, Holger Brülls and Achim Preiss (Weimar, 1995), p. 123.

[38] Militzer, 'Collen eyn kroyn', ill.3.

[39] The closest parallel that I have found to the Augsburg images is an engraved title page for a 1617 edition of Surius' *Vitae sanctorum*. On this title page the Virgin and Child sit in front of Cologne, surrounded by a crowd of other saints. Annette Frese, *Barocke Titelgraphik am Beispiel der Verlagsstadt Köln (1570–1700)*, Dissertationen zur Kunstgeschichte 31 (Cologne and Vienna, 1989), ill. 8.

Figure 47. Master of the Glorification of the Virgin, saints before Cologne, c.1480 (WRM, Cologne)

buildings, and who is crowned by angels above.[40] An altarpiece commissioned by provost and canon Alexander Symonis for the Sebastian altar in the church of St Gereon in 1635 in thanks for Cologne's preservation from the Swedes shows a multiplicity of local saints (figure 48). Ferdinand von Bayern is depicted, as elector rather than as archbishop, in the midst of saints and eminent predecessors such as Archbishop Anno II, benefactor of St Gereon. Beneath is a panoramic cityscape. Mary appears, kneeling before the Trinity, but saints Sebastian, Helen (legendary founder of the church), Gereon and Ursula are all more visible.[41] A comparison between this painting and the two Marian monuments

[40] Bernadette Schöller, ed., *Religiöse Drucke aus Kölner Produktion: Flugblätter und Wandbilder des 16. bis 19. Jahrhunderts aus den Beständen des Kölnischen Stadtmuseums* (Cologne, 1995), no. 69.

[41] *Die Jesuitenkirche St. Mariae Himmelfahrt*, p. 152; *CR* 18–19 (2003–4), 67–70; for a similar example see *CR* 18–19 (2003–4), 407–8.

Figure 48. Johann Hulsman (?) and Johann Toussyn, altarpiece showing the saints of Cologne, c.1635 (St Gereon, Cologne)

commissioned for Munich by Maximilian I during the Thirty Years War indicates that the saintly piety promoted by members of Cologne's political elite was more diverse than that of the Bavarian court, where devotion to the Virgin was a state-sponsored programme.[42]

Although Mary was not Cologne's only saintly patron, devotion to her flourished during the fifteenth and sixteenth centuries, both at an elite and at a popular level. An altarpiece formerly thought to have been painted by Stefan Lochner but now attributed to the anonymous 'Dombild Meister' provides splendid visual testimony to the civic tradition of Marian veneration that was sponsored by Cologne's city council (figure 9). This altarpiece was probably commissioned by a group of councillors, and was installed in the early 1440s in the *Ratskapelle*, the chapel that had been built from a synagogue and dedicated in honour of St Maria in Jerusalem after the expulsion of Cologne's Jews.[43] This chapel became, in Klaus Militzer's words, 'a stage for communal self-representation and civic self-conception'. It served as the council's chapel – solemn mass was celebrated there before council sittings, before the election of a *Bürgermeister* and during the reception of foreign sovereigns and ambassadors – and was the liturgical midpoint of the free city.[44] The Dombild Meister's altarpiece depicts Mary, enthroned and splendidly crowned, holding the Christ Child and surrounded by Cologne's principal patrons and defenders, the Three Kings, St Gereon and St Ursula. Through placing this altarpiece, along with relics of Ursula's virgins and members of the Theban Legion, in the *Ratskapelle* Cologne's council appropriated for itself part of the city's 'sacred capital', making an explicit connection between the secular government and the saints' cults that were otherwise under the control of the archbishop and ecclesiastical foundations.[45] Mary's prominence – she occupies centre stage in the altarpiece, and the chapel also contained two richly clothed statues of her – testifies to her importance for Cologne's political elite.[46]

The church of St Maria im Kapitol was another important focus for civic devotion to the Virgin. This church had a distinguished history: it had been founded by Plectrudis, wife of Pippin of Herstal (635–714) who served as palace mayor to the Frankish king. In the twelfth century St Maria im Kapitol became a *Damenstift*, a collegiate foundation composed of female canons drawn from the ranks of the lay nobility.[47] The church fulfilled no parish functions until the nineteenth century yet it occupied a very prominent role in the devotional lives of local citizens.[48] Members of Cologne's patrician class sought to acquire burial

[42] Above, pp. 188–94. [43] See chapter 1, pp. 44–5.
[44] Militzer and Schmid, 'Das Inventar der Kölner Ratskapelle von 1519', 229.
[45] Chaix, 'De la cité chrétienne à la métropole catholique', pp. 73–5.
[46] Militzer and Schmid, 'Das Inventar der Kölner Ratskapelle von 1519', 232.
[47] Wolfgang Stracke, 'St Maria im Kapitol', *CR* 11 (1996), 79–84. [48] Ibid., 89.

sites within St Maria im Kapitol, endowed altars and donated furnishings. At least four lay confraternities were based there, three dedicated to the veneration of the Virgin and one to the Holy Cross. The *Marienbruderschaft vom silbernen Bild und zur großen Glocke* was Cologne's most socially exclusive confraternity, and the *Marienbruderschaft Salve Regina* was likewise dominated by eminent citizens. Throughout the early modern period these two brotherhoods continued to draw many of their members from amongst the city's leading families, the *Geschlechter*.[49] The function and significance of these Marian brotherhoods will be explored in greater detail below, but their composition suggests that a close bond existed between the church and the city council. This bond was also reflected in the number of important civic rituals that took place in the church. In times of war and plague supplicatory processions composed of clergy and members of the city council went from the cathedral to St Maria im Kapitol. A service of thanksgiving was held in St Maria im Kapitol in the presence of the town council after the appointment of a new *Bürgermeister*, and the solemn exequies that followed the death of a *Bürgermeister* were also celebrated there. Furthermore until 1637, when the west tower collapsed, the city's *Sturmglocke*, the bells rung in times of civic emergency, hung in the church.[50]

Like the *Ratskapelle* of St Maria in Jerusalem, the collegiate church of St Maria im Kapitol provides evidence of the political elite's appropriation and promotion of the cult of the Virgin. The church had two important cult images, a 'Crucifixus dolorosus' dating from the early fourteenth century, and a silver statue of the Virgin Mary. Mid-fourteenth-century statutes of the *Marienbruderschaft vom silbernen Bild und zur großen Glocke* mention an image of Our Lady that members of the confraternity were obliged to accompany as it was carried in procession around the church on high feast days and as it joined in major civic processions. The *Salve Regina* confraternity required its members to do the same on its feast day, the Ascension.[51] This image should probably be identified with the 'silver Marian image' mentioned in an inventory of 1405 and described in detail by the collector Franz Ferdinand Wallraf before it was melted down in 1798: 'an old gothic seated image of the Mother of God with the little Jesus Child, which was carried in processions – inside it was a carved wooden carcass'.[52] Statutes of the *Marienbruderschaft vom silbernen Bild und*

49 Militzer, ed., *Quellen*, vol. 1, pp. lxvi–lxx and vol. 2, pp. 908–1005; Mallinckrodt, *Struktur und kollektiver Eigensinn*, p. 266.

50 Paul Clemen, ed., *Die Kunstdenkmäler der Rheinprovinz*, vol. 7, part I: *Die Kunstdenkmäler der Stadt Köln*, vol. 2: *Die kirchlichen Denkmäler der Stadt Köln* (Düsseldorf, 1911), pp. 191–2.

51 Militzer, ed., *Quellen*, vol. 2, pp. 911, 60.

52 HAStK, Stifter und Klöster, Best. 247, St. Maria im Kapitol, Akten, 3e. HAStK, Stifter und Klöster, Best. 295, GA, 175 A, fol. 1r. Two comparable silver images of the Virgin survive today: the Walcourt Madonna and the Essen Madonna. Stracke, 'St Maria im Kapitol', 86 and n. 66; Angela Kulenkampff, 'Die Marienbruderschaft von St. Maria im Kapitol und ihre Bedeutung für das kirchliche Leben in vortridentinischer Zeit (ca. 1350–1634)', *JbKGV* 60 (1989), 8.

zur großen Glocke dating from 1405 record that members of this confraternity were also bound to maintain candles on the beam that stood before 'der loesingen unss herren', an image plausibly identified by Angela Kulenkampff as a *pietà* or *Vesperbild*.[53] In addition to these cult images, the church contained, of course, other sculpted, painted and stained-glass images of Mary.[54] A window from the east apse, which was donated by Emperor Maximilian I before 1518, shows, for example, Mary with Maximilian and his grandsons, the future Charles V and Ferdinand I.[55] Mary wears a white cloak embroidered with Maximilian's device, the pomegranate. This elite tradition of Marian veneration, with its implicit celebration of Cologne's status as a free city, survived throughout the early modern period.

Cologne's councillors not only celebrated Mary through images and liturgy, they also, like other Catholic magistrates, took it upon themselves to defend her honour. Anxious to avoid provoking divine wrath, the council, from 1372 onwards, threatened to punish those who spoke ill of God, his mother and his saints.[56] Concern about blasphemy, Marian and otherwise, was intensified by the turmoil of the Reformation years.[57] In 1544 the council prescribed the wearing of the 'hölzerne Heucke', a wooden drum from which only the offender's head and feet protruded, as the normative punishment for all blasphemy. Offenders were required to parade through the city's streets and to appear before, or even in, their local church on Sunday wearing this mantle of shame. Thus the dishonouring of God and his saints was punished by the dishonouring of the blasphemer.[58] In an edict issued in 1555 blasphemy was explicitly linked with religious heresy: this edict threatened to punish 'Anabaptists, sacramentarians, and other seditious, seductive and evil teaching' along with 'those who blaspheme against God Our Lord and his sacraments; likewise his blessed mother Mary and the saints'.[59] The *Morgensprachen*, public proclamations read out once a year on the occasion of the *Gottestracht*, also testify to a heightened concern about blasphemy, and to the crime's perceived association with heresy. Their prohibitions on blasphemy became harsher during the 1550s, and they forbade blasphemers, Lutherans, Zwinglians, Anabaptists and iconoclasts from participating in the *Gottestracht*, Cologne's great annual display of civic unity.[60]

53 Militzer, ed., *Quellen*, vol. 2, pp. 916–17; Kulenkampff, 'Die Marienbruderschaft', 8, 10.

54 Heal, 'A woman like any other?', pp. 103–11.

55 Stracke, 'St Maria im Kapitol', 92–3.

56 Schwerhoff, 'Blasphemie', 46–7.

57 Ibid., 92–5. In 1532 the council declared its determination to punish blasphemers in accordance with the 1530 *Reichspolizeiordnung*: HAStK, Reichsstadt, Best. 30, Verf. u. Verw., V126A fols. 243r–246v. Here fol. 245v.

58 Schwerhoff, 'Blasphemie', 72–4; HAStK, Reichsstadt, Best. 14, Edikte 1, fol. 102.

59 HAStK, Reichsstadt, Best. 14, Edikte 1, fol. 166. This wording was repeated in an edict from 1578. Ibid., fol. 169.

60 The *Morgensprachen* already dealt with blasphemy in the Middle Ages, e.g. HAStK, Reichsstadt, Best. 30, Verf. u. Verw., 126b, fol. 40r–v (1479). In 1554 the *Morgensprachen* prescribed the 'hölzerne Heucke', then, for repeat offenders, stocks and expulsion: HAStK, Reichsstadt, Best. 30, Verf. u. Verw., 127 fol. 36r–v. *Morgensprachen* from 1556 to 1560 condemned

Cologne's criminal sources are, unfortunately, not as comprehensive as Augsburg's, but a steady trickle of Marian cases recorded either in the council minutes or in the *Turmbücher* indicates that Cologne's magistrates made some effort to enforce their decrees.[61] Sometime between 1468 and 1474 Thonis van Wesslynghe was brought before the council because he had spoken 'very unchristian and unsuitable words' about the birth of God, his blessed mother and other articles of belief. According to one witness, Thonis had denied the miracle of Christ's conception and birth, saying: 'our Lord God was conceived from Our Lady, his blessed mother, from human nature and born as other people . . . and Joseph was our Lord God's father'.[62] In 1487 another citizen, Dietrich Flass, who was the archbishop's personal physician, was tried for various blasphemies, including one about Mary that was, according to one witness, too heinous to be spoken again or recorded.[63] Both Thonis and Dietrich pleaded their innocence and were released. Not all offenders were so fortunate: in 1516–17 Heinrich 'der Abt' [the abbot], who had blasphemed against God and his mother, was threatened with various punishments, including penitential pilgrimage to Trier and to Einsiedeln, and was eventually forced to wear the 'hölzerne Heucke' to avoid expulsion from the city.[64] In 1526 Kneuvel Hensgen had to do the same 'because he had gone around blaspheming against God and his dear blessed mother together with all of God's saints'.[65] In February 1529 the *Turmmeister* were instructed by the council to arrest 'the one who had claimed that Mary had had two children after Christ's birth'. The council at first thought to punish him by sending him on a pilgrimage but later settled for demanding a gesture of respect.[66] Again in May 1532 the *Turmmeister* were asked to take action against those who had insulted the Mother of God.[67]

'Aufrührerischer' blasphemers: ibid., fol. 40r. For blasphemers and heretics excluded from the *Gottestracht* see HAStK, Reichsstadt, Best. 30, Verf. u. Verw., 126b, fol. 245r (1526 – blasphemers); fol. 266r (1534 – Lutherans, Zwinglians, Anabaptists and blasphemers); HAStK, Reichsstadt, Best. 30, Verf. u. Verw., 127, fol. 63r (1569 – as before, plus iconoclasts).

61 For a full discussion of Cologne's criminal sources see Schwerhoff, *Köln im Kreuzverhör*, pp. 471–5. For the period 1510/11 and 1515–23 the 'Liber Malefactorum' gives alphabetically ordered names and a brief description of offences. For 1524/5 and from 1555 onwards *Turmbücher* record more detail, including examination of prisoners, witness statements and verdicts. There is also a separate *Bestand* for *Kriminalakten*. The information in the *Kriminalakten* is often fragmentary. *Ratsprotokolle* give brief, often cryptic, references to cases.

62 HAStK, Reichsstadt, Best. 125, Kriminalakten 1, fols. 19r–21r.

63 Ibid., fols. 135–7, especially 135r. On both cases see Manfred Groten, 'In glückseligem Regiment: Beobachtungen zum Verhältnis Obrigkeit–Bürger am Beispiel Kölns im 15. Jahrhundert', *Historisches Jahrbuch* 116 (1996), 313–15. On the reluctance to record the wording of Marian blasphemies see Schwerhoff, *Zungen wie Schwerter*, p. 246.

64 Schwerhoff, 'Blasphemie', 72–3 n. 132.

65 HAStK, Reichsstadt, Best. 30, Ver. u. Verw., G 205 (Turmbücher), fols. 36r–37r.

66 Manfred Groten, ed., *Beschlüsse des Rates der Stadt Köln: 1320–1550*, 5 vols., Publikationen der Gesellschaft für rheinische Geschichtskunde 45 (Düsseldorf, 1990), vol. 3, nos. 130, 243.

67 HAStK, Reichsstadt, Best. 10, Ratsprotokolle 8, fol. 203v.

In addition to this 'conventional' Marian blasphemy, which tended to impugn Mary's honour by disputing the doctrine of her perpetual virginity, some cases indicate the impact of Reformation teaching.[68] In July 1526 the weaver Hans Hesse appeared before the magistrates 'because he had scoffed at the worthy mother of God and all other saints'. A witness, one Lysbeth Scholepper, reported that she had 'scolded him and said, hey you Lutheran rogue, how can you sit and joke about the birth of our dear Lady?' Hans replied: 'She is a woman like another woman, God is above all and above his mother.' He then went into the room where three images stood and called them idols saying that 'the saints have no power as those from Cologne believe'. Hesse's master testified on his behalf, saying that the accused had, in conversation with him, stated his belief in Mary's perpetual virginity.[69] His master's defence was apparently successful: no sentence is recorded.[70] In September 1538 the *Gewaltrichter* were instructed to arrest someone from Protestant Marburg (Hesse) 'who blasphemed and spoke mockingly about the blessed mother of God, the maid Mary'.[71] In May 1611 Thonieß von Wesseling, a blind beggar, was brought before Cologne's magistrates for his role in a fight that began when he asked a passer-by on the eve of the feast of the Annunciation whether the Virgin Mary was 'better than other women' [Ist die dan beßer alß Andere Frawen]. When two men defended Mary and threatened to get Thonieß imprisoned, he responded by hitting one of them. Having compounded Marian blasphemy with physical violence, Thonieß was expelled from the city.[72] Legislation and trial records thus indicate a determination on the part of Cologne's magistrates to punish Marian heresy, a determination that was not new at the time of the Reformation, but that was given greater urgency by the religious uncertainty of the period.

Marian devotion was important not just at a civic but also at a parochial level. The parish church of St Laurenz, for example, which served the area to the west of Cologne's town hall inhabited primarily by councillors and wealthy craftsmen, provides particularly interesting evidence of the longevity of traditional expressions of Marian veneration.[73] The church's sculpted images seem to have played a particularly important role in its devotional life. An inventory of the church's furnishings drawn up in 1528 and revised in 1530 mentions nine sculptures, including three of the Virgin Mary. One sculpture of the Virgin and Child adorned the high altar, which was dedicated to the Virgin. Another, known by

68 On the traditional focus on Mary's virginity see Schwerhoff, *Zungen wie Schwerter*, pp. 247–9.
69 HAStK, Reichsstadt, Best. 30, Verf. u. Verw., G 205 (Turmbücher), fols. 37v–38r.
70 Schwerhoff, 'Blasphemie', 83–4.
71 HAStK, Reichsstadt, Best. 10, Ratsprotokolle, 10, fol. 58v.
72 HAStK, Reichsstadt, Best. 30, Verf u. Verw., 239 (Turmbücher), fols. 154v–155v, 162v–163r, 165r–v, 170r.
73 H. Keussen, *Topographie der Stadt Köln im Mittelalter*, 2 vols. (Bonn, 1910), vol. 1, pp. 192–3.

the name of its donor, Lodowich von St Truiden, showed Mary surrounded by rays of sun. The third sculpture of the Virgin was described in inventories as the 'parish Mary', suggesting that it was especially venerated.[74] The statues were clothed in rich robes and were adorned with crowns and other precious objects. The 1528/30 inventory records that the 'parish Mary' was dressed in a red velvet robe embroidered with pearls and had another robe that was made of black velvet with a golden border. The Madonna donated by Lodowich von St Truiden had a black velvet robe. The image of Our Lady on the high altar had two velvet robes, and other saints' images had similar robes. Amongst the treasures listed in the 1528/30 inventory there were also various ornaments that were used to adorn the statues of the Virgin and Child and other saints: gilded crowns (some decorated with pearls), necklaces and rosaries. The crowns and other ornaments are listed amongst the treasures that were kept in the church's sacristy rather than being described *in situ* decorating the statues themselves.[75] At this time it seems that they were used only occasionally, probably on particular feast days or when the statues were carried in procession.

The number of sculpted images in the church of St Laurenz increased during the later sixteenth and early seventeenth centuries. By 1617 there were at least seven and perhaps as many as nine Marian statues.[76] It is clear from the inventories that these statues continued to be adorned with robes and treasures. The church accounts for 1545 and 1546 record payments made for robes belonging to the Marian image on the high altar and for a gilded silver crown belonging to the 'parish Mary'. In 1550 a covering for a Madonna was 'improved'.[77] Between 1551 and 1617 a number of new robes were acquired. Most of the crowns, necklaces and other treasures listed in the 1528/30 inventory were still in the sacristy in 1617, along with a few extra ornaments. By 1617, however, the images in the church also seem to have been more richly decorated on a daily basis. The statues of female saints all wore crowns, veils and other ornaments. The Virgin Mary on the high altar had a coral rosary and a small silver ring. The Apocalyptic Woman on the second Marian altar wore a red robe embroidered with pearls, a transparent veil and a crown and had a pearl ornament in her hand. The smaller Madonna beside her also wore a robe, transparent veil and

[74] HAEK, Alte Kölner Pfarrarchive, Dom, St Laurenz, D II 17, 'Anstellung des Offermans und Inventare der ihm übergebenen Kirchengeräte', 1530–1652, fol. 4r; HAEK, Dom, St Laurenz, D II 6, 'Verzeichniß der H. Gefäß und sämtlichen Kirchengeräthen der St Laurenz-Pfarrkirche', 1551, fols. 6v and 7r. The inventory of St Brigida from 1508 contains a similar entry: 'Item ein gulden kroene mit eine Iesus mu°tzgen zo der Kirchspelsmarien'. A. Ditges, 'Eine Kölner Gerkammer im 16. Jahrhundert', *Annalen des Historischen Vereins für den Niederrhein* 45 (1886), 123.

[75] HAEK, Dom, St Laurenz, D II 17, 'Anstellung . . .', fol. 2r–v, fol. 4r–v.

[76] HAEK, Dom, St Laurenz, D II 6, 'Inuentarium sacrorum uasorum Indumerntorum sacerdotalium . . .' [1572] and 'Instrumentum Inuentarii bonorum et rerum Ecclesiæ S. Laurentii . . .' [1617].

[77] HAEK, Dom, St Laurenz, D II 176, Kirchenrechnungen 1545, 1546, 1550.

crown. The statues of the Virgin and St Barbara on the Barbara altar both had veils, crowns and rosaries, and the statue of the Virgin above St Michael's altar was clothed in a robe embroidered with flowers, wore a transparent veil and had a small crown for her Christ Child.[78] St Laurenz was by no means the only church in Cologne to contain richly clothed statues. The *Ratskapelle* had two such Madonnas, for example, and members of the Marian brotherhood at the parish church of St Brigida donated robes for the statue of Our Lady that they carried in procession on feast days.[79]

To some observers such adornment smacked of idolatry. Philip Melanchthon, when he was called to Bonn to help implement Hermann von Wied's plans for reform, complained that the piety of the city's inhabitants consisted of excessive veneration.[80] In a tract justifying the need for a Reformation in Cologne published in 1543 he again wrote that: 'it is regarded now as a particular piety to call on Mary and to overload her with gifts'.[81] The adornment of statues attracted criticism from Catholic as well as Protestant reformers, even though it was a long-established practice.[82] In December 1563 the Council of Trent, as part of its attempt to eliminate all traces of superstition from the use of sacred images, decreed that 'all sensual appeal must be avoided, so that images are not painted or adorned with seductive charm'.[83] Yet in Cologne the custom of adorning images of the Virgin and other saints flourished during the later sixteenth and early seventeenth centuries. In 1586 the former priest of St Maria Ablaß and canon of St Ursula, Stephan Isaac, published a defence of a sermon he had preached three years earlier, *Against the Veneration and Carrying around of the Idols or Images*.[84] The prevalence of this practice in Cologne provoked him to complain that although iconophobes erred too far in one direction, 'we Catholics are [also] mistaken . . . [for] we do not let it remain at the historical use of pictures and paintings, but decorate the same with beautiful clothes, gold and silver . . . fall down before them, light lamps to them, carry them around with drums and pipes, which is all against God's word'.[85] Despite such reproofs Cologne's citizens continued to adorn statues of the Virgin and of other saints believing, as Isaac said, 'that one did the dear saints in heaven a favour

78 HAEK, Dom, St Laurenz, D II 6, 'Instrumentum Inuentarii bonorum et rerum Ecclesiæ S. Laurentii . . .'

79 Militzer, ed., *Quellen*, vol. 1, pp. 289–96.

80 Carolus Gottlieb Bretschneider, ed., *Corpus Reformatorum* (Halle, 1838), vol. 5, no. 2700.

81 W. Rotscheidt, ed., *Warum eine Reformation im 'hilligen Cöln'? Eine Antwort Melanchthons aus dem Jahre 1543* (Cologne, 1904), p. 19.

82 Above, pp. 99–102.

83 Tanner, ed., *Decrees*, pp. 775–6. It was not until 1662 that Cologne's archbishops turned their attention to the thorough reform of the cult of images. J. Hartzheim, *Concilia Germaniae* (Cologne, 1771), vol. 9, p. 957.

84 On Isaac see Ennen, *Geschichte*, vol. 5, pp. 421–41.

85 Isaac, *Wahre und einfältige Historia*, fol. 13v.

when one decorated or clothed their images'.[86] It seems likely that during the sixteenth century such votive offerings also acquired a demonstrative character, serving as testimony to Catholics' continued confidence in the efficacy of images.[87]

Cologne's traditional processional practices also endured and even flourished despite reformers' attempts to limit them. In Cologne, unlike in Augsburg, public processions continued throughout the sixteenth century. Intended to invoke or to celebrate the blessing of God and his saints they served as a visible sign of the holiness of the city and were an important form of communal self-representation. The greatest, the *Gottestracht*, took place on the second Friday after Easter and was organized under the aegis of the city council.[88] Civic officials, clergy, canons, members of religious orders and confraternities and other citizens all participated in this procession, carrying the sacrament, relics and images of the saints around the city walls.[89] There were also additional supplicatory processions in times of crisis, for example in 1564 because of plague, in 1571 because of the Turks and in 1594 because of the Turks and against the division of Christendom. These *Bittprozessionen* went from the cathedral to St Maria im Kapitol.[90] Processions were also held to mark events that were of significance for the Catholic cult. In 1622, for example, the Jesuit college organized a procession to celebrate the canonization of Ignatius Loyola and Francis Xavier and in 1633 the translation of the relics of the local saint, Engelbert, was marked by another elaborate procession.[91]

Images of the Virgin Mary played a prominent role in such major processions, as well as in the smaller ones organized by individual confraternities and congregations. Fourteenth-century statutes from the *Marienbruderschaft vom silbernen Bild und zur großen Glocke* at St Maria im Kapitol decreed that the brothers must assemble at the church and help to carry the silver image of the Virgin during the *Gottestracht* and during supplicatory processions.[92] Processions with this silver image also marked several of the most important feast days of the liturgical year within the collegiate foundation itself. On the feast day of the Purification the brothers went to the church at eight in the morning to receive candles and process with their statue. They then proceeded to the

[86] Ibid., fol. 14r. On the practice of clothing images see Trexler, 'Der Heiligen neue Kleider' and Nikolaus Gussone, 'Zur Krönung von Bildern: heutige Praxis und neuzeitlicher Ritus', *Jahrbuch für Volkskunde*, n.s. 10 (1987).

[87] Chaix, 'De la cité chrétienne à la métropole catholique', p. 925.

[88] Joseph Klersch, *Volkstum und Volksleben in Köln* (Cologne, 1979), p. 236.

[89] Scholten, 'Die Stadt als Kultraum', 109–15.

[90] Militzer, 'Collen eyn kroyn', 21; Herborn, 'Fast-, Fest- und Feiertage', 46–8; HAStK, Reichsstadt, Best. 14, Edikte, 16, fols. 66–7 (1571) and 1, fol. 140 (c.1594).

[91] Scholten, 'Die Stadt als Kultraum', 112–17.

[92] Militzer, ed., *Quellen*, vol. 1, p. 910.

master's house, where they had an elaborate meal.[93] This pattern continued into the seventeenth century.[94] A handbook written in 1634 by the rector of the St Aegidius altar records that the silver statue was also carried on the festival of Mary's Assumption, on St Vitalis' day and on the anniversary of the church's dedication.[95] On these feast days the procession left the confines of the church building and went around the graveyard, i.e. the area covered by the church's immunity. Members of the church's second Marian confraternity, the *Marienbruderschaft Salve Regina*, also processed with the silver image on the vigil of their feast day, the Ascension.[96]

The silver Madonna from St Maria im Kapitol appears to have enjoyed an especially high status: certainly no other image was carried in procession so frequently. But other churches did also honour their Marian images in this way. Statutes from the second half of the fifteenth century from the *Marienbruderschaft der Riemenschneider* at St Brigida stated that whenever the image of Our Lady was carried in procession the brothers should accompany it. The confraternity's masters held the image itself and lesser members were required to follow in pairs according to their rank.[97] The 1500 statutes of the Marian confraternity at the parish church of St John the Baptist also stated that on the feast of Corpus Christi the masters of the confraternity were to order its members to follow the statue of Our Lady in pairs.[98] At the parish church of St Laurenz a Marian image, almost certainly the statue referred to in the church inventories as the 'parish Mary', was carried twice a year, during the parish Corpus Christi procession ('vnsere Gotzdracht') and during the patronal festival of St Laurenz.[99] The financial records of the *Kirchenmeister* from the 1580s and 1590s mention payments made to the 'Megden' [maids] who carried the 'Hailligen' [saints' relics and/or images], to individuals who carried the flags and cross and to musicians who accompanied the procession. An entry from 1594 specifies that the maids had carried a 'Marien bildt' and in the following year the records mention that the Marian image was carried with a 'Himmel', i.e. a canopy. Entries from 1596 onwards also mention a 'grösse luchtt' [great light]. It seems that the procession was becoming more elaborate towards the end of the sixteenth century. On St

93 Ibid., vol. 2, p. 917.

94 Statutes from 1616 still mention the custom, HAStK, Stifter und Klöster, Best. 295, GA, Nr. 173 fol. 17v, as does a handbook composed in 1634 by the rector of the Aegidius altar, HAEK, Alte Kölner Pfarrarchive, St Maria i. Capitol, A II 16, fol. 7r. On the canonesses' participation see HAStK, Stifter und Klöster, Best. 295, GA, Nr. 170, fol. 2v.

95 HAEK, St. Maria i. Capitol, A II 16, fols. 7r, 18r, 32v, 40v.

96 Militzer, ed., *Quellen*, vol. 2, p. 960.

97 Ibid., vol. 1, p. 287.

98 HAEK, Alte Kölner Pfarrarchive, St Johann Bapt., A II 25 fols. 2r–3v.

99 Above, p. 224. On the local Corpus Christi processions see Eduard Hegel, 'Prozessionen und Wallfahrten im alten Erzbistum Köln im Zeitalter des Barock und der Aufklärung', *Zeitschrift des Aachener Geschichtsvereins* 84/5 (1977/8), 302.

Laurenz's day the maids again carried the saints' images or relics, and flags and a cross were also carried. This time, however, the Marian image was carried by two priests.[100]

Catholic reformers had an ambivalent attitude towards such processions. On the one hand they served an important spiritual and demonstrative purpose, as we have seen in the case of Augsburg. On the other, they encouraged superstition and immorality. In 1549 a provincial synod, presided over by Archbishop Adolf von Schauenberg, attempted to reform some aspects of processional practice. A decree issued by this synod stated that processions in which the host was carried with images of the saints should be cleansed of their abuses. Whatever did not contribute to the devotional aspects of the processions should be discontinued and they must, henceforth, be calm, grave and modest. In a particularly interesting passage the synod specified that: 'nor should more than one image of the Blessed Virgin, or of any other saint, be carried around from one place to another, lest we should see great and small, cult and non-cult statues, and think about a material object rather than concentrate our thoughts on heaven above'.[101] Multiple competing images of the Virgin would prevent worshippers from comprehending the true significance of the processional ritual. The attention of both participants and spectators should therefore be focused on one great image, an image like the silver statue from St Maria im Kapitol, whose cult status had been vindicated by centuries of veneration. The main points of the 1549 decree were reiterated by a diocesan synod in 1551, apparently without effect.[102] In 1583 Stephan Isaac complained about the persistence of what he described as a 'truly idolatrous and heathen practice': images of the saints were decorated and carried in procession by 'beautiful young maids', each of whom had a male staff carrier beside her. What devil had, he asked, inspired the inhabitants of Cologne to such actions? In Italy, Spain and France, even in Rome itself, images were not carried with such pomp.[103] In 1651 and in 1662 Archbishop Max Heinrich made further attempts to reform processional practice and threatened to punish the holding of processions that had not been approved by the archbishop.[104] Yet, as we have seen, processions organized by confraternities and parishes survived and even grew increasingly elaborate. And new processions, in particular those organized by the Jesuits, followed longer routes and were even more spectacular than their traditional counterparts.

[100] HAEK, Dom, St Laurenz, D II 177a, fols. 23r, 27v, 29v, 58v, 59v, 61v and so on.

[101] J. Hartzheim, ed., *Concilia Germaniae* (Cologne, 1765), vol. 6, p. 557. See also H. L. Cox, 'Prozessionsbrauchtum des späten Mittelalters und der frühen Neuzeit im Spiegel obrigkeitlicher Verordnungen in Kurköln und den vereinigten Herzogtümern', *Rheinsch-Westfälische Zeitschrift für Volkskunde* 22 (1976), 63–4.

[102] Hartzheim, ed., *Concilia Germaniae*, vol. 6, p. 792.

[103] Isaac, *Wahre und einfältige Historia*, fol. 14v.

[104] Hartzheim, *Concilia Germaniae*, vol. 9, pp. 729–40, 950; Mallinckrodt, *Struktur und kollektiver Eigensinn*, p. 248.

The vitality of traditional forms of civic and parochial devotion to the Virgin suggests that Cologne's religious culture was shaped more by the city's medieval patrimony than by the forces of the Counter-Reformation. The Marian paintings that adorned Cologne's churches also testify to this continuity. In Cologne medieval Marian images did not fall victim to the purifying zeal of iconophobic reformers, as they had done in Augsburg. Local Protestants caused some disruption, and there was a temporary decline in pious artistic commissions during the middle of the sixteenth century because of the uncertainty generated by the Reformation.[105] But most images survived this period of trauma: late medieval paintings of Mary with the sickle moon beneath her feet, of the glorification of the Virgin, of the *Schutzmantelmadonna* and of scenes from Mary's life continued to adorn Cologne's churches.[106] And during the later sixteenth century patrons once again began to commission conventional images of the Virgin, which echoed earlier iconographies. Figure 5, for example, shows Mary interceding before Christ, showing the breast with which she nursed him.[107] This iconography generally fell from favour in the post-Tridentine period when images of Mary's bare breast were condemned for their lack of decorum, but it reappeared in a painting from around 1556 for the church of St Kunibert and in a print produced in Cologne in the 1630s.[108] A comparison between triptych wings painted by Bartholomäus Bruyn the Elder in around 1530 (figure 49) and three panels dating from the late sixteenth century also indicates the continued popularity of traditional Marian images. On the Bruyn panels, which were probably part of an altarpiece from St Maria im Kapitol, the donor, probably Canon Johannes Hilpoet of Neuss, kneels before St Stephen. Mary appears holding the Christ Child, crowned, standing on a sickle moon and surrounded by a mandorla of light.[109] The three late sixteenth-century panels show the Virgin and Child in a similar way, crowned and surrounded by light (figures 50, 51 and 52). The donors – two canons from St Andreas and a Carthusian monk – kneel or stand before the Virgin and Child, their hands clasped in prayer.[110] These panels testify to a Marian piety that was shaped not by the Italianate and post-Tridentine sensibilities of the Fuggers and Wittelsbachs, but by local visual and devotional precedents.

[105] In 1538, for example, the council reported that images and liturgical vessels had been stolen from several of the city's churches by 'adherents of the Anabaptist sect and [of] unchristian teaching' HAStK, Best. 20, Briefbücher, Nr. 60, fols. 139v–140r. Also Groten, ed., *Beschlüsse*, vol. 4, p. 519. Wolfgang Schmid, *Stifter und Auftraggeber im spätmittelalterlichen Köln* (Cologne, 1994), p. 207.

[106] For examples of medieval Marian images see *CR* 10 (1995) and *CR* 11 (1996).

[107] For another example see *CR* 11 (1996), 121, ill. 5.

[108] *CR* 18–19 (2003–4), 323–4; Schöller, ed., *Religiöse Drucke*, cat. no. 28.

[109] Frank Günter Zehnder, *Katalog der Altkölner Malerei*, Kataloge des Wallraf-Richartz-Museums 11 (Cologne, 1990), pp. 47–9.

[110] *CR* 16–17 (2001–2), 85–6, 93, 141. For an example from c.1556 see *CR* 18–19 (2003–4), 323.

Figure 49. Bartholomäus Bruyn the Elder, wings from an altarpiece (Virgin and Child, and donor with St Stephen), c.1530 (WRM, Cologne)

Evidence concerning the display of *Hausmadonnen* also testifies to the longevity of local Marian piety. The *Cronica van der hilliger Stat van Coellen*, printed by Johann Koelhoff in 1499, records that Archbishop Walram von Jülich (1322–49) was the first to erect a *Hausmadonna* on a Cologne street. The archbishop's statue had a lamp in front of it and apparently ('als ich hain hoeren sagen') anyone who recited the Ave Maria before it would receive an

Figure 50. Wings of the so-called Drolshagen altar, after 1581 (St Andreas, Cologne)

indulgence.[111] Such *Hausmadonnen* were favoured by the civic as well as the ecclesiastical elite. The two houses on Heumarkt that provided a base for Cologne's cloth guild were destroyed in 1372 but the *Hausmadonna* that had adorned these buildings was saved at the behest of the city council. It was transferred to the church of Groß St Martin where it was placed before the entrance to the sacristy. The council endowed a perpetual income for the brotherhood of St Martin and St Nicholas that assumed responsibility for its illumination.[112]

[111] *Chroniken*, vol. 14, p. 672.

[112] Klaus Militzer, *Ursachen und Folgen der innerstädtischen Auseinandersetzung in Köln in der zweiten Hälfte des 14. Jahrhunderts* (Cologne, 1980), pp. 137–8 and Militzer, ed., *Quellen*, vol. 2, p. 1104.

Figure 51. Panel showing the Virgin and Child with donor, 1594 (St Andreas, Cologne)

Herman Keussen's comprehensive study of the topography of medieval Cologne mentions five other fourteenth- and fifteenth-century *Hausmadonnen*, and payments for the illumination of another, which adorned the linen trading-house on Aldermarkt, appear in the records of council expenditure for 1504 and 1508.[113] No equivalent study has been undertaken for the period after 1500 but there is plenty of evidence to indicate that medieval *Hausmadonnen* survived and

[113] Keussen, *Topographie*, vol. 1, pp. 27, 76, 97, 264; vol. 2, pp. 113, 282.

Figure 52. Virgin and Child with a Carthusian monk, c.1600 (WRM, Cologne)

that, unlike in Nuremberg, new ones continued to be erected. The diary of the Cologne councillor Hermann von Weinsberg mentions two, an old one on the corner of an inn on Waidmarkt and a newly renovated one that was placed on a recently constructed house in 1593.[114] The practice of adorning houses with images of the Virgin continued throughout the seventeenth century and enjoyed an upswing during the eighteenth.[115] In his study of Cologne houses Hans Vogts estimates that there were over a hundred *Hausmadonnen* on the city's streets in the eighteenth century and they are certainly plentiful on illustrations of buildings that were later destroyed.[116]

Cologne's wealthy citizens adorned the interiors as well as the exteriors of their homes with paintings and sculptures of the Virgin. Evidence from household inventories suggests that after scenes from Christ's life and Passion, Marian images were the most popular for domestic devotion.[117] Most of these Marian images were painted wooden panels or sculptures, though a few were more unconventional. In the *Saal* (living room) of Joist Wiltperg's house, for example, was a chandelier made from an antler with iron candle holders and an image of Our Lady.[118] Cologne inventories provide evidence of a whole spectrum of different domestic devotional environments. At the top end of this spectrum was the house chapel, a self-contained space furnished with wall paintings, stained glass, panels and sculptures. Hans Vogts noted in 1912 that there were more house chapels (or at least visual records of house chapels) surviving in Cologne than in any other city in northern Germany.[119] Even houses without a purpose-built chapel sometimes had specific areas set aside for religious devotion. The 1580 inventory of goods inherited by the sisters Gundula and Margaretha Schopman mentions a 'small prayer room in which there used to be many religious panels, letters, pictures and crucifixes, for which the two above-named virgins . . . were responsible'.[120] At the bottom end of the spectrum were the simple, altar-like arrangements within bedrooms or living rooms that are mentioned in a number of the inventories.[121] The habit of displaying devotional images in this way seems to have enjoyed particular currency in the Netherlands and in the Rhineland. An example is depicted in Joos van Cleve's altarpiece for the chapel of the Hackeney family's house on Neumarkt (figure 53).

114 Hermann von Weinsberg, *Das Buch Weinsberg: Kölner Denkwürdigkeiten aus dem 16. Jahrhundert*, 5 vols., Publikationen der Gesellschaft für rheinische Geschichtskunde 3, 4 and 16 (Leipzig and Bonn, 1886–1926), vol. 5, p. 376.

115 For other examples see Isabelle Kirgus, *Renaissance in Köln: Architektur und Ausstattung 1520–1620*, Sigurd Greven-Studien, 3 (Bonn, 2000), pp. 54–5 and 59.

116 Hans Vogts, *Das Kölner Wohnhaus bis zur Mitte des 19. Jahrhunderts* (Neuss, 1966), p. 147.

117 A sample of 29 sixteenth-century inventories revealed 22 mentions of images of Christ, 16 of images of Mary and 11 of images of other specific saints. Heal, 'A woman like any other?', pp. 153–58.

118 Hans Vogts, 'Das Haus Groenendal auf der Brückenstrasse', *JbKGV* 38/9 (1963/5), 62.

119 Hans Vogts, 'Kölner Hauskapelle', *Zeitschrift für christliche Kunst* 25 (1912), 195.

120 HAStK, Stifter und Klöster, Best. 223, Jesuiten, U2/481, fol. 2v.

121 See, for example, ibid., fols. 1v, 3r.

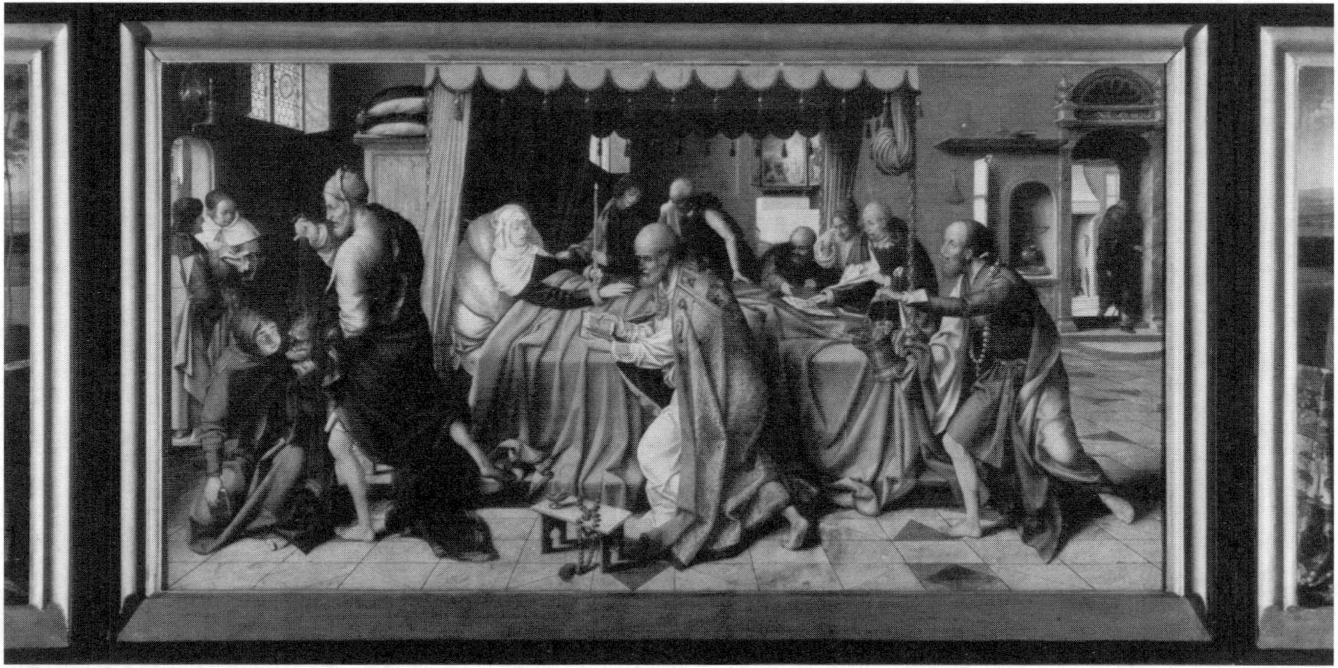

Figure 53. Joos van Cleve, house altar showing the death of the Virgin (WRM, Cologne)

Here a triptych showing the creation of Eve stands on a cupboard behind the bed in which Mary lies dying.[122] The strong interest in domestic devotion to Christ and the Virgin testifies to what Chaix describes as the 'privatization of religiousness'.[123] This 'privatization' was, he argues, a product of the long-lived influence in Cologne of the *devotio moderna*, with its emphasis on individual prayer and contemplation.[124] Once again, we see Cologne's sixteenth-century religious culture being influenced by late medieval patterns of piety.

THE IMPACT OF MARIAN INNOVATION

Because there was no caesura in Cologne's religious practice, and because many of the city's ecclesiastical and lay patrons remained steeped in local devotional traditions, the sixteenth century witnessed no significant transformation in the cult of the Virgin. This does not mean, however, that Cologne remained indefinitely cut off from Counter-Reformation Mariology. While long-established civic and parochial Marian rituals and conventional Marian images remained important, by the mid seventeenth century there were also innovations in the ways in which Mary was invoked. Some of Cologne's churches acquired characteristically Counter-Reformation Marian altarpieces, baroque in style and markedly acclamatory in subject matter. As in Augsburg, the Assumption was a favoured theme.[125] In 1618 Cologne's first significant baroque church, Mariä Himmelfahrt, was founded for the Jesuits by members of the Wittelsbach family. It provided a fitting setting for militant displays of Marian piety of the type favoured by the Jesuits and Wittelsbachs in Bavaria. Moreover, as post-Tridentine Germany's most important Catholic printing centre, Cologne played an important role in disseminating baroque devotional texts and images. And through the work of the Wittelsbach archbishops, the Jesuits and other reforming orders, some indigenous Marian devotions – the veneration of the Immaculate Conception and local pilgrimage cults – were given a distinctly Counter-Reformation gloss.

Gérald Chaix maintains that iconography provides a poor indication of the evolution of forms of devotion in Cologne because there are so many gaps in the historical record: too much of the city's ecclesiastical art has disappeared over time.[126] It is certainly true that conclusions about transformations in the visual cult of the Virgin must remain tentative, since Cologne's ecclesiastical imagery

122 On Mary as second Eve see Ernst Guldan, *Eva und Maria: eine Antithese als Bildmotiv* (Graz, 1966). Joos van Cleve was active in Antwerp from 1511 to 1540.

123 Chaix, 'Von der Christlichkeit zur Katholizität', p. 240.

124 On the influence of the *devotio moderna* in Cologne see Janssen, *Das Erzbistum Köln*, pp. 326–30.

125 Robert Grosche, *Der Kölner Altarbau im 17. und 18. Jahrhundert* (Cologne, 1978), p. 65.

126 Chaix, 'De la cité chrétienne à la métropole catholique', p. 687.

is exceptionally difficult to trace. Some paintings were transferred to private collections during the French occupation and secularization (1794–1814), some baroque altarpieces were removed during nineteenth-century 'purification' campaigns that sought to restore the city's churches to their medieval state, and many were destroyed during the Second World War.[127] Surviving artefacts and written records, in particular the travel diary of the Netherlandish artist Vincent van der Vinne, give some insight, however, into the appearance of Cologne's churches during the seventeenth century.[128] In Cologne, as in southern Germany, Rubens's work was highly valued and highly influential. The Flemish master, who had spent part of his childhood in Cologne, painted altarpieces for the parish church of St Peter and for the Capuchin monastery of St Franziskus.[129] Amongst the local artists of the period Johann Hulsman (c.1610–46), who had completed his training in Antwerp and elsewhere in the Netherlands, enjoyed the greatest reputation.[130]

A number of new Marian altarpieces entered the city's churches from the 1620s onwards. In around 1638 the Antwerp artist Cornelis Schut, a follower of Rubens, painted a panel for the St Mauritius altar in St Gereon that showed Mary as Queen of Heaven adored by Mauritius, Gereon and other saints.[131] St Agatha, the church of the female Benedictines, had a small Assumption of the Virgin by Johann Hulsman.[132] In 1643 Hulsman completed another Assumption for the collegiate foundation of St Aposteln (figure 54). This painting, which today serves as the high altarpiece of the church of Mariä Himmelfahrt, shows the donor, Johann Adolph Wolff von Metternich, with his family, kneeling in prayer as Mary is taken up into heaven on banks of clouds supported by angels.[133] In both its subject matter and its style, this painting is very like Rubens's and Lanfranco's altarpieces for Augsburg churches (figures 37 and 39). Its Counter-Reformation credentials are strong: it entered the church in 1643, the year in which Cologne's suffragan bishop, Georg Pauli-Stravius, decided to remove certain other paintings and statues from the church in accordance with a decree against 'monstrous and fictional and therefore offensive works'.[134]

127 Toni Diederich, 'Die Säkularisation in Köln während der Franzosenzeit', in *Lust und Verlust: Kölner Sammler zwischen Trikolore und Preussenadler*, ed. Hiltrud Kier and Frank Günter Zehnder (Cologne, 1995). See also *CR* 16–17 (2001–2) and *CR* 18–19 (2003–4).

128 Grosche, *Der Kölner Altarbau*.

129 *CR* 16–17 (2001–2), 251; Grosche, *Der Kölner Altarbau*, pp. 63–4.

130 Barbara Herrmann, *Johann Hulsman: ein Kölner Maler des 17. Jahrhunderts*, Europäische Hochschulschriften 314 (Frankfurt am Main, 1998), p. 33.

131 *CR* 18–19 (2003–4), 66, ill. 20.

132 *CR* 16–17 (2001–2), 38.

133 Hans Peter Hilger, 'Die ehemalige Jesuitenkirche St. Mariae Himmelfahrt in Köln', in *Die Jesuitenkirche St. Mariae Himmelfahrt in Köln: Dokumentation und Beiträge zum Abschluss ihrer Wiederherstellung 1980* (Düsseldorf, 1982), p. 22; *CR* 16–17 (2001–2), 109, ill. 6; Herrmann, *Johann Hulsmann*, pp. 61–6. Wolf-Metternich also gave a chapel to the church of Maria Ablaß: *CR* 18–19 (2003–4), 373.

134 *CR* 16–17 (2001–2), 106.

Figure 54. Johann Hulsman, Assumption of the Virgin from St Aposteln, Cologne, 1643 (St Mariae Himmelfahrt, Cologne)

In 1646 Hulsman painted an altarpiece showing the Virgin and Child enthroned and surrounded by saints for the parish church of St Christopher. It celebrates Mary's divine status in equally unapologetic terms.[135] Several paintings of the Holy Family, a popular Counter-Reformation theme, were also commissioned for Cologne churches during the 1640s, and in 1666 the Carthusian church of St Barbara acquired an Assumption for its high altar.[136]

The Jesuit church of Mariä Himmelfahrt was Cologne's first significant baroque church. Founded in 1618 and financed by Duke Maximilian of Bavaria, his brother Ferdinand, archbishop-elector of Cologne, and his cousin Franz Wilhelm von Wartenburg, bishop of Osnabrück, it was described by Ferdinand as a monument to Wittelsbach piety.[137] In comparison to the church of St Michael in Munich, another Wittelsbach-financed Jesuit foundation, Mariä Himmelfahrt is very traditional in appearance. Its external architecture references Cologne's medieval churches, and its internal structure is essentially gothic.[138] Yet it provided a backdrop for the kind of militant Marianism that we have come to expect from the Jesuits and their Wittelsbach patrons. In 1627, in the shell of the yet-to-be-completed church, the Jesuits staged a spectacular play. Involving a cast of 125, it told how Stephen (c.975–1038), king and patron saint of Hungary, had overcome his enemies with the help of the Virgin and converted his lands to Christianity. Performed partly in German before an audience of invited guests, both male and female, and general passers-by (who on the first two nights disrupted the production with noise and laughter), the play sought to inculcate the values of the Jesuits' Marian sodalities – virtue and victory through pious devotion to the Virgin.[139]

When completed, the church of Mariä Himmelfahrt also contained many visual invocations of the Virgin. The iconographical programme of the church was primarily Christocentric, but accorded Mary a prominent place. The nave of the church was adorned with statues of Mary, Christ and the Twelve Apostles, and each bay had a cartouche with a Marian emblem at the apex of its arch. These emblems were mnemonic prompts for the Litany of Loreto. On the frame of the high altarpiece, donated by Archbishop Ferdinand in 1628, carved angels,

[135] *CR* 16–17 (2001–2), 178; Herrmann, *Johann Hulsmann*, pp. 73–6.

[136] *CR* 16–17 (2001–2), 138, 167, 179. Some of Cologne's religious orders also promoted their own Marian cults: on the Discalced Carmelites and the scapular see *CR* 18–19 (2003–4), 231, 234 and Mallinckrodt, *Struktur und kollektiver Eigensinn*, pp. 107–8; on the Servites and their *Gnadenbild* from S. Annunziata in Florence see *CR* 18–19 (2003–4), 348–9.

[137] Hilger, 'Die ehemalige Jesuitenkirche St Mariae Himmelfahrt', p. 148; Smith, *Sensuous Worship*, pp. 165–87.

[138] Smith, *Sensuous Worship*, pp. 169–70.

[139] Joseph Kuckhoff, 'Das erste Jahrhundert des Jesuitenschauspiels am Tricoronatum in Köln,' *JbKGV* 10 (1928), 27–30. The Latin and German programmes are preserved in the HAStK, Univ. 1057, fols. 1r–4r and 5r–11r.

prophets and patriarchs adored the Virgin and Child. The altarpiece was divided into three zones, each of which had space for a painting that could be changed in accordance with the liturgical seasons. The paintings that were prepared for it showed episodes in the lives of Christ, Mary and St Francis Xavier.[140] The pulpit, which was crowned by a figure of St Michael trampling Lucifer, was adorned with scenes from the lives of Christ and the Virgin, including Mary's Assumption and Coronation. There were scenes from the life of the Virgin above the confessionals, intended to prepare the penitent for confession by emphasizing the sacrifices of Christ and the compassion of Mary.[141] And lining the sanctuary were painted landscapes by Johann Toussyn showing scenes from the life of the Virgin and from Christ's infancy that could be removed to reveal the church's relic collection.[142]

In the church's Marian chapel stood an altar with a retable from 1628, donated by Franz Wilhelm von Wartenburg, bishop of Osnabrück. It contained a fourteenth-century alabaster statue of the Virgin and Child, which was one of the few objects that the Jesuits had managed to preserve when their previous church, the Achatiuskapelle, burned in 1621. In typically baroque fashion this *Gnadenbild* was staged for maximum devotional effect: it was set in a new altar, and was kept covered for most of the year by a painting of the Assumption, a variant on a design by Rubens. Mary's coronation was depicted above.[143] The church's most unequivocal statement of Counter-Reformation Marianism would not, however, have been immediately apparent to its congregation. In 1631, at the request of Elector Maximilian of Bavaria, Tilly, commander of the Catholic League, sent to Cologne eleven of the Swedish cannons that had been captured during the sack of Magdeburg. Magdeburg, which had been one of the few imperial free cities to defend itself successfully against Emperor Charles V during the Schmalkaldic War, had become a symbol of heroic Protestant resistance. Part of its armoury was now used to cast bells to summon Catholics to worship at Cologne's Jesuit church. Mariä Himmelfahrt was literally crowned by a trophy of the Catholic triumph over heresy.[144]

Baroque altarpieces and a Jesuit church were by no means Cologne's only manifestations of Counter-Reformation Marianism. Indeed, as home to many reformed and Counter-Reformation religious orders and as Germany's greatest Catholic printing centre, Cologne played a pivotal role in disseminating new

140 Hilger, 'Die ehemalige Jesuitenkirche St Mariae Himmelfahrt', pp. 21–2, 175, fig. 2.

141 Walter Schulten, 'Die Beichtstuhlbilder der Kirche St. Mariae Himmelfahrt in Köln', in *Die Jesuitenkirche St Mariae Himmelfahrt in Köln*.

142 Anton Legner, 'Reliquienpräsenz und Wanddekoration', in *Die Jesuitenkirche St Mariae Himmelfahrt in Köln*, p. 282.

143 Hilger, 'Die ehemalige Jesuitenkirche St Mariae Himmelfahrt', p. 149 and fig. 83.

144 *Die Jesuitenkirche St Mariae Himmelfahrt*, pp. 320–3.

devotional texts and images.[145] Mary's cult was affirmed and promoted in works such as the 1570–5 *De probatis Sanctorum historiis*, written by the Cologne Carthusian Laurentius Surius, a friend of Peter Canisius.[146] Surius' six-volume collection of saints' lives was hugely influential. It was translated into German immediately for Albrecht V of Bavaria, and later Latin editions (of which there were four within half a century) expanded Surius' original text.[147] The collection remained the Catholic Church's most important hagiographical work until the Jesuit Jean Bolland and his followers began their definitive critical edition of the saints' lives, the *Acta sanctorum*, in the seventeenth century. Surius' work recounts the story of Mary's life and death, drawing on authors such as the Byzantine Simeon Metaphrastes in accordance with the traditions of the Catholic Church. Intended to edify the reader, and to strengthen Catholic belief, the text has a distinctly Counter-Reformation flavour. Surius invokes Mary, for example, as the 'fortress of the faith of Christians, and defender of those who place their hope in you'.[148]

Printed images also testify to the intensified promotion of Marian piety by reformed Catholic and Counter-Reformation orders.[149] The Jesuits probably made most effective use of printed *Andachtsbildern*, cheap images of Christ, the Virgin and saints that they distributed free to members of their Marian sodalities.[150] But it was not only the Jesuits who recognized the devotional value of such prints. In 1659, for example, Peter Overadt's publishing house had issued a single-sheet Marian print (figure 55). It was probably produced at the behest of one of Cologne's Franciscan houses, as it includes a prayer attributed to the founder of the Friars Minor. Mary is shown as the Woman of the Apocalypse with long, loose hair, hovering above the earth, an iconography that should probably, given the print's Franciscan connection, be read as referring to her Immaculate Conception. Around this central image are devotional directives that emphasize in particular the importance of Marian images. They range from the duty of praying an Ave Maria every hour to the obligation to defend Mary's honour with goods and with blood. The reader is told to carry Mary's image constantly either around his neck or on a rosary. Every Saturday he should pray to the Virgin and then light a candle before her image. Throughout his life he

[145] Wilfried Enderle, 'Die Buchdrucker der Reichsstadt Köln und die katholische Publizistik zwischen 1555 und 1648', in *Köln als Kommunikationszentrum*, ed. Mölich and Schwerhoff; Dietmar Spengler, *Spiritualia et Pictura: die graphische Sammlung des ehemaligen Jesuitenkollegs in Köln. Die Druckgraphik* (Cologne, 2003), pp. 94–7.

[146] Laurentius Surius, *De probatis Sanctorum historiis*, 6 vols. (Cologne, 1570–5).

[147] Laurentius Surius, *Bewerter Historien der lieben Heiligen Gottes*, 6 vols. (Munich, 1574).

[148] Surius, *De probatis Sanctorum historiis* (1573), vol. 4, p. 679.

[149] Spengler, *Spiritualia et Pictura*, pp. 316–23.

[150] Bernadette Schöller, *Kölner Druckgraphik der Gegenreformation: ein Beitrag zur Geschichte religiöser Bildpropaganda zur Zeit der Glaubenskämpfe mit einem Katalog der Einblattdrucke des Verlages Johann Bussenmacher* (Cologne, 1992), pp. 125–7.

Figure 55. 'Ehren=Taffel', single-leaf print showing Mary as the Woman of the Apocalypse, produced by Peter Overadt's publishing house, 1659 (GNM, Graphische Sammlung, Nuremberg)

should have Mary's image 'in the living room or most honourable room of [his] house' as well as in the bedroom, where he 'should venerate her daily with bended knee', and at the hour of his death he should have an image of Mary beside him or before his eyes. In its prescriptions concerning both public and private Marian piety Overadt's 'Ehrentafel' echoes many of the themes that were central features of religious devotion for the Jesuits' Marian *sodales*.

In the post-Tridentine era some of Cologne's traditional Marian devotions were also given a new, Counter-Reformation gloss. The Immaculate Conception had long been of great significance in Cologne. The Franciscan Johannes Duns Scotus (c.1265–1308), who died in Cologne in 1308, was an important defender of the doctrine, and members of the Order of Friars Minor continued to promote it throughout the sixteenth century.[151] It was not only Cologne's Franciscans, however, who declared their belief in Mary's sinless conception. From the early fifteenth century members of Cologne's cathedral chapter were given golden stars showing the *Immaculata*, with the inscription 'virgin conceived without stain'. And in the final decade of the fifteenth century the theological faculty of Cologne's university decided to bar opponents of the doctrine from lectures and to refuse doctorates to those who had not sworn their belief in it.[152] The cult gained added impetus from its Empire-wide promotion during the Thirty Years War. The Jesuits were, as we have seen, keen defenders, and under the patronage of the Habsburgs the *Immaculata* became the figurehead of the Catholic Church's struggle against heresy.[153] The Jesuits' *Litterae Annuae* describe in considerable detail a procession organized in 1639 in Cologne to mark the German jubilee year called by the pope because of the Thirty Years War. The sodalities that participated in this procession carried statues depicting their titular saints, and the sodality of the *B. Maria Annunciata Maior* presented a silver statue of Mary as the Woman of the Apocalypse surrounded by golden rays and standing on a globe. Seas, continents and islands could be recognized on this globe, and it was encircled by a dreadful dragon.[154] The message was clear: the Immaculate Virgin would triumph over heresy throughout the world.[155]

Cologne's Wittelsbach archbishops brought together these indigenous and post-Tridentine traditions. Emperor Ferdinand II prescribed the celebration of the feast of the Immaculate Conception in 1629 in the aftermath of the Edict of Restitution.[156] In Cologne Mary's conception had been celebrated throughout the sixteenth century, but in 1629 Archbishop Ferdinand von Bayern ordered the

[151] Graef, *Mary*, vol. 1, pp. 300–2. On the Franciscans in Cologne see Tekath, 'Die Unbefleckte Empfängnis Mariens', p. 60.

[152] Cologne was the first German university to adopt such draconian measures. Tekath, 'Die Unbefleckte Empfängnis Mariens', pp. 61, 66.

[153] Above, pp. 196, 200.

[154] HAStK, Stifter und Klöster, Best. 223, Jesuiten, A9, Litterae Annuae des Kölner Jesuiten Kollegs 1552–1660, fol. 368r–v. Scholten, 'Die Stadt als Kultraum', 117–19.

[155] Spengler, *Spiritualia et Pictura*, p. 319. A print produced in 1652 by Peter Overadt also emphasizes the role of the *Immaculata* as victor. The print gives twenty-nine events from Mary's life for contemplation, and depicts at its centre the Woman of the Apocalypse trampling a serpent. Beneath her is a globe. Schöller, ed., *Religiöse Drucke*, cat. no. 27.

[156] Above, pp. 152–3.

celebration to be extended to the vigil of the feast, which was to be marked by a fast. A Franciscan text of 1648 reported that Ferdinand also, with the agreement of the cathedral chapter, put the whole archbishopric under the protection of the *Immaculata*. In 1645 Aegidius Gelenius recorded that Cologne's inhabitants regarded the feast of the Immaculate Conception as their *Patronsfest*, and its status was confirmed in 1662 when Archbishop Max Heinrich's diocesan synod gave as patron for the archdiocese of Cologne the 'feast of the conception of the God-bearing Virgin Mary and of Our Lord'.[157] During this period the Franciscans also continued to promote the cult within the diocese. The church of St Franziskus, where Duns Scotus was buried, acquired a number of visual reminders of his Marian veneration: an archaic carved limewood sculpture of the *Immaculata* in 1629 and two paintings of the doctor venerating the Virgin in the 1640s.[158] In 1651 St Agnes, the church of the Observant Franciscans that had hosted a brotherhood dedicated to the Immaculate Conception since sometime before 1647, acquired a lattice screen with a door, above which was an image of the *Immaculata*.[159] And in 1644 Archbishop Ferdinand gave permission for a brotherhood dedicated to the Immaculate Conception in the Franciscan church at Bonn, which he, Max Heinrich and Bishop Franz Wilhelm of Osnabrück joined in 1647.[160]

The promotion of cult images and pilgrimages was also, of course, an important part of post-Tridentine Marian piety. Of the cities considered in this book, Cologne was the only one that had important Marian *Gnadenbilder* within its walls. The most venerable was the Milan Madonna, which according to Gelenius had been brought to Cologne from Italy together with the relics of the Three Kings in 1164 (though the existing statue dates from the late thirteenth century). This Madonna was housed beneath a baldachin in the cathedral's Marian chapel. In 1622 it was joined by a second Marian statue, which the cathedral chapter sought successfully to promote as another focus of devotion.[161] In 1662–3, as part of a campaign to refurbish the cathedral choir and to provide a fitting setting for its key relics, the Milan Madonna was given a new baroque altar, Italianate in style and possibly modelled on the Cappella Paolina in S. Maria Maggiore in Rome.[162] In a letter of 1658 to Archbishop Max Heinrich asking him to

157 Tekath, 'Die Unbefleckte Empfängnis Mariens', pp. 60–3.

158 *CR* 16–17 (2001–2), 236–40.

159 Tekath, 'Die Unbefleckte Empfängnis Mariens', p. 66; *CR* 16–17 (2001–2), 47; Mallinckrodt, *Struktur und kollektiver Eigensinn*, p. 103.

160 Tekath, 'Die Unbefleckte Empfängnis Mariens', pp. 61–2. While devotion to the Immaculate Virgin was especially strong in Cologne, the cult of the Virgin of Loreto, which flourished in southern Germany during the later sixteenth and early seventeenth centuries, took much longer to get established. Cologne's Jesuits promoted the use of the Loretan Litany, but the city did not acquire a Loretan pilgrimage site until the final quarter of the seventeenth century. *CR* 18–19 (2003–4), 418–21.

161 Schöller, *Kölner Druckgraphik*, pp. 60–2.

162 Ingo Matthias Deml, 'Der Altar der Mailänder Madonna und die Neuausstattung des Kölner Domes im 17. Jahrhundert', *Kölner Domblatt: Jahrbuch des Zentral-Dombau-Vereins* 64 (1999).

persuade the pope to prolong the indulgence for the altar, the cathedral chapter spelled out the Counter-Reformation aims of the new installation. Their request should, they argued be granted because of 'the worship practised up until now with special edifying traffic of the common folk in the aforementioned chapel of Our Dear Lady for attainment of constant peace and unity of the Catholic princes and potentates, the abolition of heresy and the glorification of the holy church'.[163] The altar's donor, the suffragan bishop Adrian van Walenburch, had been involved in recatholicization of parts of the Rhineland.[164] As a result he was, perhaps, like Peter Canisius and the Jesuits, especially attuned to the polemical value of Marian pilgrimage.

The parish church of St Maria Ablaß had another important Marian image, a wall painting that had been venerated since the late fourteenth or early fifteenth century. Its popularity escalated in 1583, when Stephan Isaac, parish priest at Maria Ablaß, attacked its cult. In his defence of his sermon against idolatry, published in 1586, he gave his account of events. Unable to tolerate the idolatry occurring in his church, Isaac had sold the wax votive offerings that had accumulated at the Madonna's shrine. The wall painting began to sweat, 'like other stone walls', because of a change in the weather. Its devotees, however, reported that they had seen it crying in response to Isaac's actions. There was a popular outcry against the priest, fomented, he reported, by female zealots. The Jesuits also stirred up opposition to Isaac, an archiepiscopal commission forbade him from preaching and he left the city in 1584.[165] The image's cult flourished: a painted *ex voto* from 1707 lists numerous miracles that were attributed to its intercession. As for the Milan Madonna, the era of the Thirty Years War was especially important. In 1627, at the time of Ferdinand von Bayern's witch hunt, a 'Zauberinne', who could find peace from Satan only before the image, gave herself up to the authorities and was 'judged blessed'. In 1630 the duchess of Bavaria was safely delivered of a child thanks to her devotion to the Madonna. In 1633 a thirteen-year-old boy who dared to throw a snowball at the image died of a protracted illness. In 1635 the chapel, which had been closed off with an iron bar, was miraculously reopened ('ohne Menschen Hülff'). And in 1642, as the elector's castle of Lechenich was besieged by French troops, Ferdinand von Bayern took refuge in the chapel, and the enemy fled as a result.[166]

The Milan Madonna and St Maria Ablaß's miraculous wall painting were traditional cults, given new impetus by the traumas of the Thirty Years War. Two other cults were new to Cologne in this period. The first focused on a statue venerated under the title 'Maria vom Frieden', which had been bequeathed to the female Discalced Carmelites in the Schnurgasse by Marie de' Medici in 1642. Louis XIII's mother, who had escaped from France to the Spanish Netherlands

[163] HAEK, Dom, A II 112. [164] Deml, 'Der Altar der Mailänder Madonna', 206.

[165] Isaac, *Wahre und einfältige Historia*, pp. 25–6. For a description of events see Ennen, *Geschichte*, vol. 5, pp. 429–41.

[166] *CR* 18–19 (2003–4), pp. 367–76; Ennen, *Geschichte*, vol. 5, pp. 710–11.

in 1631, spent the final years of her life in Cologne, bringing with her this statue, carved from the wood of the oak tree at Scherpenheuvel in Brabant on which a miraculous image of the Virgin had been found. Marie's Madonna, which showed Mary crowned as Queen of Heaven, was on public display from 1643, began to attract devotion and was housed in a baroque altar in the recently completed church of St Maria vom Frieden in 1685.[167]

Scherpenheuvel itself also became an important pilgrimage site for the inhabitants of Cologne. Archdukes Albert and Isabella, who shared sovereignty over the Spanish Netherlands with Philip III, promoted the shrine of Scherpenheuvel. In 1603, in thanks for conquest of 's-Hertogenbosch, the archdukes had a stone chapel built at the site. In true Habsburg fashion, Albert (the nephew of Philip II) called on the Virgin as patron of his troops and attributed in particular the 1604 Spanish victory over the Dutch at Ostende to her intercession.[168] In thanks for this victory Albert and Isabella gave Scherpenheuvel the status of a town and began to fortify the site. In 1609, during the festivities that marked the signing of the Twelve Years' Truce, they laid the foundation stone for a monumental new church. The whole town was a shrine to the archdukes' Marian piety: its church, the garden (a Marian *hortus conclusus*) that surrounded it and even the fortified city walls had a heptagonal plan, symbolizing the seven sorrows and seven joys of the Virgin.[169]

In the Spanish Netherlands Justus Lipsius played a part in promoting the Scherpenheuvel cult with his *Diva Sichemiensis sive Aspricollis, Nova eius beneficia et admiranda* of 1605.[170] In Cologne the pilgrimage was promoted through prints and through confraternities. Figure 56, an engraving produced in 1607 perhaps on behalf of Cologne's rosary brotherhood or a Marian sodality, shows the Virgin and Child in an oak surrounded by a rosary and by rays of sun. Supplicants, including a cripple and a possessed woman, kneel beneath, with other saints to their left and Archdukes Albert and Isabella and their companions to their right. Votive offerings hang from the tree, and the stone pilgrimage shrine can be seen in the background. Above are the arms of Prince Philipp-Wilhelm of Orange-Nassau, in whose domain Scherpenheuvel lay.[171] In 1628 the Marian confraternity at the Cologne church of St Cäcilia, which belonged to the female Augustinians, was refounded in order to promote pilgrimage to

[167] *CR* 18–19 (2003–4), pp. 385–90; Marion Opitz, 'Das Kölner Gnadenbild "Maria vom Frieden" im Spiegel des kleinen Andachtsbildes', *Kölner Museums-Bulletin. Berichte und Forschungen aus den Museen der Stadt Köln* 1 (2000). Marie gave a second Marian image made from the miraculous oak to Cologne's city council.

[168] Luc Duerloo, 'Archducal piety and Habsburg power', in *Albert and Isabella: essays*, ed. Werner Thomas and Luc Duerloo (Brussels, 1998), pp. 270–6.

[169] Amt für rheinische Landeskunde, ed., *Wallfahrt im Rheinland*, pp. 33–7; Schöller, *Kölner Druckgraphik*, pp. 56–60.

[170] Thomas and Duerloo, eds., *Albert and Isabella*, p. 275.

[171] Schöller, *Kölner Druckgraphik*, ill. 11 and pp. 56–60.

Figure 56. The miraculous Virgin of Scherpenheuvel, 1607 (Staatsbibliothek, Berlin)

Scherpenheuvel. This confraternity flourished during the Thirty Years War: from 1635 there was an annual pilgrimage to the shrine, and between 1637 and 1640 the brotherhood attracted 139 new members.[172] The pilgrimage, which took nine days, is shown on a panel by Johann Toussyn dated to around 1640

[172] Mallinckrodt, *Struktur und kollektiver Eigensinn*, pp. 244–5, 287.

(figure 57).[173] A procession winds up the hill from the left, reaching a wayside shrine and an oak with a Marian image. The pilgrimage church, built between 1609 and 1624, dominates the right of the picture, and the older brick chapel can be seen behind. Mary appears in the clouds above.[174]

The militant Virgin of the Counter-Reformation had been repeatedly invoked by Catholics during the civil wars in the Low Countries. In 1580, for example, witnesses reported that when the Calvinist administration of Brussels attacked Hal, a city with an important thirteenth-century cult image, Mary appeared above the city walls catching cannonballs in her lap.[175] In 1587, two years after Antwerp was recovered for the Spanish crown by Alessandro Farnese, duke of Parma, a statue of Silvius Brabo, a legendary Roman hero, on the city's town hall was replaced with one of the Virgin and Child.[176] As the Jesuit Franz Coster reported, the town 'recognized and received the Virgin Mary Mother of God, oppressed and rejected by the heretics, for its Lady, its guardian and its advocate'.[177] Like the Spanish kings on whose behalf they ruled, Albert and Isabella were ardent supporters of the Immaculate Conception. They were also dedicated to the cult of the Seven Sorrows of the Virgin, and venerated Our Lady of Sorrows as protectress of the union of the Netherlands.[178] It is scarcely surprising, therefore, that they chose to promote the Marian shrine at Scherpenheuvel during their continued struggle with the Dutch rebels. But neither Scherpenheuvel, nor Marie de' Medici's image taken from its miraculous oak, celebrates the militant Madonna of the Immaculate Conception, trampling heretics beneath her feet. Instead, they invoke Mary of Peace.[179] In Cologne in 1644 students of the Jesuit *Gymnasium* performed a play, *Maria Virgo Mater Dei, Regina Pacis, quae invenit gratiam apud Deum*, in which Mary rescued Europe from the plagues of war, discord, hunger and death. This play was repeated three times, and the same theme reappeared in later decades in times of war.[180] Moreover, as we have seen, in 1658 Cologne's cathedral chapter told Archbishop Max Heinrich that the common folk visited the Milan Madonna 'for the attainment of constant peace'.[181] Devotion to the *Regina Pacis* became

[173] *CR* 16–17 (2001–2), 170.

[174] On later Marian pilgrimages near Cologne see Amt für rheinische Landeskunde, ed., *Wallfahrt im Rheinland*, pp. 67–78 (Kevelaer); Bäumer and Scheffczyk, eds., *Marienlexikon*, vol. 6, pp. 714–15 (Werl).

[175] Thomas and Duerloo, eds., *Albert & Isabella*, p. 274.

[176] Smith, *The Northern Renaissance*, p. 406. On the invocation of Mary by Farnese's army see Chaline, *La Bataille de la Montagne Blanche*, p. 312.

[177] Quoted in Châtellier, *The Europe of the Devout*, p. 8.

[178] Thomas and Duerloo, eds., *Albert & Isabella*, pp. 271–2.

[179] Claudia Banz, 'Anmerkungen zum Ausstattungsprogramm der Marienwallfahrtskirche in Scherpenheuvel', in *Albert and Isabella*, ed. Thomas and Duerloo. On the designation of the Cologne image as *Maria Pacis* see Opitz, 'Das Kölner Gnadenbild', 14.

[180] HAStK, Univ. 1057, fols. 49r–50v. Kuckhoff, 'Das erste Jahrhundert', 36–7.

[181] Above, p. 245.

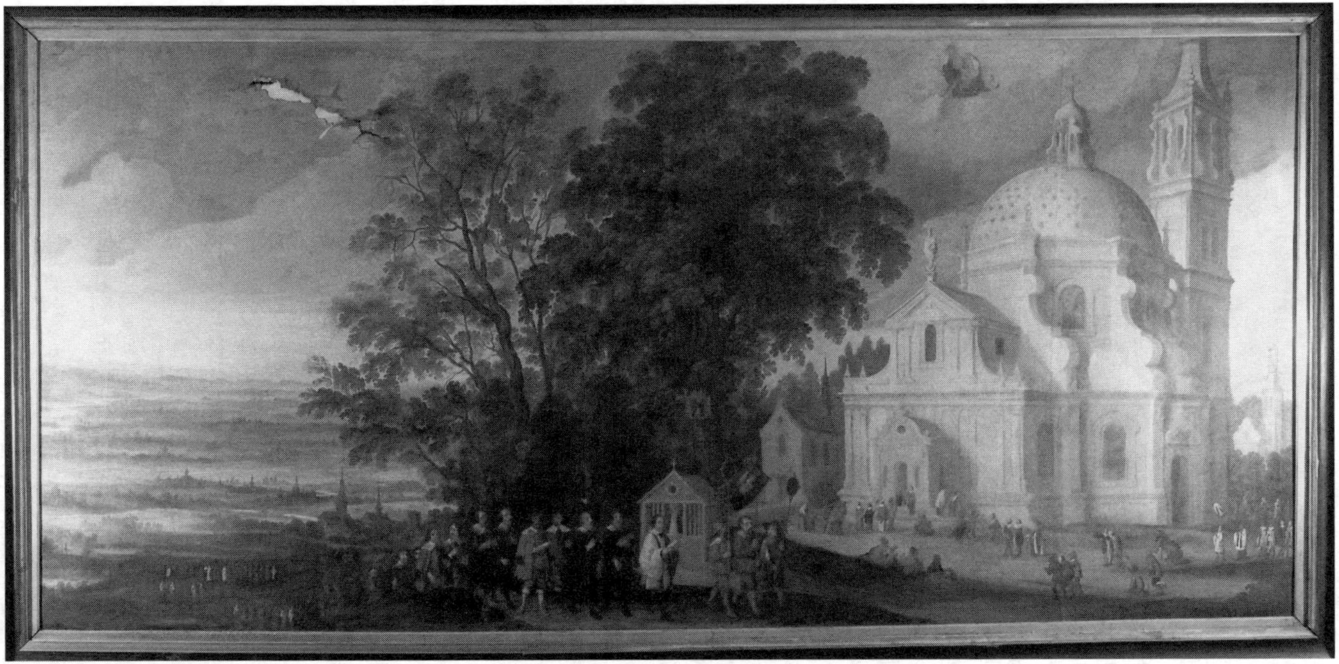

Figure 57. Johann Toussyn, pilgrimage to Scherpenheuvel, c.1640 (St Peter (Pfarrhaus), Cologne)

increasingly important north of the Alps as the inhabitants of Germany and the Netherlands suffered the impact of decades of warfare.

MARIAN BROTHERHOODS

In the seventeenth century there were innovations in Cologne's Marian cult, from the commissioning of baroque altarpieces to the emergence of new pilgrimages. But we should not overstate their importance: in general, continuity was as important as change. In St Maria im Kapitol, for example, which was the centre of civic devotion to the Virgin, the key cult image was still the gothic silver Madonna. This image was carried in procession on feast days as it had been for centuries, and Wallraf's inventory from 1795/98 indicates that it was still adorned with ornaments at that date.[182] In 1666 the 'Crux miraculosa' was placed on the Holy Cross altar at the centre of the rood screen, and in 1677 the church acquired a new marble high altar showing the resurrected Christ and two saints. Otherwise the appearance of this important Marian church remained largely unaltered until the later eighteenth century.[183]

Cologne's confraternity life also demonstrates the vitality of the city's medieval religious heritage, as well as the circumscribed impact of the Jesuits' concerted Counter-Reformation campaign. Confraternities were especially numerous in the Rhineland metropolis: while Nuremberg had fewer than ten on the eve of the Reformation and Augsburg had only seven, Cologne had over 120 during the later sixteenth and seventeenth centuries.[184] Rebekka von Mallinckrodt estimates that during the seventeenth century perhaps as much as 90 per cent of Cologne's adult male lay population belonged to at least one confraternity. These brotherhoods therefore constituted a key part of the religious and social life of the city.[185] They also provide a good indication of the importance of Marian piety: nearly one-third of Cologne's confraternities (thirty-five in the sixteenth century and forty in the seventeenth) were dedicated to the Virgin.[186] By contrast only nine or ten were dedicated to the next most popular patron, the Blessed Sacrament. Few records survive from the majority of Cologne's confraternities: their existence is often attested to only by a brief reference in a will, in a set of accounts or in Aegidius Gelenius' *De admiranda, sacra, et civili magnitudine Coloniae* (1645). In a number of cases, however, manuscripts containing statutes and membership lists or printed 'handbooks'

[182] HAStK, Stifter und Klöster, Best. 295, GA, 175 A, fol. 1r.

[183] Sabine Czymmek, 'Schattenrisse – zur barocken Ausstattung von St. Maria im Kapitol', *CR* 3 (1988).

[184] Militzer, ed., *Quellen*, vol. 1, p. xxviii, vol. 3, pp. xi–xvii; Mallinckrodt, *Struktur und kollektiver Eigensinn*, p. 31.

[185] Ibid., p. 381

[186] Ibid., p. 119; Militzer, ed., *Quellen*, vol. 3, p. xxi.

survive, making it possible to consider in more detail the devotional practices of the confraternities' members.

The type of piety promulgated by confraternities, and by Marian confraternities in particular, is generally thought to have changed during the later sixteenth and seventeenth centuries. Traditional brotherhoods, where members' key duties consisted of attendance at liturgical rituals and social events, were replaced by confraternities with solely religious aims, which sought to reform the spiritual lives not only of their members but also of the whole community. This change was, of course, initiated during the 1570s by the Jesuits' Marian sodalities, which, as Louis Châtellier has shown, hoped to transform Christian society in its entirety.[187] In southern Germany the shift from medieval confraternity to baroque sodality was marked. In Augsburg, as we have seen, traditional brotherhoods were abolished at the Reformation and during the later sixteenth and seventeenth centuries the Jesuits' sodalities dominated the city's confraternity life. In Munich the Marian sodalities were actively promoted by Bavaria's Wittelsbach dukes, and membership became a way for courtiers to demonstrate their Catholic credentials.[188] In Cologne the situation was more complex. The mid sixteenth century was an unpropitious time for the city's confraternities, and membership waned as a result of the uncertainty generated by the criticisms of the Protestant reformers. Cologne's confraternity system took time to recover, but unlike Augsburg's it was never entirely interrupted.[189] The Jesuits' sodalities had, therefore, to fit into an existing pattern of confraternity life: traditional foundations such as the *Marienbruderschaft vom silbernen Bild und zur großen Glocke* and the *Marienbruderschaft Salve Regina* at St Maria im Kapitol survived and flourished during the first half of the seventeenth century. Indeed, as Mallinckrodt has shown, during the post-Tridentine era new confraternities with traditional spiritual and social aims even continued to be founded. As a result, the Marian piety of Cologne's confraternities, like the city's Marian imagery and liturgy, comprised a rich mixture of local tradition and Counter-Reformation innovation.

Traditional confraternities had a small number of members: few had more than 200 and none more than 300.[190] As Mallinckrodt has pointed out, the religiosity of these assemblies was primarily communal, integrative and representative. Fines were imposed on members who threatened the cohesion of the confraternity or who refused to attend public rituals such as processions.[191] The confraternities' chief religious objective was the commemoration of the dead, and they also expressed devotion to their patron saints in various ways. Some confraternities were defined by their association with particular cult images,

187 Châtellier, *The Europe of the Devout*, p. 8. 188 Ibid., pp. 92, 119.
189 Chaix, 'De la cité chrétienne à la métropole catholique', pp. 684–7.
190 Mallinckrodt, *Struktur und kollektiver Eigensinn*, pp. 65, 63. 191 Ibid., pp. 59–61.

for example the *Marienbruderschaft vom silbernen Bild und zur großen Glocke* at St Maria im Kapitol, the 'broederschafft Unser Liever Frauen des groissen bildtz' at the church of the Augustinian Hermits and the 'broiderschaff Unsser Liever Vrauwen des groissen bylden jn dem cleynen choire' at the Carmelite monastery. In a number of cases the Marian images had been commissioned by or on behalf of the confraternity. A document from 1450 describing the establishment of the *Marienbruderschaft Salve Regina* at the Benedictine church of Groß-St Martin refers to two images of Our Lady 'that we have given on behalf of the aforementioned brotherhood to praise and honour God and Our Lady'. The abbot and prior, their descendants and the brotherhood were bound to protect these images, and the ornaments that belonged to them.[192] In addition to commissioning and adorning such images, Marian confraternities, as we have seen, processed with them on particular festivals and were sometimes responsible for their illumination. Some confraternities also undertook to provide for the singing of Marian hymns and antiphons.[193]

As we saw in chapter 1, the rosary confraternity founded in 1475 by Jakob Sprenger, prior of Cologne's Dominican convent and *Provinzial* of western and southern Germany, was exceptional in both organizational and religious terms.[194] Like other brotherhoods founded by the clergy rather than by the laity, the rosary confraternity promoted the internalization of religious practice. Its members had no communal corporate life, and as a result their relationship to the Virgin was expressed primarily through private prayer and devotion rather than through public ritual. Sprenger stated that a member offered up prayer to the Virgin on behalf of him- or herself and the whole brotherhood 'so that they all acquire the grace of justification from sins from her dear son'.[195] A book, dated by Klaus Militzer to 1509–10, describing the foundation of the *Bruderschaft der Sieben Freuden Mariens* by Cologne's Augustinian Canons at the church of Corpus Christi (Herrenleichnam) enumerates more fully the spiritual benefits that a member of such a Marian brotherhood might hope to receive from the Virgin. During his lifetime Mary would console him in all his sufferings and strengthen him in all his endeavours. A man who turned his heart to Mary and inwardly honoured and venerated her seven joys would never, because of Mary's intercession, die an unprepared death. At his last hour Mary would stand by him and bring his soul into the joy of eternal life. Every man 'who had affinity [ynichait]' with the most holy Virgin Mary and who pledged to serve and honour her should trust that she would save him from eternal damnation and from hellish torment. For although Mary would not contradict divine judgment by placing in heaven someone who had died in a state of mortal

[192] Militzer, ed., *Quellen*, vol. 1, no. 15; vol. 2, nos. 53 and p. 1056.
[193] Above, p. 39.
[194] Mallinckrodt, *Struktur und kollektiver Eigensinn*, pp. 67–72.
[195] Militzer, ed., *Quellen*, vol. 1, p. 512.

sin she would, through her prayer and with the consent of her son, lessen the torment of purgatory for those who truly rejected and repented of their sins.[196]

In their social inclusiveness, in their emphasis on prayer and in their use of printed devotional texts the Dominicans' rosary confraternity, the Augustinian Canons' *Bruderschaft der Sieben Freuden Mariens* and other clerical foundations served as models for the Jesuits' post-Tridentine sodalities.[197] Indeed, in 1575 Father Franz Coster specified that anyone who wished to join his Marian sodality should first become a member of the Dominicans' rosary confraternity.[198] The Jesuits, however, introduced important innovations to Cologne's confraternity life. Pre-Reformation confraternities had made little attempt to regulate or improve the lives and general devotional habits of their members. This was a primary objective of the Jesuits' Marian sodalities. Franz Coster wrote that the purpose of the Marian sodality that he founded for students at Cologne's Jesuit *Gymnasium* in 1575 was to encourage piety, good customs and study. The *sodales* confessed every eight days and received communion once a month. They were also required to promote such exemplary practices amongst their acquaintances.[199] When a sodality was established for Cologne's lay citizens in 1608 its members were expected to behave in an equally exemplary fashion. In a 'Handbuchlein', published in 1610, Francis Copper wrote that the members of the *Bürger-Sodalität* 'should rather with honourable customs and behaviour and in all their works conduct themselves so that everyone recognizes as worthy those who live under the shield and protection [Schutz und Schirm] of the heavenly Queen in her brotherhood'. They should confess and take communion each month, attend mass every day and participate in a devotional assembly each Sunday after mass.[200]

Both private piety and public proclamation were expected of the Marian *sodales*. The prefect of the Cologne group reported in 1577 that some members had pledged themselves to make a particular contemplation every day: the sufferings of Christ on Mondays, Wednesdays and Fridays, the life and virtues of the Virgin on Tuesdays, Thursdays and Saturdays and the gospel reading for the day on Sundays.[201] They also defended their faith against those who erred in their beliefs, thereby bringing some back to the church and strengthening others who had wavered in their commitment.[202] They brought to light and destroyed heretical books and sought to discourage calumny, lying, swearing, the eating of meat on Fridays and Saturdays and dishonourable behaviour in

[196] Ibid., vol. 3, pp. 10–18. [197] Mallinckrodt, *Struktur und kollektiver Eigensinn*, p. 73.
[198] Châtellier, *The Europe of the Devout*, p. 4.
[199] Duhr, *Geschichte der Jesuiten im XVI. Jahrhundert*, pp. 358–60.
[200] Quoted in Mallinckrodt, *Struktur und kollektiver Eigensinn*, p. 146.
[201] Duhr, *Geschichte der Jesuiten im XVI. Jahrhundert*, pp. 359–60.
[202] J. B. Kettenmeyer, *Die Anfänge der marianischen Sodalität in Köln*, Katholisches Leben und Kämpfen im Zeitalter der Glaubensspaltung 2 (Münster, 1928), pp. 16–18.

church. Copper's 'Handbuchlein' indicates that a similar combination of contemplation and action was expected of the members of the *Bürger-Sodalität*. The 'Handbuchlein' contains liturgical songs, psalms and litanies for public gatherings, prayers and readings for private devotion and doctrinal polemic to enable *sodales* to counter the invective of their Protestant opponents.[203] The members of the various Jesuit sodalities also participated in public processions.

The sodalities were, of course, specifically Counter-Reformation foundations. They were closely bound to Rome – all congregations were affiliated to the Roman college's congregation of the Annunciation – and their members were required to swear the Tridentine confession.[204] Their mission was, as Canisius told Coster in 1577, to preserve the Catholic Church in Germany.[205] Not surprisingly, therefore, their Marian piety had a distinctly polemical edge to it. In their oath of consecration, the *sodales* pledged not only to dedicate themselves to Mary but also to defend her from slanderous attacks.[206] Public Marian piety was required of them: directives issued in Cologne in 1576 stated that every *sodalis* should carry a rosary, that whenever Jesus' or Mary's name was spoken he should uncover or bow his head and that on entering a church he should always kneel and recite the Hail Mary.[207] In the Rhineland Archbishop Gebhard Truchseß's attempts to secularize the archbishopric gave the Jesuits' struggle against heresy a particular impetus during the sodalities' early years. In the introduction to his *Libellus Sodalitatis* Coster wrote that as a result of the 'cunning' of members of the confraternity 'it happened (the most Holy Mother of God supporting and assisting them) that the senate of Cologne held very resolutely to the Catholic faith, and most courageously repulsed and surmounted the great perils presented by the enemy'.[208] During the Thirty Years War this triumphalism was more than mere rhetoric for some of Germany's *sodales*. In 1633, for example, the fortress of Eichstätt was captured from the Swedes by an army composed mostly of members of Ingolstadt's Marian sodalities.[209]

In Cologne the Jesuits' sodalities recruited many members. By September 1576 the original foundation had two hundred, and in 1581 it was large enough to be split into five sections: one for academics, one for clergy and three for different types of student. It was first opened to a lay audience in 1608, when a sodality for local citizens was founded. One for unmarried journeymen followed

203 Mallinckrodt, *Struktur und kollektiver Eigensinn*, pp. 182–3.
204 Ibid., p. 144; Châtellier, *The Europe of the Devout*, p. 9.
205 Kettenmeyer, *Die Anfänge der Marianischen Sodalität*, p. 36; Canisius, *Beati Petri Canisii, Societatis Iesu, epistulae et acta*, vol. 7, pp. 422–3.
206 Mallinckrodt, *Struktur und kollektiver Eigensinn*, p. 145.
207 Kettenmeyer, *Die Anfänge der Marianischen Sodalität*, p. 9.
208 Franz Coster, *Libellus Sodalitatis: Hoc est, Christianarum Institutionum Libri Quinque, In gratiam Sodalitatis B. Virginis Mariae* (Cologne, 1603), fol. 5. Translation from Châtellier, *The Europe of the Devout*, 7.
209 Châtellier, *The Europe of the Devout*, p. 117.

in 1610.[210] During the Thirty Years War Cologne had a total of nine sodalities, five Latin ones for the clergy, academics and students of the university and *Gymnasium* and four German ones for citizens, single artisans, apprentices and soldiers.[211] Châtellier speculates that by the mid seventeenth century these sodalities had a total of two thousand members.[212] The few surviving membership lists confirm this impression of extensive recruitment: Cologne's *Bürger-Sodalität* had 136 members in 1608, the year of its foundation. During the 1630s and 1640s it won acceptance amongst the city's political elite, and by 1654 its membership had increased to 600.[213] The Jesuit sodalities therefore represented a new stage in Cologne's confraternity life: they recruited widely, but unlike the Dominicans' rosary confraternity they combined this social inclusiveness with a coherent structure and concrete obligations for their members. We should not assume, however, that the polemical Marian piety promulgated by the Jesuits entirely displaced the older forms espoused by the traditional confraternities. As Mallinckrodt has pointed out, in seventeenth-century Cologne there were only 9 Jesuit sodalities out of a total of 123 confraternities, and 3 of these Jesuit foundations were aimed at children. The remaining 114 confraternities were either other 'reformed Catholic' foundations or surviving or newly established traditional brotherhoods.[214] In Cologne the Jesuit sodalities only ever constituted a part of the local confraternity landscape.

Other 'reformed Catholic' confraternities shared the Jesuit sodalities' concern for education and good conduct and for the Tridentine ideal of uniformity and centralization. Most were founded by religious orders, by Cologne's archbishops or by its papal nuncios, and were branches of mother congregations. In 1633, for example, Archbishop Ferdinand founded an arch-brotherhood dedicated to the Seven Sorrows of the Virgin at the pilgrimage church at Kreuzberg near Bonn, and in 1635 he chose the church of St Maria im Kapitol for its urban branch.[215] Some were renewals of traditional foundations, given a Counter-Reformation gloss: in 1628, for example, the Marian brotherhood at St Cäcilia was re-established as an arch-brotherhood to promote communal pilgrimage to Scherpenheuvel.[216] In terms of Marian devotion, the dedications

[210] Joseph Hansen, ed., *Rheinische Akten zur Geschichte des Jesuitenordens 1542–1582*, Publikationen der Gesellschaft für rheinische Geschichtskunde (Bonn, 1896), pp. 706, 745; Brigitte Garbe, 'Reformmaßnahme und Formen der katholischen Erneuerung in der Erzdiözese Köln (1555–1648)', *JbKGV* 47 (1976), 166–7.

[211] Bernhard Duhr, *Geschichte der Jesuiten in den Ländern deutscher Zunge in der ersten Hälfte des XVII. Jahrhunderts*, 2 vols. (Freiburg im Breisgau, 1913), vol. 2, p. 84.

[212] Châtellier, *The Europe of the Devout*, p. 51.

[213] Mallinckrodt, *Struktur und kollektiver Eigensinn*, pp. 143, 195. [214] Ibid., pp. 131, 133.

[215] Eduard Hegel, *Das Erzbistum Köln zwischen Barock und Aufklärung*, *Geschichte des Erzbistums Köln*, vol. 4 (Cologne, 1979), p. 352. See also Simon Heinrich, *Regii natales confraternitatis septem dolorum B. Mariae Virginis ab ordine Servitarum religiosissimo quondam Praemonstratae* (Cologne, 1635) (UStBK, GB IV 5977).

[216] Mallinckrodt, *Struktur und kollektiver Eigensinn*, pp. 243–5.

given to seventeenth-century confraternities suggest the prominence of particular cults: the Seven Sorrows and Seven Joys, the Immaculate Conception and the Assumption.[217]

As Mallinckrodt points out, the prayer and song collections disseminated in printed devotional books by these 'reformed Catholic' brotherhoods were usually translations of medieval texts, which helped to demonstrate the Catholic Church's historical legitimacy. The confraternities' piety was, in this respect, conservative.[218] Saintly intercession and the remission of sins remained important devotional objectives, as a painting from 1621 showing the distribution of rosaries and the rescuing of souls from purgatory indicates (figure 58).[219] This painting also, however, shows rosary devotion in a Counter-Reformation light: here it unites the whole of Christendom – represented by a seemingly endless crowd of figures – in worship of the heavenly Virgin. In a 'Handbuchlein' from 1635 written by Jakob Plenck, the spiritual father and head of the Dominicans' rosary brotherhood, the value of rosary devotion as *demonstratio catholica* was expressed in concrete terms. Members of the rosary confraternity were now expected to confess and take communion frequently, to attend prayer assemblies and to participate in processions on the first Sunday of every month and on important Marian feast days.[220] The public nature of their Marian piety was all important. The rosary prayer changed from a quiet meditation to a confessional display. Plenck emphasized, for example, 'how useful it is to pray the holy rosary in public, communally, with loud voices and with choral song', and the 'Handbuchlein' offered indulgences for the public, as opposed to hidden, carrying of the rosary.[221]

As we saw in chapter 3, in Augsburg the confessional connotations of the rosary had been recognized as early as 1529, when the local citizen Heinrich Meckenloher stated that he carried one so that Berthold Aichelin, the imperial official responsible for the persecution of Anabaptists in the region, did not catch him. In Cologne these confessional connotations gained official recognition over a century later. After citing the rosary's anti-heretical credentials – in particular, its legendary role in St Dominic's thirteenth-century struggle against the Albigensians – Plenck went on to write:

> that the rosary and the profession of belonging to this brotherhood is a true sign of a true and keen Catholic Christian. If one doubts of what religion or faith an unknown person is, when one sees the rosary with him, one recognizes him immediately for a Catholic Christian; because the rosary reveals that one

217 Ibid., p. 117. 218 Ibid., pp. 271, 295. 219 *CR* 18–19 (2003–4), 282–3.

220 Jacob Plenck, *Handbu°chlein / der Bru°der und Schwerstern / der Vhralter / vnd weitberu^e hmbter / bey den Predigern gepflantzter ErtzBruderschafft IESV, vnd MARIÆ Rosenkrantz* (Cologne, 1635), pp. 252–4.

221 Ibid., pp. 259, 222.

Figure 58. The distribution of rosaries, 1621 (St Andreas, Cologne)

is an obedient child of the Catholic Church and not an adherent of an adverse sect or heresy.[222]

[222] Ibid., p. 158. Since the fifteenth century the 1213 victory over the Albigensians at Muret in southern France had been associated with Mary's gift of the rosary to St Dominic. Mallinckrodt, *Struktur und kollektiver Eigensinn*, p. 261 n. 54.

Plenck's 1635 'Handbuchlein' was much more polemical in tone than the 'liber fraternitatis rosacee corone' produced for the brotherhood in 1510.[223] Both texts emphasized the power of the rosary, dedicating whole chapters to miracles brought about by its recitation. Plenck recorded, for example, the rosary's role in exorcisms, in military victories, in healing the sick and in bringing the dead back to life, and told of the divine punishments meted out on those who persecuted it.[224] Such stories served to legitimate rosary devotion and to provide a proper historical pedigree for contemporary practice.[225] Plenck's account of the origins of the brotherhood also emphasized, to a new extent, Mary's role as protector and victor. Plenck gives as the immediate occasion for the founding of the brotherhood the threat to Cologne from Charles the Bold of Burgundy, who in 1474 promised Archbishop Ruprecht his assistance in subjugating the city and archdiocese of Cologne. Cologne's council asked the Dominican Jakob Sprenger for advice, and he recommended a rosary brotherhood.[226] Mary was, according to Plenck, especially effective in the struggle against religious as well as political opponents. The 1635 text made no explicit mention of contemporary Catholic–Protestant conflict, but talked of the arch-brotherhood of the rosary as 'a justifiable and necessary means to uproot heresies and sins' and cited not only Dominic's victory over the Albigensians but also the Battle of Lepanto as examples of the potency of rosary prayer.[227] Aegedius Gelenius recorded in his 1645 *De Admiranda, Sacra et Civili Magnitudine Coloniae* that in 1642, as French troops threatened Cologne, Archbishop-Elector Ferdinand von Bayern inscribed his name in the brotherhood's book, and donated an image of the Annunciation to the Dominican church. Because this image revived the populace's devotion to Mary, the enemy was defeated.[228]

This militant Virgin of the Rosary featured on a seventeenth-century single-leaf print inviting members of the confraternity to celebrate the feast of the rosary (figure 59). Mary tramples Turks beneath her feet. She holds a sword in her right hand and the Christ Child clutches the bloody head of one of her victims. Behind her the sea battle of Lepanto rages, and an inscription asks 'Queen of the most sacred rosary, fight for us.'[229] There is a marked difference between this violent image and the serene *Schutzmantelmadonna* of around 1500 sheltering members of the Cologne confraternity beneath her cloak (figure 7).

While such 'reformed Catholic' confraternities, with their typically polemical Marian piety, were undoubtedly important in seventeenth-century Cologne, they were exceeded in number and also, perhaps, in social influence by old-style

[223] Militzer, ed., *Quellen*, vol. 3, pp. 75–6. [224] Plenck, *Handbu^ochlein*, pp. 163–200.
[225] Mallinckrodt, *Struktur und kollektiver Eigensinn*, p. 260.
[226] Plenck, *Handbu^ochlein*, pp. 15–20. [227] Ibid., pp. 8, 186–7.
[228] Erzbischöfliches Diözesanmuseum Köln, *500 Jahre Rosenkranz*, pp. 107–8.
[229] Mallinckrodt, *Struktur und kollektiver Eigensinn*, p. 262.

TRIUMPHUS
SS.mi ROSARII,
Daß ist/
Das Glorwürdige und Sieghaffte Fest der Himmel-Königin
MARIÆ
Unter dem Nahmen des allerheyligsten Rosenkrantzes.

BEgrüsset seyst Du Königin Mutter der Barmhertzigkeit. Das Leben/ Süssigkeit und unsere Hoffnung sey gegrüst. Zu dir schreyen wir elende Kinder Evæ. Zu dir seufftzen wir/ trawrende und weinende in diesem Thal der Zäher. Eja unsere Fürsprecherin/ drum kehre deine barmhertzige Augen zu unß. Und nach diesem Elend zeige Unß Jesum die gesegnete Frucht deines Leibs/ O gütige/ o milte/ o süsse Jungfraw MARIA.

CLIPEUS CHRISTIANORUM

Regina Sacratissimi Rosarij pugna pro nobis

WEilen alle Jahr den ersten Sontag Monats Octobris/ bey den Predigeren das Sieghaffte Fest des H. Rosenkrantz hochfeyrlich zur schüldigster Dancksagung Gottes gehalten wird/ wegen des Siegs und Victori, so die Christenheit wider den Türcken auff dem Meer im Jahr 1571. Zur Zeit des H. Pabsts Pii V. durch das Gebett des H. Rosenkrantz wunderbarlicher weiß von Gott erhalten hat Alß werden zu demselben alle Hochgeehrte/ einverleibte Herrn Brüder und Schwesteren der löblichen/ uhralten Bruderschafft des H. Rosenkrantz: Wie dan auch alle eiffrige Liebhaber und Verehrer der H. Jungfrawen MARIAE mit diesem Zettel eingeladen/ und freundlichst ersucht/ an diesem Fest die Himmels-Königin MARIAM, alß ein gewisse Helfferin in allem Streit/ besonders aber in den letzten gefährlichen Todt-Kampff/ mit einem Wachsliecht zu verehren: Nach dero tröstlicher und gewisser Zusag/ und Verheissung Eccl. cap. 24. v. 31. Die mich erklären/ die werden das ewige Leben (und ewige Liecht) erhalten.

Bitt für uns O Königin des allerheyligsten Rosenkrantz.

Figure 59. 'Triumphus SS.mi Rosarii', invitation to the feast of the rosary for members of the Dominicans' rosary confraternity, seventeenth century (Graphische Sammlung, Historisches Stadtmuseum, Cologne)

confraternities promoting traditional forms of devotional practice.[230] Some of these had a continuous history, for example the *Marienbruderschaft vom silbernen Bild und zur großen Glocke* and the *Marienbruderschaft Salve Regina* at St Maria im Kapitol. Others, such as the fourteen brotherhoods established during the seventeenth century, were new foundations in the old style.[231] They were local institutions, not tied to a mother congregation, to a religious order or to Rome. They remained more interested in social cohesion than in outreach and pedagogy. Some were deliberately exclusive: the *Marienbruderschaft vom silbernen Bild und zur großen Glocke* limited its membership to forty people.[232] They did not prescribe weekly assemblies or monthly communion, and continued to focus instead on traditional forms of piety: care for the dead and participation in processions and other communal religious duties.[233] Their processions retained, as Mallinckrodt points out, a representative character, but did not seek, like those of the Jesuits' Marian sodalities, to engage the whole community. Those at St Maria im Kapitol, for example, remained within the confines of the church and churchyard.[234] But the limited membership and geographical scope of these traditional confraternities should not blind us to their considerable significance. The *Marienbruderschaft vom silbernen Bild und zur großen Glocke*, for example, retained the social prominence that it had enjoyed before the Reformation, and counted *Bürgermeister*, councillors, elite clergy, nobles and imperial and ecclesiastical dignitaries amongst its members, while the *Salve Regina* brotherhood at the same church was favoured by younger civic leaders.[235] In Cologne's confraternity life, as in its visual and liturgical culture, traditional Marian devotion flourished alongside Counter-Reformation innovation.

The Jesuits' militant Marian piety has been seen as the dominant prototype for devotion to the Mother of God in the post-Tridentine era. Johannes Burckhardt writes, for example, of the 'selective' reconstruction of Mary's cult in the aftermath of the Reformation that exalted the Virgin as Queen of Heaven, as patron of Catholic dynasties and lands and as military helper.[236] This Counter-Reformation Virgin was indeed prominent in Wittelsbach Bavaria and in Habsburg Austria. She also dominated the Catholic cult in the biconfessional city of Augsburg, where religious discontinuity and competition fomented change in forms of devotional practice. Here Marian piety acquired a demonstrative character and had a polemical and political edge. Cologne's Marian cult, by contrast, was shaped by the strength and continuity of local institutions and religious traditions. The plurality of ecclesiastical authority within the city ensured that the

[230] Ibid., pp. 297, 373. [231] Ibid., pp. 304–6. [232] Ibid., p. 360. [233] Ibid., p. 323.
[234] Ibid., p. 327 and above, pp. 226–7. [235] Ibid., p. 360.
[236] Burckhardt, *Das Reformationsjahrhundert*, p. 109.

influence of Counter-Reformation orders, in particular of the Jesuits, was less strong in Cologne than in parts of southern Germany. Moreover, throughout the early modern period civic devotion to the Virgin, with its implicit celebration of Cologne's independence, parochial Marian piety and traditional Marian brotherhoods remained important. Counter-Reformation innovations – baroque images and texts, new pilgrimage cults, the Jesuits' sodalities – were merely part of a larger landscape of Marian devotion. Traditional and Counter-Reformation Marianism were not, of course, incompatible: in the cults of the Immaculate Conception and of the rosary, for example, Mary was celebrated both as patron of Cologne and as leader of the universal Catholic struggle against heresy. But the diversity of Marian devotion in 'holy' Cologne shows that we must not overestimate the Counter-Reformation's ability to dictate a uniform style of religious life throughout Germany.

6. *Marian devotion and gender*

In 1523 Dr Georg Hauer, a member of the University of Ingolstadt, preached three impassioned defences of the Marian antiphon *Salve Regina*. Luther and his followers had, Hauer argued, perverted the text of the *Salve* by transferring its supplications from Mary to Christ. In so doing they had impugned Mary's honour. No punishment could be too harsh for such blasphemers: Hauer reported with pleasure that the previous summer a 'defiler of Mary' had been executed in Munich while in Freiburg im Breisgau another who had 'dishonoured Mary' had had his tongue torn out. Some of Hauer's harshest criticism was directed, however, neither at male blasphemers nor at the leaders of the evangelical movement but at women. As a result of Luther's attack on the *Salve* 'the women in many cities . . . revolt against Mary the virgin, crane their necks, tear down the pride of your mother, abandon and despise Mary's humility, and say Mary is a woman like I am one, our lady is a woman like any other'. Hauer was horrified by the expression of such sentiments: even Luther himself had not written so shamelessly of Mary. For Hauer, Mary was humble, chaste and pure, unlike all other 'daughters of Eve'. The evangelically inspired assertion that she was a woman like any other prompted him to provide a bitter catalogue of the failings of 'sinful women'. Whereas Mary, for example, had been brought up in the temple, 'you, sinful creature, prone to evil from childhood, never did anything good, and even if you are raised in a cloister or brought up honourably you do not stick with it, do not improve through such education [zucht], but only become more evil, reckless and devilish'.[1]

The cult of the Virgin cannot, as Hauer's text indicates, be properly analysed without taking into account early modern notions of womanhood. Although few commentators contrasted the Virgin with real women as explicitly and harshly as Hauer, assumptions about proper female behaviour underlay both Catholic and Protestant Marian teaching. The implications of the promotion and celebration

[1] Georg Hauer, *Drey christlich predig vom Salve regina / dem Eua[n]geli vnnd heyligen schrift gemeß* (Ingolstadt, 1523), Aiii, Gii, Giii.

of this idealized woman have been much debated by historians. Understandably, given the sentiments expressed by churchmen such as Hauer, feminist historians writing from a Catholic perspective have seen the cult of the Virgin as a device designed to facilitate the imposition of misogynist values. They argue that male churchmen set up Mary as an unattainable ideal of female virtue. In her discussion of fourteenth-century Italian paintings of the Virgin Margaret Miles speaks of 'images designed to criticise and denigrate . . . [women's] bodies, their personalities, and their accomplishments', while Marina Warner describes the Virgin as the 'instrument' of an 'argument from the Catholic Church about the structure of society, presented as a God-given code'.[2] Reformation historians have tended to assume, by contrast, that the cult of the Virgin provided women with inspiration. Merry Wiesner points out that the Catholic cult of the Virgin 'did describe at least one woman in totally positive terms'.[3] The female saints, and Mary in particular may, Lyndal Roper acknowledges, have been regarded as unattainable ideals, but they did at least 'allow women some female figures with which to identify'.[4] Indeed, the notion that through destroying Mary's cult the Protestant reformers deprived women of an important role model has become a commonplace of Reformation scholarship. Johannes Burckhardt states, for example, that Mary was the most important female figure whom Christians could relate to and take as their example.[5]

In this debate, the realities of early modern Marian devotion have become obscured. Scholars have failed to take into account the diversity of both Protestant and Catholic Marian piety. While in some Protestant areas Marian images and feast days disappeared, in others they were successfully assimilated into post-Reformation devotional life. Within the Catholic Church Georg Hauer's type of militant Marianism was, as this book has demonstrated, only one possible prototype for devotion to the Mother of God. We need to acknowledge this diversity and to consider how Mary was depicted and described in different places and at different times. Was she presented as a human mother, a figure with whom real women might well have felt some immediate affinity, or as a distant and divine being? Where possible, we also need to assess how women responded to the various manifestations of Mary's cult. Despite the problems

[2] Miles, *Image as Insight*, p. 87. Miles does go on to acknowledge that women might have found such images enriching: they 'provided models of a spiritual life liberated from immersion in the potentially overwhelming biological contingencies of childbearing and the physical and environmental necessities of the household . . .' (p. 88); Warner, *Alone of All Her Sex*, p. 338. Some anthropologists have reached similar conclusions. In her study of the Mexican cult of the Virgin of Guadalupe Ena Campbell writes, for example, that 'in the west, the worship of the Virgin stands alongside the self-abnegation of women and the patriarchal, authoritarian attitudes of males', 'The Virgin of Guadalupe and the female self-image: a Mexican case history', in *Mother Worship: theme and variations*, ed. J. J. Presto (Chapel Hill, 1982), p. 21.

[3] Wiesner, 'Luther and women', p. 303. [4] Roper, *The Holy Household*, p. 263.

[5] Burckhardt, *Das Reformationsjahrhundert*, p. 109.

that inevitably beset attempts to recover early modern women's own opinions, we can glean some indication of women's spiritual priorities from the few personal testimonies that survive as well as from indirect evidence concerning participation in Marian rites and rituals. Finally we need to recognize that the mainstream evangelical Reformation rarely created an exclusively masculine religious landscape. Even when Marian images and feast days were abolished, Christians' devotion was redirected towards a Christ who was described and depicted in maternal as well as in paternal terms. The relationship between a religious symbol such as Mary or Christ and gendered social reality is therefore considerably more complex than most previous studies have acknowledged.

CATHOLIC DEVOTION

In Nuremberg much late medieval art survived intact, and it is clear that both before and after the Reformation women would have seen images celebrating Mary's motherhood whenever they worshipped in the city's main churches. Here, as elsewhere in Germany, devotion to Mary's maternity and to all of Christ's earthly kindred flourished during the late fifteenth and early sixteenth centuries. Images of the Virgin and Child, of the Holy Family and of the Holy Kindred depicted Mary as a young, human mother, and seemed therefore, at least at first glance, to validate the experiences of normal women. Images of the Virgin Mary and Christ emphasized the lively and affectionate bond between mother and son. Adam Kraft's Pergenstorffer epitaph of 1498, for example, showed a conspicuously human baby kicking as if trying to escape from his mother's grasp (figure 11), and Albrecht Dürer produced numerous examples of touchingly maternal Marian iconography. Between 1504 and 1515 the Lorenzkirche received three images showing the Virgin and Child with St Anne or with their extended family: an epitaph showing the Holy Kindred commemorating the young Johannes Löffelholz, son of a local patrician (figure 24); a carved wooden altarpiece showing the Virgin and Child with St Anne donated by a woman, Ottilia Mayr; and a painted altarpiece showing the Holy Kindred and four other saints commissioned by Kunz Horn and his wife to adorn the altar of their chapel in the graveyard of the church (figure 25).[6]

As Klaus Arnold and others have argued, such images probably reflect the increasing emphasis amongst Germany's burghers on the importance of marriage, motherhood and the home.[7] Strong familial sentiment obviously informed at least two of the Nuremberg commissions: the epitaph for twelve-year-old

[6] On the Löffelholz epitaph see Strieder, *Tafelmalerei*, p. 233 and on Kunz Horn's donation see Schleif, *Donatio et Memoria*, pp. 103–14.

[7] Klaus Arnold, 'Die Heilige Familie: Bilder und Verehrung der Heiligen Anna, Maria, Joseph und des Jesuskindes in Kunst, Literatur und Frömmigkeit um 1500', in *Maria in der Welt*, ed. Opitz *et al.*, p. 156.

Johannes Löffelholz, and the altarpiece for Kunz Horn's chapel. According to its foundation document this chapel was dedicated to the Trinity, the Virgin Mary, Anne, Joachim, their lineage and all souls, and was endowed for the salvation of Horn, his wife, their cousins, mothers and forefathers. As an elderly childless couple Horn and his wife looked towards their ancestors and relations, and concerned themselves with their salvation.[8] Similarly in several early sixteenth-century depictions of the Holy Kindred the association between Christ's earthly kindred and the donor's own lineage was made explicit through the inclusion of portraits.[9] In a painted wing panel (c.1522) from the high altarpiece of Nuremberg's Frauenkirche the donor's wife, Ehrentraut von Thumenberg, is depicted visiting St Anne in her lying-in chamber, dressed, as befitted the wife of a prominent local citizen, in a church bonnet and silk-lined mantle (figure 2).

The prominence of such images, as well as the inclusion in late fifteenth- and early sixteenth-century liturgical calendars of the feast day of Mary's mother, Anne, served to elevate and sanctify motherhood. Understandings of the holy and even, in the case of Mary, miraculous motherhoods of Christ's female relatives validated, to a certain extent, the maternal experiences of normal women. On the south portal of Nuremberg's Frauenkirche there was even a fourteenth-century statue of the Annunciation that showed a heavily pregnant Virgin.[10] Of course Mary was a mother to her devotees as well as to the Christ Child. Two votive panels painted by Bernhard Strigel in 1517 for the Augsburg merchant Conrad Rehlinger make this relationship explicit (figure 60). Rehlinger places himself and his eight children under the protection of God and the Virgin. On the textile hanging behind the figure of Rehlinger is an inscription that reads: 'O Lord, in all your goodness, save the children and me from sin.' The equivalent inscription above the children reads: 'We pray to you, Mary pure, that you will be our mother.' The children's own mother had died two years previously, and the plea put into their mouths by their father explicitly asks the Virgin to take her place. In the background Mary appears on a bank of cloud, her voluminous cloak partially spread out by cherubs. The reference to the traditional iconography of the *Schutzmantelmadonna* is clear.

While such images undoubtedly testify to Mary's accessibility, to read them as mere celebrations of maternity and domesticity is to understand only a small part of their significance. Religious images were never straightforward

[8] Schleif, *Donatio et Memoria*, p. 103.

[9] This device seems to have enjoyed particular favour amongst patrons connected with Emperor Maximilian I. See Hans Georg Thümmel, 'Bernhard Strigels Diptychon für Cuspinian', *Jahrbuch der kunsthistorischen Sammlungen in Wien* 76 (1980), 108 and K. Ashley and P. Sheingorn, eds., *Interpreting Cultural Symbols: Saint Anne in late medieval society* (Athens, GA, and London, 1990), p. 189.

[10] Metropolitan Museum of Art and Germanisches Nationalmuseum, eds., *Gothic and Renaissance Art*, pp. 118–19.

Figure 60. Bernhard Strigel, Conrad Rehlinger and his children, 1517 (Alte Pinakothek, Munich)

expressions of social reality. As Caroline Walker Bynum points out, 'pictures of the Holy Family are themselves theological statements', statements about Christ's incarnation and about Mary's role in the story of salvation.[11] Take, for example, Lucas Cranach's altar for the Marienkirche in Torgau (figure 61), surely, for modern observers, one of the most touchingly maternal images of the Holy Kindred. In this image the divine is domesticated: on the left-hand wing panel Mary Cleophas nurses her baby, while on the right Mary Salome picks nits from the hair of her son. Two other young children play in the foreground. Delight in domestic detail is part of the appeal of such images, yet Cranach's painting, and others like it, in fact break the conventions of the real world. Mary

[11] Caroline Walker Bynum, *Fragmentation and Redemption: essays on gender and the human body in medieval religion* (New York, 1991), p. 80.

Figure 61. Lucas Cranach the Elder, Holy Kindred (the Torgau altar), 1509 (Städelsches Kunstinstitut, Frankfurt am Main)

sits with her hair uncovered, an obvious reference to her status as the ultimate paradox, the virginal mother. The object in her hand that Christ reaches for is an apple, a symbol of his role as Redeemer of mankind's Original Sin. Although Mary Cleophas' attire is courtly and contemporary, her position – seated on the ground and breastfeeding her son – reflects the iconography of the Madonna of Humility rather than the behaviour of a real noblewoman. And the young child reading at her feet reinforces the spiritual significance of Christ's playfellows, all of whom were venerated as saints.[12]

Mary may have been depicted in a domestic setting, but as a closer examination of Cranach's Torgau altar and of other similar images suggests, her motherhood inevitably retained a certain detachment from the world of normal female experience. Klaus Schreiner's assertion that 'medieval women experienced Mary not as unreachable superhuman, but as woman, to whom the dangers and sufferings of the female sex happened: pregnancy, delivery, poverty, isolation, hardship amongst refugees, the loss of her son' is an oversimplification.[13] Textual sources confirm that although Mary was celebrated as a mother she was not, according to Catholic reckoning, a mother like any other. Indeed, the differences between Mary and the sinful daughters of Eve were a constant theme in Catholic teaching. In accounts of Mary's life events that might have found parallels in the lives of human mothers were described in ways that served to emphasize Mary's special status. As Georg Hauer emphasized, her pregnancy and delivery were painless and uncomplicated, and she remained a virgin: 'Mary gives birth without pain and loss of her virginity, you poor woman with great pain and infirmity. Angels with songs of praise surrounded Mary's birth, around you weak woman midwives stand crying and screaming.'[14] Although she subsequently adhered to the Levitical prescription for postnatal ritual purification (Luke 2:22–39), she did so, Catholic authors argued, only because of her admirable humility.[15] For normal mothers the ritual of churching represented the moment at which they were reintegrated into the local community after childbirth and the period of lying-in. During this ritual their impurity, and hence their heightened receptivity to the forces of evil, was banished.[16] The feast of Candlemas celebrated the equivalent moment in the life of the Virgin, but emphasized her purity. As Canisius wrote in his discussion of this feast, Mary, who was pure in body and spirit, had nothing in common with other new mothers. Indeed, the blessing of candles that formed the central

[12] Friedländer and Rosenburg, *Die Gemälde von Lucas Cranach*, cat. no. 18. Cranach's altarpiece also has a political subtext: the figures of Alpheus and Zebedee on the two side panels are portraits of Elector Frederick the Wise of Saxony and his brother Duke John the Steadfast, while the middle man on the central panel (one of Anne's three husbands) has been identified as Emperor Maximilian.

[13] Schreiner, *Maria*, p. 500. [14] Hauer, *Drey christlich predig*, Giii.

[15] See for example Voragine, *The Golden Legend*, vol. 1, p. 144.

[16] Karant-Nunn, *The Reformation of Ritual*, pp. 72–8.

liturgical event of the feast day symbolized Mary's perpetual virginity, as well as Christ's role as Light of the World.[17]

For Catholics Mary's motherhood was important more because it conferred salvific power upon her than because it reflected real female experience. Bound by the ties of filial obedience, her omnipotent son could refuse her nothing. Images of the 'double intercession' and the 'ladder of salvation' express clearly this link between Mary's corporal maternity and her intercessory power. In double intercessory images Christ and Mary present themselves before God the Father, Christ showing his wounds and Mary displaying her breast. In a version painted in 1508 by Hans Holbein the Elder for the Augsburger Ulrich Schwarz a text above Christ reads 'Father, see my red wounds, help men in their need, through my bitter death.' Another above Mary pleads: 'Lord, sheath your sword that you have drawn, and see my breast, where your son has sucked.'[18] In images showing the ladder of salvation Mary exercises her power through the mediation of Christ rather than turning directly to God the Father. A panel painted in Cologne by the Master of the Holy Kindred during the second half of the fifteenth century shows a donor keeling before God the Father (figure 5).[19] His prayers are received first by the saints surrounding him on earth then by the bare-breasted Virgin then by Christ himself. In a plague altarpiece painted by the Ulm artist Martin Schaffner in around 1515 Mary holds her breast and shelters supplicants beneath her cloak, whilst the arrows sent by God to wreak havoc on his people break harmlessly in mid-air, deflected by the pleas of Christ and his mother (figure 6).[20]

Phyllis Mack and Ulinka Rublack have pointed out that early modern sensibilities did associate human motherhood with power, at least to a certain extent: pregnant women were accorded specially privileged status, and nursing mothers were perceived to be potent as well as comforting.[21] But the power associated with Mary's maternity was infinitely more consequential than the mere moral and spiritual authority with which normal motherhood was imbued. Indeed Mary's maternity entitled her to a form of power that, in secular usage, was specifically associated with fathers rather than mothers: the power to protect dependents. In her study of parenthood in the fourteenth and fifteenth centuries Claudia Opitz argues that one of the prime duties of fathers was to protect their offspring. This duty found expression in legal documents as well as in records

17 Canisius, *De Maria Virgine incomparabili*, pp. 410–11.

18 On double intercessory images see Bynum, *Fragmentation and Redemption*, pp. 106–8. On Holbein's image see Martin Schawe, *Staatsgalerie Augsburg: Altdeutsche Malerei in der Katharinenkirche* (Munich, n.d.), pp. 59 and 85.

19 Above, p. 34.

20 Germanisches Nationalmuseum, ed., *Die Gemälde des 16. Jahrhunderts*, pp. 443–6.

21 Phyllis Mack, *Visionary Women: ecstatic prophecy in seventeenth-century England* (Berkeley, Los Angeles and Oxford, 1992), pp. 35–44 and Ulinka Rublack, 'Pregnancy, childbirth and the female body in early modern Germany', *Past & Present* 150 (1996).

of men seeking help for sick children and carrying out pilgrimages on their behalf.[22] The fact that this duty and right was, in the spiritual realm, transferred to a female figure should come as no surprise. As Caroline Walker Bynum has pointed out, in late medieval spirituality God was often described using maternal imagery. Just as Christ could assume the female role of nurturer so Mary could assume the male role of protector. In the religious realm, medieval people blurred the boundaries between male and female with an ease that is surprising to modern sensibilities.[23]

Thus while Mary's motherhood may have validated the experiences of normal women in some ways, in late medieval spirituality it also raised her above the gender boundaries that pervaded everyday society. Mary's role in Christ's Passion, which was as frequently commemorated in the visual and devotional culture of the Catholic Church as her relationship with her infant son, also emphasized her universal significance. In Passion imagery, and in particular in the *pietà* (the sorrowing Virgin alone with Christ's body), Mary was a witness to the sufferings of Christ. Her role was not, Christine Peters argues, gender specific: 'Mary's grief, far from striking a chord amongst mothers alone, was more commonly understood to stand for the general grief of mankind for the necessity of Christ's sacrifice.'[24] A prayer invoking Mary's compassion in the 1635 handbook of the Cologne rosary brotherhood asked: 'What man [Mensch] will not weep, when he sees the pure mother, in such great agony and torment.'[25] Mary's *compassio* or co-suffering also reinforced her salvific power.[26] In a woodcut designed by Wolf Traut and printed by Hieronymus Holtzel in Nuremberg in the late fifteenth century, for example, Mary and Christ appear side by side surrounded by the instruments of the Passion. Mary's pain is graphically depicted in the form of a sword transfixing her breast, and in the verses that originally accompanied the image Christ promised his mother that because his Passion had pierced her through they would both come together into the realm of glory.[27] At her Assumption – an event frequently depicted in paintings and prints – Mary is welcomed by Christ and crowned as Queen of Heaven. Seated beside him, she can intercede to save her devotees from damnation.

22 Claudia Opitz, 'Mutterschaft und Vaterschaft im 14. und 15. Jahrhundert', in *Frauengeschichte – Geschlechtergeschichte*, ed. Karin Hausen and Heide Wunder (Frankfurt and New York, 1992), p. 141.

23 Caroline Walker Bynum, *Jesus as Mother: studies in the spirituality of the high Middle Ages* (Berkeley, Los Angeles and London, 1984) and Bynum, *Fragmentation and Redemption*, p. 182.

24 Peters, *Patterns of Piety*, p. 77.

25 Plenck, *Handbuͦchlein*, p. 432.

26 See Otto G. von Simson, 'Compassion and co-redemptio in Roger van der Weyden's Descent from the Cross', *Art Bulletin* 35, no. 1 (1953) and Amy Neff, 'The pain of compassion: Mary's labor at the foot of the Cross', *Art Bulletin* 80, no. 2 (1998).

27 Robert W. Scribner, 'Wolf Traut, Imago pietatis und Mater dolorosa', in *Glaube Hoffnung Liebe Tod*, ed. Christoph Geissmar-Brandi and Eleonora Louis (Vienna, 1995).

During the turmoil of the Reformation and Counter-Reformation period the invocation of Mary's independent power as an advocate and protector generally came to take precedence over interest in her maternal and familial roles. Devotion to the Holy Family was certainly an important strand of post-Tridentine piety in parts of Europe. And in areas of Germany in which traditional expressions of religiosity survived Mary's motherhood continued to provide a significant devotional focus. In Cologne, for example, the iconography of the bare-breasted Virgin endured for an unusually long time.[28] In southern Germany especially, however, Marian devotion emphasized the divine rather than the domestic. Notions of Mary's exceptional merit and virtue were reaffirmed in response to Protestant criticism. In Ingolstadt Georg Hauer's impassioned defence of Mary's unique status as Queen of Heaven was made in the aftermath of Lutheran attacks on her cult. In his 1577 *De Maria Virgine incomparabili* Peter Canisius also reacted strongly against Luther's account of Mary's humble origins, reproducing the apocryphal story of her exceptional upbringing in the temple at Jerusalem. He defended traditional Catholic belief in the vow of virginity that Mary had made before her marriage to Joseph, upheld the doctrine of the Immaculate Conception and affirmed the notion of Mary's personal merit.[29] Canisius added that whilst in all normal women the emotions were more formed than the intellect, a state that led to impatience, hate, lamentation and immoderation, in Mary there was nothing worthy of condemnation. Mary was the only truly blessed one amongst the feminine sex.[30] In response to evangelical attacks on the excesses of Mary's cult, Catholics exalted her even further beyond the realm of normal female experience.

Right from the start, Jesuit Marian devotion had been suffused with knightly sentiment, thanks to Ignatius Loyola's own chivalrous relationship with the Virgin. In their consecration oath the Jesuits' Marian *sodales* pledged to honour and serve Mary, and took her as their patroness.[31] Mary's motherhood could not, of course, be forgotten. In Christoph Schwarz's painted panels for Munich's Jesuit college and for Augsburg's Jesuit church, for example, Mary is still depicted as a young mother, human rather than regal (figure 32). Yet she is raised above the earthly realm on banks of cloud and surrounded by worshipping angels. In the Loretan Litany, the use of which was, as we have seen, promoted in Germany by the Jesuits, Mary is again invoked first of all as 'mother', but as 'mother most chaste', 'mother most pure', 'mother inviolate'

28 Above, p. 229.

29 Canisius, *Maria, die unvergleichliche Jungfrau und hochheilige Gottesgebärerin*, pp. 88–90, 133–40, 206. At their fifth General Congregation leaders of the Jesuit order made the defence of the doctrine of the Immaculate Conception into a general duty of the order. Beissel, *Geschichte der Verehrung Marias im 16. und 17. Jahrhundert*, p. 240.

30 Canisius, *De Maria Virgine incomparabili*, p. 425. See also Gössman and Bauer, eds., *Maria*, p. 64.

31 See above, pp. 200 and 253–4.

and 'mother undefiled'. The litany goes on to invoke her as powerful and merciful Virgin, and as queen of the angels, patriarchs, prophets, apostles, martyrs, confessors, virgins and saints.[32] The Virgin's power was manifest in her victory over demons and heretics. In 1570, for example, Peter Canisius exorcized Mark Fugger's maidservant at Altötting, using the Loretan Litany and Marian images to drive an evil spirit from the unfortunate woman's body.[33] In 1571 the victory of the Holy League over the Ottoman fleet at the Battle of Lepanto was ascribed to Mary's intercession, an event commemorated in a bloodthirsty seventeenth-century woodcut for Cologne's rosary confraternity (figure 59). After the Battle of the White Mountain (1620) Mary was invoked as 'the best and greatest patron of Bavaria . . . the special protector of princes . . . the victorious helper' and dedications to 'Maria Hilf' flourished.[34] The climax of this Counter-Reformation trend was the Habsburg devotion to the Virgin of the Immaculate Conception. Embodying purity and power rather than maternity and domesticity, the *Immaculata* was often depicted without her child.[35]

Fifteenth- and sixteenth-century images of the Holy Family and Holy Kindred may have affirmed the value of domesticity, but the differences between the holy mother Mary and the sinful daughters of Eve were a constant theme in Catholic teaching. Moreover, with the advent of the Counter-Reformation Mary's domestic role was overshadowed by invocation of her divine power. Personified by the childless *Immaculata*, the Virgin of the Counter-Reformation no longer had any obvious connection to the realm of normal female experience. Yet to suggest, as some scholars have done, that women inevitably found Mary's perfection and power alienating and oppressive is to fail to appreciate the complex nature of late medieval and early modern religious devotion.[36] Mary's status may have been exceptional, but it is clear that women could nonetheless find spiritual fulfilment in her cult. Some religious women took her as a role model, and laywomen often sought her aid, particularly in matters relating to childbirth and childrearing. Virgins and mothers did not necessarily turn to Mary because she was a woman like them. They turned to her because she was a powerful intercessor. The appeal of Mary's cult transcended all gender boundaries, although, as we shall see, men's and women's experiences of Marian devotion

[32] John W. O'Malley, ed., *The Jesuits: cultures, sciences and the arts 1540–1773* (Toronto, 1999), p. 585.

[33] Above, pp. 155–6. [34] Above, pp. 158–60 and 193.

[35] In seventeenth-century Spain, for example, where veneration of the *Immaculata* reached its apogee, Francisco Pacheco stated that Mary should be painted without her child because the iconography of the Immaculate Conception was derived from St John's description of the Woman of the Apocalypse. Robert Enggass and Jonathan Brown, *Italy and Spain 1600–1750: sources and documents*, Sources and Documents in the History of Art (Englewood Cliffs, NJ, 1970), pp. 115–16.

[36] See for example Gössman and Bauer, eds., *Maria*, p. 65.

were inevitably shaped by the gender asymmetries that permeated every aspect of early modern life.

The pre-Reformation cult of the Virgin may have been constructed and promoted by male churchmen, but Mary undoubtedly played an important role in the lives of some female celibates, as the records of mystical visions from fourteenth-century south German Dominican convents demonstrate. In their spiritual autobiographies a number of Dominican nuns recorded their close identification with the Mother of God: in visions Mary offered the Christ Child to them to hold or nurse.[37] The child interacted with them in a very personal way. Margaretha von Ebner, for example, told how he persuaded her to give him her breast, saying 'if you will not suckle me then I will depart from you when you love me most'. The testimony of Friedrich Sunder, chaplain of a female Dominican convent near Nuremberg, demonstrates that although this strand of piety was primarily a female phenomenon, on occasion male mystics could also change places with the Virgin and suckle the Christ Child.[38] As Bynum points out, in the realm of medieval religiosity gender boundaries were remarkably fluid.[39] All such visions were, of course, part of a quest for mystical union with Christ. Johannes Tauler, a Dominican preacher, told his audience that whoever wanted spiritual motherhood, 'this birth in her soul', must be separated from everything, as Mary had been at the Annunciation.[40] This type of esoteric mystical spirituality was of little relevance to ordinary parishioners, but the testimonies of the Dominican nuns do at least indicate the important role that Mary might play in the piety of female celibates.[41]

The writings of Margareta Lynnerie (1576–1621), the daughter of a Cologne patrician, demonstrate the extent to which this role changed over the course of the sixteenth century. In Germany at least the great age of medieval mysticism was over: for Margareta the Virgin Mary was to be emulated in daily life not imitated in fervent visions. With the support of her parents, Margareta founded a small community of devout virgins in Münstereifel (south-west of Bonn) in the final decade of the sixteenth century. The members of this community dedicated themselves to prayer, to the reading and writing of religious texts, to handiwork, to visiting the sick and to teaching girls.[42] According to the statutes that Margareta wrote for the community, in all of these activities Mary was to be

37 Rosemary Hale, 'Imitatio Mariae: motherhood motifs in devotional memoirs', *Mystics Quarterly* 16, no. 4 (1990).

38 Ulinka Rublack, 'Female spirituality and the Infant Jesus in late medieval Dominican convents', in *Popular Religion in Germany and Central Europe, 1400–1800*, ed. Robert W. Scribner and T. Johnson (Basingstoke and London, 1996), pp. 22 and 26.

39 Bynum, *Fragmentation and Redemption*, p. 182.

40 Hale, 'Imitatio Mariae', 199.

41 On the Marian devotion of the beguines see Martina Wehrli-Johns, 'Haushälterin Gottes: zur Mariennachfolge der Beginen', in *Maria, Abbild oder Vorbild*, ed. Hedwig Röckelein (Tübingen, 1990).

42 Conrad, 'Nähe und Distanz', pp. 107–8.

the virgins' model: 'it is my intention, that the virgins of Christ and inhabitants of this house of St Salvator should everywhere keep the Virgin Mary before their eyes as an example, mirror and patron, whether they are walking or standing, speaking or keeping silent, praying or reading, contemplating or working, and whether they are alone or with others'.[43] In the details of their daily lives as well as in their exercise of the traditional female virtues of humility, gentleness, obedience, chastity and piety they should follow Mary's example. They should care for their house, and should spend their time spinning and sewing or alone in contemplation, shunning unnecessary company as Mary had done. Margareta's text contains characteristically Counter-Reformation elements: the members of the community should invoke Mary as their protectress, and should not be ashamed to confess 'our ancient, holy, Catholic, Roman-apostolic faith, which alone makes blessed', just as Mary had professed her faith publicly when she stood beneath Christ's cross.[44] Perhaps not surprisingly, however, given its Cologne context, Margareta's text focuses more on Mary's traditional attributes. The humble, obedient and domestic Virgin is here used by a woman as a positive role model for other women.

It is, of course, much more difficult to find evidence concerning the devotional interests of laywomen. Very few German laywomen left behind spiritual autobiographies or records of belief equivalent to Margareta Lynnerie's. We are therefore dependent upon indirect evidence concerning women's actions: the writings of religious reformers, visitation records, records of endowments and bequests, and descriptions of pilgrimage and confraternity life. Such sources are hardly, as we shall see, problem free, but they do at least allow us a glimpse into the elusive realm of women's spirituality.

Polemic by both Catholic and Protestant reformers suggests that Mary played a prominent role in this spirituality. A passage in Thomas More's 1528 *Dialogue Concerning Tyndale* provides the most famous example of reformers' condemnation of the weaker sex's Mariolatry. The messenger in the *Dialogue*, who has supposedly been sent by a friend of More's to ask him about matters of faith that have been called into question by the evangelical reformers, reports a conversation that he had overheard between two women: '"Of all our ladies," saith one, "I love best our lady of Walsingham." "And I," saith the other, "our lady of Ipswich."' For the messenger this conversation was a sure indication of women's propensity for idolatrous veneration: 'In which words what meaneth she but her love and her affection to the stock that standeth in the chapel of Walsingham or Ipswich?'[45] In Germany too Protestant reformers saw

[43] P. Salesius Elsner, *Die Ursulinen von St Salvator* (Trier, 1913), pp. 32–3. [44] Ibid., p. 31.

[45] W. E. Campbell, *The Dialogue Concerning Tyndale by Sir Thomas More* (London, 1927), p. 62. More replies: 'take the simplest fool that ye can choose, and she will tell you that our Lady herself is in heaven. She will also call an image an image, and she will tell you a difference between an image of an horse and an horse indeed' (ibid., p. 164).

women as the chief proponents of Marian devotion. The ecclesiastical officials who conducted Nuremberg's 1560/1 rural visitation criticized women's role in maintaining particular Marian cults: in the villages of Tennelohe and Eltersdorf it was women who visited the 'idolatrous statues' and 'held them in higher esteem than God' and in Rasch it was 'old wives from the countryside' who made offerings before the Madonna behind the church.[46] In Cologne Stephan Isaac, the priest of St Maria Ablaß and canon of St Ursula, claimed that it was chiefly women who venerated the Marian image on the wall of his church.[47] Isaac reported sceptically that 'an infertile woman became fertile through this dear Lady, or perhaps through a monk, of whom so many are busy in this chapel'. Isaac also complained that it was women who led the hue and cry against him when he attacked the idolatrous cult.[48]

Some of these comments can, of course, be dismissed as mere stereotypes of female foolishness. As Peters points out, such stereotypes were 'a gift to the polemicist who wished to denigrate the religious practices of his opponents'.[49] It was easy to belittle the cult of the Virgin by describing it as a product of female credulity. 'The female sex', Erasmus wrote in his Apology against Alberto Pio, 'loves to hear the praise of a woman rather than of Christ.'[50] But evidence for women's devotion to Mary, and in particular for the association of her cult with childbirth and child rearing, goes beyond mere polemic. As well as making general accusations against women and 'old wives', Nuremberg's ecclesiastical commissioners also found two individuals who had made pilgrimages and offerings to Marian shrines in order to seek assistance in bearing and raising children. Stefan Rummer's wife from the village of Rasch admitted that she had twice pledged her seven-year-old daughter before the miraculous Marian image at Trautmannshofen in the Upper Palatinate.[51] The wife of Fritz Linberger had made an offering to the Madonna at Hüll 'so that our God would confer grace on her birth'.[52] Protestant visitations continued to turn up such cases: in 1582, for example, visitors to the parish of Ühlfeld in Protestant Ansbach reported that local women persisted in suckling their children before a specific image of the Virgin and Child after the completion of their churching ceremonies.[53]

In a Catholic context such pilgrimages, offerings and rituals were generally encouraged rather than condemned (despite the concerns of reformers such as Erasmus). The confraternity of the Seven Joys of Our Lady at the Cologne cloister of the Augustinian Canons had a chapel that, according to a description published in 1509–10, was founded so that all Christian people, but especially pregnant women, could call on the glorious Virgin Mary. In order to guarantee safe childbirth women invoked Mary's aid there with seven candles and seven

[46] Above, p. 113. [47] Above, p. 245. [48] Isaac, *Wahre und einfältige Historia*, p. 25.
[49] Peters, *Patterns of Piety*, p. 40. [50] *CWE*, vol. 84, p. 251.
[51] Hirschmann, *Die Kirchenvisitation*, pp. 183, 190–1. [52] Above, p. 111.
[53] Dixon, *The Reformation and Rural Society*, p. 172.

masses in honour of her seven joys.[54] Stephan Isaac's bane, the Marian image at St Maria Ablaß in Cologne, could offer the same service. An *ex voto* panel of 1707 reported that in 1630 the pregnant duchess of Bavaria had held masses and lit a candle before the image for a period of six weeks, and on the last day had been safely delivered of a baby.[55] Certain Marian pilgrimage images, for example one at St Gallen near Lake Constance and another at the Augustinian cloister at Eberhardsklausen near Trier, specialized in offering miraculous cures for barrenness, and objects such as rosaries and candles blessed at the feast of the Purification were sometimes placed on women's beds during labour by midwives.[56] Such traditional religious practices persisted throughout the early modern period.

Given such evidence, it is perhaps hardly surprising that some historians have assumed that virgins and mothers turned to Mary because she was a woman like them. While Schreiner asserts that women experienced Mary as a 'woman, to whom the dangers and sufferings of the female sex happened', Claudia Opitz states that although the gender-specific elements of medieval Marian veneration have yet to be fully analysed, it seems likely that the experiences and needs of women played an important role in promoting Mary's cult.[57] The notion that the cult was particularly important for members of the female sex finds support in anthropological studies that claim that female-referring symbols are especially attractive to women.[58] Bynum points out, however, that 'gender-related symbols, in their full complexity, may refer to gender in ways that affirm or reverse it, support or question it; or they may, in their basic meaning, have little at all to do with male and female roles'.[59] We must, therefore, eschew oversimplified, schematic views of the relationship between religious symbols and social reality. As Peters argues, 'female saints are tokens that female sanctity is attainable, but the possibilities of identification and aspiration are much more complex: female and male saints do not simply speak to women and men respectively'.[60] In order to demonstrate that devotion was driven by more than simply perceived similitude we have only to remember that the patron saint of childbirth was not, in fact, the mother Mary but Margaret, a virgin martyr who never herself gave birth but who, according to legend, emerged unscathed after being swallowed by a dragon.

While some women undoubtedly found comfort in Mary's cult, reformers were wrong to describe it as a primarily female phenomenon. The first great

[54] *Van der broderschaff der 7 vreuden Unser Liever Vrauwen*, Hessische Landes- und Hochschulbibliothek Darmstadt, W 3619/130. I am grateful to Prof. Dr Klaus Militzer for allowing me access to a transcript of this text.

[55] *CR* 18–19 (2003–4), 375.

[56] Schreiner, *Maria*, pp. 57–60.

[57] Ibid., p. 500 and Opitz, 'Mutterschaft und Vaterschaft', p. 144.

[58] For a summary of this debate see Bynum, Harrell and Richman, eds., *Gender and Religion*, especially p. 9.

[59] Ibid., p. 2.

[60] Peters, *Patterns of Piety*, p. 97.

blossoming of Marian devotion took place in the twelfth century under the inspiration of male monastics. Bernard of Clairvaux's rapturous praises of the Virgin as queen and fair spouse of the Song of Songs and his intense personal commitment to her, with its echoes of contemporary courtly love poetry, set the tone for monastic Marian veneration throughout Europe.[61] Bynum has described the special devotion that members of Bernard's Cistercian order felt for Mary.[62] The Virgin's cult was subsequently promoted by the mendicant orders, in particular the Franciscans, who celebrated her humility and maternity. Laymen also played a crucial role in maintaining Mary's cult: Rebekka Habermas's statistical sample of German miracle collections indicates that during the sixteenth century miracles performed on men at Marian shrines slightly outnumbered those performed on women.[63] Miracle collections are hardly, of course, problem-free sources: the stories in them were recorded by male churchmen with the aim of promoting particular saints' cults. Moreover, patterns of pilgrimage were undoubtedly determined as much by the socio-cultural and financial constraints as by religious preference. It would have been considerably easier, for example, for a woman to visit a local shrine, regardless of its dedication, than to travel a great distance to reach a particular Marian relic or image. Yet despite these provisos, the fact that men seem to have outnumbered women at Habermas's Upper Bavarian Marian shrines at least alerts us to the dangers of taking at face value reformers' polemic.

Peters suggests that the pilgrimages that women went on were an extension of their roles as housewives and nurturers. Women were expected, she argues, to perform ritual acts designed to procure the wellbeing of the family.[64] Some German evidence bears out this assertion. The miracle that, according to the Jesuit Jacobus Irsing, writing in 1643, initiated the Altötting cult in Bavaria back in 1489 provides an example of a mother's care for her child. A three-year-old boy fell into some water and was eventually pulled out quite dead. His mother, 'out of great trust in the Mother of God', carried the dead child to the chapel, laid him on the altar and pleaded for his life, which was duly restored.[65] There are many such stories (according to Habermas's survey one-third of sixteenth-century miracles involved children), but it was by no means always mothers who took responsibility for sick children.[66] The first miracle recorded in the earliest surviving printed miracle book from Altötting (1494/5) concerns a father and his daughter: Hans Kurz from a village near Regensburg

[61] Graef, *Mary*, vol. 1, pp. 235–41. [62] Bynum, *Jesus as Mother*, p. 137.
[63] Rebekka Habermas, 'Die Sorge um das Kind: die Sorge der Frauen und Männer. Mirakelerzählungen im 16. Jahrhundert', in *Ordnung und Lust: Bilder von Liebe, Ehe und Sexualität im Spätmittelalter und Früher Neuzeit*, ed. Hans-Jürgen Bachorski (Trier, 1991), p. 173, n. 19.
[64] Peters, *Patterns of Piety*, pp. 15–7.
[65] Quoted in Robert Bauer, *Die Bayerische Wallfahrt Altötting* (Munich, 1970), p. 6.
[66] Habermas, 'Die Sorge um das Kind', pp. 169–70.

brought his seven-year-old daughter, who was crippled in her hands and feet, to the shrine where she was restored to health.[67] As Habermas shows, the majority of vows were in fact undertaken by fathers. For the child-orientated wonders recorded at Hohenpeißenberg (south-west of Munich), 40 per cent of betrothals were carried out by fathers, 28 per cent by both parents together and only 19 per cent by mothers alone. These proportions varied significantly from shrine to shrine, but the miracle collections do suggest that fathers generally played a greater role than mothers in entrusting children to the Virgin's protection.[68]

The appeal of traditional Marian veneration may have been universal, but as Bynum points out, 'religious experience is the experience of men and women, and in no human society is this experience the same'.[69] Records of endowments and bequests made in honour of Mary demonstrate that gender roles affected the ways in which laymen and women expressed their devotion to Mary. Most Marian altars and altarpieces, masses and antiphons were donated by wealthy men. Only occasionally did a woman's independent financial status allow her to make such a benefaction. In 1510, for example, Ottilia Mayer founded the St Anne altar in Nuremberg's Lorenzkirche and adorned it with a carved altarpiece showing Mary, Christ and Anne, using funds from the business interests left to her by her merchant husband who had died ten years previously. In 1512 Katherine, widow of the Cologne city councillor Costyn van Lyßkirchen, gave a perpetual income for a candle to illuminate the Madonna in the local church of the Augustinian Hermits.[70] It seems, however, that on the rare occasions on which women were able to make such independent endowments they were not especially likely to select Mary as the beneficiary of their largesse. In 1509 in the church of St Laurenz in Cologne, for example, Catharina Plettenbergh established perpetual masses that were to be celebrated on the feast days of saints Erasmus, Augustine and Brice and on the day after Paul's conversion, and in 1525 in the same church Sophia Tack provided income for a lamp before the crucifix in the church's choir that was to be lit on high feast days.[71]

Although most substantial Marian endowments were made by men, evidence from Cologne indicates that women sometimes made minor bequests commensurate with their subordinate legal and financial status. Some Marian confraternities undertook, as we have seen, to illuminate cult statues of the Virgin, and men also donated robes and jewels to particularly favoured images. In 1491, for example, members of the Marian brotherhood at St Brigida contributed jointly to the cost of making a robe for an image of Our Lady.[72] But many of the

[67] *Vermarckt dye Grossenn wunder zaichen So dye Junckfraw Maria hye zu° alten O^e tting würcken ist an Vil Cristen menschen* (Augsburg, 1494/5) (SStBA, 4⁰ INK.125).
[68] Habermas, 'Die Sorge um das Kind', p. 171 n. 17.
[69] Bynum, Harrell and Richman, eds., *Gender and Religion*, p. 2.
[70] Haas, 'Die mittelalterliche Altaranordnung', p. 80; Militzer, ed., *Quellen*, vol. 1, p. 197.
[71] HAEK, Dom, St Laurenz, D II 34, fols. 149r–152v and 168r.
[72] Militzer, ed., *Quellen*, vol. 1, pp. 289–96. See also vol. 2, pp. 1110, 1221.

city's statues also received gifts of clothes, girdles, jewellery and rosaries from individual female devotees. These gifts reflected their donors' domestic interests.[73] In Germany rosaries in particular were often passed down from mother to daughter, so to give one to Mary was to make a very intimate gesture of devotion.[74] In 1484, for example Wendel, a widow, gave a girdle and a rosary to the Madonna in the Cologne church of St Jakob. In 1502 Druytgyn, another widow, gave her 'bridal rosary made from coral, a golden ring and her belt' to the Marian brotherhood in the same church, presumably to adorn its statue. And in 1518 Engyn, wife of Peter Rostenmecher van Hymmellgeyst, gave a pearl girdle to the statue, and was admitted into the brotherhood in return. Similar donations were made to the Madonnas in the Cologne churches of St Kunibert, St Paul and St Brigida.[75] Whereas wealthy men could endow Marian altars and masses, their wives and widows usually offered only personal possessions as testimony to their devotion to the Virgin.

For men, both rich and poor, confraternities provided another important forum for Marian piety. As we have seen, it is possible that during the seventeenth century as much as 90 per cent of Cologne's adult male population belonged to at least one confraternity. These confraternities had, of course, been founded by men, and all their office holders were male. Some confraternities allowed only men to join and others limited female membership to the wives of existing brothers. Even when no such formal restrictions applied, the financial and institutional commitment attendant upon membership of such a body could make it difficult for women to participate.[76] As Schwerhoff points out, most confraternities did, in fact, incorporate at least some women (several of Cologne's Marian brotherhoods certainly admitted women), but as 'second-class' members who could participate in the religious rituals but not in governance.[77] The only exception was the rosary brotherhood founded in 1475 by the Dominican

[73] Peters, *Patterns of Piety*, pp. 49–52.

[74] A prayer book from 1215 specified that 'daughters should inherit from their mothers yarn, bedding, golden jewelry, rosaries, prayerbooks and all books pertaining to church services which are usually read by women'. Quoted in Cornelia Niekus Moore, *The Maiden's Mirror: reading material for German girls in the sixteenth and seventeenth centuries*, Wolfenbütteler Forschungen 36 (Wiesbaden, 1987), p. 78. In her will, drawn up in 1536 in Lutheran Nuremberg, Agatha Weilend gave to her daughter, who had remained in the convent of St Klara, a yellow amber rosary 'as a sign of my maternal love for her that remains undiminished'. StaatsAN, Rep. 8, 158, Nr. 778.

[75] Militzer, ed., *Quellen*, vol. 2, pp. 674–6, 836, 1232; vol. 1, 289–96.

[76] Ibid., vol. 1, pp. lxi, lxiii. On fifteenth-century journeymen's guilds dedicated to the Virgin see Wilfried Reininghaus, *Die Entstehung der Gesellengilden im Spätmittelalter* (Wiesbaden, 1981), pp. 108–12.

[77] Gerd Schwerhoff, '"Vereinswesen" und Religiosität in der spätmittelalterlichen Stadt: eine neue Quellenedition zur Geschichte der Kölner Laienbruderschaften', *Geschichte in Köln* 45 (1999), 118–21. See, for example, HAEK, St Joh. Bapt, A ii 25, the brotherhood book of the Marian confraternity at St Johann Baptist covering the period 1500–1680, where sisters' as well as brothers' names are listed. The two socially exclusive Marian brotherhoods at St Maria im Kapitol did not admit women: Mallinckrodt, *Struktur und kollektiver Eigensinn*, p. 384.

Jakob Sprenger that demanded no entrance fee and had no fixed organizational structure. Here women could participate on equal terms with men. A surviving brotherhood book from Colmar records 6,461 members in 1500, more than half of whom were women.[78] The rosary brotherhood, which included both clergy and laymen (from Emperor Frederick III right down to obscure artisans and servants) as well as numerous women amongst its members, testifies to the universal popularity of Marian piety within the Holy Roman Empire in the late fifteenth century.[79]

The Jesuits' Marian confraternities were built on the foundations laid by the rosary brotherhood.[80] By the early seventeenth century they were seeking, as the Dominican foundation had done before them, to reach all levels of society, though for the purposes of pastoral care members were divided into different congregations according to social status and level of education.[81] Unlike the rosary brotherhood most Jesuit foundations did not, however, admit women.[82] Moreover, in 1586 the Jesuit General Claudius Aquaviva forbade members of his order from having any dealings with women's congregations modelled on the Marian sodalities. Women were excluded from the Jesuits' confraternity life partly, Aquaviva argued, 'because of the many suspicions that might arise' from Jesuits' involvement with women, and partly perhaps because of the Marian sodalities' initial focus on the intellectual elite, the pupils of the Jesuit colleges.[83] The conviction that the weaker sex lacked the ability to exercise religious self-determination, perhaps compounded by a sense that it would have been inappropriate for women to take the *sodales'* chivalrous oath of consecration that required each man to promise to defend Mary's honour from attacks by those subordinate to him, may also have played a role in determining women's exclusion. Although in some areas Aquaviva's direction was disregarded and female congregations were founded, elsewhere women were entirely shut out of the Jesuits' Marian sodalities.[84] Their deliberate debarring from the very bodies that played such a key role in promulgating the Counter-Reformation cult of the Virgin demonstrates the importance of paying proper attention to chronological and geographical variations in Marian piety. In the late sixteenth century Catholic women played a more prominent role in public Marian piety in Cologne, where traditional liturgical practices and confraternities survived,

[78] Militzer, ed., *Quellen*, vol. 1, pp. cxix–cxxii.
[79] Erzbischöfliches Diözesanmuseum Köln, *500 Jahre Rosenkranz*, pp. 109–10.
[80] Above, p. 253. [81] Mallinckrodt, *Struktur und kollektiver Eigensinn*, p. 142.
[82] On 16 June 1587 Aquaviva wrote that women were excluded from the congregations. Ibid., p. 143 n. 42.
[83] Duhr, *Geschichte der Jesuiten im XVI. Jahrhundert*, pp. 369–70, 480–1.
[84] Mallinckrodt, *Struktur und kollektiver Eigensinn*, pp. 143, 145. See also Anne Conrad, *Zwischen Kloster und Welt: Ursulinen und Jesuitinnen in der Katholischen Reformbewegung des 16./17. Jahrhunderts*, Veröffentlichungen des Instituts für Europäische Geschichte Mainz 142 (Mainz, 1991), pp. 105–7.

than in Augsburg, where the Jesuit model of Marianism was the only one available.[85]

Excluded from the Jesuit movement and from its Marian sodalities, some women established equivalent organizations themselves. Like the Jesuits, some of whom encouraged female foundations despite Aquaviva's directives, these women wanted to dedicate their lives to God but to remain active in the world, teaching and proselytizing. They took a vow of chastity, but did not wish to be enclosed within convent walls. Some took as their model the Ursuline order, which had been founded by Angela Merici in northern Italy in the 1530s and had then spread through France and Germany. In Flanders and the Lower Rhine area there were numerous smaller, less formal groups whose adherents were referred to as 'Devotessen', 'virgines devotae', 'Jesuitessen' or 'Jesuitinnen'.[86] Mary Ward's foundation, whose members were known as the English Ladies, was established in the second decade of the seventeenth century, in order, Ward wrote, to serve the pope in disseminating the faith.[87] For some of these women, such as Margareta Lynnerie, the Virgin Mary provided an important spiritual focus and a role model. For others, for example the Frenchwomen Anne de Xainctogne and Alix Le Clerc, she was a patron. Mary Ward's initial plan was for a 'Schola Beatae Mariae', and in her subsequent design for a pious institute she cited Mary alongside Christ himself as a model of the mixed form of life to be adopted by the English Ladies.[88]

Anne Conrad points out that the Virgin Mary did not, however, play as central a role in the devotional lives of these female organizations as in the piety of their male prototypes. Some were dedicated to Mary, in order that they might be seen as counterparts to the Society of Jesus, but in their self-awareness and spirituality Christ and various female martyrs were often more important than the Mother of God.[89] In Cologne in 1606, for example, Ida Schnabels and nine other women formed the 'S. Ursulae Sodalitet', which was officially recognized as a brotherhood in 1611–12. When new members were admitted to this brotherhood they were required to recite a prayer that was very like the oath taken by those entering the Jesuits' Marian sodalities. But the women of the Cologne Ursulagesellschaft took as their personal protector and intercessor not only Mary but also Ursula and her 11,000 virgins.[90] For most members of women's religious organizations Christ and the female martyrs and confessors

[85] Interestingly, women participated alongside the *sodales* in the splendid procession organized by the Jesuits in Cologne in 1639 to mark the German jubilee year. See above, p. 243. HAStK, Stifter und Klöster, Best. 223, Jesuiten, A 9, Litterae Annuae des Kölner Jesuitenkollegs 1552–1660, fols. 367r ff.

[86] Conrad, *Zwischen Kloster und Welt*, p. 108.

[87] Mathilde Köhler, *Maria Ward: ein Frauenschicksal des 17. Jahrhunderts* (Munich, 1989), pp. 86–7.

[88] Conrad, *Zwischen Kloster und Welt*, pp. 70 n. 22, 75ff., 191.

[89] Conrad, 'Nähe und Distanz', 183–8.

[90] Conrad, *Zwischen Kloster und Welt*, p. 142.

such as Ursula, Agnes, Agatha, Cecilia and Catherine of Alexandria provided more important devotional lodestones than Mary.[91] Women who were actively engaged in the Catholic reform movement, often in defiance of ecclesiastical authority, tended to choose as their role model not the humble and obedient Mother of God, but a saint such as Ursula who had struggled and died for her faith.[92] Mary's appeal may have transcended gender boundaries, but she did not provide a suitable role model for women seeking an apostolate within either the Catholic or the Protestant church, as we shall see when we consider female evangelical pamphleteers.

THE PROTESTANT VIRGIN

If both women and men could find comfort and inspiration in the Catholic cult of the Virgin, how are we to evaluate the significance for the laity of Protestant attacks on that cult? The notion that the Reformation removed Mary from the devotional landscape, thereby destroying an important focus for female identification, needs to be modified. As Christine Peters argues in relation to Reformation England, 'it is oversimplistic to see an attack on Marian veneration as getting rid of the Virgin Mary to the detriment of women and their access to a female role model'.[93] Mary did not disappear at the Reformation. In Lutheran Germany, as we saw in chapter 2, her images and feast days survived. In areas that turned to Reformed Protestantism her role may have been reduced, but no mainstream church could afford to abandon altogether the guarantor of Christ's humanity. We need to acknowledge that the Reformation rarely created, as has been supposed, an exclusively masculine religious landscape. Mary was still present. She was no longer invoked as a powerful intercessor, but was instead confined to the characteristically female role of housemother. As we shall see in the final sections of this chapter, her protective functions were transferred to Christ. Stripped of her divine power she became a model for all Christians, though gender asymmetries continued to shape experiences of Marian devotion as they had done in the pre-Reformation period. To both men and women Mary was presented as an example of faith, obedience and humility, but to women in particular she was also presented as a model of chastity and domestic virtue.

The Catholic Church described Mary as uniquely virtuous. She was exceptional amongst women because in her there was nothing worthy of condemnation. Catholics accused evangelicals of believing, by contrast, that Mary was no better than other women. As we have seen, in 1523 Georg Hauer reported that urban women, inspired by Luther's attack on the antiphon *Salve Regina*, had impugned Mary's honour by saying that 'Mary is a woman like I am one,

[91] Ibid., pp. 190–201. [92] Conrad, 'Nähe und Distanz', 179.
[93] Peters, *Patterns of Piety*, p. 223.

our lady is a woman like another.'[94] His accusation was perhaps not entirely unfounded: in 1523, for example, Berne city council fined the wife of the municipal doctor because she had defended the marriage of clergy and 'had also expressed the opinion that Mary had no claim to special veneration, and that the Mother of God was a woman like any other'.[95] In the same year Hieronymus Gebwiler of Strasbourg published a tract defending Mary against the wicked blasphemers who dared to say that Mary was not the Mother of God but was merely 'a woman like another woman'.[96] The Augsburg chronicler Clemens Sender, who looked on the Reformation movement with suspicion, reported that the Zwinglian preacher at the city's Barfüßerkirche also said that Mary was 'a woman like another ordinary woman'.[97] Similar sentiments were recorded in the blasphemy trials discussed in chapter 5 of this book: in Cologne in 1526 the 'Lutheran rogue' Hans Hesse supposedly said of Mary that 'she is a woman like another woman', and in 1611 the blind beggar Thonieß von Wesseling was brought before the city's magistrates on account of a fight that began when he asked a passer-by whether the Virgin Mary was 'better than other women'.[98]

By mainstream Protestant standards, the notion that Mary was a woman like any other was not entirely orthodox. The Mother of God could never be unexceptional. As Luther wrote in his 1521 *Commentary on the Magnificat*: 'for in this there follows all honour, all blessedness, and her unique place in the whole of mankind, among which she has no equal, namely, that she had a child by the Father in heaven, and such a Child'.[99] She played an exceptional role in the story of salvation. As Ambrosius Lobwasser wrote in his hymn celebrating the birth of Christ:

Frew dich, du weibliches geschlecht!	Rejoice, you female sex!
von dir ist der geboren	From you is he born
Der wider bringen sol zu recht	who will bring again to right
was durch ein weib verloren.[100]	what was lost through a woman.

Mary also remained, according to orthodox Protestant teaching, a virgin both before and after the birth of her son, something no normal woman could hope to achieve. Luther wrote that she was blessed amongst women 'not only because she gave birth without labour and pain and without care, unlike Eve and all other women, but because she also became fertile and conceived a bodily fruit

94 Hauer, *Drey christlich predig*, Gii.
95 Quoted in Alice Zimmerli-Witschi, *Frauen in der Reformationszeit* (Zurich, 1981), p. 129.
96 Hieronymus Gebwiler, *Beschirmung des lobs und eren der hochgelobte[n] hymelischen künigin Marie aller heiligen gottes, auch der wolangesetzten ordnungen der Christlichen kirchen wider die freuenliche[n] heilige[n]schmeher* (Strasbourg: Grüninger, 1523)
97 *Chroniken*, vol. 23, pp. 215–16. 98 Above, p. 223.
99 *WA*, vol. 7, p. 572; Pelikan, ed., *Luther's Works*, vol. 21, p. 326.
100 Wackernagel, *Das deutsche Kirchenlied*, vol. 4, no. 1297. For another example see Wackernagel, *Das deutsche Kirchenlied*, vol. 3, no. 1373.

from the Holy Ghost without any sin'.[101] Such sentiments were echoed by other evangelical preachers: in a sermon published in 1525 Andreas Keller, pastor in Wasselnheim near Strasbourg, reiterated that Mary had been able to give birth without pain, to remain a virgin and to conceive through the Holy Spirit without sin.[102] For Luther and his contemporaries Mary's experiences of childbearing could not be compared to those of any other woman.

Mary may not have been a woman like any other for Luther, but there can be no doubt that the 'blasphemous' statements of ordinary evangelicals recorded by hostile Catholic observers reflected a genuine transformation in teaching on the Virgin. At the Reformation Mary was demystified. She lost her supernatural power, and where Protestant ideas took hold she was no longer invoked as an intercessor or protector. The humble and family-orientated Virgin who had featured in late medieval images of the Holy Kindred remained, but her domestic role was no longer offset by authority in the heavenly sphere. While the notion that Mary engaged in household chores was by no means a new one, Luther emphasized her housewifery to a greater extent than Catholic commentators. In his 1521 *Commentary on the Magnificat* he wrote that after the Annunciation Mary 'seeks not any glory, but goes about her meals and her usual household duties, milking the cows, cooking the meals, washing pots and kettles, sweeping out the rooms, and performing the work of a maidservant or housemother [hauszmackt odder hauszmutter] in lowly and despised tasks'.[103] In a 1532 sermon on the feast day of the Visitation, as in other discussions of Mary's visit to Elizabeth, he likewise dwelt on her exemplary humility and domesticity. Mary helped Elizabeth with her housework, and acted as a 'kinder magdlein' to the young John the Baptist, caring for him and washing his nappies.[104] Luther was by no means the first to use the story of Mary's journey to Elizabeth as an opportunity to discuss female virtues – Ambrosius had interpreted the Visitation in the same way – but at the moment at which Luther and his fellow reformers deprived Mary of her heavenly authority her role as housemother assumed a new prominence.[105]

As a humble human mother Mary could serve as a model for all Christians. As we saw in chapter 1, Lutheran reformers advocated the use of saints as exemplars. In Melanchthon's *Apology for the Augsburg Confession*, in sermons and in church calendars such as that of Caspar Goldtwurm (1559) they were presented as patterns for ordinary Christians.[106] As Robert Kolb suggests, 'without the burden of providing cures for human problems, the saints diminished to their human shape and size for Lutheran hearers and could serve as models

[101] Quoted in Schimmelpfennig, *Die Geschichte der Marienverehrung*, p. 13.
[102] Kreitzer, 'Reforming Mary', p. 67.
[103] *WA*, vol. 7, p. 575; Pelikan, ed., *Luther's Works*, vol. 21, p. 329.
[104] *WA*, vol. 36, pp. 207–14; Düfel, *Luthers Stellung*, pp. 102–3, 181.
[105] Ibid., 181. [106] Above, pp. 60–1.

for godly living'.[107] Mary in particular provided an example of the grace of God and of Christian faith.[108] The fact that many postils contained sermons for three, four or even five Marian festivals meant that throughout the year Mary was presented to parishioners as an example of godly virtue.[109] Her story also provided a message of hope for all Christians. Catholic authors had emphasized Mary's virtues: Erasmus wrote in his *Paean* to Mary, for example, that 'a huge gulf stretches between your exalted state and my lowliness, between your more than angelic purity and my uncleanness, between your splendour and my darkness'.[110] By contrast, Lutheran preachers' willingness to describe the Mother of God as a fallible human perhaps made her more accessible as a role model than she had ever been before. This willingness to criticize Mary was, Beth Kreitzer argues, particularly marked after the middle of the sixteenth century: in 1548, for example, Philip Melanchthon spoke of Mary's 'negligence' in losing the twelve-year-old Christ in the temple at Jerusalem (Luke 2:41–52), while in a postil printed in 1594 Martin Chemnitz stated that 'Mary is a sinner, exactly like us.'[111]

Alongside this general Marian message aimed at all Christians the reformers promulgated another about chastity and domesticity aimed specifically at women. As Kreitzer argues, 'Mary was used to support and model the preachers' image of the ideal female, wife, and mother.'[112] Mary was by no means the only biblical woman to be used in this way, but Luther himself valued her example particularly highly.[113] In his 1544 *Hauspostille* Luther used the image of a rose garland to enumerate the virtues that Mary teaches 'to us all, but especially to the womenfolk'. The garland was adorned with three especially beautiful roses representing the virtues of faith, humility, and 'fine and chaste conduct'. Women should not, Luther said, be irresponsible and nosy, gossiping and flitting here and there, but instead should stay at home. When out on the streets they should behave modestly and focus on their tasks, as Mary had done when she went to visit Elizabeth. Regrettably, he added, girls today are unable to imitate Mary's virtues: 'they are insolent and crude in their words, immodest in their behaviour'. They have been set bad examples by their mothers, who make no effort to instil modesty and propriety in their daughters. The feast day of the Visitation would therefore, he hoped, teach the womenfolk 'to conduct themselves in all decency [zucht], respectability, and humility'.[114]

[107] Kolb, *For All the Saints*, p. 622.
[108] Above, pp. 61–3.
[109] Kolb, *For All the Saints*, p. 623.
[110] *CWE*, vol. 69, p. 20.
[111] Kreitzer, 'Reforming Mary', pp. 159, 76.
[112] Ibid., p. 43.
[113] Susan Karant-Nunn, 'Kinder, Küche, Kirche: social ideology in the sermons of Johannes Mathesius', in *Germania Illustrata: essays on early modern Germany presented to Gerald Strauss*, ed. Andrew C. Fix and Susan Karant-Nunn (Kirksville, MO, 1992), p. 131.
[114] *WA*, vol. 52, pp. 682–8; Kreitzer, 'Reforming Mary', pp. 94–6.

Mary was, as Luther's *Hauspostille* suggests, a model for both virgins and wives. While marriage and motherhood were seen as women's true vocations, Mary's virginity remained relevant since pre-marital sexuality had to be regulated. Indeed, in 1524 Huldrych Zwingli suggested that the money that had previously been invested in Mary's cult should instead be used to protect the honour of girls and women whose chastity was in danger because of their poverty.[115] In a sermon of 1539 Luther told his congregation that Mary's chaste conduct during her journey to Elizabeth provided an example for all 'women and virgins'.[116] In 1548 Caspar Huberinus commended the 'pretty' example of Mary as a lesson to all 'virgins and brides'. She was, he said, 'home-loving and secluded, for the angel came inside to her, not in the streets or at a dance'. Moreover, 'she is bashful [schamhafft], [for] she is frightened and horrified by the angel; . . . she is also modest, pure, and chaste, for she says "I know no man"; she is also humble, for she said to the angel, "See, I am the handmaid of the lord [des Herren Magdt]".'[117] Other Lutheran preachers repeated the same message,[118] and it was reiterated in hymns such as Johannes Hesse's *Ein new geystlich Lied, Von einer holdseligen Junckfrawen Maria*, which again used the image of Mary's garland with three roses, this time representing faith, humility and love of Christ. In verse 17 Hesse said explicitly:

Diß Liedlein ist inn eyl gemacht	This little song was made in a hurry
Vnd plötzlich in den truck gebracht	and printed immediately
Dir, Weiblichem geschlecht,	for you, female sex,
Das du fortan solt leben	so that you should live from now on
Fein erbarlich vnd recht.[119]	nicely, honourably and rightly.

Lutheran preachers may have used Mary to embody their restrictive prescriptions concerning women's comportment, but their domesticated Virgin did at least reflect quotidian female experience more closely than the divine Virgin of the Catholic tradition, whose exceptional status was, as we have seen, constantly emphasized. Conrad Porta, Lutheran pastor in Eisleben, discussed the value of Mary's example in his 1580 *Jungfrawenspiegel*, a text intended specifically for women. At the wedding at Cana, Porta wrote, Mary did not conduct herself with pride but helped to cook and serve. Citing Luther's *Hauspostille*, Porta suggested that a God-fearing and pious housemaid who had to perform such tasks around the home should console herself and be happy in the knowledge

115 Campi, *Zwingli und Maria*, p. 79. 116 *WA*, vol. 47, pp. 827–8.
117 Quoted in Kreitzer, 'Reforming Mary', p. 80. 118 See, for example, ibid., pp. 81, 88, 111.
119 Wackernagel, *Das deutsche Kirchenlied*, vol. 3, no. 1139. Published in the mid sixteenth century (Kreitzer, 'Reforming Mary', p. 94 n. 27). For other hymns that use Mary as example for women see Schimmelpfennig, *Die Geschichte der Marienverehrung*, p. 46.

that Mary had done the same.[120] The feast day of Mary's Purification – the story of her trip to the temple in Jerusalem after Christ's birth – also provided an opportunity for preachers to relate Mary's life to that of normal women. This feast day survived because it recorded a scriptural event in the life of Christ, but it also pertained to the contemporary ritual of churching, the liturgical blessing of new mothers after a period of confinement in accordance with Mosaic law.

By the fifteenth century churching was an important rite of passage for women who had recently given birth. The festive ceremony marked their reintegration into the community at the end of forty days during which they were considered, in popular belief at least, impure and dangerous. Some Protestant reformers condemned the ritual as superstitious, but in most Lutheran areas it survived.[121] The feast day of Mary's Purification provided preachers with an opportunity to justify churching. They commended Mary's humility and obedience: Luther, for example, said that although according to Mosaic law she did not need to be purified because she had remained a virgin, she nonetheless went to the temple like other women.[122] Contemporary women were also no longer bound by the abrogated Jewish law, and were not considered impure after childbirth, but for primarily practical reasons they should nonetheless follow Mary's example and observe a period of confinement, the end of which should be marked by a service of thanksgiving.[123] In his 1587 church calendar Andreas Hohndorff wrote an entry for the feast day of the Purification that included the following typically Lutheran explanation of women's postnatal confinement:

> Although in the New Testament the Law of Moses concerning the purification of the post-parturient woman is repealed . . . still natural decency, the need of the woman lying in to return to bodily strength and health and the warm love of the married couple for one another require that the husband spares his wife with hard work for six weeks, and looks after her more with drink and food, so that mother and the new-born child grow strong.[124]

For the sake of their own health and that of their child, women should follow the example given by Mary and remain apart from society until they were welcomed back in the churching ritual.

[120] Conrad Porta, *Jungfrawen Spiegel. Aus Gottes Wort / vnd D. M. Lutheri Schrifften / nach Ordnung der heiligen zehen Gebot / mit vleis zugerichtet. Sampt angehengten kurtzen Historien / der heiligen Jungfrawen / welcher Namen im Calender stehen* (Eisleben: Vrban Graubisch, 1580), fol. 40r. For a discussion of Porta's text see Moore, *The Maiden's Mirror*, p. 91.

[121] Karant-Nunn, *The Reformation of Ritual*, pp. 72–81.

[122] Kreitzer, 'Reforming Mary', pp. 128–9.

[123] Ibid., pp. 127–36 and 147.

[124] Hohndorff, *Calendarium sanctorum & historiarum*, p. 74. For another example see Veit Dietrich, *Kinder Postilla vber die Sontags / vnd der fu^e rnembsten Fest Euangelia / durch das gantze Jar* (Nuremberg: Johann von Berg and Ulrich Newber, 1549), p. cclxxvi.

If it is difficult, as we saw in the first section of this chapter, to reconstruct Catholic women's responses to the cult of the Virgin then it is nigh on impossible to assess how Lutheran women felt about the humble, domestic Virgin presented to them in post-Reformation sermons, books and hymns. In a Lutheran context we do not even have indirect evidence of the type provided by pilgrimage and confraternity records. We can do little more than speculate about the impact of Protestant teaching on the Virgin on women's spiritual and material lives. The Lutheran revaluing of the Virgin can be seen, at a certain level, as a disadvantageous development. There is a powerful strand of Reformation scholarship that regards the early modern period as, in Merry Wiesner's words, 'a time of continual reinforcement of gender hierarchies and patriarchal structures'.[125] In her study of sixteenth-century Augsburg Lyndal Roper shows, for example, that 'the institutionalized Reformation was most successful when it most insisted on a vision of women's incorporation within the household under the leadership of their husbands'.[126] The Lutheran shift in teaching on the Virgin Mary reinforced this patriarchal trend. No longer described as a powerful goddess, Mary was instead, Kreitzer argues, 'promoted as a role model for females in ways that served to constrain and domesticate women, placing them more firmly under male authority'.[127]

The sermons quoted above demonstrate that Luther and his fellow reformers did indeed use Mary to personify their ideal of obedient, domesticated womanhood. It is hardly surprising, therefore, that women who challenged the early modern status quo found little comfort in Mary's example. Mary could not provide inspiration or justification for those who sought an apostolic role, as the writings of female pamphleteers demonstrate. Mary did not feature as a role model in the writings of either Argula von Grumbach or Katharina Schütz Zell, the two most prominent female polemicists. Argula was a Bavarian noblewoman who petitioned the University of Ingolstadt and other Catholic authorities in defence of the evangelical cause in 1523–4, while Katharina, wife of the Strasbourg reformer Mattäus Zell, published throughout her adult life (d.1562) in support of her local Reformation.[128] As Ulrike Zitzlsperger points out, both women used a variety of devices to justify their presumptuousness. They wrote in times of danger, they claimed, because men had failed to do so. Both also invoked the example of biblical women. In her last published writing Argula referred to the Old Testament heroine Judith, while Katharina compared herself

[125] Merry E. Wiesner, *Women and Gender in Early Modern Europe*, 2nd edn, New Approaches to European History (Cambridge, 2000), p. 311.

[126] Roper, *The Holy Household*, p. 2. [127] Kreitzer, 'Reforming Mary', p. v.

[128] Peter Matheson, *Argula von Grumbach: a woman's voice in the Reformation* (Edinburgh, 1995) and Elsie Anne McKee, *Katharina Schütz Zell*, vol. 1: *The Life and Thought of a Sixteenth-Century Reformer*, ed. Heiko A. Oberman, Studies in Medieval and Reformation Thought 69 (Leiden, 1999).

to Mary Magdalene and to the prophetess Anna. She was not, she claimed, *trying* to act as a preacher or apostle, but her situation was like that of the Magdalene, 'who became an apostle without planning to do so and was forced by the Lord himself to tell the disciples Christ had risen'.[129] Despite these biblical models, and both women's obeisance to the rhetoric of motherhood and domesticity, neither Argula nor Katharina made any significant personal identification with the Mother of God in their writings.[130]

The Virgin Mary did not, it seems, appeal to the few exceptional women who sought active apostolates within the movements for either Protestant or Catholic reform. In both traditions the messages of humility and obedience with which Marian teaching was associated held little attraction for them. The fact that Georg Hauer's vitriolic comparison between real women and the divine mother of God was inspired in part, Peter Matheson argues, by Argula von Grumbach's writings, indicates how problematic Mary's model might be for such women.[131] Yet these women were not typical. It is tempting, given the paucity of documentation relating to women's ideas and experiences, to regard figures such as Argula and Katharina as representative of womankind. But we must remember that most women, from noblewomen to middle-class city dwellers and beyond, spent their lives working within the boundaries of patriarchal society rather than fighting against them.

Luther's belief that marriage and motherhood were the only vocations suitable for women does not endear him to a modern audience and certainly also alienated some sixteenth-century women. The Nuremberg abbess Caritas Pirckheimer, for example, mounted a spirited defence of her nuns' communal way of life. But given the fact that after the Reformation the vast majority of women spent their days not reading, writing or preaching but engaged in household tasks, it seems possible that the figure of the housewife-Madonna provided an important role model. As Peters argues, 'the effect of deflecting attention from Mary as Queen of Heaven was to make the model of Mary more accessible, and more powerful, for godly men and women'.[132] As a humble housemother and a fallible human, Mary was more easily emulated than as a divine goddess. Indeed, in Lutheran writings for the first time the virtues for which Mary was singled out corresponded exactly with the virtues for which real women were praised: maternal devotion, domestic competence and humble submission to male authority. Mary could affirm the value of women's day-to-day occupations for her house was, like that of all her sisters, her 'calling and office [beruffs vnd ampts]', as the pastor Christoph Vischer put it in 1575.[133] This

[129] Ulrike Zitzlsperger, 'Mother, martyr and Mary Magdalene: German female pamphleteers and their self-images', *History* 88, no. 3 (2003), especially p. 389.

[130] Matheson, *Argula von Grumbach*, p. 42; McKee, *Katharina Schütz Zell*, vol. 1, p. 381.

[131] Matheson, *Argula von Grumbach*, p. 19.

[132] Peters, *Patterns of Piety*, p. 224.

[133] Kreitzer, 'Reforming Mary', p. 107.

domestic 'calling and office' was, for Lutheran commentators, as worthwhile and holy as any other occupation.[134] While we will never know for sure how the majority of Protestant women felt about this domesticated Virgin, we should at least consider the possibility that as a woman *almost* like any other, who milked cows, cooked meals, washed pots, swept rooms and yet became the Mother of God, Mary provided inspiration for Lutheran women who served God through their housewifery.

REPLACING MARY: THE PARENTHOOD OF GOD

As this book has shown, Mary remained prominent in Lutheran Germany. Many of her images and feast days survived, and she was presented to Lutheran congregations as a model of faith, humility, chastity and domesticity. Her continued prominence was partly, as we have seen, a product of Lutheran reformers' concerns about the pace of religious change. Luther, for example, in his 1523 *Order of Mass and Communion for the Church at Wittenberg*, wrote that while Wittenberg had abandoned all feast days except for those of Christ this decision was not intended to be binding for all evangelicals: 'Let others act according to their own conscience or in consideration of the weakness of some.'[135] Likewise the feast of the Assumption (15 August) was retained as a holiday in Nuremberg because of its popularity 'amongst the common folk'.[136] Such concessions meant that unlike Reformed Protestants in some other parts of Europe, German Lutherans were not suddenly required to adjust to a devotional landscape from which all visual and liturgical traces of the saints had been removed, and Mary's continued presence may, for some, have facilitated the transition from Catholic to Protestant belief. Even in Reformed territories, where Marian images and feast days did generally disappear, Mary retained an important role as an example of God's grace and as a model of faith, obedience and humility.

Yet despite this continuity, in areas that adhered to any kind of Protestant confession a major theological shift had to be accommodated in the day-to-day devotional lives of laymen and women. Mary's humility and domesticity may still have been extolled, as they traditionally had been in images of the Holy Family and Holy Kindred. But in the pre-Reformation period these qualities had played only a relatively minor role in determining Mary's appeal. Even the most intimate depiction of the Virgin and Child referred, in its original context, as much to divine intercession as to human motherhood. The cult of the Virgin had celebrated, above all, Mary's ability to provide material assistance in this world and to save souls. Her role was described, for example, in a devotional book of 1509–10 that recounted the foundation of one of Cologne's

[134] Kolb, *For All the Saints*, p. 155. [135] *WA*, vol. 12, pp. 208–9. [136] Above, p. 86.

Marian brotherhoods: Mary consoled and strengthened her devotees during their lifetimes; she ensured, through her intercession, that they would never die an unprepared death; she saved them from eternal damnation; and she lessened the torment of purgatory for those who truly rejected and repented of their sins.[137] Luther's domesticated Virgin, honoured though she was, fulfilled none of these functions. We must therefore consider what replaced Mary. How did the reformers fill the spiritual gulf that opened up when they deprived Mary of her divine authority?

Part of the answer to this question undoubtedly lies, as Keith Thomas and others have argued, in Protestants' increased emphasis on divine providence.[138] The knowledge that day-to-day events – even the most menial things – reflected the working-out of God's purpose compensated believers, to some extent at least, for the loss of what Thomas describes as the medieval church's 'apparatus of supernatural assistance'.[139] Whereas the intercession of Mary, Margaret and other saints had traditionally been sought during the travails of childbirth, for example, Lutheran reformers taught women to turn to God and to take comfort from the knowledge that they were doing his work. The *Hauß vnd Kirchenschatz* of the Augsburg pastor Bernhard Albrecht gave a prayer for women to use when the hour of birthing was at hand:

> Now, dear God, merciful father, the hour of birth has come, now no one can help me but only you. You are the right helper in the time of need. I place my hope and trust in you alone, and beseech you warmly that you will now look kindly upon me in this your work, for the sake of your dear son Jesus Christ. Amen.[140]

In 1570 Christoph Vischer reminded his readers that it was wrong to teach that blessed objects – herbs from the feast of the Assumption, salt and water – would ward off evil during childbirth. Instead, God would send his angels to keep the mother safe.[141] Luther's own message to parturient women was surely the most austere. He stated that women should be comforted and encouraged not by the repetition of 'St Margaret legends and other silly old wives' tales', but with the following words: 'Dear Grete, remember that you are a woman, and that this work of God in you is pleasing to him . . . Work with all your might to bring forth the child. Should it mean your death, then depart happily, for you will

137 Above, pp. 252–3. Militzer, ed., *Quellen*, vol. 3, pp. 10–18.

138 Keith Thomas, *Religion and the Decline of Magic: studies in popular beliefs in sixteenth- and seventeenth-century England* (London, 1971), pp. 90–132.

139 Ibid., p. 89.

140 Bernhard Albrecht, *Hauß vnd Kirchenschatz: Das ist / Außerlesene Andaechtige Gebett vnd Dancksagungen / auff jede Tag in der woche[n] / Item auff die fuernemste Fest vnnd Zeiten im Jahr: Deßgleichen auff alle begebende Faell in dem Menschlichen Leben: beedes fuer Junge vnnd Alte / Gesunde vnd Krancke / ausser vnnd inner der Creutz / daheim zu Hauß / vnd in der Kirchen / nutzlich vnnd heylsamlich zu gebrauchen*, 3rd edn (Ulm, 1620), p. 569.

141 Kreitzer, 'Reforming Mary', p. 132.

die in a noble deed and in subservience to God.'[142] While there was surely a limit to the degree of consolation that could be derived from such a message, it is possible that for some the knowledge that they were doing God's work and that events were firmly under divine direction lessened the need for saintly intercession.

Emphasis on Christ's mediatory role also, of course, compensated for the loss of the saints. Protestant reformers derided the non-scriptural doctrine of purgatory and taught that works of satisfaction, penance for sins and the intercession of the saints played no role in the process of salvation. Christ was, they emphasized, the only route to salvation. Robert Kolb argues in his study of late Lutheran preachers that 'alternative avenues to the mercy of God seemed unnecessary given the constant theme of Christ as way, truth, and life, which permeated the homiletical efforts of these preachers'.[143] While it is certainly true that for the preachers themselves a proper focus on Christ removed the need for saintly intercession, the reformers recognized that for the laity this transition would be a difficult one to make. Fear of the Godhead was, they observed, a prevalent emotion, and accounted for popular recourse to the saints. As Zwingli commented in his 1523 *Kurze christliche Einleitung*: 'Perhaps I will say: I may not come before God, because I am foolish, sinful, worthless and evil.'[144] Melanchthon's *Apology for the Augsburg Confession* explained that 'men suppose that Christ is more severe and the saints more approachable so they trust more in the mercy of the saints than in the mercy of Christ and they flee from Christ and turn to the saints'.[145] Luther also lamented in a commentary on Psalm 110 printed in 1539 that in accordance with the pope's doctrine Christ had been presented as a terrifying judge: 'His exacting and serious wrath was impressed on the people to such a degree that they had to flee from Him.' The church therefore 'directed us further to the saints in heaven; these were supposed to be the mediators between us and Christ'.[146]

Of course this wrathful God did not disappear at the Reformation. Indeed as Francisca Loetz argues in her study of blasphemy in early modern Zurich, 'for Reformed Christians God was an angry God of revenge, a strict, authoritarian father, who could nonetheless prove merciful'.[147] In theological treatises, in sermons, in catechisms and in discipline ordinances parishioners were warned of the dire consequences of incurring God's wrath. But this characteristically

[142] *WA*, vol. 10, part II, p. 296 (*Vom ehelichen Leben*, 1522); Pelikan, ed., *Luther's Works*, vol. 45, p. 40.

[143] Kolb, 'Festivals of the Saints', p. 621.

[144] Quoted in Campi, *Zwingli und Maria*, p. 89.

[145] *Die Bekenntnisschriften der evangelisch-lutherischen Kirche*, p. 319; translation from Tappert, ed., *The Book of Concord*, p. 231.

[146] *WA*, vol. 41, p. 198; Pelikan, ed., *Luther's Works*, vol. 13, p. 326. For another equivalent example see his sermons on the Gospel of John delivered in 1530–2, Pelikan, ed., *Luther's Works*, vol. 23, p. 57.

[147] Loetz, *Mit Gott handeln*, pp. 472–3.

Reformed emphasis on obedience and discipline was tempered, in the Lutheran and Zwinglian churches at least, by rhetoric that stressed God's parental love for his children and Christ's approachability. In his 1549 *Kinder Postilla* the Nuremberg preacher Veit Dietrich wrote that a Christian should fear God in the way that a pious child fears its parents: 'Because it accepts its father and mother as its best, most dear friends, it knows that where father and mother are absent it will have no consolation, no help [and] no protection in the wide world. Therefore it fears father and mother, takes care not to do anything against their will, never angers or insults them.'[148] God was both mother and father to his children, providing refuge and protection as well as discipline and guidance.[149]

The early Protestant Church assimilated the religious rhetoric of motherhood only with caution; there was nothing to parallel the 'feminization of religious language' that had characterized late medieval piety.[150] Yet the reformers did invoke God's maternal care. Echoing Jesus' exhortation to the inhabitants of Jerusalem, reported in Matthew 23:37 and in Luke 13:34, Luther wrote that God 'wants to gather us under this Clucking Hen [i.e. Christ], lest we go astray and fall prey to the hawk'. Similarly:

> The love of a mother's heart cannot forget its child. This is unnatural. A mother would be ready to go through fire for her children. So you see how hard women labour in cherishing, feeding, and watching. To this emotion God compares Himself, as if to say, 'I will not forsake you, because I am your mother. I cannot desert you.'[151]

Such images apparently struck a chord with at least some lay hearers. In her own writings Katharina Schütz Zell, for example, compared Christ's love directly with that of a mother for her child, saying that in his suffering Christ 'so hard and bitterly bore us, nourished us and made us alive, gave us to drink from his breast and side with water and blood (John 19:34), as a mother nurses her child'.[152]

As well as invoking God's maternal care, reformers also emphasized Christ's approachability. Zwingli asked his readers: 'do you not hear God say that Christ is our wisdom, innocence, beauty, justice and salvation? Do you not hear that he calls to us who are heavily laden?' We must, he told them, place our trust in Christ as in a father.[153] Luther also reminded his audience in a sermon delivered in the early 1530s that 'Christ does not want to be a tyrant or a jailer; He does

148 Dietrich, *Kinder Postilla*, p. cccvv.
149 On God's parental persona see Peters, *Patterns of Piety*, pp. 232–3.
150 Bynum, *Jesus as Mother*, p. 129.
151 *WA* , vol. 47, p. 198 and vol. 31, part II, p. 405; Pelikan, ed., *Luther's Works*, vol. 22, p. 490 and vol. 17, p. 183. From a 1539 sermon on the Gospel of John and one of the lectures on Isaiah delivered in 1527–30.
152 Zitzlsperger, 'Mother, martyr and Mary Magdalene', pp. 386, 390 and McKee, *Katharina Schütz Zell*, vol. 1, pp. 385–7.
153 Campi, *Zwingli und Maria*, p. 89.

not want to cast you out or drive you from Him.'[154] Such messages surely comforted their hearers, and helped console them for the loss of saintly support. Their continuing relevance and power is indicated by the trial of Christof Glatz, a fisherman brought before Augsburg's Catholic magistrates in 1630 at a time of real crisis for German Protestants. Glatz was accused of possessing a song that opposed the Edict of Restitution, and amongst the records relating to his interrogation is a copy of a small prayer book, *Etliche schoͤne trostreiche Gebet vnnd Andachten Fuͤr alle fromme Christen / vnnd sonderlich fuͤr die ienigen / welche wegen deß H. Evangelii angefochten vnnd betraͤnget werden*, printed in Nuremberg in 1629. This book includes a prayer for divine assistance during the misery of exile, which invokes Jesus in terms that Luther would undoubtedly have approved: 'I place my hope and trust in you, and flee to you, like a chick to the clucking hen his mother, and pray to you from the bottom of my heart that you will take me under your all-powerful and gracious wings.'[155]

In Lutheran and Zwinglian sermons and prayers emphasis on God's parental or maternal love for his children and on Christ's approachability compensated, to some extent at least, for the disappearance of Mary's protective presence. Hymns and images also suggest that in the evangelical church devotion to Christ in some sense replaced devotion to Mary. Music played an important role in spreading Lutheran ideas.[156] As we have seen, a number of traditional Marian hymns were 'corrected' to eliminate all mention of Mary's mediating role.[157] Instead, these 'corrected' hymns now spoke of the comfort the believer could expect to derive from Christ's intercession. Wackernagel's collection of German church songs contains, for example, four versions (one Latin and three vernacular) of the *Salve Regina* where Christ's name has been substituted for Mary's.[158] The text, which traditionally invoked Mary as our advocate, now began:

Salve, Jhesu Christe! Misericordia,	Hail Jesus Christ, Our mercy,
Vita, dulcedo et spes nostra, salve!	life, sweetness and hope, hail!

The Nuremberg cobbler and *Meistersinger* Hans Sachs likewise 'changed' and 'corrected in a Christian manner' two popular hymns, 'Maria zart' and 'Die

[154] *WA*, vol. 33, p. 84; Pelikan, ed., *Luther's Works*, vol. 23, p. 57. On the importance of Christ's humanity to Luther see Oberman, 'The Virgin Mary in evangelical perspective', p. 243.

[155] On this case see Fisher, *Music and Religious Identity*, pp. 62, 282. StadtAA, Reichsstadt, Strafamt, Nr. 105 (Strafbuch 1615–1632), p. 682 and K 211 (Urgicht). *Etliche schoͤne trostreiche Gebet vnnd Andachten Fuͤr alle fromme Christen / vnnd sonderlich fuͤr die ienigen / welche wegen deß H. Evangelii angefochten vnnd betraͤnget werden* (Nuremberg: Simon Halbmayern, 1629), p. 48.

[156] Oettinger, *Music as Propaganda*.

[157] Above, pp. 90–1.

[158] Wackernagel, *Das deutsche Kirchenlied* (1870), vol. 3, nos. 549 and 569–72.

fraw von hymmel'.[159] Both now referred to Christ's consoling role. The first verse of Sachs's new version of 'Die fraw von hym[m]el' invoked him thus:

Christum von hym[m]el ruͦff ich an	Christ from heaven I call on you
in dysen grossen noͤtten mein!	in my hour of need!
Im[m] Gsetz ich mich verschuldet han,	According to the Law I have indebted myself
zuͦ leyden ewig helle peyn,	to suffer the eternal torments of hell
Gen deim vater:	against your father:
o Christe, ker	Oh Christ, turn
sein zorn von mir,	his wrath from me,
mein zuͦflucht ist allein zuͦ dir,	my refuge is only with you,
hilff, ee daß ich verzweyffel schir!	help, before I despair almost!

With hymns, as with images and feast days, Lutherans showed a marked propensity for retaining traditional forms while changing their theological content. Rebecca Wagner Oettinger has analysed the significance of contrafacta, the practice of giving old melodies new words. Through contrafacta the reformers were able, she argues, to use 'devotional song, Catholicism's foothold with the common people, as a weapon against traditional belief'. In 'correcting' and improving texts, they replaced 'undesirable' beliefs with suitably evangelical sentiments.[160] It seems that even more radical Protestant groups recognized the value of reworking well-known songs. An Anabaptist songbook published in 1570, for example, includes a corrected version of a text that dates, Wackernagel estimates, from the early sixteenth century: 'Ach gott, wem soll ichs klagen'. This corrected version subsequently appeared in a Lutheran collection of psalms and hymns published by Abraham Wagenmann in Nuremberg in 1605. It condemns confession and penance without repentance, and invokes Christ alone instead of both Mary and Christ, as the original had done.[161] Placing the opening verses of the two versions side-by-side provides a perfect illustration of the devotional shift from Mary to Christ that occurred at the Reformation:

1. Ach gott, wem soll ichs klagen,	Ach Gott, wem soll ichs klagen,
mir ligt groß kummer an,	mir ligt gros kummer an:
Mein hertz will mir verzagen,	Mein hertz wil mir verzagen,
ich hab vil sünd gethan.	Ich hab vil sünde gethan:
Ich dörfft beücht, buß vnd rewe,	Dan was hilfft beicht ohn rewen?
Wöllt ich gegen gott bestan:	mag nit vor Gott bestahn,
So rüeff ich an mit trewe	drumb ruͤff ich an mit trewen
Mariam die wolgethan,	sein eingebornen Sohn,

[159] Ibid., vol. 3, pp. 80, 81.
[160] Oettinger, *Music as Propaganda*, pp. 89–136, especially 90 and 108.
[161] Wackernagel, *Das deutsche Kirchenlied*, vol. 3, pp. 498–9.

2. Das sy mir gnad erwerbe
Gegen gott dem schöpffer mein,
Dz wir nit ewig sterbenn,
in trewen ich dz main.
Sy kan vns wol bewaren,
die kayserliche maid,
wann wir von hynnen faren,
sy geitt vnß frid vnd glaitt.
3. An vnßrem lettstenn ende
Kan sy vns helffen schon
Vnd mag vnß gnad her sende
Wol auß dem hoͤchstenn thron.
Kom vnns zu hülff, Maria,
Behüett vns alle tag,
Kläglich so thüe wir schreyen:
Maria, wend vnßer klag.
4. Auff dich hab ich gebawen,
du wellest mich nit verlon,
Dz thu ich dir vertrawen,
du bist gar wolgethan.
Ich will mich dir ergeben,
gantz vnderthaͤnig sein,
in deinem willenn leben
biß auff dz ende mein.

Das er mir gnad erwerbe
bey Gott dem Vatter sein,
Das ich nit ewig sterbe,
Jesum Christum ich mein,
Der kan mich wol bewaren,
wie er hat zu geseit;
wenn ich von hin sol fahren,
Gibt er mir fried vnd gleidt.
An meinem letsten ende
kan er mire helffen schon,
Vnd mag mir gnad her senden
Wol von des Vatters thron,
Vnd mir meine sünde verzeihen,
so ichs von hertzen klag:
zu Jesu wil ich schreyen,
Der mir wol helffen mag.
Auff Jesum wil ich bawen,
er wirdt mich nicht verlan.
Das wil ich ihm vertrawen,
ohn allen argen wahn
Wil ich mich ihm ergeben,
gantz vnderthenig sein,
nach seinem willen zu leben
biß das ende mein.

1. Ah God, to whom should I cry,
I have great cares,
My heart will despair,
I have committed many sins.
I would need confession, penance and repentance,
if I were to prove myself before God:
So I call faithfully on
Mary the fair,
2. so that she obtains grace for me
from God my creator,
so that we do not die forever,
this I mean faithfully.
She can protect us well,
the noble maid,
when we pass from here,
she gives us peace and protection.

Ah God, to whom should I cry,
I have great cares:
My heart will despair,
I have committed many sins:
For what does confession help without repentance?
I cannot prove myself before God,
So I call faithfully on
his only-begotten Son,
so that he obtains grace for me
from God his father,
so that I do not die forever,
I mean Jesus Christ,
he can protect me well,
as he promised;
when I will pass from here,
he gives me peace and protection.

3. In our final hour	In my final hour
she can help us well	he can help me well,
and can send grace to us	and can send grace to me
from the highest throne.	from the father's throne,
Come to help us Mary,	and forgive me my sins,
protect us every day,	so I cry from my heart:
pitifully we cry:	to Jesus I will cry,
Mary, end our lamentation.	he can help me.
4. Upon you I rely,	I will trust in Jesus,
you will not abandon me,	he will not abandon me.
in that I trust you,	In that I will trust him
you are very fair.	unreservedly
I will surrender to you,	I will surrender to him,
entirely subject myself to you,	entirely subject myself to him,
live according to your will	live according to his will
until my end.	until my end.

Such reworkings of traditional hymns sought to inculcate evangelical piety and to strengthen devotion to Christ. Of course we cannot be sure how people responded to these alterations. Sebald Heyden, rector of Nuremberg's Sebalduskirche, tried to replace the traditional *Salve* with the revised *Salve Jhesu Christe* in 1523, but his innovation was quickly abandoned because the changes in the text were thought too subtle for the majority of the population, who had no knowledge of Latin, to comprehend.[162] As we have seen, Nuremberg's eventual abolition of the *Salve Regina* met with some resistance: Peter Imhoff, who had endowed its singing in the Lorenzkirche, demanded to know why 'such praise and honour had been withdrawn and turned away from God the Almighty and the Mother of God'.[163] It seems likely, however, that despite such teething troubles, over the course of time the Christocentric devotion promoted by the reformers in sermons, prayers and hymns was accepted by the majority of parishioners. As we saw in the case of Nuremberg, in well-established Protestant areas with decent educational provision pilgrimage and other manifestations of improper prayer to the Virgin did eventually die out.[164]

In Lutheran areas, where authorities adopted a tolerant attitude towards religious imagery, shifts in visual culture sometimes reinforced the devotional message contained in the reformers' sermons and texts. In Lutheran drawings and paintings the Virgin's traditional duties of protection and consolation were transferred to Christ. The popular image of the Madonna of Mercy or

162 Zeltner, *Kurtze Erläuterung*, p. 11, 17. Above, p. 91.
163 Dormeier, 'St Rochis, die Pest und die Imhoffs in Nürnberg vor und während der Reformation', 54. Above, pp. 86–7.
164 Above, pp. 109–14.

Schutzmantelmadonna – Mary sheltering supplicants beneath her cloak – was condemned by Luther because it drew people away from Christ: 'it is idolatry, that one points people away from Christ towards the cover of Mary's mantle'.[165] Several German artists provided an evangelical substitute for this censured image: the *Schutzmantelchristus*. While images of Christ spreading his mantle over supplicants were not entirely unknown in the Catholic Church, they had a particular resonance in a Reformation context.[166] In the late 1530s Lucas Cranach the Elder produced a drawing, perhaps intended as a design for an altarpiece, showing the resurrected Christ in Limbo sheltering figures beneath his outstretched cloak, just as Mary had once done (figure 62).[167] In an epitaph commemorating the Stuttgart *Bürgermeister* Sebastian Welling who died in 1532, Martin Schaffner likewise depicted the resurrected Christ spreading his cloak above supplicants, in this case Welling and his family (figure 63). The inscription in the centre of this image, 'Come here to me all who labour and are heavily laden, I will give you rest (Matth. XI) because to me is given all power in heaven and on earth', reinforces the Reformation understanding of this iconography: in times of trouble we must turn only to the all-powerful Christ.[168]

Of course not all paintings in Lutheran churches depicted Christ: we have seen the extent to which pre-Reformation images of saints survived in places such as Nuremberg. Where new images were commissioned, however, Lutheran patrons certainly tended to select as their subjects episodes from Christ's life and Passion, narrative scenes from the Old or New Testament or allegories of salvation. The altarpiece by Lucas Cranach that was installed in the Stadtkirche in Wittenberg in 1547 showed the Last Supper, a scene particularly recommended by Luther himself, and representations of baptism, confession and preaching. In its predella the crucified Christ appears before the preacher's pulpit as he (Luther) expounds the word of God.[169] In 1555 the sons of Johann Friedrich of Saxony (d.1554) erected in Weimar's Stadtkirche a triptych showing Christ's crucifixion and a depiction of justification, with portraits of Luther, Cranach the Elder (d.1553) and the former elector and his family.[170] Augsburg's key

165 *WA*, vol. 47, p. 276; for a later Lutheran sermon condemning this image see Martin Sharfe, *Evangelische Andachtsbilder: Studien zu Intention und Funktion des Bildes in der Frömmigkeitsgeschichte vornehmlich des schwäbischen Raums* (Stuttgart, 1968), pp. 175–6.

166 For discussions of Catholic examples see Immenkötter, 'Glaubensbilder', p. 174 and Suzanne Lustenberger, *Martin Schaffner, Maler zu Ulm* (Zug, 1961), p. 115. For an embroidered example from around 1590 from Munich showing supplicants with rosaries beneath the cloak of the resurrected Christ see Paul Mai, ed., *Schatzstücke der Münchner Peterskirche* (Munich, 1985), back cover.

167 Immenkötter, 'Glaubensbilder', pp. 174–5; Bott, ed., *Martin Luther und die Reformation in Deutschland*, no. 477; Oskar Thulin, *Cranach-Altäre der Reformation* (Berlin, 1955), p. 133.

168 Lustenberger, *Martin Schaffner*, pp. 113–16.

169 On this altarpiece see Koerner, *The Reformation of the Image*.

170 Friedländer and Rosenburg, *Die Gemälde von Lucas Cranach*, p. 434.

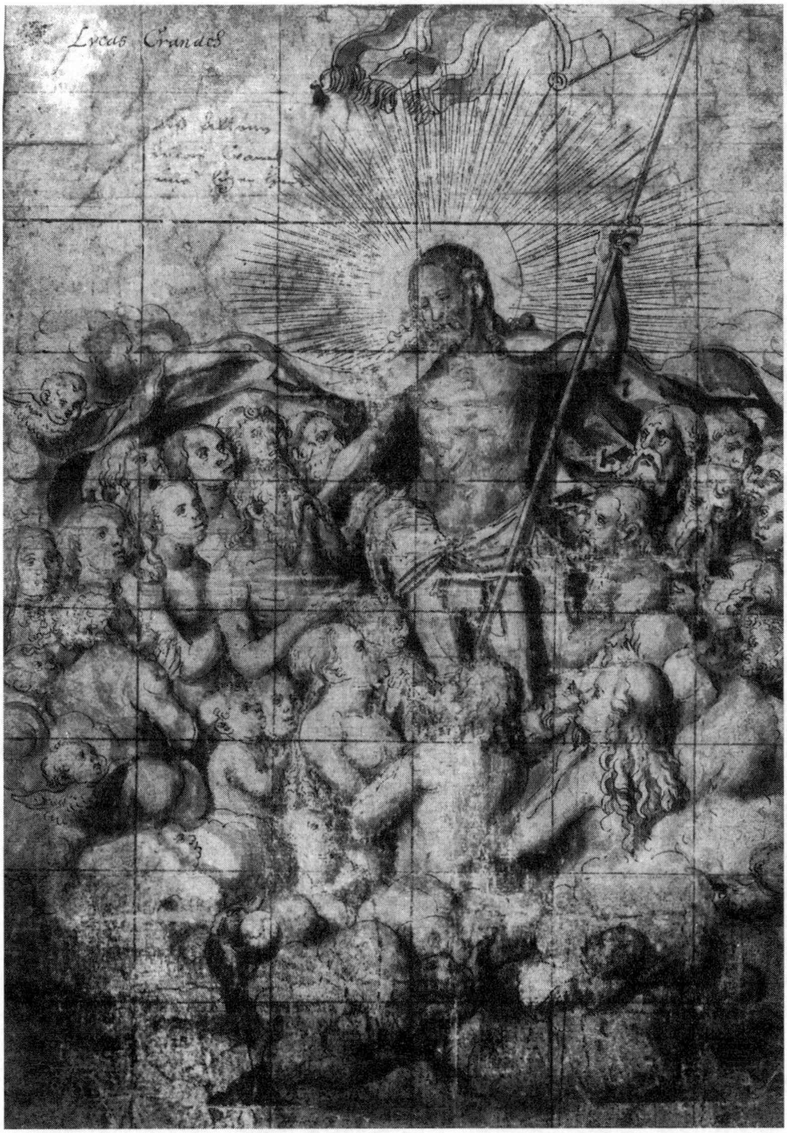

Figure 62. Lucas Cranach the Elder, *Schutzmantelchristus* / Christ in Limbo, 1530s (Kupferstichkabinett, Staatliche Museen zu Berlin)

Figure 63. Martin Schaffner, epitaph of Sebastian Welling, c.1532 (Hamburger Kunsthalle)

Protestant church, St Anna, provides an interesting example of a south German church redecorated in accordance with Lutheran Christocentric devotional priorities.[171] Iconophobes had removed the church's late medieval furnishings during the first half of the sixteenth century, so local evangelical patrons were presented with a blank slate in the aftermath of the 1555 Peace of Augsburg. During the second half of the sixteenth century they installed in the church's

[171] Above, pp. 120–22.

cloister epitaphs showing allegorical and narrative scenes that emphasized the importance of God's word, of faith in Christ and of grace. In the seventeenth century paintings of scenes from Christ's life and Passion, as well as portraits of Protestant preachers and Old Testament stories, were donated to the church.[172]

Several iconographies that were favoured by evangelical patrons emphasized Christ's approachable and forgiving nature. Paintings and prints of Christ with the woman taken in adultery (John 8:1–11), many of which were produced in the Cranach workshop from around 1520 onwards, and of Christ as the Good Shepherd served to negate the idea of a wrathful, vengeful God.[173] From the 1530s onwards Cranach's workshop also began to produce images of Christ blessing the children (Mark 10:13–16), a theme that was previously unknown in panel painting.[174] Perhaps developed initially as part of the Lutheran campaign to defend infant baptism against its Anabaptist critics, this iconography remained popular throughout the sixteenth and seventeenth centuries.[175] The depiction of Christ surrounded by babies and infants, presented to him by their mothers, obviously had a lasting relevance for Lutheran patrons. In an epitaph from the workshop of Lucas Cranach the Younger the artist has included portraits of the donor, his wife, their dead child and perhaps, Dieter Koepplin suggests, a godmother amongst the figures crowded around Christ (figure 64).[176] In this image a layman expresses his acceptance of Luther's maxim that Christians could approach Christ directly and without fear, and therefore had no need of saintly intercession. In around 1670 a fifteenth-century carved wooden relief from Schlotheim near Mühlhausen in Thuringia showing the Holy Kindred was reworked and made to represent the still-popular theme of Christ amongst the children. By removing St Anne's veil and breast and replacing them with hair and a beard the carver transformed the central group from a representation of Anne with Mary and the infant Christ into an adult Christ receiving a mother and her child.[177] Here, as in the 'corrected' and 'improved' Protestant versions of traditional hymns, Christians' devotion was directed away from Mary and the saints towards a welcoming and approachable Christ.

The belief of certain feminist scholars that the Virgin Mary functioned as 'an instrument of sex-role socialization, helping to create and reinforce a norm of

[172] Heal, 'A woman like any other?', pp. 86–8.

[173] On the iconography of the woman taken in adultery see Dieter Koepplin and Tilman Falk, eds., *Lucas Cranach: Gemälde, Zeichnungen, Druckgraphik. Ausstellung im Kunstmuseum Basle, 15. Juni–8. Sept. 1974*, 2 vols. (Basle and Stuttgart, 1974), vol. 2, pp. 514–16.

[174] Ibid., pp. 516–18.

[175] See for example Friedländer and Rosenburg, *Die Gemälde von Lucas Cranach*, no. 217 and Hamburger Kunsthalle (Hofmann), ed., *Luther und die Folgen für die Kunst*, no. 117.

[176] Koepplin, 'Reformatorische Kunst', p. 509 and ill. 22.

[177] Meissner, 'Zwischen Zerstörung und Umdeutung', pp. 279–80.

Figure 64. Workshop of Lucas Cranach the Younger, Christ blessing the children, c.1560 (Schloss Gottorf, Schleswig)

social behaviour for women in a patriarchal world' contains a kernel of truth.[178] As we saw in the case of the Ingolstadt preacher Georg Hauer, Mary's virtues provided churchmen with an opportunity to decry the inability of contemporary womankind to live up to the example set by the Mother of God. This idea of Mary as an instrument of misogynist repression is only, however, a very small part of the story. Mary was the ultimate example of what the anthropologist Victor Turner described as a 'polyvalent or polysemic' symbol.[179] She may have been a representation of unattainable purity and virtue, but she was also a humble human mother, an intercessor and a powerful helper and protector. Her multiplicity of meanings ensured that her appeal transcended all gender as well as all social boundaries. As we have seen, the Catholic Church's emphasis on her paradoxical status as 'mother most pure' did not necessarily alienate real women. Many women, from the Nuremberg peasants' wives who sought her aid in caring for their own children to Margareta Lynnerie, the Cologne patrician's daughter who used Mary as a model for her company of virgins, found solace in Mary's cult.

[178] N. Broude and M. D. Garrard, *The Expanding Discourse: feminism and art history* (New York, 1992), p. 3.

[179] Bynum, Harrell and Richman, eds., *Gender and Religion*, p. 2.

While Mary's cult was never gender specific, in both Catholic and Protestant territories the gender asymmetries that permeated every aspect of early modern life did shape both men's and women's experiences of Marian piety. During the Counter-Reformation, for example, men but not women could join the Jesuits' Marian sodalities and pledge themselves to defend the Virgin's honour. In Protestant areas all adherents of the new faith were required to adjust to a devotional landscape in which trust in Mary's intercession was replaced by trust in God's providence and Christ's mercy. But Mary's story continued to provide evangelical reformers with an opportunity to extol specifically female virtues: modesty, chastity and maternity. For Luther and his followers, the Mother of God personified their ideal of an obedient, domesticated woman. In analysing Mary's significance we must also, however, remember that the impact of the Reformation and Counter-Reformation was determined as much by particular circumstances of time and place as by reformers' doctrinal and devotional prescriptions. In the later sixteenth century Catholic women could, for example, have played a more active role in Marian piety in Cologne, where traditional liturgical practices and confraternities survived, than in Augsburg, where the Jesuit model of Marianism predominated. In the same period Lutheran women were exposed to Mary on a more regular basis in Nuremberg, where church furnishings and festivals remained, than in Augsburg, where they were eliminated. If we wish to understand how the inhabitants of early modern Germany viewed the Mother of God we must, therefore, as this book has shown, recreate the specific matrices of politics, religion and society within which Marian piety developed.

Conclusion

Early modern attitudes towards the Virgin Mary seem, at first glance, to have been highly polarized. Evangelicals complained that Mary had, in popular devotion, replaced Christ, and that she was being invoked in a superstitious manner. They condemned traditional manifestations of Marian devotion, from the celebration of feast days to the recitation of the rosary, and vilified idolatrous Marian pilgrimage sites such as the one at Regensburg in southern Germany. In response, Catholics reaffirmed their belief in the value of Marian veneration and in the intercessory power of the Mother of God. Peter Canisius set the standard for Counter-Reformation Marianism when he argued in his 1577 *De Maria Virgine incomparabili* that Catholics should revere the Virgin and honour her both at home and in public, in explicit defiance of her detractors. The Wittelsbachs, in particular Duke Maximilian I of Bavaria, and the Habsburgs took such Jesuit prescriptions to heart, and made Mary into a figurehead for their campaigns of Catholic reconquest. For them she was, as Canisius had characterized her, a vanquisher of demons and heretics.[1] The Catholic victories at Lepanto and the White Mountain were attributed to her intercession and she was invoked as patron of Bavaria. As the *Immaculata*, trampling a serpent representing heresy beneath her feet, she presided over the Habsburgs' lands into the eighteenth century.[2]

There is no denying the importance of this dichotomy between Protestant and Catholic attitudes towards Mary. In some areas the Virgin did indeed disappear, more or less, from evangelical devotion. In Protestant Augsburg, for example, where Reformed theologians shaped local religious life, Mary's images were removed, her feast days were abolished and blasphemy against her was no longer treated as a punishable offence. When Catholicism was restored in Augsburg, in the aftermath of Charles V's victory over the Schmalkaldic League, Bishop Otto Truchseß von Waldburg and his supporters were presented with a

[1] Canisius, *De Maria Virgine incomparabili*, pp. 599–600.
[2] Coreth, *Pietas Austriaca*, pp. 62–8.

tabula rasa with regard to Marian devotion. In the visual and devotional void created by the Protestant iconoclasts Otto, the Jesuits and their Fugger patrons actively promoted Mary's cult. During the later sixteenth and seventeenth centuries Counter-Reformation Marianism flourished in Augsburg. New Marian altarpieces, many of which depicted the Virgin's apotheosis using the dramatic compositions and heightened emotionalism characteristic of baroque art, were installed in the city's Catholic churches. Marian rituals such as processions and pilgrimages flourished: local Catholics flocked to the Loreto chapel on the Kobel hill and to Maria Hilf chapel on the Lechfeld. And the Jesuits' Marian sodalities dominated Augsburg's confraternity life. Marian devotion became a way in which Catholics, both rich and poor, distinguished themselves from their Protestant neighbours.

Overall, however, the situation in Germany was much more complex than Augsburg's polarity suggests. As this book has demonstrated, Mary remained important in some evangelical territories. Luther's reluctance to force the pace of religious change and willingness to reinterpret traditional Catholic symbols left open the possibility of a legitimate evangelical devotion to Mary. In some areas this Lutheran temperateness combined with the political circumspection and cultural concerns of the local patrician elite to permit the survival of numerous Marian images and feast days. The churches of Lutheran cities such as Nuremberg and Lübeck still contained medieval carved altarpieces, statues, paintings and stained-glass windows depicting the Virgin, and some Lutheran congregations even commissioned new images of the Mother of God. Most Lutheran churches continued to celebrate at least three Marian feast days, and some retained as many as five. Where possible, reformers reinterpreted these images and feast days, cleansing them of their popish associations and giving them a new meaning. Mary was celebrated as an exemplary recipient of God's grace and as a model of right belief and conduct.

The comparison between the Marian practice of Lutheran Nuremberg and that of post-1555 Lutheran Augsburg demonstrates that German Lutheranism cannot be understood in isolation from other confessions. In Augsburg Lutheran Marianism continued, throughout the seventeenth century, to look very much like Reformed Marianism looked elsewhere: the Mother of God remained largely absent from the visual and liturgical culture of the city's Protestant churches. When different confessions co-existed in close proximity to each other, as they often did in Germany, devotional life was shaped not only by theological precept and social and political context, but also by the interactions of the various religious groups. Nuremberg's citizens could assimilate many manifestations of pre-Reformation Marian devotion because they were not under immediate threat of recatholicization. In areas such as Brandenburg and Danzig, where Calvinism emerged as a new force, Marian images and liturgy became even more closely associated with Lutheran identity. In 1589–90, for example, Lutheran church fathers in Danzig used a statue of the Virgin to drive away a Calvinist preacher. Augsburg's evangelical citizens, on the other hand, were faced on a daily basis with the Jesuits' militant Marianism. In Augsburg legitimate Lutheran Marianism did not develop because of the excessive Marian devotion of the city's Catholic inhabitants.[3]

Within the Catholic Church, we cannot simply assume that one Jesuit-led model of Marianism dominated post-Tridentine piety. In Augsburg Marian piety had a demonstrative character and a polemical edge because the city's Catholics were surrounded by Mary-hating heretics. But when the Jesuits took Counter-Reformation Marianism to Cologne the strength of that city's own religious traditions ensured that the militant Virgin did not conquer Catholic devotional practice as she had done in the south. Traditional manifestations of Marian devotion, from old iconographies to pre-Reformation confraternities, survived into the eighteenth century.[4] This diversity of Marian practice indicates that both Protestant and Catholic piety were fluid and adaptable. We should not expect to find linear evolutions in religious life, from Luther's moderation to Calvin's extremism or from Erasmus' reformed Catholicism to the Jesuits' crusading zeal. Instead, we should acknowledge that different devotional traditions, shaped by local circumstances, continued to exist within the Holy Roman Empire. Lutheran cultural moderation remained an important force throughout the seventeenth and eighteenth centuries, as the flourishing of Lutheran architecture and music demonstrates. In Catholic Germany the scene may have been set, by the mid-seventeenth century, for the triumph of baroque piety, but this triumph did not necessarily take place at the expense of long-established devotional customs.

Mary's continued prominence during the religious turmoil of the sixteenth and seventeenth centuries testifies to her adaptability. She could, as Canisius recommended, be a symbol of the triumphant Catholic Church. She could lead Catholic troops into battle against the infidel and heretics. She could also, however, be the saint to whom war-weary Germans turned when they sought peace. She could be a protector of cities and of corporations, but she also interceded on behalf of individual supplicants, from wounded soldiers to pregnant women. No other saint was so versatile, as the Lutherans' self-confident manipulation of her images and feast days demonstrates. She became, for them, a defender of their moderate evangelical identity and a model holy housemother. This versatility has important implications for the ongoing scholarly debate about women's experiences of religious change.[5] For churchmen such as the Ingolstadt preacher Georg Hauer the promotion of Mary's cult went hand-in-hand

[3] Meinhold, 'Die Marienverehrung', p. 43.
[4] Mallinckrodt, *Struktur und kollektiver Eigensinn*, pp. 397–408.
[5] Lyndal Roper, 'Gender and the Reformation', *Archiv für Reformationsgeschichte* 29 (2001).

with the denunciation of the manifold failings of real women. But some Catholic women nonetheless found inspiration in Mary's cult: the relationship between religious symbolism and social reality was a complex one. On the Protestant side, it is impossible to know how the majority of women reacted to Luther's demystified Virgin. She reinforced the patriarchal message promulgated by the reformers, but she also affirmed the value of women's domestic vocation. In considering women's experiences, we must at least acknowledge that the Reformation did not create an exclusively masculine religious landscape. Even Reformed Protestants could not do away with Mary entirely. For, as Erasmus' 'Virgin from the Rock' reminded Zwingli and the iconoclasts who threatened to expel her from their places of worship, a church without Mary was a church without Christ.[6]

6 *CWE*, vol. 40, p. 628.

Bibliography

ARCHIVAL SOURCES CITED

Stadtarchiv Nürnberg

Rep. A6, Sammlung der (gedruckten) Mandate, Urkunden und Verordnungen der Reichsstadt und Stadtverwaltung Nürnberg, 1219 bis Gegenwart: 1525 Mai 24.; 1526 März 3.; 1529; B 31/1.

Rep. B14/III, Inventarbücher: Nr. 8 (1529–1531); Nr. 11 (1544–1551); Nr. 12 (1548–1586).

Rep. E1, Familienarchiv Spengler: Nr. 47.

Rep. F1, Nürnberger Chroniken: Nr. 127.

Staatsarchiv Nürnberg

Rep. 8: 158 (Testament).

Rep. 44e, Losungsamt, Akten: S.I.L.130, Nr. 7a; S.I.L. 131, Nr. 10, Nr. 13, Nr. 14, Nr. 15, Nr. 22.

Rep. 52a, Handschriften: Nr. 46.

Rep. 52b, Reichsstadt Nürnberg, Amts- und Standbücher: 209 (Achtbuch, 1578–1581); 221 (Malefizurteilsbücher 1487–1558).

Rep. 56, Nürnberger Druckschriften: 97a (Agendbüchlein).

Rep. 60b, Ratsbücher: Nr. 15.

Reichsstadt Nürnberg, Kirchen und Ortschaften auf d. Lande: 454 (1560–1 Kirchenvisitation).

Archiv des Bistums Augsburg

HS (Handschriften): Nr. 34.

Fr 30 (*Missale Augustense*, 1510); Fr 34 (*Missale secundum ritum Augustensis ecclesie*, 1555).

Stadtarchiv Augsburg

Reichsstadt, Anschläge und Dekrete, 1490–1649, Nr. 1–86: Nr. 70.

Reichsstadt, Evangelisches Wesens Archiv (E. W. A.): Nr. 666; Nr. 941.

Reichsstadt, Katholisches Wesens Archiv (K. W. A.): B. 10^2–14.
Reichsstadt, Ratsbücher: Nr. 16 (1529–42), Nr. 26; Geh. Ratsbücher Nr. 2, Nr. 3.
Reichsstadt, Ratserlasse: 1507–99.
Reichsstadt, Schätze: Nr. ad 36/3, Nr. ad 36/7 (Zucht- und Polizeiordnungen); Nr. 165 (Augsburger Pflegschaftsbuch von 1501–42).
Reichsstadt, Schuld-, Klag-, und Apellationsakten: Teil 2, Karton 14; Teil 2, Karton 20.
Reichsstadt, Spreng'sche Notariatsakten: 100/1 (1567–80); 100/2 (1581–93).
Reichsstadt, Strafamt: Nr. 105 (Strafbuch, 1615–32); Nr. 106 (Strafbuch, 1633–53).
Reichsstadt, Strafamt, Urgichten Sammlung: Nr. 7 (15. Juni 1529, Georg Zeindlweber); Nr. 400–1 (1579–80, Paul Hector Mair); Nr. 235 (19. März 1612, Anna Maria Stengler); K 211 (7. März, 1630, Christoph Glatz); K 212 (1630 August bis 1631 Dezember, Martin Haller); Nr. 322 (August 1636, Abraham Raiffinger); K 217 (1636 Januar bis 1637 Mai, Marx Heiß, Hannß Fischer, Hannß Wagner, Hannß Klökhler).
Literalien, 1576–9: 9/11 1577.

Staats- und Stadtbibliothek Augsburg

2°Cod. Aug. 88 (Paul v. Welser, Inventar 1615).
2°Cod. Aug 346 (De initiis et progressu omnium Fraternitatum, quæ in alma hac Vrbe Augustana fuerunt diuersis temporibus erectæ a Christi fidelibus, narratio MDCXVII).
4° Aug. 524 (Gymnasium St Salvator (Jesuiten). Dissertationen, Schulkomödien, Sing- und Fastnachtspiele).
4° Bild 1–25 (Trivmph Der Gebenedeyten Junckfrawen vnnd Himmelkuenigin Maria, 1617).

Historisches Archiv der Stadt Köln

Reichsstadt, Best. 10, Ratsprotokolle: Nr. 8, Nr. 10.
Reichsstadt, Best. 14, Edikte: Nr. 1, Nr. 16.
Reichsstadt, Best. 20, Briefbücher, Nr. 60.
Reichsstadt, Best. 30, Verfassung und Verwaltung (Verf. u. Verw.): G 205 (Turmbücher); 239 (Turmbücher); V 126 a, V 126 b, 127 (Morgensprachen).
Reichsstadt, Best. 125, Kriminalakten: Nr. 1.
Reichsstadt, Best. 150, Univ. 1057.
Stifter und Klöster, Best. 223, Jesuiten: U2/481 (Inventare); A9, Litterae Annuae des Kölner Jesuiten Kollegs 1552–1660.
Stifter und Klöster, Best. 247, St Maria im Kapitol: Akten, 3e (Inventar, 1405).
Stifter und Klöster, Best. 295, Geistliche Abteilung (GA): 170, 173, 175A (St Maria im Kapitol).

Historisches Archiv des Erzbistums Köln

Dom: A II 112.
Alte Kölner Pfarrarchive, Dom, St Laurenz: D II 6; D II 17; D II 34; D II 176; D II 177a.
Alte Kölner Pfarrarchive: St Johann Bapt.: A II 2, A II 25.
Alte Kölner Pfarrarchive: St Maria im Kapitol: A II 16.

PRINTED PRIMARY SOURCES

Albrecht, Bernhard, *Hauß vnd Kirchenschatz: Das ist / Außerlesene Anda^{e}chtige Gebett vnd Dancksagungen / auff jede Tag in der woche[n] / Item auff die fu^{e}rnemste Fest vnnd Zeiten im Jahr: Deßgleichen auff alle begebende Fa^{e}ll in dem Menschlichen Leben: beedes fu^{e}r Junge vnnd Alte / Gesunde vnd Krancke / ausser vnnd inner der Creutz / daheim zu Hauß / vnd in der Kirchen / nutzlich vnnd heylsamlich zu gebrauchen.* 3rd edn. Ulm: Johann Meder, 1620.

Die Bekenntnisschriften der evangelisch-lutherischen Kirche. Göttingen, 1959.

Bretschneider, Carolus Gottlieb, ed. *Corpus Reformatorum*. Halle, 1834–.

Canisius, Peter, *Beati Petri Canisii, Societatis Iesu, epistulae et acta*, ed. Otto Braunsberger. 8 vols. Freiburg im Breisgau, 1896–1923.

De Maria Virgine incomparabili, et dei genitrice sacrosancta, libri qvinqvi. Ingolstadt, 1577.

Maria, die unvergleichliche Jungfrau und hochheilige Gottesgebärerin, trans. Carl Telch. Warnsdorf, 1933.

Die Chroniken der deutschen Städte vom 14. bis ins 16. Jahrhundert. 36 vols. Leipzig, 1862–1931.

Coster, Franz, *Libellus Sodalitatis: Hoc est, christianarvm institvtionvm libri qvinqve, in gratiam sodalitatis B. Virginis Mariae*. Cologne: Hierat, 1603.

Decreta synodalia dioeces. August. Augsburg: Simon Utzschneider, 1693.

Dietrich, Veit, *Kinder Postilla vber die Sontags / vnd der fu^{e}rnembsten Fest Euangelia / durch das gantze Jar*. Nuremberg: Johann von Berg and Ulrich Newber, 1549.

Egli, Emil, *Actensammlung zur Geschichte der Zürcher Reformation in den Jahren 1519–1533*. Zurich, 1879.

Eisengrein, M., *Vnser liebe Fraw zu Alten Oetting*. Ingolstadt, 1571.

Erasmus, Desiderius, *Opera Omnia Desiderii Erasmi Roterodami*. Amsterdam 1969–.

Gebwiler, Hieronymus, *Beschirmung des lobs und eren der hochgelobte[n] hymelischen künigin Marie aller heiligen gottes, auch der wolangesetzten ordnungen der Christlichen kirchen wider die freuenliche[n] heilige[n] schmeher.* Strasbourg: Grüninger, 1523.

Gedicke, Simon, *Calviniana Religio oder Calvinisterey / So fa^{e}lschlich die Reformirte Religion genennet wird / Kurtzer Ausßzug vnd Bericht / nach den fu^{e}rnembsten Hauptpunckten Christlicher Lehre vnd Ceremonien*. Leipzig: Abraham Lamberg, 1615.

Von Bildern vnd Altarn / In den Evangelischen Kirchen Augspurgischer Confession. Wolgegru^{e}ndter Bericht / sampt kurtzer Wiederlegung des newlich außgegangenen Zerbestischen Buchs / menniglich in disen letzten gefehrlichen leufften / wider die Caluinische Newrung der Bilder und Altarstu^{e}rmer / zu wissen sehr nu^{e}tzlich vnd no^{e}tig. Magdeburg: Johan Francken, 1597.

Goldtwurm, Caspar, *Kirchen Calender*. Frankfurt am Main: Christian Egenolff, 1564.

Gumppenberg, Wilhelm, *Atlas Marianus*. Munich, 1672.

Hainhofer, Philipp, *Reise-Tagebuch enthaltend Schilderungen aus Franken, Sachsen, der Mark Brandenburg und Pommers im Jahr 1617*. Stettin, 1834.

Hampe, T., ed. *Nürnberger Ratsverlässe über Kunst und Künstler im Zeitalter der Spätgotik und Renaissance.* 2 vols. Quellenschriften für Kunstgeschichte und Kunsttechnik des Mittelalters und der Renaissance, n.s. 11, 12 and 13. Vienna and Leipzig, 1904.

Hansen, Joseph, ed. *Rheinische Akten zur Geschichte des Jesuitenordens 1542–1582*. Publikationen der Gesellschaft für rheinische Geschichtskunde. Bonn, 1896.

Hartknoch, Christoph, *Preussische Kirchen-Historia*. Frankfurt am Main and Leipzig, 1686.

Hartzheim, J., ed. *Concilia Germaniae*. 11 vols. Cologne, 1759–90.

Hauer, Georg, *Drey christlich predig vom Salve regina / dem Eua[n]geli vnnd heyligen schrift gemeß*. Ingolstadt: Andreas Lutz, 1523.

Heilbrunner, Jacob, *Synopsis Doctrinae Calvinianae*, vol. 2: *Widerholte Erzehlung der Caluinischen Irrthumb*. Laugingen, 1595.

Heinrich, Simon, *Regii natales confraternitatis septem dolorum B. Mariae Virginis ab ordine Servitarum religiosissimo quondam Praemonstratae*. Cologne: Cholin, 1635.

Hirschmann, Gerhard, *Die Kirchenvisitation im Landgebiet der Reichstadt Nürnberg 1560 und 1561. Quellenedition*. Einzelarbeiten aus der Kirchengeschichte Bayerns 68. Neustadt an der Aisch, 1994.

Hohndorff, Andreas, *Calendarium sanctorum & historiarum*. Frankfurt am Main, 1587.

Hottinger, J. J., and H. H. Vögeli, eds. *Heinrich Bullingers Reformationsgeschichte*. 3 vols. Frauenfeld, 1838–40.

Isaac, Stephan, *Wahre und einfältige Historia Stephani Isaaci*. N.p., 1586.

Kempis, Thomas à, *The Imitation of Christ*, trans. Leo Sherley-Price. Harmondsworth, 1952.

Kistler, R., *Basilika, dass ist die herrliche kirchendes Frey-Reichsklosters St Ulrich und Afra in Augsburg*. Augsburg, 1712.

Mangrum, B. D., and G. Scavizzi, eds. *A Reformation Debate: Karlstadt, Emser, and Eck on sacred images. Three treatises in translation*. Toronto, 1991.

Marquard von Berg, *Ritus Ecclesiastici Augustensis Episcopatus*. Dillingen, 1580.

Militzer, Klaus, ed. *Quellen zur Geschichte der Kölner Laienbruderschaften vom 12. Jahrhundert bis 1562/63*. 4 vols. Publikationen der Gesellschaft für Rheinische Geschichtskunde 71. Düsseldorf, 1997–2000.

Militzer, Klaus, and Wolfgang Schmid, 'Das Inventar der Kölner Ratskapelle von 1519: Edition und Kommentar', *Wallraf-Richartz-Jahrbuch* 58 (1997), 229–37.

Mollen, Christoph, *Ein Predig von dem Ave Maria, vnd von anrüfung der heyligen*. Strasbourg: Christian Müller, 1575.

Montaigne, Michel de, *Montaigne's Travel Journal*, trans. Donald M. Frame. San Francisco, 1983.

Müller, G., and Gottfried Seebass, eds. *Andreas Osiander d. Ä: Gesamtausgabe*. 10 vols. Gütersloh, 1975–97.

Müller, Karl, *Die Bekenntnisschriften der reformierten Kirche*. Leipzig, 1903.

Murr, Christoph Gottlieb von, *Beschreibung der vornehmsten Merkwürdigkeiten in des H. R. Reichs freyen Stadt Nürnberg und auf der hohen Schule zu Altdorf*. Nuremberg, 1778.

Osiander, Andreas, *Zwo Predig. Eine von den heiligen / wie man sie ehren sol. Die ander / vonn Verstorbnen / wie man fu^{e}r sie bitten sol*. N. p., 1547.

Pelikan, Jaroslav, ed. *Luther's Works*. 55 vols. St Louis / Philadelphia, 1958–67.

Pfeiffer, Gerhard, ed. *Quellen zur Nürnberger Reformationsgeschichte. Von der Duldung liturgischer Änderungen bis zur Ausübung des Kirchenregiments durch den Rat (Juni 1524 – Juni 1525)*. Einzelarbeiten aus der Kirchengeschichte Bayerns 45. Nuremberg, 1968.

Plenck, Jacob, *Handbu^{o}chlein / der Bru^{o}der und Schwerstern / der Vhralter / vnd weitberu^{e}hmbter / bey den Predigern gepflantzter ErtzBruderschafft IESV, vnd MARIÆ Rosenkrantz*. Cologne, 1635.

Porta, Conrad, *Jungfrawen Spiegel. Aus Gottes Wort / vnd D. M. Lutheri Schrifften / nach Ordnung der heiligen zehen Gebot / mit vleis zugerichtet. Sampt angehengten kurtzen Historien / der heiligen Jungfrawen / welcher Namen im Calender stehen.* Eisleben: Vrban Gaubisch, 1580.
Rupprich, H., ed. *Dürer: schriftlicher Nachlass.* 3 vols. Berlin, 1956–70.
Schuler, Johannes, *Etliche Christliche Predigen.* Stuttgart, 1612.
Schuler, Melchior, and Johannes Schulthess, eds. *Huldreich Zwinglis Werke.* 8 vols. Zurich, 1828–42.
Sehling, Emil, ed. *Die evangelischen Kirchenordnungen des XVI. Jahrhunderts.* 16 vols. Leipzig and Tübingen, 1902–77.
Steiner, J. A., ed. *Acta Selecta Ecclesiae Augustanae.* N.p., 1785.
Stetten, Paul von, *Beschreibung der Reichs-Stadt Augsburg, nach ihrer Lage.* Augsburg, 1788.
Geschichte der Heil. Ro^{e}m. Reichs Freyen Stadt Augsburg. Frankfurt and Augsburg, 1743.
Stupperich, Robert, ed. *Martin Bucers deutsche Schriften. Martini Buceri opera omnia,* ser. 1. Gütersloh, 1960–.
Surius, Laurentius, *Bewerter Historien der lieben Heiligen Gottes.* 6 vols. Munich: Berg, 1574.
De probatis Sanctorum historiis. 6 vols. Cologne: Calenius and Quentel, 1570–5.
Tanner, Norman P., ed. *Decrees of the Ecumenical Councils.* 2 vols. Washington, DC, 1990.
Tappert, Theodore G., ed. *The Book of Concord: the confessions of the evangelical Lutheran Church.* Philadelphia, 1959.
Tappolet, Walter, ed. *Das Marienlob der Reformatoren.* Tübingen, 1962.
Vermarckt dye Grossenn wunder zaichen So dye Junckfraw Maria hye zu^{o} alten O^{e}tting würcken ist an Vil Cristen menschen. Augsburg, 1494/5 (SStBA, 4^{0} INK.125).
Voragine, Jacobus de, *The Golden Legend: readings on the saints,* trans. William Granger Ryan. 2 vols. Princeton, NJ, 1993.
Wackernagel, Philipp, *Das deutsche Kirchenlied von der ältesten Zeit bis zu Anfang des XVII. Jahrhunderts.* 5 vols. Leipzig, 1864–77.
Würfel, Andreas, *Diptycha Cappellae B. Mariae.* Nuremberg, 1761.
Diptycha Ecclesiæ Laurentianæ. Nuremberg, 1756.
Zeltner, Gustav Georg, *Kurtze Erläuterung der Nürnbergischen Schul- und Reformationsgeschichte / aus dem Leben und Schriften des berühmten Sebald Heyden / Rectoris bey S. Sebald.* Nuremberg, 1732.
Zwingli, Huldrych, *Huldreich Zwinglis sämtliche Werke.* Corpus Reformatorum. Leipzig, 1904–.

SECONDARY SOURCES

Albrecht, Dieter, *Maximilian I. von Bayern 1573–1651.* Munich, 1998.
Amt für rheinische Landeskunde, ed. *Wallfahrt im Rheinland.* Cologne, 1981.
Andersson, Christiane, 'Religiöse Bilder Cranachs im Dienste der Reformation', in *Humanismus und Reformation als kulturelle Kräfte in der deutschen Geschichte,* ed. L. W. Spitz, pp. 43–79. Berlin and New York, 1980.
Andresen, Carl, and Adolf Martin Ritter, eds. *Handbuch der Dogmen- und Theologiegeschichte.* 3 vols. 2nd edn. Göttingen, 1998–9.
Anzelewsky, Fedja, *Dürer: his art and life,* trans. Heide Grieve. Fribourg, 1980.

Arndt, Johannes, 'Köln als kommunikatives Zentrum im Zeitalter des Dreißigjährigen Krieges', in *Köln als Kommunikationszentrum: Studien zur frühneuzeitlichen Stadtgeschichte*, ed. Georg Mölich and Gerd Schwerhoff, pp. 116–38. Cologne, 1999.

Arnold, Klaus, 'Die Heilige Familie. Bilder und Verehrung der Heiligen Anna, Maria, Joseph und des Jesuskindes in Kunst, Literatur und Frömmigkeit um 1500', in *Maria in der Welt: Marienverehrung im Kontext der Sozialgeschichte 10.–18. Jahrhundert*, ed. Claudia Opitz, Hedwig Röckelein, G. Signori and G. P. Marchal, pp. 153–74. Zurich, 1993.

Ashley, K., and P. Sheingorn, eds. *Interpreting Cultural Symbols: Saint Anne in late medieval society*. Athens, GA, and London, 1990.

Aston, Margaret, *England's Iconoclasts*, vol. 1: *Laws against Images*. Oxford, 1988.

Baader, Joseph, ed. *Nürnberger Polizeiordnungen aus dem XIII. bis XV. Jahrhundert*. Stuttgart, 1861.

Banz, Claudia, 'Anmerkungen zum Ausstattungsprogramm der Marienwallfahrtskirche in Scherpenheuvel', in *Albert and Isabella: essays*, ed. Werner Thomas and Luc Duerloo, pp. 161–71. Brussels, 1998.

Baron, Hans, 'Religion and politics in the German imperial cities during the Reformation', *English Historical Review* 52 (1937), 405–27, 614–33.

Bauer, Robert, *Die Bayerische Wallfahrt Altötting*. Munich, 1970.

Bäumer, Remigius, and Leo Scheffczyk, eds. *Marienlexikon*. 6 vols. St Ottilien, 1988–94.

Baumstark, Reinhold, ed. *Rom in Bayern: Kunst und Spiritualität der ersten Jesuiten. Katalog zur Ausstellung des Bayerischen Nationalmuseums München, 30. April bis 20. Juli 1997*. Munich, 1997.

Baxandall, Michael, *The Limewood Sculptors of Renaissance Germany*. New Haven, CT, and London, 1980.

Painting and Experience in Fifteenth-Century Italy. 2nd edn. Oxford, 1988.

Bayerische Verwaltung der staatlichen Schlösser, Gärten und Seen, *Residenz München: amtlicher Führer*. Munich, 1937.

Bayerisches Nationalmuseum and Adalbert Stifter Verein, eds. *Wallfahrt kennt keine Grenzen: Ausstellung im Bayerischen Nationalmuseum, München, 28. Juni bis 7. Oktober 1984*. Munich, 1984.

Beissel, Stephan, *Geschichte der Verehrung Marias im 16. und 17. Jahrhundert*. Freiburg im Breisgau, 1910.

Belting, Hans, *Likeness and Presence: a history of the image before the era of art*, trans. Edmund Jephcott. Chicago and London, 1994.

Benedict, Philip, 'Towards the comparative study of the popular market for art: the ownership of paintings in seventeenth-century Metz', *Past & Present* 109 (1985), 100–17.

Benzing, Josef, *Lutherbibliographie: Verzeichnis der gedruckten Schriften Martin Luthers bis zu dessen Tod*. Bibliotheca bibliographica Aureliana 10, 16, 19. Baden-Baden, 1966.

Biedermann, Gottfried, *Katalog – Alte Galerie am Landesmuseum Joanneum. Mittelalterliche Kunst*. Graz, 1982.

Blickle, P., A. Holenstein, H. R. Schmidt and F.-J. Sladeczek, eds. *Macht und Ohnmacht der Bilder*. Beihefte der Historischen Zeitschrift 33. Munich, 2002.

Bluhm, Heinz, 'Luther's translation and interpretation of the *Ave Maria*', *Journal of English and German Philology* 51 (1952), 196–211.

Bosbach, Franz, 'Die katholische Reform in der Stadt Köln', *Römische Quartalschrift für christliche Altertumskunde und Kirchengeschichte* 84 (1989), 120–59.

Bossy, John, 'The Counter-Reformation and the people of Catholic Europe', *Past & Present* 47 (1970), 135–52.

Bott, Gerhard, ed. *Martin Luther und die Reformation in Deutschland*. Frankfurt am Main, 1983.

Brady, Thomas A., 'Confessionalization: the career of a concept', in *Confessionalization in Europe, 1555–1700: essays in honor and memory of Bodo Nischan*, ed. John M. Headley, Hans J. Hillerbrand and Anthony J. Papalas. Aldershot, 2004.

'Settlements: the Holy Roman Empire', in *Handbook of European History, 1400–1600: late Middle Ages, Renaissance, and Reformation*, ed. Thomas A. Brady, Heiko A. Oberman and James D. Tracy, pp. 349–83. Leiden and New York, 1994–5.

Braun, Karl, *Nürnberg und die Versuche zur Wiederherstellung der alten Kirche im Zeitalter der Gegenreformation, 1555–1648*. Einzelarbeiten aus der Kirchengeschichte Bayerns 1. Nuremberg, 1925.

Bräutigam, Günther, 'Nürnberg als Kaiserstadt', in *Kaiser Karl IV: Staatsmann und Mäzen*, ed. Ferdinand Seibt, pp. 339–43. Munich, 1978.

Breuer, Tilman, *Die Stadt Augsburg*. Munich, 1958.

Brisch, Carl, *Geschichte der Juden in Cöln und Umgebung aus ältester Zeit bis auf die Gegenwart*. 2 vols. Cologne, 1879 and 1882.

Broadhead, Philip, 'Politics and expediency in the Augsburg Reformation', in *Reformation Principle and Practice: essays in honour of Arthur Geoffrey Dickens*, ed. P. N. Brooks, pp. 53–70. London, 1980.

Brooks, Peter Newman, 'A lily ungilded? Martin Luther, the Virgin Mary and the saints', *Journal of Religious History* 13 (1984–5), 136–49.

Broude, N., and M. D. Garrard, *The Expanding Discourse: feminism and art history*. New York, 1992.

Brückner, Wolfgang, ed. *Volkserzählung und Reformation: ein Handbuch zur Tradierung und Funktion von Erzählstoffen und Erzählliteratur im Protestantismus*. Berlin, 1974.

Burckhardt, Johannes, *Das Reformationsjahrhundert: deutsche Geschichte zwischen Medienrevolution und Institutionenbildung, 1517–1617*. Stuttgart, 2002.

Bushart, Bruno, *Die Fuggerkapelle bei St Anna in Augsburg*. Munich, 1994.

'Die Hochaltarblätter des Barock in Augsburg', *JbVAB* 25 (1991), 190–225.

'Kunst und Stadtbild', in *Geschichte der Stadt Augsburg: 2000 Jahre von der Römerzeit bis zur Gegenwart*, ed. G. Gottlieb, pp. 363–85. Stuttgart, 1984.

Bynum, Caroline Walker, *Fragmentation and Redemption: essays on gender and the human body in medieval religion*. New York, 1991.

Jesus as Mother: studies in the spirituality of the high Middle Ages. Berkeley, Los Angeles and London, 1984.

Bynum, Caroline Walker, Stevan Harrell and Paula Richman, eds. *Gender and Religion: on the complexity of symbols*. Boston, 1986.

Campbell, Ena, 'The Virgin of Guadalupe and the female self-image: a Mexican case history', in *Mother Worship: theme and variations*, ed. J. J. Presto, pp. 5–21. Chapel Hill, 1982.

Campbell, W. E., *The Dialogue Concerning Tyndale by Sir Thomas More*. London, 1927.

Campenhausen, Hans, 'Die Bilderfrage in der Reformation', *Zeitschrift für Kirchengeschichte* 68 (1957), 96–128.

Campi, Emidio, *Zwingli und Maria: eine reformationsgeschichtliche Studie*. Zurich, 1997.

Chaix, Gérald, 'De la cité chrétienne à la métropole catholique: vie religieuse et conscience civique à Cologne au XVIe siècle', thèse pour le Doctorat d'Etat, L'Université des Sciences Humaines de Strasbourg, 1994.

'Von der Christlichkeit zur Katholizität: Köln zwischen Traditionen und Modernität (1500–1648)', in *Frühe Neuzeit – Frühe Moderne? Forschungen zur Vielschichtigkeit von Übergangsprozessen*, ed. Rudolf Vierhaus, pp. 233–44. Göttingen, 1992.

Chaline, Olivier, *La Bataille de la Montagne Blanche (8 Novembre 1620): un mystique chez les guerriers*. Paris, 1999.

Chartier, Roger, *Cultural History: between practices and representations*, trans. Lydia G. Cochrane. Cambridge, 1988.

Châtellier, Louis, *The Europe of the Devout: the Catholic Reformation and the formation of a new society*, trans. Jean Birrell. Cambridge, 1989.

Christensen, Carl, 'Iconoclasm and the preservation of ecclesiastical art in Reformation Nuremberg', *Archiv für Reformationsgeschichte* 61 (1970), 205–21.

Cieslak, Katarzyna, 'Die "zweite Reformation" in Danzig und die Kirchenkunst', in *Historische Bildkunde: Probleme – Wege – Beispiele*, ed. B. Tolkenmitt and R. Wohlfeil, *Zeitschrift für historische Forschung*, supplementary volume 12, pp. 165–73. Berlin, 1991.

Clemen, Paul, ed. *Die Kunstdenkmäler der Rheinprovinz*, vol. 7, part I: *Die Kunstdenkmäler der Stadt Köln*; vol. 2: *Die kirchlichen Denkmäler der Stadt Köln*. Düsseldorf, 1911.

Cohn, Henry J., 'The territorial princes in Germany's Second Reformation, 1559–1622', in *International Calvinism, 1541–1715*, ed. Menna Prestwich, pp. 135–65. Oxford, 1985.

Conrad, Anne, 'Nähe und Distanz – katholische Frauen im Spannungsfeld der frühneuzeitlichen Mariologie', in *Maria in der Welt: Marienverehrung im Kontext der Sozialgeschichte 10.– 18. Jahrhundert*, ed. Claudia Opitz, Hedwig Röckelein, G. Signori and G. P. Marchal, pp. 175–90. Zurich, 1993.

'Stifterinnen und Lehrerinnen: der Anteil von Frauen am jesuitischen Bildungswesen', in *Petrus Canisius SJ (1521–1597): Humanist und Europäer*, ed. R. Berndt, pp. 205–24. Berlin, 2000.

Zwischen Kloster und Welt: Ursulinen und Jesuitinnen in der Katholischen Reformbewegung des 16./17. Jahrhunderts. Veröffentlichungen des Instituts für Europäische Geschichte Mainz 142. Mainz, 1991.

Coreth, Anna, *Pietas Austriaca: österreichische Frömmigkeit im Barock*. 2nd edn. Schriftenreihe des Instituts für Österreichkunde. Munich, 1982.

Cox, H. L., 'Prozessionsbrauchtum des späten Mittelalters und der frühen Neuzeit im Spiegel obrigkeitlicher Verordnungen in Kurköln und den vereinigten Herzogtümern', *Rheinsch-Westfälische Zeitschrift für Volkskunde* 22 (1976), 51–85.

Creasman, Allyson, 'The Virgin Mary against the Jews: anti-Jewish polemic in the pilgrimage to the Schöne Maria of Regensburg, 1519–25', *Sixteenth Century Journal* 33, no. 4 (2002), 963–80.

Cuneo, P. F., 'Propriety, property, and politics: Jörg Breu the Elder and issues of iconoclasm in Reformation Augsburg', *German History* 14, no. 1 (1996), 1–20.

Czymmek, Sabine, 'Schattenrisse – zur barocken Ausstattung von St. Maria im Kapitol', *CR* 3 (1988), 99–111.

Dannenbauer, H., 'Die Nürnberger Landgeistlichen bis zur zweiten Nürnberger Kirchenvisitation', *Zeitschrift für bayerische Kirchengeschichte* 4 (1927), 207–36.

Delius, Walter, *Geschichte der Marienverehrung*. Munich and Basle, 1963.

Dellsperger, Rudolf, 'Wolfgang Musculus (1497–1563): Leben und Werk', in *Wolfgang Musculus (1497–1563) und die oberdeutsche Reformation*, ed. Rudolf Dellsperger, Rudolf Freudenberger and Wolfgang Weber, pp. 23–36. Berlin, 1997.

Deml, Ingo Matthias, 'Der Altar der Mailänder Madonna und die Neuausstattung des Kölner Domes im 17. Jahrhundert', *Kölner Domblatt: Jahrbuch des Zentral-Dombau-Vereins* 64 (1999), 183–226.

Diederich, Toni, 'Die Säkularisation in Köln während der Franzosenzeit', in *Lust und Verlust: Kölner Sammler zwischen Trikolore und Preussenadler*, ed. Hiltrud Kier and Frank Günter Zehnder, pp. 77–83. Cologne, 1995.

Ditges, A., 'Eine Kölner Gerkammer im 16. Jahrhundert', *Annalen des Historischen Vereins für den Niederrhein* 45 (1886), 117–37.

Dixon, C. Scott, *The Reformation and Rural Society: the parishes of Brandenburg–Ansbach–Kulmbach, 1528–1603*. Cambridge Studies in Early Modern History. Cambridge, 1996.

The Reformation in Germany. Historical Association Studies. Oxford, 2002.

ed. *The German Reformation: the essential readings*. Oxford, 1999.

Dormeier, H., 'St. Rochis, die Pest und die Imhoffs in Nürnberg vor und während der Reformation', *Anzeiger des Germanischen Nationalmuseums* (1985), 7–72.

Dorn, Ludwig, 'Aus dem Atlas Marianus: die Marienwallfahrten des Bistums Augsburg im Jahre 1672', *JbVAB* 11 (1977), 66–83.

'Das Mirakelbuch der Wallfahrt Maria Hilf in Speiden', *JbVAB* 20 (1986), 141–5.

Dotterweich, Helmut, *Der junge Maximilian: Jugend und Erziehung des bayerischen Herzogs und späteren Kurfürsten Maximilian I. von 1573 bis 1593*. Munich, 1962.

Duerloo, Luc, 'Archducal piety and Habsburg power', in *Albert and Isabella: essays*, ed. Werner Thomas and Luc Duerloo, pp. 267–83. Brussels, 1998.

Düfel, Hans, *Luthers Stellung zur Marienverehrung*. Göttingen, 1968.

'Die Marienverehrung im Licht des reformatorischen "sola scriptura"', in *De culto Mariano saeculo 16 [decimo sexto]. Acta congressus Mariologici-Mariani Internationalis Caesaraugustae anno 1979 celebrati*, pp. 1–24. Rome, 1985.

Duhr, Bernhard, *Geschichte der Jesuiten in den Ländern deutscher Zunge im XVI. Jahrhundert*. Freiburg im Breisgau, 1907.

Geschichte der Jesuiten in den Ländern deutscher Zunge in der ersten Hälfte des XVII. Jahrhunderts. 2 vols. Freiburg im Breisgau, 1913.

Dülmen, Richard van, *Kultur und Alltag in der Frühen Neuzeit*, vol. 3: *Religion, Magie, Aufklärung 16.–18. Jahrhundert*. Munich, 1994.

'Volksfrömmigkeit und konfessionelles Christentum im 16. und 17. Jahrhundert', in *Volksreligiosität in der modernen Sozialgeschichte*, ed. Wolfgang Schieder, *Geschichte und Gesellschaft* 11, special issue, pp. 14–30. Göttingen, 1986.

'Wider die Ehre Gottes: Unglaube und Gotteslästerung in der Frühen Neuzeit', *Historische Anthropologie. Kultur. Gesellschaft. Alltag* 2, no. 1 (1994), 20–38.

Dupeux, Cecile, Peter Jezler and Jean Wirth, eds. *Bildersturm: Wahnsinn oder Gottes Wille?* Munich, 2000.

Dussler, Hildebrand, 'Die Restaurierung des Augsburger Domes von 1547/48', *JbVAB* 5 (1971), 95–110.

Ellington, Donna Spivey, *From Sacred Body to Angelic Soul: understanding Mary in late medieval and early modern Europe*. Washington, 2001.

Elsner, P. Salesius, *Die Ursulinen von St Salvator*. Trier, 1913.

Enderle, Wilfried, 'Die Buchdrucker der Reichsstadt Köln und die katholische Publizistik zwischen 1555 und 1648', in *Köln als Kommunikationszentrum: Studien zur frühneuzeitlichen Stadtgeschichte*, ed. Georg Mölich and Gerd Schwerhoff, pp. 167–82. Cologne, 1999.

'Die katholischen Reichsstädte im Zeitalter der Reformation und der Konfessionsbildung', *Zeitschrift der Savigny-Stiftung für Rechtsgeschichte. Kanonistische Abteilung* 75 (1989), 228–69.

Enggass, Robert, and Jonathan Brown, *Italy and Spain 1600–1750: sources and documents*. Sources and Documents in the History of Art. Englewood Cliffs, NJ, 1970.

Ennen, L., *Geschichte der Stadt Köln*. 5 vols. Cologne, 1863–80.

Erzbischöfliches Diözesanmuseum Köln, *500 Jahre Rosenkranz: Köln 1475–1975*. Cologne, 1975.

Essenwein, Adolf, *Der Bildschmuck der Liebfrauenkirche zu Nürnberg*. Nuremberg, 1881.

Evans, R. J. W., *The Making of the Habsburg Monarchy, 1500–1700*. Oxford, 1979.

Fisher, Alexander J., *Music and Religious Identity in Counter-Reformation Augsburg, 1580–1630*. St Andrews Studies in Reformation History. Aldershot, 2004.

Foerster, Hans, *Reformbestrebungen Adolfs III. von Schaumburg (1547–56) in der Kölner Kirchenprovinz*. Reformationsgeschichtliche Studien und Texte 45/46. Münster, 1925.

Foister, Susan, 'Paintings and other works of art in sixteenth-century English inventories', *The Burlington Magazine* 123, no. 938 (1981), 273–82.

Ford, James Thomas, 'Unter dem Schein der Concordien und Confession: Wolfgang Musculus and the confessional identity of Augsburg, 1531–1548', in *Wolfgang Musculus (1497–1563) und die oberdeutsche Reformation*, ed. Rudolf Dellsperger, Rudolf Freudenberger and Wolfgang Weber, pp. 111–29. Berlin, 1997.

Forster, Marc, *Catholic Revival in the Age of the Baroque: religious identity in southwest Germany, 1550–1750*. Cambridge, 2001.

The Counter-Reformation in the Villages: religion and reform in the bishopric of Speyer, 1560–1720. Ithaca, NY, and London, 1992.

'With and without confessionalization: varieties of early modern German Catholicism', *Journal of Early Modern History* 1 (1997), 315–43.

François, Etienne, *Die unsichtbare Grenze: Protestanten und Katholiken in Augsburg 1648–1806*. Sigmaringen, 1991.

Franz, E., *Nürnberg, Kaiser und Reich: Studien zur reichsstädtischen Außenpolitik*. Munich, 1930.

Franzen, August, *Bischof und Reformation: Erzbischof Hermann von Wied in Köln vor der Entscheidung zwischen Reform und Reformation*. 2nd edn. Münster, 1971.

Freedberg, David, *Iconoclasm and Painting in the Revolt of the Netherlands, 1566–1609*. Outstanding Theses in Fine Arts from British Universities. New York, 1988.

The Power of Images: studies in the history and theory of response. Chicago and London, 1989.

Freitag, Werner, *Volks- und Elitenfrömmigkeit in der frühen Neuzeit: Marienwallfahrten im Fürstbistum Münster*. Paderborn, 1991.

Frese, Annette, *Barocke Titelgraphik am Beispiel der Verlagsstadt Köln (1570–1700)*. Dissertationen zur Kunstgeschichte 31. Cologne and Vienna, 1989.

Friedländer, Max, and Jakob Rosenburg, *Die Gemälde von Lucas Cranach*. Berlin, 1932.

Fritz, Johann Michael, ed. *Die bewahrende Kraft des Luthertums: mittelalterliche Kunstwerke in evangelischen Kirchen*. Regensburg, 1997.

Fuchs, Peter, ed. *Chronik zur Geschichte der Stadt Köln. Band 2: von 1400 bis zur Gegenwart*. 2nd edn. Cologne, 1993.

Garbe, Brigitte, 'Reformmaßnahme und Formen der katholischen Erneuerung in der Erzdiözese Köln (1555–1648)', *JbKGV* 47 (1976), 136–77.
Garside, Charles, *Zwingli and the Arts*. New Haven, 1966.
Gebessler, August, *Stadt und Landkreis Dinkelsbühl*. Bayerische Kunstdenkmale 15. Munich, 1962.
Germanisches Nationalmuseum, ed. *Spiegel der Seligkeit: Privates Bild und Frömmigkeit im Spätmittelalter*. Nuremberg, 2000.
ed. *Veit Stoß in Nürnberg: Werke des Meisters und seiner Schule in Nürnberg und Umgebung*. Munich, 1983.
Germanisches Nationalmuseum, Nürnberg (Kurt Löcher), ed. *Die Gemälde des 16. Jahrhunderts*. Stuttgart, 1997.
Germann, W., *D. Johann Forster der Hennebergische Reformator*. Meiningen, 1894.
Glaser, Herbert, ed. *Wittelsbach und Bayern*. 6 vols. Munich, 1980.
Glüber, Wolfgang, '"Die Judengaßen thet man zerstören / der hymelkünigin zu eren". Synagogenzerstörung und Marienkirchenbau', in *Maria – Tochter Sion? Mariologie, Marienfrömmigkeit und Judenfeindschaft*, ed. Johannes Heil and Rainer Kampling. Paderborn, 2001.
Goeters, J. F. Gerhard,'Genesis, Formen und Hauptthemen des reformierten Bekenntnisses in Deutschland. Eine Übersicht', in *Die reformierte Konfessionalisierung in Deutschland – das Problem der 'zweiten Reformation'*, ed. H. Schilling, pp. 44–59. Gütersloh, 1986.
'Die Reformation in Kurköln', in *Kurköln. Land unter dem Krummstab: Essays und Dokumente*, ed. Nordrhein-Westfälischen Hauptstaatsarchiv Düsseldorf, pp. 191–4. Kevelaer, 1985.
Gombrich, E. H., *Art and Illusion: a study in the psychology of pictorial representation*. London, 1960.
Gordon, Bruce, *The Swiss Reformation*. Manchester and New York, 2002.
Gössman, E., and D. R. Bauer, eds. *Maria – für alle Frauen oder über alle Frauen?* Freiburg im Breisgau, 1989.
Götz, J. B., *Die religiösen Wirren in der Oberpfalz von 1576 bis 1620*. Reformationsgeschichtliche Studien und Texte 66. Münster in Westfalen, 1937.
Graef, Hilda, *Mary: a history of doctrine and devotion*. 2nd edn, 2 vols. combined. London, 1985.
Graf, Klaus, 'Maria als Stadtpatronin in deutschen Städten des Mittelalters und der frühen Neuzeit', in *Frömmigkeit im Mittelalter: politisch-soziale Kontexte, visuelle Praxis, körperliche Ausdrucksformen*, ed. Klaus Schreiner, pp. 125–54. Munich, 2002.
Graff, P., *Geschichte der Auflösung der alten gottesdienstlichen Formen in der evangelischen Kirche Deutschlands*, vol. 1: *Bis zur Eintritt der Aufklärung und des Rationalismus*. 2nd edn. Göttingen, 1937.
Grimm, Jacob, and Wilhelm Grimm, *Deutsches Wörterbuch*. 16 vols. Leipzig, 1854–1954.
Grosche, Robert, *Der Kölner Altarbau im 17. und 18. Jahrhundert*. Cologne, 1978.
Grote, Ludwig, *Die Tucher: Bildnis einer Patrizierfamilie*. Munich, 1961.
Groten, Manfred, 'In glückseligem Regiment: Beobachtungen zum Verhältnis Obrigkeit–Bürger am Beispiel Kölns im 15. Jahrhundert', *Historisches Jahrbuch* 116 (1996), 303–20.
'Die nächste Generation: Scribners Thesen aus heutiger Sicht', in *Köln als Kommunikationszentrum: Studien zur frühneuzeitlichen Stadtgeschichte*, ed. Georg Mölich and Gerd Schwerhoff, pp. 110–13. Cologne, 1999.
ed. *Beschlüsse des Rates der Stadt Köln: 1320–1550*. 5 vols. Publikationen der Gesellschaft für rheinische Geschichtskunde 45. Düsseldorf, 1990.

Guggisberg, H. R., *Basle in the Sixteenth Century*. St Louis, MO, 1982.
Guldan, Ernst, *Eva und Maria: eine Antithese als Bildmotiv*. Graz, 1966.
Gümbel, Albert, ed. *Das Mesnerpflichtbuch von St Lorenz in Nürnberg vom Jahre 1493*. Einzelarbeiten aus der Kirchengeschichte Bayerns 8. Munich, 1928.
Gussone, Nikolaus, 'Zur Krönung von Bildern. Heutige Praxis und neuzeitlicher Ritus', *Jahrbuch für Volkskunde*, n.s. 10 (1987), 151–64.
Haas, Walter, 'Die mittelalterliche Altaranordnung in der Nürnberger Lorenzkirche', in *500 Jahre Hallenchor St Lorenz zu Nürnberg 1477–1977*, ed. Herbert Bauer, Gerhard Hirschmann and Georg Stolz, pp. 63–108. Nuremberg, 1977.
Habermas, Rebekka, 'Die Sorge um das Kind: die Sorge der Frauen und Männer. Mirakelerzählungen im 16. Jahrhundert', in *Ordnung und Lust: Bilder von Liebe, Ehe und Sexualität im Spätmittelalter und Früher Neuzeit*, ed. Hans-Jürgen Bachorski, pp. 165–83. Trier, 1991.
Habsburg, Max von. 'The devotional life: Catholic and Protestant translations of Thomas à Kempis' Imitatio Christi, c.1420–c.1620', unpublished PhD thesis, University of St Andrews, 2001.
Hagen, Bernd von, and Angelika Wegener-Hüssen, *Stadt Augsburg*. Denkmäler in Bayern 7/83. Munich, 1994.
Hahn, Andreas, 'Die St.-Anna-Kirche in Augsburg', in *'. . . wider Laster und Sünde'. Augsburgs Weg in der Reformation. Katalog zur Ausstellung in St Anna, Augsburg, 26. April bis 10. August 1997*, ed. Josef Kirmeier, Wolfgang Jahn and Evamaria Brockhoff, pp. 71–82. Cologne, 1997.
Hale, Rosemary, 'Imitatio Mariae: motherhood motifs in devotional memoirs', *Mystics Quarterly* 16, no. 4 (1990), 193–203.
Halkin, Léon-E., *Erasmus: a critical biography*, trans. John Tonkin. Oxford, 1994.
'La mariologie d'Erasme', *Archiv für Reformationsgeschichte* 68 (1977), 32–55.
Hamburger Kunsthalle (Werner Hofmann), ed. *Luther und die Folgen für die Kunst*. Munich and Hamburg, 1983.
Hampe, T., 'Kunstfreunde im alten Nürnberg und ihre Sammlungen', *MVGSN* 16 (1904), 57–124.
Die Nürnberger Malefizbücher als Quellen der reichsstädtischen Sittengeschichte vom 14. bis zum 18. Jahrhundert. Neujahrsblätter 17. Bamberg, 1927.
Harper, J., *The Forms and Orders of Western Liturgy from the Tenth to the Eighteenth Century: a historical introduction and guide for students and musicians*. Oxford, 1991.
Hasse, Max, 'Maria und die Heiligen im protestantischen Lübeck', *Nordelbingen: Beiträge zur Kunst- und Kulturgeschichte* 34 (1965), 72–81.
Heal, Bridget. 'A woman like any other? Images of the Virgin Mary and Marian devotion in Nuremberg, Augsburg and Cologne, c.1500–1600', unpublished PhD thesis, University of London, 2001.
Hecht, Christian, *Katholischen Bildertheologie im Zeitalter von Gegenreformation und Barock*. Berlin, 1997.
Hegel, Eduard, *Das Erzbistum Köln zwischen Barock und Aufklärung. Geschichte des Erzbistums Köln*, vol. 4. Cologne, 1979.
'Prozessionen und Wallfahrten im alten Erzbistum Köln im Zeitalter des Barock und der Aufklärung', *Zeitschrift des Aachener Geschichtsvereins* 84/5 (1977/8), 301–19.
Heming, Carol Piper, *Protestants and the Cult of the Saints in German-Speaking Europe, 1517–31*. Sixteenth Century Essays and Studies 65. Kirksville, MO, 2003.
Herborn, W., 'Fast-, Fest- und Feiertage im Köln des 16. Jahrhunderts', *Rheinisches Jahrbuch für Volkskunde* 25 (1985), 27–61.

'Die Protestanten in Schilderung und Urteil des Kölner Chronisten Hermann von Weinsberg', in *Niederland und Nordwestdeutschland*, ed. W. Ehbrecht and H. Schilling, pp. 136–53. Cologne, 1983.

Herold, M., *Alt-Nürnberg in seinen Gottesdiensten: ein Beitrag zur Geschichte der Sitte und des Kultus*. Gütersloh, 1890.

Herrmann, Barbara, *Johann Hulsman: ein Kölner Maler des 17. Jahrhunderts*. Europäische Hochschulschriften 314. Frankfurt am Main, 1998.

Herzig, Arno, *Der Zwang zum wahren Glauben: Rekatholisierung vom 16. bis zum 18. Jahrhundert*. Göttingen, 2000.

Hesse, H. K., *Adolf Clarenbach: ein Beitrag zur Geschichte des Evangeliums im westen Deutschland*. Theologische Arbeiten aus dem wissenschaftlichen Prediger-Verein der Rheinprovinz, n.s. 25. Neuwied am Rhein, 1929.

Hilger, Hans Peter, 'Die ehemalige Jesuitenkirche St. Mariae Himmelfahrt in Köln', in *Die Jesuitenkirche St Mariae Himmelfahrt in Köln: Dokumentation und Beiträge zum Abschluss ihrer Wiederherstellung 1980*, pp. 9–30. Düsseldorf, 1982.

Hirschmann, Gerhard, 'The second Nürnberg church visitation', in *The Social History of the Reformation*, ed. L. P. Buck and J. W. Zophy, pp. 355–80. Columbus, OH, 1972.

Hoeynck, F. A., *Geschichte der kirchlichen Liturgie des Bisthums Augsburg*. Augsburg, 1889.

Hoffmann, Carl A., 'Konfessionell motivierte und gewandelte Konflikte in der zweiten Hälfte des 16. Jahrhunderts – Versuch eines mentalitätsgeschichtlichen Ansatzes am Beispiel der bikonfessionellen Reichsstadt Augsburg', in *Konfessionalisierung und Region*, ed. Peer Friess and Rolf Kiessling, pp. 99–120. Constance, 1999.

Hsia, R. Po-Chia, *Social Discipline in the Reformation: central Europe 1550–1750*. London and New York, 1989.

Hubensteiner, Benno, *Vom Geist des Barock: Kultur und Frömmigkeit im alten Bayern*. Munich, 1978.

Hutchison, Jane Campbell, *Albrecht Dürer: a biography*. Princeton, NJ, 1990.

Hütl, Ludwig, *Marianische Wallfahrten im süddeutsch-österreichischen Raum*. Kölner Veröffentlichungen zur Religionsgeschichte 6. Cologne and Vienna, 1985.

Immenkötter, Herbert, 'Glaubensbilder der Renaissance in Deutschland', in *Das 16. Jahrhundert: europäische Renaissance*, ed. Hildegard Kuester, pp. 167–79. Regensburg, 1995.

'Kirche zwischen Reformation und Parität', in *Geschichte der Stadt Augsburg: 2000 Jahre von der Römerzeit bis zur Gegenwart*, ed. G. Gottlieb *et al.*, pp. 391–412. Stuttgart, 1984.

Isenmann, Eberhard, 'Die Reichsstadt in der Frühen Neuzeit', in *Köln als Kommunikationszentrum: Studien zur frühneuzeitlichen Stadtgeschichte*, ed. Georg Mölich and Gerd Schwerhoff, pp. 39–87. Cologne, 1999.

Janssen, Wilhelm, *Das Erzbistum Köln im späten Mittelalter*, vol. 2, part II. Cologne, 2003.

Die Jesuitenkirche St Mariae Himmelfahrt in Köln: Dokumentation und Beiträge zum Abschluss ihrer Wiederherstellung 1980. Beiträge zu den Bau- und Kunstdenkmälern im Rheinland. Düsseldorf, 1982.

Johnson, T., 'The recatholicization of the Upper Palatinate', unpublished PhD thesis, University of Cambridge, 1992.

'"Victoria a Deo missa?" Living saints on the battlefields of the central European Counter-Reformation', in *Confessional Sanctity (c.1500–c.1800)*, ed. Jürgen Beyer, Albrecht Burkardt, Fred van Lieburg and Marc Wingens, pp. 319–35. Mainz, 2003.

Jongh, Eddy de, and Ger Luijten, *Mirror of Everyday Life: Genreprints in the Netherlands 1550–1700*, trans. Michael Hoyle. Amsterdam, 1997.

Karant-Nunn, Susan, 'Kinder, Küche, Kirche: social ideology in the sermons of Johannes Mathesius', in *Germania Illustrata: essays on early modern Germany presented to Gerald Strauss*, ed. Andrew C. Fix and Susan Karant-Nunn, pp. 121–40. Kirksville, MO, 1992.

The Reformation of Ritual: an interpretation of early modern Germany. London and New York, 1997.

Kaufmann, Thomas, 'Die Bilderfrage im frühneuzeitlichen Luthertum', in *Macht und Ohnmacht der Bilder: Reformatorischen Bildersturm im Kontext der europäischen Geschichte*, ed. Peter Blickle, André Holenstein, Heinrich Richard Schmidt and Franz-Josef Sladeczek, pp. 407–54. Munich, 2002.

Kettenmeyer, J. B., *Die Anfänge der marianischen Sodalität in Köln*. Katholisches Leben und Kämpfen im Zeitalter der Glaubensspaltung 2. Münster, 1928.

Keussen, H., *Topographie der Stadt Köln im Mittelalter*. 2 vols. Bonn, 1910.

Kiessling, R., 'Augsburg in der Reformationszeit', in *'. . . wider Laster und Sünde', Augsburgs Weg in der Reformation. Katalog zur Ausstellung in St Anna, Augsburg, 26. April bis 10. August 1997*, ed. Josef Kirmeier, Wolfgang Jahn and Evamaria Brockhoff, pp. 17–43. Cologne, 1997.

Bürgerliche Gesellschaft und Kirche in Augsburg im Spätmittelalter: ein Beitrag zur Strukturanalyse der oberdeutschen Reichsstadt. Augsburg, 1971.

Kirgus, Isabelle, *Renaissance in Köln: Architektur und Ausstattung 1520–1620*. Sigurd Greven-Studien 3. Bonn, 2000.

Kirmeier, Josef, Wolfgang Jahn, and Evamaria Brockhoff, eds. *'. . . wider Laster und Sünde'. Augsburgs Weg in der Reformation. Katalog zur Ausstellung in St Anna, Augsburg, 26. April bis 10. August 1997*. Cologne, 1997.

Kittelson, James, 'Successes and failures in the German Reformation', *Archiv für Reformationsgeschichte* 73 (1982), 153–75.

Klaus, B., *Veit Dietrich. Leben und Werk*. Einzelarbeiten aus der Kirchengeschichte Bayerns 32. Nuremberg, 1958.

Kleinehagenbrock, Frank, 'Würzburg als gegenreformatorisches Zentrum', *Würzburger Diözesan-Geschichtsblätter* 67 (2005), 63–77.

Klersch, Joseph, *Volkstum und Volksleben in Köln*. Cologne, 1979.

Knötel, Paul, *Kirchliche Bilderkunde Schlesiens*. Glatz, 1929.

Koepplin, Dieter, 'Reformatorische Kunst aus der zweiten Hälfte des 16. Jahrhunderts', in *Die lutherische Konfessionalisierung in Deutschland*, ed. H.-C. Rublack, pp. 495–544. Gütersloh, 1992.

Koepplin, Dieter, and Tilman Falk, eds. *Lucas Cranach: Gemälde, Zeichnungen, Druckgraphik. Ausstellung im Kunstmuseum. Basle, 15. Juni–8. Sept. 1974*. 2 vols. Basle and Stuttgart, 1974.

Koerner, Joseph Leo, *The Reformation of the Image*. London, 2004.

Kohlberger, Alexandra, *Maria Hilf auf dem Lechfeld. 400 Jahre Wallfahrt*. Augsburg, 2003.

Köhler, Mathilde, *Maria Ward: ein Frauenschicksal des 17. Jahrhunderts*. Munich, 1989.

Kolb, Robert, *Confessing the Faith: reformers define the church, 1530–1580*. St Louis, 1991.

'Festivals of the saints in late Reformation Lutheran preaching', *The Historian: a Journal of History* 52 (1990), 613–26.

For All the Saints: Changing Perceptions of Martyrdom and Sainthood in the Lutheran Reformation. Macon, GA, 1987.

Kosel, Karl, 'Ein vergessener Altar im Augsburger Dom und sein Gemälde', *JbVAB* 21 (1987), 117–22.

Kraus, Andreas, *Maximilian I. Bayerns großer Kurfürst*. Graz etc., 1990.

Kreitzer, Beth, 'Reforming Mary: changing images of the Virgin Mary in Lutheran sermons of the sixteenth century', unpublished PhD thesis, Duke University, 1999.

Reforming Mary: changing images of the Virgin Mary in Lutheran sermons of the sixteenth century. Oxford Studies in Historical Theology. Oxford and New York, 2004.

Kroon, Marijn de, 'Bucer und die Kölner Reformation', in *Martin Bucer and Sixteenth Century Europe. Actes du colloque de Strasbourg (28–31 août 1991)*, ed. Christian Krieger and Marc Lienhard, pp. 493–506. Leiden, 1993.

Kuckhoff, Joseph, 'Das erste Jahrhundert des Jesuitenschauspiels am Tricoronatum in Köln', *Jahrbuch des kölnischen Geschichtsvereins e.V.* 10 (1928), 1–49.

Kulenkampff, Angela, 'Die Marienbruderschaft von St. Maria im Kapitol und ihre Bedeutung für das kirchliche Leben in vortridentinischer Zeit (ca. 1350–1634)', *JbKGV* 60 (1989), 1–29.

Lansemann, Robert, *Die Heiligentage besonders die Marien-, Apostel-, und Engeltage in der Reformationszeit*. Göttingen, 1939.

Legner, Anton, 'Reliquienpräsenz und Wanddekoration', in *Die Jesuitenkirche St Mariae Himmelfahrt in Köln: Dokumentation und Beiträge zum Abschluss ihrer Wiederherstellung 1980*, pp. 269–96. Cologne, 1982.

Lenk, Leonhard, *Augsburger Bürgertum im Späthumanismus und Frühbarock (1580–1700)*. Augsburg, 1968.

Lieb, Norbert, *Die Fugger und die Kunst im Zeitalter der hohen Renaissance*. Munich, 1958.

Octavian Secundus Fugger (1549–1600) und die Kunst. Tübingen, 1980.

Lieball, Josef, *Martin Luthers Madonnenbild*. Stein am Rhein, 1981.

Lieske, Reinhard, *Protestantische Frömmigkeit im Spiegel der kirchlichen Kunst des Herzogtums Württemberg*. Munich and Berlin, 1973.

Lochner, G. W. K., *Die noch vorhandenen Abzeichen Nürnberger Häuser*. Nuremberg, 1855.

Loetz, Francisca, *Mit Gott handeln: von den Zürcher Gotteslästern der frühen Neuzeit zu einer Kulturgeschichte des Religiösen*. Veröffentlichungen des Max-Planck-Instituts für Geschichte 177. Göttingen, 2002.

Lustenberger, Suzanne, *Martin Schaffner, Maler zu Ulm*. Zug, 1961.

MacCulloch, Diarmaid, 'Mary and sixteenth-century Protestants', in *The Church and Mary*, ed. R. N. Swanson, pp. 191–217. Woodbridge and Rochester, 2004.

Reformation: Europe's house divided, 1490–1700. London, 2003.

Mack, Phyllis, *Visionary Women: ecstatic prophecy in seventeenth-century England*. Berkeley, Los Angeles and Oxford, 1992.

Mader, Feliz, *Stadt Amberg*. Die Kunstdenkmäler des Königreichs Bayern 2. Regierungsbezirk Oberpfalz und Regensburg 16. Munich, 1909.

Mai, Paul, ed., *Schatzstücke der Münchener Peterskirche*. Munich, 1985.

Mallinckrodt, Rebekka von, *Struktur und kollektiver Eigensinn: Kölner Laienbruderschaften im Zeitalter der Konfessionalisierung*. Veröffentlichungen des Max-Planck-Instituts für Geschichte 209. Göttingen, 2005.

Matheson, Peter, *Argula von Grumbach: a woman's voice in the Reformation*. Edinburgh, 1995.

Matsche, Franz, 'Gegenreformatorische Architekturpolitik: Casa-Santa-Kopien und Habsburger Loreto-Kult nach 1620', *Jahrbuch für Volkskunde*, n.s. 1 (1978), 81–118.

McKee, Elsie Anne, *Katharina Schütz Zell*, vol. 1: *The Life and Thought of a Sixteenth-Century Reformer*. Studies in Medieval and Reformation Thought 69. Leiden, 1999.

Meinhold, Peter, 'Die Marienverehrung im Verständnis der Reformatoren des 16. Jahrhunderts', *Saeculum* 32 (1981), 43–58.

Meissner, Karl-Heinz, 'Zwischen Zerstörung und Umdeutung: Kunst-Schicksale in den Kirchen der lutherischen Reformation', *Kunst und Kirche* 4193 (1993), 278–80.

Merkl, Franz Josef, 'Kunst und Konfessionalisierung – das Herzogtum Pfalz-Neuburg 1542–1650', *JbVAB* 32 (1998), 188–211.

Metropolitan Museum of Art and Germanisches Nationalmuseum, eds. *Gothic and Renaissance Art in Nuremberg, 1300–1550*. New York and Munich, 1986.

Metzner, J., 'Stephan Schulers Saalbuch der Frauenkirche in Nürnberg', in *Zweiunddreissigster Bericht über das Wirken und den Stand des historischen Vereins zu Bamberg im Jahre 1869*, pp. 1–113. Bamberg, 1869.

Michalski, S., 'Die Ausbreitung des reformatorischen Bildersturms 1521–1537', in *Bildersturm: Wahnsinn oder Gottes Wille?*, ed. Cecile Dupeux, Peter Jezler and Jean Wirth, pp. 46–51. Munich, 2000.

'Inscriptions in Protestant paintings and in Protestant churches', in *Ars Ecclesiastica: the church as a context for visual arts*, pp. 34–47. Helsinki, 1996.

The Reformation and the Visual Arts. London, 1993.

Miles, M. R., *Image as Insight: visual understanding in western Christianity and secular culture*. Boston, 1985.

Militzer, Klaus, 'Collen eyn kroyn boven allen steden schoyn: zum Selbstverständnis einer Stadt', *CR* 1 (1986), 15–32.

Ursachen und Folgen der innerstädtischen Auseinandersetzung in Köln in der zweiten Hälfte des 14. Jahrhunderts. Cologne, 1980.

Minty, J. M., '*Judengasse* to Christian quarter: the phenomenon of the converted synagogue in the late medieval and early modern Holy Roman Empire', in *Popular Religion in Germany and Central Europe, 1400–1800*, ed. Robert W. Scribner and Trevor Johnson, pp. 58–86. London, 1996.

Molitor, Hansgeorg, 'Frömmigkeit im Spätmittelalter und früher Neuzeit als historisch-methodisches Problem', in *Festgabe für Ernst Walter Zeeden zum 60. Geburtstag am 14. Mai 1976*, ed. Horst Rabe, Hansgeorg Molitor and H.-C. Rublack, pp. 1–20. Münster, 1976.

'Gegenreformation und kirchliche Erneuerung im niederen Erzstift Köln zwischen 1583 und 1688', in *Kurköln. Land unter dem Krummstab: Essays und Dokumente*, ed. Nordrhein-Westfälischen Hauptstaatsarchiv Düsseldorf, pp. 199–214. Kevelaer, 1985.

'Die untridentinische Reform: Anfänge katholischer Erneuerung in der Reichskirche', in *Ecclesia Militans: Studien zur Konzilien- und Reformationsgeschichte; Remigius Bäumer zum 70. Geburtstag gewidmet*, ed. Walter Brandmüller, Herbert Immenkötter and Erwin Iserloh, pp. 399–431. Paderborn, 1988.

Moore, Cornelia Niekus, *The Maiden's Mirror: reading material for German girls in the sixteenth and seventeenth centuries*. Wolfenbütteler Forschungen 36. Wiesbaden, 1987.

Morrall, Andrew, *Jörg Breu the Elder: art, culture, and belief in Reformation Augsburg*. Histories of Vision. Aldershot, 2001.

Muir, Edward, *Ritual in Early Modern Europe.* New Approaches to European History. Cambridge, 1997.

Muller, Frank, 'Der Bildersturm in Strassburg 1524–1530', in *Bildersturm. Wahnsinn oder Gottes Wille?*, ed. Cecile Dupeux, Peter Jezler and Jean Wirth, pp. 84–9. Munich, 2000.

Müller, G., 'Protestant veneration of Mary: Luther's interpretation of the Magnificat', in *Humanism and Reform: the church in Europe, England, and Scotland, 1400–1643. Essays in honour of James K. Cameron*, ed. James Kirk, pp. 99–111. Oxford, 1991.

Muller, Jeffrey M., 'Private collections in the Spanish Netherlands: ownership and display of paintings in domestic interiors', in *The Age of Rubens*, ed. Peter C. Sutton, pp. 195–206. Boston, 1993.

Müller, Michael G., 'Zur Frage der zweiten Reformation in Danzig, Elbig und Thorn', in *Die reformierte Konfessionalisierung in Deutschland – das Problem der 'Zweiten Reformation'*, ed. H. Schilling, pp. 251–65. Gütersloh, 1986.

Müller, Nikolaus, *Der Dom zu Berlin*. Berlin, 1906.

Müller, Rainer A., 'De Christiani Principis Officio – Religion und katholische Konfession in ausgewählten Fürstenspiegeln der Frühen Neuzeit', in *Die katholische Konfessionalisierung: Wissenschaftliches Symposion der Gesellschaft zur Herausgabe des Corpus Catholicorum und des Vereins für Reformationsgeschichte 1993*, ed. Wolfgang Reinhard and Heinz Schilling, pp. 332–47. Gütersloh, 1995.

Müller, Siegfried, 'Repräsentationen des Luthertums – Disziplinierung und konfessionelle Kultur in Bildern', *Zeitschrift für historische Forschung* 29 (2002), 217–55.

Mullett, Michael A., *The Catholic Reformation*. London and New York, 1999.

Münch, Paul, 'Changing German perceptions of the historical role of Albrecht Dürer', in *Dürer and his Culture*, ed. Dagmar Eichberger and Charles Zika, pp. 181–99. Cambridge, 1998.

Neff, Amy, 'The Pain of Compassion: Mary's Labor at the Foot of the Cross', *Art Bulletin* 80, no. 2 (1998), 254–73.

Nestler, Martin, *Ulm. Geschichte einer Stadt*. Erfurt, 2003.

Netzer, Susanne, *Johann Matthias Kager: Stadtmaler von Augsburg (1575–1634)*. Neue Schriftenreihe des Stadtarchivs München 113. Munich, 1980.

Nischan, Bodo, *Lutherans and Calvinists in the Age of Confessionalization*. Aldershot, 1999.

Prince, People, and Confession: the second Reformation in Brandenburg. Philadelphia, 1994.

Oberman, Heiko A., *The Roots of Anti-Semitism in the Age of Renaissance and Reformation*, trans. James I. Porter. Philadelphia, 1984.

'The Virgin Mary in evangelical perspective', in *The Impact of the Reformation*, ed. Heiko A. Oberman, pp. 225–52. Edinburgh, 1994.

Oettinger, Rebecca Wagner, *Music as Propaganda in the German Reformation*. St Andrews Studies in Reformation History. Aldershot, 2001.

O'Malley, John W., *The First Jesuits*. Cambridge, MA, 1993.

ed. *The Jesuits: cultures, sciences and the arts 1540–1773*. Toronto, 1999.

Opitz, Claudia, 'Mutterschaft und Vaterschaft im 14. und 15. Jahrhundert', in *Frauengeschichte – Geschlechtergeschichte*, ed. Karin Hausen and Heide Wunder. Frankfurt and New York, 1992.

Opitz, Claudia, Hedwig Röckelein, Gabriela Signori and Guy Marchal, eds. *Maria in der Welt. Marienverehrung im Kontext der Sozialgeschichte 10.–18. Jahrhundert*. Zurich, 1993.

Opitz, Marion, 'Das Kölner Gnadenbild "Maria vom Frieden" im Spiegel des kleinen Andachtsbildes', *Kölner Museums-Bulletin. Berichte und Forschungen aus den Museen der Stadt Köln* 1 (2000), 10–25.

Ostrow, Steven F., *Art and Spirituality in Counter-Reformation Rome: the Sistine and Pauline Chapels in S. Maria Maggiore*. Cambridge, 1996.

Pabel, Hilmar M., *Conversing with God: prayer in Erasmus' pastoral writings*. Toronto, 1997.

Pelikan, Jaroslav, *Mary Through the Centuries: her place in the history of culture*. New Haven and London, 1996.

Obedient Rebels: Catholic substance and Protestant principle in Luther's Reformation. London, 1964.

Peters, Christine, *Patterns of Piety: women, gender and religion in late medieval and Reformation England*. Cambridge, 2003.

Peters, F. J., *Beiträge zur Geschichte der Kölnischen Messliturgie: Untersuchungen über die gedruckten Missalien des Erzbistums Köln*. Colonia Sacra 2. Cologne, 1951.

Pettegree, Andrew, *Reformation and the Culture of Persuasion*. Cambridge, 2005.

Pfeiffer, Gerhard, *Nürnberg – Geschichte einer europäischen Stadt*. Munich, 1971.

'Nürnberg und das Augsburger Bekenntnis 1530–1561', *Zeitschrift für bayerische Kirchengeschichte* 49 (1980), 2–19.

Planer, Oskar, *Verzeichnis der Gustav Adolf Sammlung mit besonderer Rücksicht auf die Schlacht am 6./16. November 1632*. Leipzig, 1916.

Pohl, Horst, ed. *Willibald Imhoff, Enkel und Erbe Willibald Pirckheimers*. Nuremberg, 1992.

Pörtner, Regina, *The Counter-Reformation in Central Europe. Styria 1580–1630*. Oxford Historical Monographs. Oxford, 2001.

Pötzl, Walter, *Loreto – Madonna und Heiliges Haus: die Wallfahrt auf dem Kobel. Ein Beitrag zur europäischen Kult- und Kulturgeschichte*. Beiträge zur Heimatkunde des Landkreises Augsburg 15. Augsburg, 2000.

'Loreto in Bayern', *Jahrbuch für Volkskunde* 2 (1979), 187–218.

Rabb, Theodore K., *The Struggle for Stability in Early Modern Europe*. New York, 1975.

Rajkay, Barbara, 'Die Bevölkerungsentwicklung von 1500 bis 1648', in *Geschichte der Stadt Augsburg: 2000 Jahre von der Römerzeit bis zur Gegenwart*, ed. G. Gottlieb *et al.* Stuttgart, 1984.

Rasmussen, Jörg, 'Bildersturm und Restauration', in *Welt im Umbruch: Augsburg zwischen Renaissance und Barock*, ed. Städtische Kunstsammlung Augsburg and Zentralinstitut für Kunstgeschichte Munich, pp. 95–114. Augsburg, 1981.

'Der Englische Gruß', in *Veit Stoß in Nürnberg: Werke des Meisters und seiner Schule in Nürnberg und Umgebung*, ed. Germanisches Nationalmuseum, pp. 202–4. Munich, 1983.

Reinhard, Wolfgang, 'Katholische Reform und Gegenreformation in der Kölner Nuntiatur 1584–1621', *Römische Quartalschrift für christliche Altertumskunde und Kirchengeschichte* 66 (1971), 8–65.

'Was ist katholische Konfessionalisierung?', in *Die katholische Konfessionalisierung: wissenschaftliches Symposium der Gesellschaft zur Herausgabe des Corpus Catholicorum und des Vereins für Reformationsgeschichte 1993*, ed. Wolfgang Reinhard and Heinz Schilling, pp. 419–52. Gütersloh, 1995.

ed. *Augsburger Eliten des 16. Jahrhunderts: Prosopographie wirtschaftlicher und politischer Führungsgruppen 1500–1620*. Berlin, 1996.

Reininghaus, Wilfried, *Die Entstehung der Gesellengilden im Spätmittelalter*. Wiesbaden, 1981.

Renger, Konrad, *Peter Paul Rubens: Altäre für Bayern*. Munich, 1991.

Renner, P., 'Spätmittelalterliche Klosterpredigten aus Nürnberg', *Archiv für Kulturgeschichte* 41 (1959), 201–17.

Repgen, Konrad, 'Der Bischof zwischen Reformation, katholischer Reform und Konfessionsbildung (1515–1650)', in *Der Bischof in seiner Zeit: Bischofstypus und Bischofsideal im Spiegel der Kölner Kirche*, ed. P. Berglar, pp. 245–314. Cologne, 1986.

Röckelein, Hedwig, 'Marienverehrung und Judenfeindlichkeit in Mittelalter und früher Neuzeit', in *Maria in der Welt: Marienverehrung im Kontext der Sozialgeschichte*, ed. Claudia Opitz, Hedwig Röckelein, G. Signori and G. P. Marchal, pp. 279–307. Zurich, 1993.

ed. *Maria, Abbild oder Vorbild: zur Sozialgeschichte mittelalterlicher Marienverehrung*. Tübingen, 1990.

Roeck, Bernd, *Als wollt die Welt schier brechen: eine Stadt im Zeitalter des Dreißigjährigen Krieges*. Munich, 1991.

Eine Stadt in Krieg und Frieden: Studien zur Geschichte der Reichsstadt Augsburg zwischen Kalenderstreit und Parität. 2 vols. Göttingen, 1989.

Rohling, Ludwig, *Die Kunstdenkmäler der Stadt Flensburg*. Munich and Berlin, 1955.

Rolle, Theodor, 'Die Anfänge der marianischen Kongregationen in Augsburg', *JbVAB* 23 (1989), 27–68.

Heiligkeitsstreben und Apostolat: Geschichte der Marianischen Kongregation am Jesuitenkolleg St Salvator und am Gymnasium der Benediktiner bei St Stephan in Augsburg 1589–1989. Augsburg, 1989.

Roper, Lyndal, 'Gender and the Reformation', *Archiv für Reformationsgeschichte* 29 (2001), 290–302.

The Holy Household: women and morals in Reformation Augsburg. 2nd edn. Oxford, 1991.

Oedipus and the Devil: witchcraft, sexuality and religion in early modern Europe. London and New York, 1994.

Rosen, Wolfgang, 'Rat, Bürger und geistliche Institutionen: zur Amortisationsgesetzgebung im frühneuzeitlichen Köln', in *Köln als Kommunikationszentrum: Studien zur frühneuzeitlichen Stadtgeschichte*, ed. Georg Mölich and Gerd Schwerhoff, pp. 286–320. Cologne, 1999.

Roth, Elisabeth, *Volkskultur in Franken*, vol. 1: *Kult und Kunst*. Bamberg and Würzburg, 1990.

'Wallfahrten zu evangelischen Landkirchen in Franken', *Jahrbuch für Volkskunde*, n.s. 2 (1979), 135–60.

Roth, Friedrich, *Augsburgs Reformationsgeschichte*. 4 vols. Munich, 1901–11.

Rotscheidt, W., ed. *Warum eine Reformation im 'hilligen Cöln'? Eine Antwort Melanchthons aus dem Jahre 1543*. Cologne, 1904.

Rott, H., 'Kirchen- und Bildersturm bei der Einführung der Reformation in der Pfalz', *Neues Archiv für die Geschichte der Stadt Heidelberg und der rheinischen Pfalz* 6, no. 4 (1905), 229–54.

Rublack, Ulinka, 'Female spirituality and the Infant Jesus in Late Medieval Dominican Convents', in *Popular Religion in Germany and Central Europe, 1400–1800*, ed. Robert W. Scribner and T. Johnson, pp. 16–37. Basingstoke and London, 1996.

'Pregnancy, childbirth and the female body in early modern Germany', *Past & Present* 150 (1996), 84–110.

Rummel, Peter, 'Die Augsburger Diözesansynoden: historischer Überblick', *JbVAB* 20 (1986), 9–69.

'Petrus Canisius und Otto Kardinal Truchsess von Waldburg', in *Petrus Canisius – Reformer der Kirche. Festschrift zum 400. Todestag des zweiten Apostels Deutschlands*, ed. Julius Oswald and Peter Rummel, *JbVAB* 30 (1996), 41–66.

Sabean, David, *Power in the Blood: popular culture and village discourse in early modern Germany*. Cambridge, 1984.

Sandner, Ingo, *Spätgotische Tafelmalerei in Sachsen*. Dresden and Basle, 1993.

Sargent, Steven, 'Miracle books and pilgrimage shrines in late medieval Bavaria', *Historical Reflections* 13 (1986), 455–71.

Schad, Martha, *Die Frauen des Hauses Fugger von der Lilie (15.–17. Jahrhundert). Augsburg – Ortenburg – Trient*. Tübingen, 1989.

Schäfke, Werner, ed. *Die Kölner Kartause um 1500. Aufsatzband*. Cologne, 1991.

Scharfe, Martin, 'Der Heilige in der protestantische Volksfrömmigkeit', *Hessische Blätter für Volkskunde* 60 (1969), 93–106.

Schawe, Martin, *Staatsgalerie Augsburg: altdeutsche Malerei in der Katharinenkirche*. Munich, n.d.

Schemmel, Bernhard, *Figuren und Reliefs an Haus und Hof in Franken*. Würzburg, 1978.

Schiller, Gertrud, *Ikonographie der christlichen Kunst*. 8 vols. Gütersloh, 1966–90.

Schiller, W., *Die St Annakirche in Augsburg: ein Beitrag zur Augsburger Kirchengeschichte*. Augsburg, 1938.

Schilling, Heinz, *Niederländische Exulanten im 16. Jahrhundert: ihre Stellung im Sozialgefüge und im religiösen Leben deutscher und englischer Städte*. Schriften des Vereins für Reformationsgeschichte 187. Gütersloh, 1972.

Religion, Political Culture and the Emergence of Early Modern Society: essays in German and Dutch history. Leiden, 1992.

Schimmelpfennig, Reintraud, *Die Geschichte der Marienverehrung im deutschen Protestantismus*. Paderborn, 1952.

Schleif, Corine, *Donatio et Memoria: Stifter, Stiftungen und Motivationen an Beispielen aus der Lorenzkirche in Nürnberg*. Munich, 1990.

Schlemmer, K., *Gottesdienst und Frömmigkeit in der Reichsstadt Nürnberg am Vorabend der Reformation*. Würzburg, 1980.

Schlichtenmaier, Harry, 'Studien zum Werk Hans Rottenhammers des Älteren (1564–1625) Maler und Zeichner mit Werkkatalog', PhD dissertation, Eberhard-Karls-Universität, 1988.

Schmid, Wolfgang, *Stifter und Auftraggeber im spätmittelalterlichen Köln*. Cologne, 1994.

Schmidt, Anja, *Augsburger Ansichten: die Darstellung der Stadt in der Druckgraphik des 15. bis 18. Jahrhunderts*. Schwäbische Geschichtsquellen und Forschungen 19. Augsburg, 2000.

Schmidt, Heinrich Richard, *Reichsstädte, Reich und Reformation: korporative Religionspolitik 1521–1529/30*. Veröffentlichungen des Instituts für Europäische Geschichte Mainz 122. Stuttgart, 1986.

Schöffler, H., *Deutsches Geistesleben zwischen Reformation und Aufklärung*. 2nd edn. Frankfurt am Main, 1956.

Schöller, Bernadette, *Kölner Druckgraphik der Gegenreformation: ein Beitrag zur Geschichte religiöser Bildpropaganda zur Zeit der Glaubenskämpfe mit einem Katalog der Einblattdrucke des Verlages Johann Bussenmacher*. Cologne, 1992.

ed. *Religiöse Drucke aus Kölner Produktion: Flugblätter und Wandbilder des 16. bis 19. Jahrhunderts aus den Beständen des Kölnischen Stadtmuseums*. Cologne, 1995.

Schöller, R. G., *Der Gemeine Hirte. Viehhaltung, Weidewirtschaft und Hirtenwesen vornehmlich des mittelalterlichen Umlandes von Nürnberg*. Schriftenreihe der Altnürnberger Landschaft 18. Nuremberg, 1973.

Scholten, Uta, 'Die Stadt als Kultraum. Prozessionen im Köln des 17. Jahrhunderts', in *Kunstgeschichtliche Studien. Hugo Borger zum 70. Geburtstag*, ed. Klaus Gereon Beuckers, Holger Brülls and Achim Preiss, pp. 109–36. Weimar, 1995.

Schreiner, Klaus, *Maria: Jungfrau, Mutter, Herrscherin*. Munich and Vienna, 1994.

Schröder, Alfred, 'Das Augsburger Dombild', *Münchner Jahrbuch der bildenden Kunst*, n.s. 7 (1930), 111–24.

Schulten, Walter, 'Die Beichtstuhlbilder der Kirche St. Mariae Himmelfahrt in Köln', in *Die Jesuitenkirche St. Mariae Himmelfahrt in Köln: Dokumentation und Beiträge zum Abschluss ihrer Wiederherstellung 1980*, pp. 248–68. Düsseldorf, 1982.

Schütz, Bernhard, *Die kirchliche Barockarchitektur in Bayern und Oberschwaben 1580–1780*. Munich, 2000.

Schwaiger, Georg, 'Maria Patrona Bavariae', in *Bavaria Sancta. Zeugen christlichen Glaubens in Bayern*, ed. Georg Schwaiger, pp. 28–37. Regensburg, 1970.

Schwemmer, Wilhelm, 'Aus der Geschichte der Kunstsammlungen der Stadt Nürnberg', *MVGSN* 40 (1949), 97–133.

'Das Mäzenatentum der Nürnberger Patrizierfamilie Tucher vom 14.–18. Jahrhundert', *MVGSN* 51 (1962), 18–59.

Schwerhoff, Gerd, 'Blasphemie vor den Schranken der städtischen Justiz: Basle, Köln und Nürnberg im Vergleich (14.–17. Jahrhundert)', *Ius Commune: Zeitschrift für europäische Rechtsgeschichte* 25 (1998), 39–120.

'Fehltritt oder Provokation? Theologisch-rechtliche Deutung und sozialen Praxis der Gotteslästerung im 15. und 16. Jahrhundert', in *Der Fehltritt. Vergehen und Versehen in der Vormoderne*, ed. Peter van Moos, pp. 403–18. Cologne, 2001.

Köln im Kreuzverhör: Kriminalität, Herrschaft und Gesellschaft in einer frühneuzeitlichen Stadt. Bonn, 1991.

'"Vereinswesen" und Religiosität in der spätmittelalterlichen Stadt: eine neue Quellenedition zur Geschichte der Kölner Laienbruderschaften', *Geschichte in Köln* 45 (1999), 107–21.

Zungen wie Schwerter: Blasphemie in alteuropäischen Gesellschaften 1200–1650. Konflikte und Kultur – Historische Perspektiven 12. Konstanz, 2005.

Scribner, Robert W., *For the Sake of Simple Folk: popular propaganda for the German Reformation*. 2nd edn. Oxford, 1994.

'The image and the Reformation', in *Disciplines of Faith: Studies in Religion, Politics and Patriarchy*, ed. J. Obelkevich and Lyndal Roper, pp. 539–50. London, 1987.

'The impact of the Reformation on daily life', in *Mensch und Objekt im Mittelalter und in der frühen Neuzeit*, ed. Österreichische Akademie der Wissenschaft, pp. 315–43. Vienna, 1990.

'Perceptions of the sacred in Germany at the end of the Middle Ages', in *Religion and Culture in Germany (1400–1800)*, ed. Lyndal Roper, pp. 85–103. Leiden, 2001.

'Ritual and popular religion in Catholic Germany at the time of the Reformation', *Journal of Ecclesiastical History* 35, no. 1 (1984), 47–77.

'Why was there no Reformation in Cologne?', *Bulletin of the Institute of Historical Research* 48 (1975), 217–41.

'Wolf Traut, Imago pietatis und Mater dolorosa', in *Glaube Hoffnung Liebe Tod*, ed. Christoph Geissmar-Brandi and Eleonora Louis, pp. 368–9. Vienna, 1995.

Seebass, Gottfried, 'Augsburg und Nürnberg – ein reformationsgeschichtlicher Vergleich', in *Wolfgang Musculus (1497–1563) und die oberdeutsche Reformation*, ed. Rudolf Dellsperger, Rudolf Freudenberger and Wolfgang Weber, pp. 91–110. Berlin, 1997.

'Die Augsburger Kirchenordnung von 1537 in ihrem historischen und theologischen Zusammenhang', in *Die Augsburger Kirchenordnung von 1537 und ihr Umfeld*, ed. Reinhard Schwarz, pp. 33–58. Gütersloh, 1988.

'Martin Bucer und die Reichsstadt Augsburg', in *Martin Bucer and Sixteenth Century Europe. Actes du colloque de Strasbourg (28–31 août 1991)*, ed. Christian Krieger and Marc Lienhard, pp. 479–91. Leiden, 1993.

'Mittelalterliche Kunstwerke in evangelisch gewordenen Kirchen Nürnbergs', in *Die bewahrende Kraft des Luthertums: mittelalterliche Kunstwerke in evangelischen Kirchen*, ed. Johann Michael Fritz, pp. 34–53. Regensburg, 1997.

Das reformatorische Werk des Andreas Osiander. Nuremberg, 1967.

Sharfe, Martin, *Evangelische Andachtsbilder: Studien zu Intention und Funktion des Bildes in der Frömmigkeitsgeschichte vornehmlich des schwäbischen Raums*. Stuttgart, 1968.

Sieh-Burens, Katarina, *Oligarchie, Konfession und Politik im 16. Jahrhundert: zur sozialen Verflechtung der Augsburger Bürgermeister und Stadtpfleger 1518–1618*. Schriften der Philosophischen Fakultäten der Universität Augsburg 29. Munich, 1986.

Simon, Matthias, *Evangelische Kirchengeschichte Bayerns*. 2nd edn. Nuremberg, 1952.

Simson, Otto G. von, 'Compassion and Co-redemptio in Roger van der Weyden's Descent from the Cross', *Art Bulletin* 35, vol. 1 (1953), 9–16.

Sladeczek, Franz-Josef, 'Bern 1528 – Zwischen Zerstörung und Erhaltung', in *Bildersturm. Wahnsinn oder Gottes Wille?*, ed. Cecile Dupeux, Peter Jezler and Jean Wirth, pp. 97–103. Munich, 2000.

Smith, Jeffrey Chipps, 'The art of salvation in Bavaria', in *The Jesuits: cultures, sciences and the arts 1540–1773*, ed. John W. O'Malley, pp. 568–99. Toronto, 1999.

German Sculpture of the Later Renaissance, c.1520–1580: art in an age of uncertainty. Princeton, NJ, 1994.

The Northern Renaissance, Art and Ideas. London, 2004.

Sensuous Worship: Jesuits and the art of the early Catholic Reformation in Germany. Princeton, NJ, 2002.

Soergel, Phil, *Wondrous in his Saints: Counter-Reformation propaganda in Bavaria*. Berkeley and London, 1993.

Spengler, Dietmar, *Spiritualia et Pictura: die graphische Sammlung des ehemaligen Jesuitenkollegs in Köln. Die Druckgraphik*. Cologne, 2003.

Städtische Kunstsammlungen Augsburg, and Munich Zentralinstitut für Kunstgeschichte, eds. *Welt im Umbruch: Augsburg zwischen Renaissance und Barock*. 3 vols. Augsburg, 1981.

Steiner, Peter Bernhard, 'Der gottselige Fürst und die Konfessionalisierung Altbayerns', in *Um Glauben und Reich: Kurfürst Maximilian I.*, ed. Hubert Glaser, pp. 252–63. Munich, 1980.

Stierhof, Horst H., *Das biblisch gemäl: die Kapelle im Ottheinrichsbau des Schlosses Neuburg an der Donau*. Forschungen zur Kunst- und Kulturgeschichte 3. Munich, 1993.

Stolz, Georg, 'Der Engelsgruß in St. Lorenz zu Nürnberg: Stiftung und Schicksal', in *Der Englische Gruß des Veit Stoß zu St Lorenz in Nürnberg*, ed. Bayerisches Landesamt für Denkmalpflege, pp. 1–22. Munich, 1983.

Stracke, Wolfgang, 'St Maria im Kapitol', *CR* 11 (1996), 79–103.

Strauss, Gerald, *Luther's House of Learning*. Baltimore, 1978.

Nuremberg in the Sixteenth Century: city politics and life between Middle Ages and modern times. Bloomington and London, 1976.

'Success and failure in the German Reformation', *Past & Present* 67 (1975), 30–63.

Strecker, Freya, *Augsburger Altäre zwischen Reformation (1537) und 1635: Bildkritik, Repräsentation und Konfessionalisierung*. Kunstgeschichte 61. Münster, 1998.

'Bilderstreit, Konfessionalisierung und Repräsentation: zur Ausstattung protestantischer Kirchen in Augsburg zwischen Reformation und Restitutionsedikt', in *Wolfgang Musculus (1497–1563) und die oberdeutsche Reformation*, ed. Rudolf Dellsperger, Rudolf Freudenberger and Wolfgang Weber, pp. 246–78. Berlin, 1997.

Strieder, Peter, *Tafelmalerei in Nürnberg 1350–1550*. Königstein im Taunus, 1993.

Szarota, E. M., *Das Jesuitendrama im deutschen Sprachgebiet*. 6 vols. Munich, 1979–87.

Tekath, Karl-Heinz, 'Die Unbefleckte Empfängnis Mariens – Hauptpatronin des Erzbistums Köln', in *Bistumspatrone in Deutschland: Festschrift für Jakob Torsy zum 9. Juni / 28. Juli 1983*, ed. August Leidl, pp. 58–77. Munich and Zurich, 1983.

Thomas, Keith, *Religion and the Decline of Magic: studies in popular beliefs in sixteenth- and seventeenth-century England*. London, 1971.

Thomas, Werner, and Luc Duerloo, eds. *Albert and Isabella, 1598–1621: essays*. Brussels, 1998.

Thon, Christina, ed. *Augsburger Barock*. Augsburg, 1968.

Thulin, Oskar, *Cranach-Altäre der Reformation*. Berlin, 1955.

Thümmel, Hans Georg, 'Bernhard Strigels Diptychon für Cuspinian', *Jahrbuch der kunsthistorischen Sammlungen in Wien* 76 (1980), 97–110.

Timmermann, Achim. 'Staging the Eucharist: late Gothic sacrament houses in Swabia and the Upper Rhine. Architecture and iconography', unpublished PhD thesis, University of London, 1996.

Trexler, R. C., 'Der Heiligen neue Kleider: eine analytische Skizze zur Be- und Entkleidung von Statuen', in *Gepeinigt, begehrt, vergessen: Symbolik und Sozialbezug des Körpers im späten Mittelalter und in der frühen Neuzeit*, ed. Klaus Schreiner and N. Schnitzler, pp. 365–402. Munich, 1992.

Valentin, Jean-Marie, *Le Théâtre des Jésuites dans les pays de langue allemande: répertoire chronologique des pièces représentées et des documents conservés (1555–1773)*. 2 vols. Stuttgart, 1983–4.

Venard, Marc, 'Volksfrömmigkeit und Konfessionalisierung', in *Die katholische Konfessionalisierung. Wissenschaftliches Symposion der Gesellschaft zur Herausgabe des Corpus Catholicorum und des Vereins für Reformationsgeschichte 1993*, ed. Wolfgang Reinhard and Heinz Schilling, pp. 258–70. Gütersloh, 1995.

Vogeler, Hildegard, *Madonnen in Lübeck: ein ikonographisches Verzeichnis der mittelalterlichen Mariendarstellungen in den Kirchen und ehemaligen Klöstern der Altstadt und des St Annen-Museums*, ed. Museum für Kunst und Kulturgeschichte der Hansestadt Lübeck. Lübeck, 1993.

Vogler, Günter, *Nürnberg 1524/25: Studien zur Geschichte der reformatorischen und sozialen Bewegung in der Reichsstadt*. Berlin, 1982.

Vogts, Hans, 'Das Haus Groenendal auf der Brückenstrasse', *JbKGV* 38/9 (1963/5), 51–72.

Das Kölner Wohnhaus bis zur Mitte des 19. Jahrhunderts. Neuss, 1966.

'Kölner Hauskapelle', *Zeitschrift für christliche Kunst* 25 (1912), 193–202.

Volk-Knüttel, Brigitte, 'Candid nach Schwarz', *Münchner Jahrbuch der bildenden Kunst*, 3rd series, 39 (1988), 113–32.

'Der Hochaltar der Münchner Frauenkirche von 1620 und seine Gemälde von Peter Candid', in *Monachium sacrum: Festschrift zur 500-Jahr-Feier der Metropolitankirche zu Unserer Lieben Frau in München*, ed. Georg Schwaiger, pp. 203–32. Munich, 1994.

Wallenta, Wolfgang, 'Grundzüge katholischer Konfessionalisierung in Augsburg 1548–1648', *JbVAB* 33 (1999), 215–32.

Wandel, Lee Palmer, 'The reform of the images: new visualizations of the Christian community at Zürich', *Archiv für Reformationsgeschichte* 80 (1989), 105–24.

Voracious Idols and Violent Hands: iconoclasm in Reformation Zurich, Strasbourg, and Basle. Cambridge, 1995.

Warmbrunn, Paul, *Zwei Konfessionen in einer Stadt: das Zusammenleben von Katholiken und Protestanten in den paritätischen Reichsstädten Augsburg, Biberach, Ravensburg und Dinkelsbühl von 1548 bis 1648*. Wiesbaden, 1983.

Warner, Marina, *Alone of All Her Sex: the myth and cult of the Virgin Mary*. London, 1976.

Wehrli-Johns, Martina, 'Haushälterin Gottes: zur Mariennachfolge der Beginen', in *Maria, Abbild oder Vorbild*, ed. Hedwig Röckelein, pp. 147–67. Tübingen, 1990.

Weiler, Peter, *Die kirchliche Reform im Erzbistum Köln*. Reformationsgeschichtliche Studien und Texte 56/57. Münster, 1931.

Weinsberg, Hermann von, *Das Buch Weinsberg: Kölner Denkwürdigkeiten aus dem 16. Jahrhundert*. 5 vols. Publikationen der Gesellschaft für rheinische Geschichtskunde 3, 4 and 16. Leipzig and Bonn, 1886–1926.

Weiss, James Michael, 'Hagiography by German humanists, 1483–1516', *Journal of Medieval and Renaissance Studies* 15, no. 2 (1985), 299–316.

Wiesner, Merry E., 'Luther and Women: the death of two Marys', in *Disciplines of Faith: Studies in Religion, Politics and Patriarchy*, ed. J. Obelkevich and Lyndal Roper, pp. 295–308. London, 1987.

Women and Gender in Early Modern Europe. 2nd edn. New Approaches to European History. Cambridge, 2000.

Wislocki, Marcin, 'Saints in Protestant theology, devotion and art in Pomerania', *Colloquia: Journal of Central European Studies* 12, nos. 1–2 (2005), 41–65.

Wolgast, Eike, 'Die Reformation im Herzogtum Mecklenburg und das Schicksal der Kirchenausstattungen', in *Die bewahrende Kraft des Luthertums: mittelalterliche Kunstwerke in evangelischen Kirchen*, ed. Johann Michael Fritz, pp. 54–70. Regensburg, 1997.

Wollschläger, Hermann Maria, *Hansestadt Köln: die Geschichte einer europäischen Handelsmetropole*. Cologne, 1988.

Zeeden, Ernst W., *Die Entstehung der Konfessionen: Grundlagen und Formen der Konfessionsbildung im Zeitalter der Glaubenskämpfe*. Munich and Vienna, 1964.

Katholische Überlieferungen in den lutherischen Kirchenordnungen des 16. Jahrhunderts. Münster, 1959.

Zehnder, Frank Günter, *Katalog der Altkölner Malerei*. Kataloge des Wallraf-Richartz-Museums 11. Cologne, 1990.

Zieger, Andreas, *Das religiöse und kirchliche Leben in Preussen und Kurland im Spiegel der evangelischen Kirchenordnungen des 16. Jahrhunderts*. Cologne and Graz, 1967.

Ziegler, Walter, 'Typen der Konfessionalisierung in katholischen Territorien Deutschlands', in *Die katholische Konfessionalisierung: wissenschaftliches Symposium der Gesellschaft zur Herausgabe des Corpus Catholicorum und des Vereins für Reformationsgeschichte 1993*, ed. Wolfgang Reinhard and Heinz Schilling, pp. 405–18. Gütersloh, 1995.

Zilliken, G., 'Der Kölner Festkalendar. Seine Entwicklung und seine Verwendung zu Urkundendatierung', *Bonner Jahrbuch: Jahrbücher des Vereins für Altertumsfreunden im Rheinlande* 119 (1910), 13–149.

Zimmerli-Witschi, Alice, *Frauen in der Reformationszeit*. Zurich, 1981.

Zitzlsperger, Ulrike, 'Mother, martyr and Mary Magdalene: German female pamphleteers and their self-images', *History* 88, no. 3 (2003), 379–92.

Zoepfl, F., *Das Bistum Augsburg und seine Bischöfe im Reformationsjahrhundert*. Augsburg, 1969.

'Die Durchführung des Tridentinums im Bistum Augsburg', in *Das Weltkonzil von Trient: sein Werden und Wirken*, ed. Georg Schreiber, pp. 135–69. Freiburg, 1951.

Zschelletzschky, Herbert, *Die 'drei gottlosen Maler' von Nürnberg: Sebald Behan, Barthel Beham und Georg Pencz. Historische Grundlagen und ikonologische Probleme ihrer Graphik zu Reformations- und Bauernkriegzeit*. Leipzig, 1975.

Index

Past and Present Publications

General Editors: Lyndal Roper, *University of Oxford*, and Chris Wickham, *University of Oxford*

Family and Inheritance: Rural Society in Western Europe 1200–1800, edited by Jack Goody, Joan Thirsk and E. P. Thompson*
French Society and the Revolution, edited by Douglas Johnson
Peasants, Knights and Heretics: Studies in Medieval English Social History, edited by R. H. Hilton*
Towns in Societies: Essays in Economic History and Historical Sociology, edited by Philip Abrams and E. A. Wrigley*
Desolation of a City: Coventry and the Urban Crisis of the Late Middle Ages, Charles Phythian-Adams*
Puritanism and Theatre: Thomas Middleton and Opposition Drama under the Early Stuarts, Margot Heinemann*
Lords and Peasants in a Changing Society: The Estates of the Bishopric of Worcester 680–1450, Christopher Dyer
Life, Marriage and Death in a Medieval Parish: Economy, Society and Demography in Halesowen 1270–1400, Ziv Razi
Biology, Medicine and Society 1740–1940, edited by Charles Webster*
The Invention of Tradition, edited by Eric Hobsbawm and Terence Ranger*
Industrialization before Industrialization: Rural Industry and the Genesis of Capitalism, Peter Kriedte, Hans Medick and Jürgen Schlumbohm*
The Republic in the Village: The People of the Var from the French Revolution to the Second Republic, Maurice Agulhon†
Social Relations and Ideas: Essays in Honour of R. H. Hilton, edited by T. H. Aston, P. R. Coss, Christopher Dyer and Joan Thirsk
A Medieval Society: The West Midlands at the End of the Thirteenth Century, R. H. Hilton
Winstanley: 'The Law of Freedom' and Other Writings, edited by Christopher Hill
Crime in Seventeenth-Century England: A County Study, J. A. Sharpe†
The Crisis of Feudalism: Economy and Society in Eastern Normandy c. 1300–1500, Guy Bois†
The Development of the Family and Marriage in Europe, Jack Goody*
Disputes and Settlements: Law and Human Relations in the West, edited by John Bossy*
Rebellion, Popular Protest and the Social Order in Early Modern England, edited by Paul Slack
Studies on Byzantine Literature of the Eleventh and Twelfth Centuries, Alexander Kazhdan in collaboration with Simon Franklin†
The English Rising of 1381, edited by R. H. Hilton and T. H. Aston*
Praise and Paradox: Merchants and Craftsmen in Elizabethan Popular Literature, Laura Caroline Stevenson*
The Brenner Debate: Agrarian Class Structure and Economic Development in Pre-Industrial Europe, edited by T. H. Aston and C. H. E. Philpin*
Eternal Victory: Triumphant Rulership in Late Antiquity, Byzantium, and the Early Medieval West, Michael McCormick†*

* Also published in paperback
† Co-published with the Maison des Sciences de l'Homme, Paris

East-Central Europe in Transition: From the Fourteenth to the Seventeenth Century, edited by Antoni Mączak, Henryk Samsonowicz and Peter Burke*

Small Books and Pleasant Histories: Popular Fiction and Its Readership in Seventeenth-Century England, Margaret Spufford*

Society Politics and Culture: Studies in Early Modern England, Mervyn James*

Horses, Oxen and Technological Innovation: The Use of Draught Animals in English Farming 1066–1500, John Langdon*

Nationalism and Popular Protest in Ireland, edited by C. H. E. Philpin*

Rituals of Royalty: Power and Ceremonial in Traditional Societies, edited by David Cannadine and Simon Price*

The Margins of Society in Late Medieval Paris, Bronislaw Geremek†

Landlords, Peasants and Politics in Medieval England, edited by T. H. Aston

Geography, Technology, and War: Studies in the Maritime History of the Mediterranean, 649–1571, John H. Pryor*

Church Courts, Sex and Marriage in England, 1570–1640, Martin Ingram*

Searches for an Imaginary Kingdom: The Legend of the Kingdom of Prester John, L. N. Gumilev

Crowds and History: Mass Phenomena in English Towns, 1790–1835, Mark Harrison*

Concepts of Cleanliness: Changing Attitudes in France since the Middle Ages, Georges Vigarello†

The First Modern Society: Essays in English History in Honour of Lawrence Stone, edited by A. L. Beier, David Cannadine and James M. Rosenheim*

The Europe of the Devout: The Catholic Reformation and the Formation of a New Society, Louis Châtellier†

English Rural Society, 1500–1800: Essays in Honour of Joan Thirsk, edited by John Chartres and David Hey

From Slavery to Feudalism in South-Western Europe, Pierre Bonnassie†

Lordship, Knighthood and Locality: A Study in English Society c. 1180–c. 1280, P. R. Coss*

English and French Towns in Feudal Society: A Comparative Study, R. H. Hilton*

An Island for Itself: Economic Development and Social Change in Late Medieval Sicily, Stephan R. Epstein*

Epidemics and Ideas: Essays on the Historical Perception of Pestilence, edited by Terence Ranger and Paul Slack*

The Political Economy of Shopkeeping in Milan, 1886–1922, Jonathan Morris*

After Chartism: Class and Nation in English Radical Politics, 1848–1874, Margot C. Finn*

Commoners: Common Right, Enclosure and Social Change in England, 1700–1820, J. M. Neeson*

Land and Popular Politics in Ireland: County Mayo from the Plantation to the Land War, Donald E. Jordan Jr*

The Castilian Crisis of the Seventeeth Century: New Perspective on the Economic and Social History of Seventeenth-Century Spain, I. A. A. Thompson and Bartolomé Yun Casalilla

The Culture of Clothing: Dress and Fashion in the Ancien Régime, Daniel Roche†*

The Sense of the People: Politics, Culture and Imperialism in England, 1715–1785, Kathleen Wilson*

Witchcraft in Early Modern Europe: Studies in Culture and Belief, edited by Jonathan Barry, Marianne Hester and Gareth Roberts*

Fair Shares for All: Jacobin Egalitarianism in Practice, Jean-Pierre Gross*

The Wild and the Sown: Botany and Agriculture in Western Europe, 1350–1850, Mauro Ambrosoli

Witchcraft Persecution in Bavaria: Popular Magic, Religious Zealotry and Reason of State in Early Modern Europe, Wolfgang Behringer*

Understanding Popular Violence in the English Revolution: The Colchester Plunderers, John Walter*

The Moral World of the Law, edited by Peter Coss
Travel and Ethnology in the Renaissance: South India through European Eyes, 1250–1625, Joan-Pau Rubiés*
Holy Rulers and Blessed Princesses: Dynastic Cults in Medieval Central Europe, Gâbor Klaniczay
Rebellion, Community and Custom in Early Modern Germany, Norbert Schindler
Fashioning Adultery: Gender, Sex and Civility in England, 1660–1740, David M. Turner
Gender in Early Modern German History, edited by Ulinka Rublack
The Origins of the English Gentry, Peter Coss*
Emperor and Priest: The Imperial Office in Byzantium, Gilbert Dagron
A Contested Nation: History, Memory and Nationalism in Switzerland, 1761–1891, Oliver Zimmer
Rethinking the Age of Reform: England 1780–1850, edited by Arthur Burns and Joanna Innes
The Peasants of Ottobeuren, 1487–1726: A Rural Society in Early Modern Europe, Govind Sreenivasan
Studies in Ancient Greek and Roman Society, edited by Robin Osborne
Crime and Law in England, 1750–1840: Remaking Justice from the Margins, Peter King
The Cult of the Virgin Mary in Early Modern Germany: Protestant and Catholic Piety, 1500–1648, Bridget Heal